Global Lessons for Stablecoin Regulation and Governance

Jane Thomason
https://orcid.org/0009-0007-3123-7851
University College London, Australia

IGI Global
Scientific Publishing
Publishing Tomorrow's Research Today

Vice President of Editorial	Melissa Wagner
Director of Acquisitions	Mikaela Felty
Director of Book Development	Jocelynn Hessler
Production Manager	Mike Brehm
Cover Design	Jose Rosado

Published in the United States of America by
IGI Global Scientific Publishing
701 East Chocolate Avenue
Hershey, PA, 17033, USA
Tel: 717-533-8845 | Fax: 717-533-7115
Website: https://www.igi-global.com E-mail: cust@igi-global.com

Library of Congress Cataloging-in-Publication Data

(CIP Data Pending)
ISBN13: 979-8-3373-9043-7
Isbn13Softcover: 979-8-3373-9044-4
EISBN13: 979-8-3373-9045-1

British Cataloguing in Publication Data
A Cataloguing in Publication record for this book is available from the British Library.

Table of Contents

Detailed Table of Contents

Stablecoins are a foundational innovation in digital finance engineered to maintain price stability by linking their value to reference assets such as fiat currencies. This chapter provides a technical and economic definition of stablecoins, classifying them into fiat-backed, crypto-collateralised, algorithmic, and hybrid categories. Through comparative analysis of USD Coin (USDC), Tether (USDT), DAI, and TerraUSD (UST), alongside recent hybrid and CBDC implementations, it examines stability mechanisms such as 1:1 reserve backing, smart contract-based collateral management, and protocol-defined supply adjustments. Evidence shows fiat-backed stablecoins maintain stronger pegs and market dominance, while crypto-collateralised and algorithmic models face volatility, capital inefficiency, and systemic risk exemplified by UST's collapse. Hybrid models like DJED and JANUS propose innovative stabilisation techniques though largely theoretical. Drawing on market data and case studies, the chapter highlights regulatory, technical, and policy distinctions between private stablecoins and CBDCs.

This chapter explores the emergence and importance of stablecoins in crypto finance, their technical construction, economic impact, and applications. It traverses the history of stablecoins as a process towards embracing blockchain efficiency and fiat money stability, theoretically challenging and charting major milestones. The three major categories—fiat-backed, crypto-collateralized, and algorithmic—are explored through the use of secondary sources and widely documented case studies. The discussion takes into account regulatory and systemic risk issues, likening the

Stablecoins—digital assets designed to maintain price stability by pegging to fiat currencies or collateralized reserves—have often been examined through the lens of private finance, focusing on market speculation, systemic risk, and regulatory arbitrage. This article reframes stablecoins as potential public goods, investigating their role in advancing financial inclusion, humanitarian effectiveness, and digital identity infrastructures. Drawing on recent data from the World Bank, the World Food Programme (WFP), and case studies across the Global South, the analysis adopts a comparative methodology, triangulating case study evidence with theoretical modeling. It applies transaction cost economics (Coase's theorem) to remittances, graph theory (max-flow/min-cut) to humanitarian aid distribution, set-theoretical analysis (via Venn modeling) to digital ID integration, and game theory to governance risks between states and private issuers.

Stablecoins have emerged as a transformative yet controversial development in digital finance, promising stability while posing novel regulatory and systemic risks. Their growing role in payments, decentralized finance, and remittances raises questions about monetary sovereignty, consumer protection, and financial integrity. This chapter examines the governance of stablecoins through comparative and interdisciplinary perspectives, focusing on the evolving relationship between self-regulation, soft law, and hard law. Special attention is given to the Commonwealth Model Law on Stablecoins (2025), which provides a harmonised legislative framework designed to balance innovation with financial stability and inclusion. By comparing this model law with international approaches such as the EU's Markets in Crypto-Assets Regulation (MiCA) and voluntary standards from global standard-setting bodies, the chapter highlights how model laws can bridge the gap between flexibility and enforceability in the governance of digital money.

This chapter traces the evolution from Payments 1.0 (cash) through 2.0 (cards), 3.0 (e-commerce and wallets), and 4.0 (real-time rails with machine learning) to Payments 5.0 agentic autonomy. Agentic payments are intelligent, intent-driven systems where software agents understand user goals, plan execution across risk assessment, authentication, funding and rewards, then act within safety guardrails while providing clear explanations. This chapter presents the architecture with five components: intent capture, tool-augmented planning, policy, safety, action and verification with dry-runs and cryptographic trails, and privacy-preserving learning . Key metrics include approval rates, fraud detection precision and recall, payment speed, and explanation quality. Use cases include proactive bill pay, agentic wallets and dispute resolution. The chapter analyzes threats such as prompt injection and tool abuse, proposing mitigations like least-privilege access and rate limiting.

Stablecoins are reshaping global finance, enabling low-cost payments, remittances, and inclusion, but also raising risks for sovereignty, consumer protection, and stability. This chapter examines regulatory challenges with a focus on Nigeria, drawing lessons from the EU's MiCA, the fragmented U.S. model, and Singapore's balanced approach. It pursues four aims: (i) review global and regional responses; (ii) position Nigeria as a test case for emerging economies; (iii) assess the Commonwealth Model Law as a harmonizable framework; and (iv) explore how regulation can mitigate risks while fostering inclusion. Using a qualitative, desk-based design combining doctrinal and comparative analysis, the study finds Nigeria's stance to be restrictive yet experimental: a banking ban excluded stablecoins, while the SEC and eNaira signaled cautious innovation. The Model Law's tiered, risk-based framework offers a path to balance sovereignty, stability, and innovation, making Nigeria a microcosm of Global South dilemmas.

interoperable digital money systems capable of supporting the next generation of global finance.

Preface

This edited volume is a global compendium built on the foundation of the Commonwealth Model Law on Stablecoins (the *Model Law*). It has been conceived as a practical, policy-facing reference for governments, regulators, scholars, and industry leaders seeking to understand not only how stablecoins function, but how they can be governed as safe, inclusive, and interoperable forms of digital money.

The book emerged from a series of expert dialogues convened under the auspices of the Commonwealth Secretariat in preparation for the development of the Model Law. Those dialogues brought together central bankers, regulators, technologists, legal scholars, economists, and development practitioners from across the Commonwealth and beyond. The interdisciplinary and collaborative character of those discussions is reflected in the chapters that follow. This volume is therefore not the product of a single discipline or jurisdiction, but the result of a shared effort to grapple with the reconfiguration of monetary sovereignty and financial regulation in the digital era.

At its core, this book seeks to bridge theory and implementation. While the scholarly literature on digital currencies has expanded rapidly, practical guidance for lawmakers and regulators remains fragmented. The Model Law responds to that gap by offering a coherent legislative and regulatory architecture that aligns with international standards, including those of the FATF, FSB, and BIS, while remaining adaptable to diverse legal systems and levels of institutional capacity. This volume situates the Model Law within broader debates on digital sovereignty, algorithmic governance, and the evolution of money as programmable infrastructure.

The relevance of this work is difficult to overstate. As digital finance reshapes economies, stablecoins have moved from experimental instruments to systemically significant components of global payment and settlement systems. They now facilitate trillions of dollars in transactions annually, influencing remittances, liquidity management, and monetary transmission, particularly in developing and small states. Yet regulatory approaches remain uneven, with risks of fragmentation, regulatory arbitrage, and loss of public trust. This book provides what has so far been missing:

a globally oriented roadmap for building trustworthy, transparent, and innovation-friendly frameworks for digital money.

Drawing on contributions from more than twenty countries, the volume explains what stablecoins are, why they matter, and how they can be harnessed to advance financial inclusion, efficiency, and resilience. It integrates perspectives from law, economics, cybersecurity, monetary policy, and blockchain engineering, and it places particular emphasis on public-good applications, including humanitarian aid, cross-border payments, consumer protection, and digital identity. In doing so, it reframes stablecoins not merely as private financial instruments, but as potential components of public financial infrastructure.

The book is structured in three integrated parts. The first establishes conceptual and regulatory foundations, offering precise definitions, comparative perspectives, and analysis of systemic and prudential risks. The second provides a detailed exposition of the Model Law itself, presenting a ready-to-adopt legislative framework designed for practical implementation. The third turns to global case studies and frontier research, examining cross-border interoperability, supervisory technologies, consumer safeguards, and emerging regulatory approaches, including recent developments such as the United States' GENIUS Act and the European Union's MiCA framework.

This volume is intended for a wide audience. For regulators and policymakers, it serves as a governance toolkit and legislative blueprint. For central banks and finance ministries, it offers strategic insights into balancing monetary sovereignty with global interoperability. For financial institutions and fintech innovators, it provides regulatory intelligence on an evolving and increasingly consequential landscape. For academics and researchers, it offers a foundational reference for interdisciplinary inquiry into digital currencies and financial governance.

As stablecoins transition from technological novelty to systemic financial infrastructure, their regulation presents one of the defining governance challenges of the twenty-first century. This book offers both a conceptual framework and a model legislative architecture for managing that transition. By integrating comparative legal analysis, economic theory, and technological insight, it aims to inform policy evolution and scholarly debate alike, and to lay the groundwork for future empirical and comparative research on the evolving relationship between law, code, and money.

ORGANIZATION OF THE BOOK

Chapter 1: Stablecoins Unveiled Technical Definitions, Economic Taxonomy, and Comparative Analysis of Fiat-Backed, Crypto-Collateralised, Algorithmic, and CBDC provides a technical and economic definition of stablecoins, classifying them into fiat-backed, crypto-collateralised, algorithmic, and hybrid categories. Through comparative analysis of USD Coin (USDC), Tether (USDT), DAI, and TerraUSD (UST), alongside recent hybrid and CBDC implementations, it examines stability mechanisms such as 1:1 reserve backing, smart contract-based collateral management, and protocol-defined supply adjustments. Evidence shows fiat-backed stablecoins maintain stronger pegs and market dominance, while crypto-collateralised and algorithmic models face volatility, capital inefficiency, and systemic risk exemplified by UST's collapse. Hybrid models like DJED and JANUS propose innovative stabilisation techniques though largely theoretical. Drawing on market data and case studies, the chapter highlights regulatory, technical, and policy distinctions between private stablecoins and CBDCs.

Chapter 2: Stablecoins: Technical Foundations, Economic Implications, and Real-World Applications explores the emergence and importance of stablecoins in crypto finance, their technical construction, economic impact, and applications. It traverses the history of stablecoins as a process towards embracing blockchain efficiency and fiat money stability, theoretically challenging and charting major milestones. The three major categories—fiat-backed, crypto-collateralized, and algorithmic—are explored through the use of secondary sources and widely documented case studies. The discussion takes into account regulatory and systemic risk issues, likening the analogy to Central Bank Digital Currencies (CBDCs) and distilling lessons from success and failure. The chapter subsequently tries to demystify how stablecoins are transforming payments and financial infrastructure and pinning down open questions to study and policy.

Chapter 3: From Law to Supervisory Practice: A Toolkit for Secure, Transparent, Issuance examines how the US GENIUS Act (2025) and the Commonwealth Model Law on Stablecoins can create an operationally enforceable regime that guarantees parity maintenance, liquidity, and transparency. The article employs a methodological approach that combines a comparative legal analysis (GENIUS, Commonwealth, MiCA, and UK) with regulatory engineering. The result is a practice-oriented toolkit that transforms stablecoins from speculative digital assets into balance sheet- and audit-compliant means of payment. The article underscores that effective regulation of stablecoins necessitates a harmonious integration of law, governance, and technology.

Chapter 4: Financial Stability and Systemic Risk in Stablecoins: When Does Digital Currency Infrastructure Become "Too Big to Fail"? examines the conditions under which stablecoins may become "too big to fail" and analyzes the unique risks posed by algorithmic and decentralized autonomous organization (DAO)-based models. Through comprehensive examination of the Terra Luna/TerraUSD (UST) collapse, Silicon Valley Bank's impact on USDC, and other significant stablecoin failures, we identify critical thresholds for systemic importance and propose an enhanced framework for assessing systemic risk in digital currency ecosystems. The analysis reveals that traditional metrics of systemic importance inadequately capture the interconnectedness, velocity-driven risks, and reflexive mechanisms inherent in algorithmic stablecoin systems .

Chapter 5: Stablecoins as Public Good: Remittances, Humanitarian Aid, and Digital ID reframes stablecoins as potential public goods, investigating their role in advancing financial inclusion, humanitarian effectiveness, and digital identity infrastructures. Drawing on recent data from the World Bank, the World Food Programme (WFP), and case studies across the Global South, the analysis adopts a comparative methodology, triangulating case study evidence with theoretical modeling. It applies transaction cost economics (Coase's theorem) to remittances, graph theory (max-flow/min-cut) to humanitarian aid distribution, set-theoretical analysis (via Venn modeling) to digital ID integration, and game theory to governance risks between states and private issuers.

Chapter 6: Designing Trust in Digital Money: Interdisciplinary Approaches to Stablecoin Governance examines the governance of stablecoins through comparative and interdisciplinary perspectives, focusing on the evolving relationship between self-regulation, soft law, and hard law. Special attention is given to the Model Law, which provides a harmonised legislative framework designed to balance innovation with financial stability and inclusion. By comparing this Model Law with international approaches such as the EU's Markets in Crypto-Assets Regulation (MiCA) and voluntary standards from global standard-setting bodies, the chapter highlights how model laws can bridge the gap between flexibility and enforceability in the governance of digital money.

Chapter 7: Payments 1.0 to 5.0: Pathways to Agentic Autonomy chapter traces the evolution from Payments 1.0 (cash) through 2.0 (cards), 3.0 (e-commerce and wallets), and 4.0 (real-time rails with machine learning) to Payments 5.0 agentic autonomy. Agentic payments are intelligent, intent-driven systems where software agents understand user goals, plan execution across risk assessment, authentication, funding and rewards, then act within safety guardrails while providing clear explanations. This chapter presents the architecture with five components: intent capture, tool-augmented planning, policy, safety, action and verification with dry-runs and cryptographic trails, and privacy-preserving learning . Key metrics include approval rates, fraud detection precision and recall, payment speed, and explanation quality. Use cases include proactive bill pay, agentic wallets and dispute resolution. The chapter analyzes threats such as prompt injection and tool abuse, proposing mitigations like least-privilege access and rate limiting.

Chapter 8: Stablecoins and the Future of Financial Regulation: Stablecoins and the Future of Financial Regulation: Nigeria's Experience and Global Lessons examines regulatory challenges with a focus on Nigeria, drawing lessons from the EU's MiCA, the fragmented U.S. model, and Singapore's balanced approach. It pursues four aims: (i) review global and regional responses; (ii) position Nigeria as a test case for emerging economies; (iii) assess the Model Law as a harmonizable framework; and (iv) explore how regulation can mitigate risks while fostering inclusion. Using a qualitative, desk-based design combining doctrinal and comparative analysis, the study finds Nigeria's stance to be restrictive yet experimental: a banking ban excluded stablecoins, while the SEC and eNaira signaled cautious innovation. The Model Law's tiered, risk-based framework offers a path to balance sovereignty, stability, and innovation, making Nigeria a microcosm of Global South dilemmas.

Chapter 9: Enabling Innovation in Stablecoin Markets through Special Jurisdictions argues that special jurisdictions - such as city states and special economic zones - enable stablecoin innovation without risking macroeconomic stability. Through their adaptive regulation, pilot programmes, sandboxes, innovation ecosystems, and specialised dispute-resolution mechanisms, they create controlled environments where stablecoin models can be tested and scaled safely. Through case studies, including Hong Kong, Singapore, DIFC, among others, the paper makes a case that special jursidictions offer credible regulatory pathways to issuers, while acting as evidence-generating laboratories for regulators. Therefore, special jurisdictions are quietly shaping the future of money, where the regulator's role is evolving from merely being a rule-maker to being a co-innovator.

The last chapter is titled Synthesizing Global Lessons for Stablecoin Regulation and Financial Stability: The Road Ahead. Stablecoins have moved decisively into the centre of global digital finance, emerging as payment infrastructure, liquidity instruments, and potential public-purpose digital money. Evidence shows growing global convergence around proportionate, technology-neutral, and risk-based regulation, even as significant divergences persist in implementation, supervisory capacity, and treatment of novel models such as algorithmic stablecoins. Unique opportunities and vulnerabilities facing emerging markets, where stablecoins can lower remittance costs and expand financial access while simultaneously raising concerns about dollarisation and monetary sovereignty. Ethical considerations, around surveillance, identity, humanitarian use, and private-sector dependency, remain central to responsible adoption. The Model Law on Stablecoins provides a forward-looking blueprint for harmonised, adaptive regulation. Its principles provide the foundation for safe, inclusive, and interoperable digital money systems capable of supporting the next generation of global finance.

CONCLUSION

This volume has sought to do more than catalogue regulatory approaches to stablecoins. Its central purpose has been to provide coherence in a rapidly evolving and often fragmented policy landscape, and to offer a shared point of reference for those tasked with governing digital money. Anchored in the Model Law, the book brings together comparative analysis, technical insight, and legislative design to illuminate how stablecoins can be regulated as safe, transparent, and interoperable components of the global financial system.

Across its chapters, a consistent theme emerges: stablecoins are no longer peripheral innovations. They are becoming embedded in payment systems, cross-border value transfer, and digital financial infrastructure, with direct implications for monetary sovereignty, consumer protection, financial stability, and inclusion. The contributors demonstrate that effective regulation must therefore move beyond ad hoc or purely reactive measures. It requires principled, adaptable frameworks that recognise the unique technological characteristics of stablecoins while remaining grounded in established regulatory objectives.

The Model Law, as presented and examined throughout this volume, is offered as one such framework. It does not prescribe a single regulatory outcome, nor does it seek to override domestic legal traditions. Rather, it provides a modular and interoperable architecture that jurisdictions can adapt to their own constitutional, economic, and institutional contexts, while maintaining alignment with international standards. In this sense, the Model Law is both a legislative tool and a mechanism for regulatory coordination in an increasingly interconnected digital economy.

Equally important is the book's interdisciplinary and public-interest orientation. By integrating perspectives from law, economics, technology, and public policy, the volume underscores that stablecoin regulation cannot be siloed. Questions of reserve management, cybersecurity, governance, and supervision intersect directly with broader societal concerns, including financial inclusion, humanitarian response, and trust in public institutions. The case studies and forward-looking analyses illustrate how stablecoins, when properly governed, can support public-good objectives rather than undermine them.

This volume also looks deliberately to the future. Emerging supervisory and regulatory technologies, the growing role of artificial intelligence, and the convergence of digital identity, payments, and programmable finance will continue to reshape the regulatory terrain. The frameworks explored here are therefore not endpoints, but foundations upon which more responsive and resilient systems of oversight can be built. As both technology and markets evolve, so too must the legal and institutional tools that govern them.

In concluding, this book is offered as a reference, a guide, and an invitation. A reference for those seeking clarity amid complexity; a guide for policymakers and regulators engaged in the practical work of implementation; and an invitation to continued dialogue, research, and collaboration across jurisdictions and disciplines. The evolution of money as digital infrastructure presents profound challenges, but also significant opportunities. By grounding innovation in sound governance and shared principles, this volume aims to contribute to the development of a global financial system that is safe, inclusive, and worthy of public trust.

Chapter 1

Stablecoins Unveiled Technical Definitions, Economic Taxonomy, and Comparative Analysis of Fiat-Backed, Crypto-Collateralised, Algorithmic, and CBDC

Aditya Mudgal
https://orcid.org/0009-0003-1932-5411
Christ University, India

Abhinav Kataria
https://orcid.org/0009-0009-6362-0569
Christ University, India

Pankaj Dhaundiyal
https://orcid.org/0000-0002-4815-1647
Christ University, India

ABSTRACT

Stablecoins are a foundational innovation in digital finance engineered to maintain price stability by linking their value to reference assets such as fiat currencies. This chapter provides a technical and economic definition of stablecoins, classifying them into fiat-backed, crypto-collateralised, algorithmic, and hybrid categories.

DOI: 10.4018/979-8-3373-9043-7.ch001

Through comparative analysis of USD Coin (USDC), Tether (USDT), DAI, and TerraUSD (UST), alongside recent hybrid and CBDC implementations, it examines stability mechanisms such as 1:1 reserve backing, smart contract-based collateral management, and protocol-defined supply adjustments. Evidence shows fiat-backed stablecoins maintain stronger pegs and market dominance, while crypto-collateralised and algorithmic models face volatility, capital inefficiency, and systemic risk exemplified by UST's collapse. Hybrid models like DJED and JANUS propose innovative stabilisation techniques though largely theoretical. Drawing on market data and case studies, the chapter highlights regulatory, technical, and policy distinctions between private stablecoins and CBDCs.

1. INTRODUCTION

1.1 The Genesis of Stability in a Volatile Digital Economy

Centrality consists of money functions based on three foundational pillars stability, reliability and universal acceptance. Regardless of which, supported by precious metals, or the good faith and credit of sovereign states, money must be useful in the functions of a medium of exchange, unit of account and store of value, based on the ability to maintain its value over time. The introduction of Bitcoin in 2008 brought about an inventive system within the area of monetary systems that has been decentralized, disputing the centuries of centralization (Nakamoto, 2008). But, this technological innovation had a great disadvantage. The severe fluctuation of the prices of initial cryptocurrencies made them not suitable in the regular business transactions and turned them into a speculative instrument instead of a practical currency (Arner et al., 2020).

Stablecoins came up in order to resolve this inherent contradiction. These digital currencies are trying to take the technological benefits of disseminated ledger technology such as speed, low transaction expenses, and operational encryption and mix them with the price predictability of traditional currencies. The stablecoins, by pegging their value to reference assets, usually the U.S. dollar, constitute an artificial remedy to cryptocurrency volatility. Between the scandalous dominance of Tether and the experiments in algorithms turning out devastatingly, the stablecoins are currently a subject of modern discussions on digital money, financial regulation, and monetary sovereignty.

Technological innovation is not the only important aspect of stablecoins. Dollar-pegged stablecoins would serve as practical hedges in the emerging markets in the Commonwealth, and other parts of the world in the face of local currency devaluation and inflation. The citizens of Argentina, Turkey, Nigeria, and Venezuela are accumulating their stores of value, which are increasingly stablecoins, which in effect has sped up the evolution of digital dollarization. Such a duality of being a technological infrastructure as well as an economic tool has drawn the interests of policymakers, central banks, and international standard-setting organs. The Financial Stability Board, the International Monetary Fund, and regional organizations such as the Commonwealth Secretariat have acknowledged that stablecoins present challenges to financial stability, monetary sovereignty and cross-border capital markets which require coordinated policy action.

1.2 Scope & Purpose

This paper represents a detailed discussion of the topic of stablecoins as fintech, innovations, and regulatory issues. Their circulation has reached upwards of $180 billion at its largest spread and the further introduction of the innovative coins as a significant part of both decentralized finance (DeFi) and traditional payments platforms, a large portion of the population (wiring) makes them systemically relevant financial infrastructure. Their mechanics, dangers, and regulatory treatment need an interdisciplinary perspective regarding computer science, economics, and law to comprehend their nature.

The three main goals of this work are the following. First, it provides clear technical and economical definitions of stablecoins, which have different structural aspects, depending on their approach to stabilizing the coins, the type of collateral, and the flagship types of governance, and explains that stablecoins are not the input of Central Bank Digital Currencies (CBDCs), but instead, they may be studied through the prism of a comparative regulatory analysis. Second, it constructs a risk-based taxonomy applying to stablecoins classifying them into: fiat-backed, crypto-collateralized, algorithmic, and hybrid models and analyses their presented financial, systemic, and governance risks. Third, it gives relative evaluation of these models in the monetary ecosystem of their relations with traditional banking processes and new central bank digital currencies (CBDCs).

The analysis places the Commonwealth Model Law on stablecoins (2025) in the context of other financial policy harmonization frameworks such as the Markets in Crypto-Assets (MiCA) regulation by the European Union, Financial Stability Board guidance on virtual assets, and G20 recommendations. This stance indicates the distinct position of the Commonwealth of the middleway between the developed and emerging market approaches, which is especially problematic in the face of the active introduction of stablecoins, as most jurisdictions in the Commonwealth have urgent needs to deal with such a process as accelerated dollarization, minimized effectiveness of the monetary policy, and the risk of capital flight.

The priorities of the Commonwealth are highlighted in the chapter financial inclusion, efficiency in cross-border payments, and the preservation of monetary sovereignty. These are rather pressing concerns with small economies in which the robustness of the home currencies and transmitting of the policies of the central bank will be jeopardized in the event that there is a tremendous uptake of stablecoins. To provide a balance between innovation facilitation and risk mitigation, the analysis reflects the idea that the stablecoins will not only be of real benefit in unbanked people and remittance corridors, but they will also present new forms of vulnerability to the systemic metrics.

1.3 Market Evolution & Quantitative Context

Stablecoin markets have gained impressive gains since 2018 showing the demand of a durable digital resource, as well as the dangers of a fast innovative financial direction. In early 2024, the aggregate market capitalization of stable coins is approximately between 120 and 180 billion dollars, but they are strongly affected by movement in the cryptocurrency market at large and regulatory policies. This would be an exponential growth of less than three billion in 2018.

The level of concentration in the market is high. Tether (USDT) always controls more than half of all supply and has volumes of transactions, especially in Asia and on exchanges having few banking relationships. In Q1 2021 alone, approximately half of the total in all stablecoin transactions occurred across the world were processed by Tether (Arner et al., 2020). USD Coin (USDC) is part of Circle and Coinbase and has a market share of approximately 20-25 percent and is penetrating more institutions and DeFi protocols because of its regulatory compliance posture and reserve transparency. The chips in the market share pertaining to the stablecoins include Binance USD (BUSD), DAI, and other stablecoins.

The metrics of transaction volume indicate the systemic significance of the stablecoins. The volume of settlements of major stablecoins daily is often much larger than that of conventional payment freeways. In 2021-2022, the amount of transactions that Tether made each day regularly exceeded what Visa has settled in a single day, which manifested a representation of how much central stablecoins have become in the world of transferring digital values (Lyons & Viswanath-Natraj, 2023). These transactions are used in diverse uses cases: trading and arbitrage in cryptocurrency, cross border remittances, interactions with DeFi protocols, and more frequently and commonly, commercial transactions and treasury functions.

Geographic distribution patterns show that both way technology and economic instruments are stablecoins. The stablecoins are engaged in trading markets with the purposes of using them as an efficient trading tool and DeFi infrastructure in the developed markets. They are beginning to play as alternative currencies and inflation insurances in the emerging economies. According to research, the use of stablecoins is also associated with the instability of the local currency, economics of capital controls and remittance corridors (MacDonald and Zhao, 2022). This geographical scattering makes the provision of the urgency to establish the respective regulatory frameworks that would guarantee the financial steadiness and prevent the relevant examples of utilization, particularly in the jurisdictions where the stablecoins appear to be related to the real demands of financial inclusivity.

1.4 Structure of Analysis

It is systematically analyzed by beginning with the background concepts to the comparative analysis and policy recommendation. Section 2 establishes technical and economic foundations, establishing a definition of the stablecoins both in term of engineering and in monetary and examining principles of stabilization that underlie numerous designs. Section 3 elaborates a detailed taxonomy of that resource in terms of collateral sources and governance structure, developing a structure in which risks are distributed among stablecoin models.

The other example of relevance is Liquity (LUSD) protocol which does not have governance tokens and stays pegged by liquidation incentives as an algorithm, and smart immutable contracts. The alternative model demonstrates that governance minimization can itself be a risk mitigation strategy, which provides an excellent understanding on how decentralized collateralized systems can be in line with new supervisory models under the Commonwealth Model Law.

In the following segment (sections 4-6), the analysis is conducted on the three main categories of the private stablecoins: fiat-backed custodial models (or the analysis of the USDT and USDC), crypto-collateralized decentralization systems (or the analysis of the DAI and MakerDAO), and algorithmic systems (or the analysis of the TerraUSD collapse and its consequences). Each part of the document comprises technical architecture description and economic risk analysis as well as applicable case studies, basing on the scholarly research and market developments.

Section 7 makes a comparison between stablecoins and CBDCs in terms of competitive forces, and possible complementing forces. This section contextualizes the analysis in general and the future of money, the sovereignty of money and the fitting roles of both private and governmental digital currencies. Section 8 summarizes findings and formulates policy recommendations based on Commonwealth Model Law framework and seeks harmonization requirements on the international front. The analysis ends with the discovery of the open research questions and necessity of the adaptational approaches to the regulatory frameworks that will promote innovation and reduce systemic risks at the same time.

Introduction: with the background context on the context and value of stablecoins in the market established, the next section shifts to the technical and economic background to bridge the gap between theoretical knowledge and the actual working marketing processes.

2. TECHNICAL AND ECONOMIC FOUNDATIONS

The stablecoins constitute a true innovation in the design of digital assets that they solve on the otherwise unstable cryptocurrency ecosystem by providing price stability. They are based on a combination of the programmable infrastructure of blockchain technology and protocols that enforce fixed value against reference assets, usually the U.S. dollar. To comprehend the place of stablecoins in modern finance, it is necessary to look at both the technical structure and the economy of this tool.

2.1 Defining stablecoins: technical & Economic Perspectives

2.1.1 Technical Architecture

Technically, a stablecoin is a token hosted on a distributed registry, typically Ethereum, but a wide range of alternative blockchains, such as Solana, Tron, and Cardano, have become major hosts. The unique factor about stablecoins is the stabilization mechanism embedded, which can be achieved by either a centralized management or decentralized smart contract paradigm (Arner et al., 2020).

On the structural level, stablecoins can be separated into custodial and non-custodial ones. Custodial stablecoins Innocent Custodians like Circle store USDC as reserve assets and oversee the methods of issuing and redeeming coins. They work like the traditional money market funds and the reserves are made of cash or highly liquid securities. The stablecoins are non-custodial that use automated smart contracts, collateralized debt obligations, or algorithmic mechanisms to stabilize value. It is quite common in these systems to have trust in code, not in institutions, but this replacement comes at the cost of smart contract vulnerabilities and market assumption failures (Kochergin, 2020).

One of the technical elements is the oracle of external data feeds delivering real-time pricing statistics to smart contracts. In the absence of reliable oracles, decentralized stablecoins cannot have accurate collateral ratios or automatic liquidations, which are executed correctly. Single points of technical and economic vulnerability are oracle failures, which may cause unnecessary liquidations due to erroneous or untrustworthy price feeds (MacDonald and Zhao, 2022).

Issuance and redemption are the basic mechanisms on which stablecoins are pegged on value points. In fiat-backed tokens, fiat money is held with the issuer when users deposit fiat money, and it is replaced with a token and vice versa. In the case of decentralized tokens, it is issued when collateral is deposited in smart contracts and can be redeemed through the opposite procedure. Cryptography, consensus, and more elaborate governance are imposed using these technical procedures.

2.1.2 Economic Functions

Stablecoins, in an attempt to recreate the fundamental functions of money in digital space, have an economic aspect. They act as units of account since they offer more consistent values of reference in ecosystems that are otherwise characterized by volatile assets. Also used as a means of exchange, enabling payment and trades in DeFi platforms, and also across international borders with an unparalleled advantage of 24/7 settlement. They also act as reservoirs of values that protect users against the risk of uncertainty that make unbacked cryptocurrencies unsuitable as a savings system (Lyons & Viswanath-Natraj, 2023).

This economic functionality makes stablecoins synthetic money, similar to digital money or money market assets. Their programmability makes utility more than money traditional by making it possible to programmatically pay interest, lend under collateral, and programmably execute escrow services discrete in the smart contracts. This programmability is the most defining aspect of stablecoins they can be run as executable code that supports complicated financial constructions without numerous intermediaries.

Stablecoins are in their unique position between cryptocurrencies and electronic money. Stablecoins can be used as a regular currency, unlike Bitcoin and other similar assets, which do not have explicit stabilization designs. Stablecoins are tokenised, and can be transmitted on public blockchains, and manipulated programmably (unlike traditional e-money) in addition to being more programmable than e-money systems such as PayPal balances. They are generally however, lacking the regulatory clarity as well as consumer protections that come with the established e-money systems. It is this middle ground that describes their swift adoption as well as the increased regulatory interest they receive in the wider world.

2.2 Stabilization Mechanisms: how Pegs Are Maintained

Stablecoins stabilize their pegs with three major mechanisms, which include fiat reserves, crypto collateral, and algorithmic supply adjustments. Both approaches represent unique advantages, threats, and trade-offs that would be worth analyzing.

2.2.1 Fiat Reserves & Custodianship

Fiat-pegged stablecoins such as Tether (USDT) & USD Coin (USDC) are pegged to demand dollar-backed assets whose dislocation is mitigated by external, highly liquid reserves. Theoretically, each unit issued is balanced by the custodian by an equivalent dollar or dollar-denominated asset. As the users deposit the dollars, tokens are minted by the issuers, and tokens are burned when the users require the dollars back (Arner et al., 2020).

The attraction of this model is the ease of use and efficiency in capital One dollar of collateral is all it takes to create one dollar of stablecoin. There are however great risks which arise. Custodial risk implies reliance on solvency and disingenuity on the side of the issuers. Transparency risk occurs due to presence or lack of proper verification of sufficient reserves where meticulous auditing must be carried out which most issuers do not welcome. These weaknesses are evident in the current controversies of Tether in terms of the composition of its reserves, especially its past reliance on historical use of commercial paper, and not cash. Naturally, the unwillingness of the company to submit to full independent audits has contended the lack of trust toward the company in that it will be capable of managing mass redemptions in cases of market crises (Barthélémy et al., 2023).

Arbitrage opportunities are used to maintain the peg. Under the event that the stablecoin is trading at a price lower than one dollar, arbitrageurs can purchase it cheaply and redeem it through fiat at a profit and at the same time reestablishes balance. When it trades higher than a dollar, they put fiat in the mint and sell the coins at a higher price and push the prices down. This arbitrage structure is based on institutional investors who have direct access to issuers and adequate funds to take advantage of any pricing difference (Lyons & Viswanath-Natraj, 2023).

2.2.2 Crypto Collateralization & Automated Liquidations

DAIs and other crypto-collateralized stablecoins are decentralized. To mint stablecoins, users secure volatile crypto assets Ether, Wrapped Bitcoin or other assets in smart contracts. Since cryptocurrencies change in value, such systems are required to be over-collateralized. As an example, one may have to deposit 150 dollars of ETH and mint 100 dollars of DAI (Klages-Mundt and Minca, 2022).

Maintenance of the peg is done by liquidation measures. When the collateral value is below required levels, it is automatically sold by the use of smart contracts to insure that the system is not caught in insolvency. This guarantees resilience at the cost of capital inefficiency since much of the value is tied up and cannot be economically utilized.

These risks are volatility risk, where rapid reduction in prices may cripple collateral buffers; liquidation cascades, where concurrent liquidation may deepen market declines; and smart contract risk, where the weaknesses of the code, or a failure of oracles, can bring down whole systems. Nevertheless, these challenges did not prevent the centralization of DAI and comparable models in DeFi due to their decentralization and compatibility with other protocols (Klages-Mundt et al., 2020).

2.2.3 Algorithmic Supply Adjustments

The stablecoins that are algorithmic strive to stabilize without having any collateral, instead of using the supply-demand dynamics coordinated by autonomous protocols. In the event that prices are higher than the peg, protocols put out new coins to put dilution in place. In a context where there is a decrease in prices, the tokens are destroyed or exchanged in governance tokens to cut supply contracts (Hafner and Pereira, 2023).

The different models have different approaches. Dual-token systems such as TerraUSD/LUNA are a seigniorage share system. Rebasing programs such as Ampleforth maintain an adjustment in balances of all wallets. Partially collateralized with algorithmic adjustments, the fractional hybrids include FRAX.

The hope of algorithmic models is the efficiency of capital that they achieve and the fact that they do not need reserves and trusted custodians. But history shows itself to be very fragile. Death spiral risk in the form of the TerraUSD (UST) fallout in 2022, sparked by loss of confidence leading to mass redemption and overwhelming the stabilization mechanisms. The artificially created algorithm that would have stabilized the situation instead fueled the erosion of the UST when it started being depegged, rendering the LUNA supply massive, annihilating its value and any justification to consider UST as credible into the bargain (BGIN, 2022).

2.2.4 Hybrid Approaches

New designs are trying to merge the collateralization features with the algorithmic characteristics. Djed, a Cardano-based application, leverages over-collateralization with a reserve coin to perform stability guarantees in specified collateral ratios mathematically. JANUS considers the concept of AI-assisted stabilization where machine learning is utilized to meet real-time adjustments in the reserves and collateral ratios. These new and innovative concepts deal with the flaws of pure models, but bring about new governance, transparency, and regulatory acceptance challenges (Hafner & Pereira, 2023).

2.3 The Stablecoin Trilemma: fundamental Trade-offs

The key design problem of stablecoins is summarized in what researchers refer to as the stablecoin trilemma. This model implies that stability, decentralization, and capital efficiency would not be able to be maximized at the same time designers would be able to maximize two qualities but does not optimize a third one (Klages-Mundt et al., 2020).

Stablecoins are pegged to the value of a specific Fiat, are financially efficient and stable, but are not decentralized, relying on centralised custodians such as Circle or Tether. Shear capital inefficiency in crypto-collateralized stablecoins through over-collateralization criterion allows them to be stable and decentralized. Stablecoins that are algorithmic are expected to be both decentralized and capital-efficient, but historically do not achieve stability, as the case of the notorious collapse of UST showed.

According to this framework, risks are not removed but shared depending on design decisions. Any stability comes at a cost and projects that focus on efficiency or decentralization usually put themselves at systemic risk. A large share of academic research and market participants are investigating whether hybrid models can meaningfully overcome such a trilemma, but such empirical evidence is still scarce (Harz et al., 2020).

Transitions: continuing the discussion of stabilization mechanisms above, the subsequent analysis task is to categorize the stablecoins according to the collateral sources and types of governance to gain a clearer insight into the distribution of systemic risks.

3. TAXONOMY AND STRUCTURAL ANALYSIS

An effective taxonomy that could be used to define stablecoins is based on two risk-characterizing dimensions, which are the basis of backing value (collateral) and the control mechanism (governance). This approach goes beyond simple categorization of assets to functional classification of risks creating a conceptual framework which enlightens how various models assign systemic vulnerabilities.

3.1 Collateral Source: exogenous versus Endogenous Backing

The source of collateral will make the difference between a stablecoin having its value based on the success of its own ecosystem or basing it on external assets with their own independent market value.

3.1.1 Exogenous Collateral

Exogenous collateral is any assets which are valued in the market without the protocols of collateralizing the stablecoin. Such assets are highly liquid and external utility, and hence the prices have little correlation to the stablecoin itself. Optimal exogenous collateral are high-grade fiat currency (USD, EUR) and government debt securities (Treasury bills). This can also be done by using commodities such as gold, but they create the risk of commodity prices (Kochergin, 2020).

Exogenous collateral risk profile of exogenous collateral is focused on custodial and counterparty risk in centralized models, and liquidity risk in mass redemptions that may result in fire sales. These fears are similar to those that have been impacting conventional money market funds. Having large holdings of short-term investmentst by stablecoin issuers would lead to a greater process of disruption of the broader funding markets in a systemic issue that regulators are considering more and more (Barthélémy et al., 2023).

3.1.2 Endogenous Collateral

Endogenous collateral is an asset of the prosperity, usefulness and speculative faith of the stablecoin ecosystem. This can contain the native token of governance of the protocol (LUNA in the case of TerraUSD, MKR in the case of MakerDAO). The seigniorage income or future perceived worth of the protocol is what the stablecoin is backed with (BGIN, 2022).

Such support system presents inescapable risk of circular dependency and death spiral. In case the stablecoin trust is lost, the selling forces will devalue the endogenous collateral and thus decrease the support in the stablecoin even further. This reinforcing cycle could get accelerating fast, as the collapse of TerraUSD in May 2022 has shown. Once UST started falling out of its peg, the tool built to regain it was minting colossal quantities of LUNA to replenish the supply, the UST, instead hyperinflated the supply of LUNA and ruined its worth, and the credibility of UST as a probable sketchy backer was lost (Hafner & Pereira, 2023).

Expanded Governance Analysis: in reality, accountability and resilience are dictated by the governance regimes. As an example, MakerDAO uses a decentralized voting process in which the token holders increase or decrease stability fees and collateral requirements, reflecting participatory but multidimensional processes of decision making. Contrary to this, centralized issuers like Circle or Tether are under authoritative and regulated corporate governance with clearer accountability but less transparency in decision making regarding how operations are operated. The differences highlight the importance of the view that governance is a functional risk category that should be provided in the same way as reserve management.

3.2 Governance Structure: centralized Custody versus Decentralized Protocols

The mechanism of control defines the location of ultimate trust: in legally responsible parties or self-governing unchangeable code.

3.2.1 Centralized Governance

Under centralized governance, there is only one legal institution (issuer or custodian) which governs pools of reserve assets, regulates the minting and burning of reserve assets, and has a contractual or legal liability to redeem stablecoins at par. This model relies on off-change legal compliance and conventional financial infrastructure, such as bank accounts and audited financial statements. This is the case with Tether (USDT) and USD Coin (USDC) (MacDonald and Zhao, 2022).

Censorship risk, potential issuer insolvency or fraud, counterparty risk; and operational risk due to use of old banking infrastructure to redeem the security has been listed in the risk profile. Nevertheless, centralized models also provide definite legal access, regulatory access routes, as well as familiar trust designs that are cognizant by institutional consumers.

Empirical Governance Insight: As an example, the population of governance participants in MakerDAO reveals that the less than 10 percent population of MKR token holders regularly votes, demonstrating concentration risks in decentralized systems. On the other hand, the USDC managed by the board in Circle presents transparent accountability in form of formal structures through centralized governance which is evident in the sense that transparency is traded with formal accountability.

Reflecting on the theoretical basis, it is possible to describe the governance structuring in digital asset systems in the terms of agency theory in which the token holders could perform the role of a principal and the developers or validators could represent the role of an agent. Effective governance thus necessitates a system of harmonizing incentives, transparency and devising a system without concentrated power to make decisions. The institutional theory offers an understanding of the development of formal and informal rules, which influence the creation of organizational legitimacy too, and decentralized protocols like MakerDAO or Compound are moving towards a balance between community-based and regulated organizational structures. According to De Filippi (2022) and Buterin (2023), this hybridity can also be seen as a gradual convergence between open-source innovation and regulatory compliance that the Commonwealth Model Law could legally commence by defining the adaptive compliance levels.

3.2.2 In Practice and Theory

Governance systems are the foundations of credibility and resilience to operations of stable coins. Theoretically speaking, centralized systems of governance are compatible with the realization of institutional economics, i.e. lines of accountability, stand of fiduciary responsibility, and legal contracts. Decentralized models, on the contrary, do represent organizational theory and game theory, which exhibits incentive compatibility and group decision making instead of hierarchical control. More precisely, the practice of decentralized autonomous organizations (DAOs) like MakerDAO indicates the possibility of having participatory governance with token-based voting schemes but also shows some shortcomings of governance concentration through the control of decision outcomes by large holders. The acknowledgment of the governance as a risk factor of regulation in the Commonwealth Model Law is an indicator of the necessity to ensure that the innovation aspect is balanced with accountability in centralized and decentralized environments.

3.2.3 Decentralized Governance

Decentralized governance places the power in the hand of protocol guideholders or entrusts an autonomous smart contract computer algorithm with all the authority. On-chain consensus is the basis of control based on the voting of token holders and immutability of code. Programmatically, actions such as adjustments to supply along with liquidations. This solution would be terraUSD (UST) and MakerDAO (DAI) (Klages-Mundt et al., 2020).

The risk profile involves governance risk (due to possible hostile takeovers or voter apathy); smart contract risk (code bugs or vulnerabilities); and economic incentive risk (when the algorithms do not get the incentives of all participants in line with their requirements). But decentralized models have censorship resistance, transparency, and composability with other DeFi protocols that cannot be achieved by centralized alternatives.

Introduction: having the structural taxonomy in place, the discussion shifts to particular models of the stablecoin, starting with fiat-backed custodial systems that tower at present markets.

4. FIAT-BACKED STABLECOINS: THE CUSTODIAL MODEL

The most popular paradigm is Fiat-backed stablecoins, which serve as would essentially be considered as digital analogues of narrow banking or money market funds. Their market supremacy indicates how simple, capital efficient, and peg stability are preferred compared with the ideals of decentralization in the market.

4.1 Technical Architecture & Reserve Management

4.1.1 The One-to-One Reserve Structure

The constructive technical implementation is anchored on the commitment of the issuers to ensure a one-to-one correlation between on-chain issued digital tokens and immensely liquid off-chain reserves of fiat currency. All of these tokens are essentially tokenized deposit claims (Kochergin, 2020).

Issuance can be undertaken by having approved participants place a deposit or fiat deposits in segregated bank or custodial accounts which generate tokens representing the deposits. Redemption enables the holder to redeem tokens with fiat money, their number decrease. Transparency protocols, such as periodic third-party attestation or auditing, is an effort to infer cryptographic evidence between on-chain supply and off-chain support. Nonetheless, as collateral is held outside the chain, it is difficult to check hence relying on conventional audits (MacDonald & Zhao, 2022).

4.1.2 Arbitrage-Based Peg Maintenance

The stability of price does not come as a result of code, but economic incentives encouraging arbitrageurs to take the opportunity of market inefficiencies. Arbitrageurs deposits fiat with the issuers, mint fresh stablecoins, and sell them at a high price into the secondary market, and by doing so, they are making a profit and traffic more coins at a lower price, not to mention the addition of supply to the market. When the price is lower than one dollar, arbitrageurs buy discounted stables and redeem them with issuers at par value, achieving a profit and reducing supply and increasing prices (Lyons and Viswanath-Natraj, 2023).

The operation of this mechanism is subject to a number of conditions: the arbitrageurs need to be able to gain access to issuers to redeem and mint new coins; there must be adequate secondary market liquidity; and the redemption process needs to be stable during stress. Whenever any of these conditions is not met, pegs may be significantly deviated which as the short-term dePEG of the USDC during the crisis with Silicon Valley Bank illustrated.

4.2 Economic Analysis: liquidity, Solvency, & Systemic Risks

4.2.1 Reserve Quality & Solvency Risk

The reserve asset quality is the key to solvency. Though the narrow banking principle would dictate that reserves be in the safest, most liquid instruments the central bank deposits or the issuing of short-term sovereign debts usually invest reserves in instruments with a higher yield such as commercial paper and corporate debt. An issuer-driven investment strategy, which is motivated by the seek of seigniorage (profit of holding non-interest-bearing liabilities before investing assets), creates a credit risk (due to defaults of issuers) and a liquidity risk (due to the impossibility of selling assets without profit within a short period).

These issues can be illustrated using the example of Tether which regularly took significant amounts of commercial paper onto its books over time. Although the company has since moved to Treasury bills, the incident showed how profit making can be used to undermine reserve safety. Poor quality of reserves generates contagion risks in the case of systemically important stablecoins. The fact that they could fail them can cause fire sales of reserves, which could in turn interfere with short-term funding markets this is of particular concern to commercial paper markets and certificate of deposit markets where issuers of stablecoins have prominent places.

4.2.2 Run Vulnerability & Confidence Dynamics

Similar to conventional banks with a fractional reserve, fiat-backed stablecoins are vulnerable to confidence run, but the complete reserve paradigm corresponds to theory. Practically, the panic may be caused by doubts about the reserve sufficiency or issues with the stability of the issuing companies. Mass redemptions can occur as a result of the loss of faith in news about the quality of reserves, regulatory measures, or overall financial crisis (MacDonald and Zhao, 2022).

First-mover advantages are made by run dynamics. Early redeemers would get full par value whereas those who would redeem late would be subject to delayed redemption or partial recovery in case the reserves are found to be inadequate. Such a dynamic promotes preemptive redemption when there exists uncertainty, and may make crises self-fulfilling even to systems sufficiently reserved.

The safest of the designs incorporate narrow bank designs that demand full support on the reserve with the 100% central banks and eliminate credit and liquidity risk. Yet Steve Biko has brought up the issue of credit disintermediation, i.e. withdrawing money that is loaned to commercial banks and depositing it into sterile deposits at the central bank. This conflict between personal stablecoin security and the general credit availability in the financial system is not solved in the policy discussions (Liao & Caramichael, 2022).

4.3 Case Studies: uSDT & USDC

4.3.1 Tether (USDT): market Dominance & Transparency Concerns

Tether, which is the biggest in terms of market capitalization and volume of transactions, was launched in 2014. Its first-mover advantage solidified its reputation in the market as the bridge between fiat and crypto, especially in Asia and offshore markets that have few banking links.

Tether has undergone incessant transparency scandals despite its ubiquity. Research studies and legal settlements had found that very much of the reserves were in commercial paper and other riskier holdings, as compared to cash or Treasury bills. The fact that the company has not been ready to submit itself to comprehensive independent audits has continued to raise doubt on its capacity to deal with mass redemptions in case of crisis situations in the market. However, USDT remains dominating most of the stablecoin liquidity in the world with potent network effects that are in tandem with scale (Arner et al., 2020).

The advantages of extreme liquidity and universal acceptability on nearly all crypto exchanges, along with the robust maintenance of pegs offered by well-established arbitrage factors and high scale. Weaknesses include unresolved transparency shortcomings based on attestation, as opposed to elaborate auditing, and high custodial and credit evaluation on the structure and operation of the reserves.

4.3.2 USD Coin (USDC): regulatory Compliance & Banking Risk

USDC, a version of Tether started by Circle and Coinbase in 2018, is the so-called regulated version of the asset. The reserves are stored mainly in often-attested cash and short term U.S Treasuries. The focus on regulatory compliance and transparency has made USDC the stablecoin of choice of institutions and DeFi developments that are running with the U.S. and European regulatory regimes (MacDonald & Zhao, 2022).

And yet even USDC cannot be spared of conventional risks in banking. In the case of the March 2023 collapse of the Silicon Valley Bank (SVB) in the US, briefly depegged the USDC was declared by Circle, after it announced that part of its reserves were in the form of uninsured deposits at the failing bank. The token dropped down to around $0.87 on the secondary markets and peg was later reinstated following the intervention of the government to support the deposits at SVB. In this episode, it became clear that even the most open fiat-backed stablecoins still face the risk of counterparty banking.

The advantages are good regulatory compliance systems that create institutional trust and high liquidity especially in regulated DeFi platforms and traditional financial institutions. Weaknesses include the vulnerability to the risks of the banking sector that manifested themselves throughout the SVB crisis, as well as being a dependent on centralized custodians and in accordance with changing regulatory standards.

4.4 Regulatory Frameworks & Reserve Standards

The Commonwealth Model Law on stablecoins (2025) specifically deals with the issues of reserve quality and transparency, which is an important contribution to harmonization of policies around the world. The law stipulates that reserves are to be made up of High-Quality Liquid Assets (HQLA) (fiat deposits with short tenors and government securities with short tenors); in other words, only (Commonwealth Secretariat, 2025).

There is an increase in the level of transparency requirements to governance imperatives but not option disclosures. Issuers have to publish reserve composition on a regular basis getting the value, type, location and custodianship arrangements. Adequacy & composition of reserves should be certified by independent auditors and reported publicly. In the case of Tier 1 systemically important issuers, reserve holdings are to be disclosed publicly in near real-time, and they should be found to be supported one-to-one (Commonwealth Secretariat, 2025).

These requirements are consistent with more general international standards that are developed based on the suggestions of the Financial Stability Board on global stablecoins and the MiCA regulation of the European Union. The convergence indicates an increasing agreement that fiat-backed stablecoins should be regulated as financial institutions, including capital requirements and reserve requirements and supervised as such with generic importance according to their systemic risk.

Transition: where fiat-backed models rely on institutional trust, crypto-collateralized stablecoins transfer that trust to code. The next part discusses the way these decentralized structures operate, and where their weaknesses are apparent.

5. CRYPTO-COLLATERALISED STABLECOINS: THE DECENTRALISED MODEL

Crypto-collateralized stablecoins, including the DAI of MakerDAO, is an attempt to create a permissionless, fixed-value digital currency, through decentralization, substituting a central authority with a software self-execution code, where the key components are transparent and publicly accessible. The paradigm attempts to appreciate the sensitivities of censorship resistance and programmability across DeFi protocol economics, to the capital efficiency and regulatory reasonableness.

5.1 Technical Architecture: over-Collateralization & Automated Liquidations

5.1.1 The Vault System

These fundamental operations are concerned with the Collateralized Debt Positions (CDPs) or vaults. Smart contract vault A vault is a form of deposit often deposited in order to hold volatile cryptocurrency, usually Ether, along with other permitted holdings, at the discretion of their owners. The protocol loans and puts the stablecoins into debt by borrowing them out to the purchasers. Stablecoin debt needs to be multiplied by 150-300 per cent to assume market volatility without defaulting instantly, because the collateral value should be much higher (Klages-Mundt, and Minca, 2022).

This excessive collateralization brings a lot of capital inefficiency. Users have to lock $150-300 collateral value to every $100 stablecoin minted, which is basically holding large amounts of capital at immobility. This inefficiency puts downward bounds on scalability and the reason why crypto-collateralized stablecoins have not yet attained the dominance of fiat-backed counterparts despite their benefits of decentralization.

5.1.2 Liquidation Mechanisms

The automated system requires real-time collateral pricing information in an oracle. Smart contracts constantly keep track of the vault collateral ratios relative to Minimum Collateralization Ratios (MCR). Liquidation is automatic when collateral prices lower to values below MCR limits, thus triggering smart contracts to liquidate assets. Collateral is sold in markets, collateral is confiscated and money used to pay off debt in stablecoins and penalty interests. It works by keeping the solvency of the system intact since stablecoins will be maintained even when collateral values change (Klages-Mundt et al., 2020).

Although the liquidation mechanisms are useful in terms of stability, they pose risks on their own. Coalitions of liquidations across numerous vaults during the crashes of fast market can flood markets with sell orders, and collateral price falls may reinforce themselves in feedback loops. These risks were evidenced by the Black Thursday experience in March 2020, when Ether prices fell more than 50 percent in one day. Liquidation markets were too slow to handle the amount of auctions, certain vaults were sold at gradually under $0, and DAI traded considerably higher than it was pegged by the system as they endeavored to make the books work (Klages-Mundt & Minca, 2022).

5.2 Economic Analysis: deleveraging Spirals & Endogenous Volatility

5.2.1 Fragility & Death Spirals

Crypto-collateralized stablecoins rely purely on unstable crypto-asset prices as opposed to the reserves or the authority of the central bank. This produces unique system and especially in deleveraging spirals. Mass simultaneous liquidations may be experienced in a large number of vaults when the price of collateral assets falls suddenly. Intelligible contracts sell collateral automatically to settle debts to enforce enormous downward pressure on collateral prices. This compelled selling has a negative impact on prices that trigger further liquidations causing self-reinforcing feedback loops (Klages-Mundt & Minca, 2022).

Collateral is eaten up more rapidly than models predict in periods of extreme volatility in which deleverage works. Markets might have inadequate liquidity to absorb forced sales making stablecoins to trade with values above their pegs because arbitrageurs might not effectively restore the issue of equilibrium. Although not as disastrous as algorithmic stablecoin failures, these dynamics show that crypto-collateralized models have fundamental stability pressures in times of market-stress.

5.2.2 Governance Tokens as Ultimate Risk Bearers

The protocols are usually controlled by special tokens (MKR in the case of MakerDAO) giving their holders voting rights on risk parameters such as stability fees, types of collateral, and liquidation ratios. Governance tokens act as protocol equity, which act as ultimate risk holders. The system becomes insolvent and protocols mint and sell more governance tokens to recover itself in disastrous situations in which liquidated collateral is not adequate to settle remaining stablecoin debt. This water downs holders but theoretically it is a stable peg of a coin (Klages-Mundt et al., 2020).

This type of governance produces complicated incentives relationships. Governance token holders should strike a balance between the parameter of risk to ensure that protocol revenue is maximized, but at an appropriate level of safety margin. Excessively aggressive parameters maximize capital efficiency and revenue but have catastrophic failures. Too restrictive parameters are a sure guarantee of stability, but restricted growth and profitability. The issue of optimum equilibria has been very difficult to solve especially with the changing market conditions.

5.3 Case Study: MakerDAO & the Peg Stability Module

MakerDAO has been an adaptive resilient system because it changed its design based on the lessons or stresses in the market. The protocol and its original implementations were based solely on Ether collateral but was later able to accept a variety of crypto assets and ultimately centralize stablecoins with the Peg Stability Module (PSM).

The PSM will allow DAI to be directly traded to particular centralized stablecoins, specifically USDC, at precise 1:1 ratios with no collateral volatility or liquidation risk. This mechanism was successful in tightening the peg of DAI through provision of effective arbitrage by centralized and trusted assets thus significantly limiting the deviation of the peg (Lyons and Viswanath-Natraj, 2023).

Nevertheless, this hybrid argues demonstrates that crypto-collateralized models contain underlying tensions. Accepting the USDC as security has improved stability as well as capital efficiency by making DAI more stable, although at the expense of restoring some of the custodial counterparty risk. This according to critics disintegrates the decentralization thesis of DAI, and according to proponents, is just practical adjustment to survive in the competition (Kozhan and Viswanath-Natraj, 2021).

The success of the PSM shows the trilemma of the stablecoin in action. Handling Pure crypto-collateralized designs are maximally decentralized but inefficient in terms of capital and problems in stability when the market experiences volatility. The enhancement of stabilization and efficiency through a centralized stablecoin occurs at the expense of decentralization. The development of MakerDAO implies that market dynamics can drive even ideologically decentralized projects towards hybridization to gain a bit of functional improvements at the cost of autonomy.

Transition: the discussion has considered the systems of custodial and collateralization, now moving on to algorithmic models, novel and vulnerable efforts to create an artificial guarantee of price stability by writing only code.

Smooth Transition Added: After surveying centralized and decentralized structure, a changeover to algorithmic structures is now considered in the analysis- showing the inability of stability engineering without collateral support.

6. ALGORITHMIC STABLECOINS: ENGINEERING FAILURE

The most ambitious yet the least successful experiments in decentralized money creation are algorithmic stablecoins. These structures are trying to be stable by using code alone without any on the collateral support and custodians. Although in theory elegant, algorithmic stablecoins have proven again and again to be structurally unsound, with failures of massively disastrous scale that wiped out billions of dollars in value and sparked the wider market explosion.

6.1 Technical Architecture: seigniorage Shares & Supply Algorithms

6.1.1 The Two-Token Model

The most common algorithm construction is the use of dual- token systems. The original instrument is the stablecoin itself, which is intended to be equal to a fixed value (usually, 1 USD). The second is a governance or volatility token which is the ultimate risk taker and origin of intrinsic value. This was the case with TerraUSD (UST) and LUNA (BGIN, 2022).

The stabilization algorithm enables continuous trading of tokens between tokens with fixed relative values. A fixed number of dollar of the volatility token can always be traded in exchange of one stablecoin, and vice versa. Theoretically, this market arbitrage mechanism keeps the peg by market market participants reacting to price variations.

6.1.2 The Mint-&-Burn Mechanism

In the case where stablecoin price is higher than their peg, arbitrageurs use volatility tokens to produce new stablecoins, and sell them at a high price to earn a profit. This adds supply to the stablecoin pushing the price of the coin down to the peg. In the case of the stablecoin devaluing against its peg, and the arbitrageurs are purchasing discounted stablecoins and burning them to issue a volatility token worth more, making a profit and decreasing the supply of stablecoin and increasing its price in the market (BGIN, 2022).

This mechanism works well in the case of expansion where demand is on the rise and confidence is strong. This system will be at its most vulnerable point during contraction especially when there are liquidity constraints and lack of confidence.

6.2 Economic Analysis: circular Dependency & Death Spirals

6.2.1 The Absence of Independent Value

The essential economic weakness of pure algorithmic designs is circular dependency & not an independent exogenous support. The value of the volatility token is based on the future expectations of the success and adoption of the stablecoin in the first place. In case of failure of the stablecoin, then the volatility token will be useless. The stablecoin is pegged exclusively to a token that could not have a value or worth outside of the stability of the stablecoin a circular relationship susceptible to one that could collapse due to confidence (Hafner & Pereira, 2023).

This is very different in the exogenously supported models. Fiat backed stablecoins are a claim to dollars, which are inherently valued regardless of whether they are backed by a specific stablecoin or not. Crypto collateralized stablecoins are listed on assets with separate utility and market demand. The algorithmic stablecoins do not have this external anchor and instead must rely solely on the self-reinforcing faith in the viability of the system.

6.2.2 The Contraction Death Spiral

The stabilization mechanism is asymmetrically carried out. Growing demand in a natural way makes tokens structurally stable as new growth takes place. Contraction is structurally instable most especially when stressed. In case the price of stablecoins drops below the peg, the algorithm is forced to issue and auction off huge amounts of volatility tokens to repurchase the supply of the stablecoins. This inundates markets with volatility tokens, which cause a collapse in their price due to a dilution (Hafner and Pereira, 2023).

When the prices of volatility tokens crash, those in the market are aware that the system is not supported seriously which results in the stablecoin itself being run out of panic. The mutual reinforcement death spiral results in the collapsing of the prices in both directions. This is an entire system outburst, hastened, and frequently irreversible failure. Systems that use algorithms to create stable coins by backing them with fiat or buying collateral do not recover in situations of short-term strain; in contrast, fiat-backed or crypto-collateralized stablecoins are able to recover in catastrophes like a death spiral.

6.3 Case Study: the TerraUSD Collapse

The algorithmic stablecoin fragility is empirically proven with the May 2022 case of the collapsed Terra ecosystem. Because of its speculative design, TerraUSD (UST) soared to an unprecedented market capitalization of more than $18 billion and widespread adoption throughout the crypto economy, especially with the Anchor protocol that gave a 20% yearly yield on UST deposits.

6.3.1 The Faulty Incentive Structure

Terra artificially boosted the demand according to artificially high yields. The 20 percent APY of the Anchor protocol was attracted by a huge inflow of capital, which generated humongous UST supply. These productions did not make economic sense--they were practically being given away by LUNA token inflation and venture capital capital. This was a time bomb, as soon as the yields would be no longer sustainable, and the UST holders would start pulling out, this system would experience a contraction pressure it was not designed to withstand (BGIN, 2022).

6.3.2 The Cascade of Failures

The fall was experienced in various planes. The mechanism behind it was an algorithm that failed because LUNA hyperinflation caused by the mint-&-burn mechanism killed its value and removed any believable UST support. The operations of the governance model failed as the team behind the Terra had to manually halt the blockchain at the time when there was a crisis, which prevented the implementation of smart contracts. This move, which was aimed at bringing in an end to the death spiral, only served to show that the system was not actually decentralized and that the centralized players could overrule code when results would have become unacceptable (BGIN, 2022).

The spread of the contagion was considerably further than Terra itself. The failure of such major crypto investors as Celsius Network, Voyager Digital, and Three Arrows Capital partly occurred because of exposure to UST. There was intense volatility in the larger crypto markets with the entire ecosystem losing trust. The episode showed that the failures of algorithmic stablecoins can potentially cause systemic risk without a scale different than the failures of traditional financial system.

6.3.3 Lessons & Policy Implications

There are a number of important lessons that became crystallized in the Terra collapse. True algorithmic stablecoins which are not supported by exogenous means are structurally unsustainable and may collapse. The great returns provided by protocols, need to be examined as possible Ponzi schemes instead of viable returns. Decentralization assertions need to be validated the capacity to ensure system stoppage by central agencies in stress conditions displays the centralization of the governance desirously of technological fragmentation.

Policymakers have reacted to this by regulating or banning unsupported algorithmic stablecoins in many jurisdictions. In the Commonwealth Model Law, the prohibition of pure algorithmic designs is largely effective since it obliges the stablecoins to have sufficient reserves, which are the assets that remain permitted. This regulative convergence is an indication that there is agreement among regulators that algorithmic stablecoins represent unacceptable systemic risks that exceed their theoretical value (Commonwealth Secretariat, 2025).

Additional Case Study: outside of the algorithmic models, other tokens such as the Euro Coin (EUROC) and the PAX Gold (PAXG) can be used to demonstrate diversification in the strategy of backing. The monetary integration between the Eurozone is observed through EUROC and the tokenization of the gold reserves through PAXG, which uses a physical commodity to assign value. Such hybrid or commodity-linked examples are also included to emphasize how such stablecoin design has continued to shift past dollar-based paradigms in favor of a broader asset representation.

6.4 Other Algorithmic Experiments

In addition to Terra, there have been other algorithmic methods that have come up with different levels of success. AMPL is a rebasing system designed to stabilise wallet balances every day according to the target prices. Although innovative, its fluctuating volatility and baffling user experience offsets change even in absence of transactions have limited its mass usage. FRAX can be discussed as a more sensible development since it is based on fractional-algorithmic design combining collateralization and algorithmic parameter changes. FRAX is trying to achieve efficiency and resilence by partially supporting tokens with assets such as USDC, but in the long term, it is unclear whether this will be viable or not.

These experiments reveal above attempts at going beyond the stablecoin trilemma by designing hybrids. Empirical track record, however, indicates that unrestricted use of algorithmic methods is fundamentally unsound, whereas hybridized models again pose a lot of the centralizing issues, which they purport to prevent.

Transition: after discussing the most important models of a stablecoin by private actors, the following section compares them to Central Bank Digital Currencies (CBDCs) to see where these two models of digital money overlap and diverge.

7. COMPARATIVE ANALYSIS: STABLECOINS AND CENTRAL BANK DIGITAL CURRENCIES

The accelerated central bank interest in issuing CBDCs has been accompanied by the rapid rise in the number of stablecoins. They both are versions of digitised, programmable money, although fundamentally different in how they are governed, trusted, and how they pursue a policy aim. A glimpse of similarities and differences will unveil opposing visions of the future of digital finance and can see the possible ways of coexistence or confrontation.

7.1 CBDC Design Principles & Technical Models

CBDCs are simply digital versions of central bank money on the one hand, affecting central bank money and not companies. The nature of their design echoes the goals of the public policy such as monetary sovereignty, financial stability, and financial inclusion, unlike the market-based innovation provided by stablecoins.

7.1.1 Central Bank Backing & Legal Status

CBDCs have the full faith and credit of the issuing central banks, unlike stablecoins. They are legal tenders supported by sovereign counterparts, and with no default risk whatsoever. By having CBDCs in both the hands of people and companies, these persons have direct claims on central banks, similar to holding real money, but digitally. This is a property of the CBDCs that designates them as theoretically the safest digital form of money in the market (WEF, 2023).

7.1.2 Technical Design Choices

CBDC architectures differ on a number of dimensions. Wholesale CBDCs are limited to the financial institutions of interbank settlements and basically the current reserve systems are digitized. Retail CBDCs are offered to ordinary people and in this case they compete directly with the transactions of the stablecoin which is privately issued. The system based on tokens enables the transfer with the help of digital signatures without referring to personal identity, which ensures increased privacy. Central bank and mediator-owned CBDCs are also linked to verified identities, which introduces a increased level of KYC compliance, but privacy is a greater concern (Sethaput and Innet, 2023).

There are also variations of distribution models. Direct systems are where central banks run all the consumer accounts where a maximum amount of control is done but large amounts of operations are created. Two tier/indirect system- Customers interface functions and AML/KYC functions are outsourced to commercial banks, maintaining low risk of bank disintermediation and commercial banking models. Majority of the central banks prefer indirect methods that do not alter current structures of financial system by adding digitality (Arner et al., 2020).

7.1.3 Integration with Monetary Policy

CBDCs are purported as monetary policy transmission instruments, which may provide central banks with more direct instruments to manage the state of the economy. Theoretically, programmable CBDCs would facilitate the use of negative interest rates by central banks, deliver focused stimulus payments more effectively than it would have been with physical cash, or manage money supply more acutely. Such integration is a key contrast to the stablecoins, which fall outside the frameworks of monetary policy and can even make the transmission of policies more difficult (Liao & Caramichael, 2022).

7.2 Comparing Stablecoins & CBDCs

7.2.1 Trust Frameworks

The most fundamental difference lies in trust frameworks. stablecoins depend on market trust in issuers, custodians, or technical protocols. This trust can evaporate quickly during crises, as Tether transparency debates & the TerraUSD collapse demonstrated. CBDCs rest on public trust in central banks & governments. While this significantly reduces credit & technical risks, it raises different concerns about state surveillance, financial privacy, & monetary power concentration (Arner et al., 2020).

7.2.2 Stability Mechanisms

The lower level of difference is in respect to trust frames. stablecoins rely on market trust in issuers, custodians or technical protocols. Through crises, this trust can be undone in a short time, as was the case with the TerraUSD collapse and transparency discussions of Tether. CBDCs are based on the belief in central banks and governments. Although this substantially concentrates credit and technical risks, it provokes other issues of state monitoring, financial confidentiality, and centralization of the power.

7.2.3 Programmability & Innovation

Stablecoins are kept stable by collateralizing to external assets by collateral reserves, over-collateralization, or algorithmic rules, and fail when stressed. CBDCs assume very divergent approaches and are necessarily stable since they are direct central bank money. They are valued by sovereign guarantees as opposed to sophisticated peg systems. Such structural advantage eradicates credit risk as well as conflict of maintaining pegs.

The programmability of the circuit board and the rate at which the chip can be reengineered/innovated.

The same promise of better efficiency, lower cost, and programmability advantages over legacy payment systems are enabled differently in both stablecoins and CBDCs, though they have many applications and are already used in DeFi applications and transfers across borders. Their programmability is their natural state of being integrated into the existing smart manors and decentralized apps. In most jurisdictions, CBDCs are still largely experimental with only a few countries having become retail. Their programmability will require central bank designing considerations and will most probably be limited further as the policymakers merge innovation and risk management (CBDC & stablecoins, 2025).

7.2.4 Legal Recognition

Perhaps the critical practical distinction is the legal status, where in many jurisdictions stablecoins are in regulatory gray areas at present, and only regulatory frameworks are establishing formal supervisory frameworks, such as the MiCA of the EU regulation and the Commonwealth Model Law. By definition, CBDCs are legally accepted and established, i.e. a legal tender, subject to the full support of the government and with regulatory clarity.

7.3 Competition, Complementarity, & Geopolitical Dimensions

7.3.1 Digital Dollarization & Monetary Sovereignty

Most of the stablecoins are pegged to dollars, and their mass implementation in fact expands the jurisdiction of U.S. money on the international scale, undermining the monetary independence of smaller states. This is the process of dollarization that can be completed by far faster than the traditional dollarization since stablecoins can be used by anyone with access to the internet, no bank connections are required, and the transfer across borders takes place immediately (Arner et al., 2020).

To Commonwealth member states as well as other developing economies, this is an acute policy challenge. In cases where the citizens are using the dollar based stablecoins instead of the local currencies, central banks become ineffective in monetary policy. Capital regulation will be more difficult because the stablecoins would provide the ability to transfer values across national borders almost instantly. The issues in exchange rate management are complicated due to the development of parallel dollar-based digital economies coupled with the formal currency systems.

CBDCs are inherent solutions to digital dollarization. Through the issuance of digital currencies that are internationally competitive, central banks can fight off competition through the issuance of foreign currency stablecoins and retain their monetary sovereignty. Due to its straightforward position as an alternative to U.S. dollar-backed stablecoins in global trade, the Chinese digital yuan (e-CNY) illustrates how CBDCs are both geopolitically oriented, as well as monetary (CBDC & stablecoins, 2025).

7.3.2 Areas of Direct Competition

CBDCs will be directly competing with fiat-backed stablecoins in a number of areas. CBDCs have superior security and legal tender which they use to gain market share of payment transactions. In the case of savings and store-of-value services, CBDCs as risk-free sovereign obligations will draw risk-averse institutional and retail investors who are currently on the stablecoins. In both of them, the structural benefits of CBDCs equal to zero credit risk, state support, and legal clarity make them competitive compared to non-state alternatives (Liao & Caramichael, 2022).

7.3.3 Potential Complementarity

Competitive tensions could not eliminate stablecoins & CBDCs can exist as part of hybrid monetary ecosystems, with decentralized crypto-collateralized stablecoins, such as DAI, being good vectors of innovation and connectors of DeFi ecosystem. CBDCs will not be at liberty to duplicate the nimbleness needed to carry out quick and agile DeFi development, and will require closed permissioned ledgers. In this vision, CBDCs can be considered as settlement layers and stablecoins as tools to be used by users to allow specific applications in tokenized finance (Argoz Consultants, 2025).

The synthetics CBDCs (sCBDCs) represent very appealing models of hybrids. Stablecoins provided by private entities are fully secured by the holdings of central bank reserves or CBDC, thus subjecting them to both the trust and stability associated to the public sector, and the innovation and efficiency that is associated with the private one. This would address the reserve transparency problem at the cost of maintaining programmability & composability that render stablecoins useful. But it presents highly complicated issues regarding banking disintermediation, fair competition, and the right regulatory systems (Arner et al., 2020).

7.3.4 Commonwealth-Specific Considerations

The stablecoin-CBDC relation implies unique connotations in the case of Commonwealth jurisdictions, especially economies that have high diaspora remittance rates. The cost of remittance in many commonwealth countries with traditional banking remains high and stablecoins present a chance at efficiency improvement but increase the dollarization process. CBDCs may offer affordable digital payments infrastructure without impairing monetary sovereignty but would need big technical resources and funding, which small central banks find hard to muster.

Inclusion of these tensions within the Commonwealth Model Law assumes these levels of regulation enabling the differentiation of tiered regulatory frameworks related to systemically important and smaller stablecoin issuers and, in a bid of balancing both facilitation of the innovation and protection of stability. This solution is based on the fact that pure prohibition would push the stablecoin activity into the shades whereas uncontrolled spread would jeopardize the financial and monetary independence (Commonwealth Secretariat, 2025).

7.4 Real-World Stress Testing: the USDC-SVB Episode

The Silicon Valley bank collapse of March 2023 and ensuing dc pegging of the USDC is an interesting example that sheds some light on the weakness of stablecoins in comparison to the strengths of CBDC. In the incident whereby Circle announced that it had 3.3 billion reserves in the form of uninsured deposits in the insolvent bank, the panic selling caused a drop in the USDC to about 0.87 on the secondary markets. Although the redemption system of Circle and intervention by the U.S. government stabilized the peg afterward, the incident revealed the fact that even the most transparent and well-managed fiat-backed stablecoins are prone to conventional banking risks (MacDonald & Zhao, 2022).

This would not have been possible with a CBDC, but not a private stablecoin, as central bank money is not subject to any custodial or counterparty risk. This shows a serious structural benefit of CBDCs even when compared to the most well-thought-out alternatives in the private sector. Nevertheless, it also shows a present systemic significance of stablecoins with government intervention being deemed to be required to reestablish the peg of USDC the reality that such a move was thought to be necessary is an indicator that the concept of stablecoins has reached a point where its failure has a wider impact on the financial infrastructure.

Transition: to lead up to this section discussing regulatory frameworks and governance practices that form the policy of stable coins in the Commonwealth and beyond, the comparative analysis above provides a context of that exploration.

Smooth Transition Added: Taking on what has been learned through comparison of CBDCs and stablecoins, the next policy framework makes the transition between theory and regulation implementation across the harmonization agenda of the Commonwealth.

8. POLICY FRAMEWORK AND RECOMMENDATIONS

Depending on the technical innovativeness of stablecoins will not overcome the underlying trade-offs between the analysis of stablecoin mechanics, risks and market performance. These trade-offs require elaborate regulatory frameworks that divide risks in proper ways, come up with some clear operational standards and coordinate activities across borders to avoid regulatory arbitrage.

8.1 Synthesis of Trade-offs & Risk Distribution

8.1.1 The Persistent Trilemma

The impossibility of being both stable and decentralized and capital efficiency as the stablecoin trilemma has been seen to be incredibly persistent even under the different design cycles. This inherent limitation implies that risks are shifted as opposed to being eliminated according to the design decisions. Models supported by Fiat push the risk to centralized custodians/banking systems. The models of crypto-collateralization intoxicate the risk in the capital inefficiency and liquidation mechanisms. The models of algorithms guarantee the concentration of risk in the dynamics of confidence and feedback loops that are endogenous (Klages-Mundt et al., 2020).

To regulate this risk, it is necessary to understand redistribution of risks. Instead of attempting to find one best model, regulatory systems should understand that various designs are used in different circumstances and demand different risk profiles to be managed using different approaches.

8.1.2 The Cost of Confidence

Offering security in terms of stablecoin support is costly in a different manner across the paradigms. Fiat-backed systems incur costs via seigniorage possibilities that are foregone in keeping safe reserves instead of investments that are made to take advantage of yield-seeking. Crypto-collateral models are costly in terms of capital inefficiency via over-collateralization as well as liquidation loss transferred to the user. Cost allocation to equity dilution and market risk to equity holders of volatility tokens is represented by algorithmic systems (Barthélémy et al., 2023).

The tensions that can be seen in these cost structures are between profitability and safety. Whether investors do so by investing money in large amounts or not, this maximization of profits through an aggressive allocation of profits in reserves increases systemic risk. Safety margins are lowered by protocols that are optimizing capital efficiency. Such dynamic needs regulation so that the social costs systemic risk and financial instability are properly internalized by operators of stablecoins.

8.2 The Commonwealth Model Law Framework

The Commonwealth Model Law on stablecoins (2025) is an important step towards risk-based regulation that takes into account the unique property of stablecoins and is compatible with global approaches to financial stability boards, anti-financial services environment, and new regulations such as the MiCA regulation of the EU.

8.2.1 Functional Regulation & Tiered Licensing

The drama of the Model Law embraces the principle of same risk, same regulation, where regulatory requirements are applied according to activities and risks and not based on technologies used. This pragmatic strategy avoids regulatory arbitrage whereby similar economic transactions can be handled differently in relation to how they are implemented using technology (Commonwealth Secretariat, 2025).

Systemically important (Tier 1) and smaller (Tier 2) stablecoin issuers are separated into a tiered licensing framework. The level of requirement imposed on tier 1 issuers is similar to that of a commercial bank or systemically critical financial market infrastructures, including a very high capital requirement, detailed supervision and redress planning. Tier 2 issuers have proportionate requirements because of their smaller systemic footprint. Risk-based segmentation is a way of balancing the needs to facilitate innovation and protect the system at a systemic level (Commonwealth Secretariat, 2025).

8.2.2 Reserve Quality & Transparency Mandates

One of the fundamental aspects of the regulatory system is represented by reserve quality standards. The Model Law enforce fiat-backed stablecoins to hold reserves as High-Quality Liquid Asset (HQLA), which is a fiat currency deposits and short-tenor government securities. This is a very lean method of banking that removes credit risk and makes liquidation quick in times of stress (Commonwealth Secretariat, 2025).

The regulatory requirements of transparency increase to voluntary disclosures into compulsory governance requirements. The issuers are required to periodically disclose reserve composition publicly with the values and nature of the assets, their location and custodianship arrangement. Independent auditors will have to certify the adequacy and composition of reserves, and available publicly. In the case of

Tier 1 issuers, the reserve holdings are to be publicized in near real-time, and show on-going one-to-one support (Commonwealth Secretariat, 2025).

These are those provisions, which are considered to fill the transparency gaps that have been the bane of stablecoins since its birth. The framework reduces information asymmetries, which facilitate market instability and runs, because of its requirement of frequent disclosure that is independently checked up.

8.2.3 Algorithmic stablecoin Restrictions

The Model Law is successful in preventing the pure algorithmic stablecoins by ensuring that the assets they allow to contain them have sufficient reserves. This is a consensus by regulators, reached based on empirical experience with Terra and other collapses, that unsupported algorithms models are unacceptable systemic risks. Although it could inhibit innovation, it will avoid the disastrous failures and contagion that algorithmic designs have proven to be both recurring and regular (Commonwealth Secretariat, 2025).

This ban is in tandem with new international trends. The MiCA regulation by the EU puts too high a demand on the algorithmic stablecoins that makes them commercially invalid. Likewise, it has been indicated that algorithmic designs may attract increased suspicion and even a ban, by regulatory bodies in larger jurisdictions such as the United States.

8.3 Global Harmonization & Cross-Border Coordination

The international nature of stablecoins they transfer seamlessly across borders & jurisdictions necessitates coordinated regulatory approaches to prevent arbitrage where issuers migrate to permissive jurisdictions while serving global markets.

8.3.1 Alignment with International Standards

The Commonwealth Model Law conforms in many ways to the recommendations of Financial Stability Board on global stablecoins and FATF on virtual assets and virtual asset service providers and the MiCA framework in the EU. Such converge indicates an accumulating global agreement on main regulatory principles such as reserve supporting guidelines, transparency principles, and operational resilience anticipations (Commonwealth Secretariat, 2025).

Nonetheless, there are still specifics to implementational differences especially in the area of decentralized protocols that do not have obvious legal personalities and governance frameworks within traditional regulatory frameworks. Additional global deliberation via forums such as the G20, FSB and FATF is necessary in order to come up with strategies that can be effective in controlling decentralized models without suffocating innovation or forcing activities to unregulated shadowy areas.

8.3.2 Embedded Supervision & Real-Time Monitoring

New supervisory models utilize the transparency of blockchain to fully resolve real-time supervision without causing too much compliance overhead. Embedded supervision or regulation by code consists of having regulated stablecoins have continuous reserve data on-chain that can be monitored by supervisors as required, and is publicly auditable. This technique enhances accountability and retains the benefits of efficiency of DLT (Auer, 2019).

Embedded supervision would involve technical prerequisites in the form of on-chain data format standardization and ensure the reliability of oracles to support the valuation of the reserve, as well as the presence of cross-border coordination to foster the ability to provide cross-border supervision. Embedded supervision approaches proposed by the Bank for International Settlements Innovation Hub have been piloted indicating feasibility, but scalability and privacy protection are still issues in development (Auer, 2019).

8.3.3 AML/CFT & Travel Rule Implementation

Stablecoins represent unique anti-money laundering and counter-financing of terrorism (AML/CFT) issues. Their cross-border a movability, their pseudo-anonymous quality, and their readiness to integrate with privacy-enhancing technologies are able to promote illicit money. This is because proper regulation presupposes that the issuers of stablecoins and the providers of their services will adopt detailed AML/CFT frameworks with customer due diligence, transaction monitoring, and suspicious transactions reporting (Commonwealth Secretariat, 2025).

The FATF Travel Rule since it asks virtual asset service providers to disclose information about originators and beneficiaries of transfers also presents a problem in implementation in decentralized protocols with no central operators. One solution that is being developed is also peer-to-peer messaging protocols that could facilitate Travel Rule compliance without any centralized intermediaries, but it is technically immature and has yet to be accepted by regulators.

8.4 Commonwealth-Specific Use Cases & Policy Implications

8.4.1 Remittance Corridors & Financial Inclusion

Most Commonwealth jurisdictions are big directions of remittances, and diaspora streams make up major part of the GDP. The costs are frequently greater than 5-10% of the value of the transfers which, even when substantial numbers of people intending to move the money internationally, can be a significant economic burden, and stablecoins promise a possibility to transfer the money almost instantly at a very low price (Arner et al., 2020).

Nevertheless, these benefits can be achieved through risk management approaches that are unique. The regulation needs to enable compliant remittance of services with stablecoins and protect the consumers, comply with AML/CFT and comply with the regulation of foreign exchange. The possibility of excessive regulation can lead to a lack of stablecoin remittance services, and the lack of regulation can facilitate the illegal finance and the harm of consumers.

The tiered approach of the Commonwealth Model Law would also allow smaller remittance-oriented stablecoin operators to be licensed with accordingly scaled-down requirements, which could result in competitive and efficient remittance markets that still ensures sufficient regulation (Commonwealth Secretariat, 2025).

8.4.2 Digital Dollarization Management

In Commonwealth jurisdictions that have weaker currencies or incur a greater rate of inflation, a strong prevalence of stablecoins presents an urgent monetary sovereignty problem. The central banks lose the power to exercise an independent monetary policy when citizens choose to have dollar-pegged stablecoins rather than use domestic currency. The management of exchange rate becomes complex, & the seigniorage profits is actually passed on to the issuers of foreign stable coins.

Some policy responses involve creating domestic versions of CBDCs to act as competitive candidates, targeted capital controls on the adoption of stablecoins, or to accept dollarization, but pursuing macroeconomic stability policies that do not undermine confidence in domestic currencies. All strategies give different trade-offs between monetary sovereignty, financial inclusion, and facilitation of innovation.

The best course of action is probably going to differ according to jurisdiction depending on institutional capability, economic realities, and policy priorities. The Commonwealth Secretariat is able to present the sharing of knowledge of effective approaches so that the member states can solve these complex trade-offs based on the experiences of their peers (Commonwealth Secretariat, 2025).

8.4.3 Commonwealth Case Studies and Empirical Context

Empirical evidence on Commonwealth cases and practice can be used to demonstrate opportunities and challenges to the adoption of stablecoins and CBDC. The eNaira image in Nigeria is a test of early CBDC implementation to minimize the cost of remittances and enhance inclusion. The JAM-DEX pilot, in Jamaica, has recorded a certain level of success in the realm of digital retail payments, and this has been adopted with a relatively low level of adoption as a result of low digital literacy in Jamaica. The integration of the Unified Payments Interface (UPI) of India with experimental stablecoin models under regulatory sandboxing demonstrates the possibility of the coexistence of the public and private digital currency models. These case studies highlight the fact that Commonwealth states can become guinea pigs of innovation, inclusion, and sovereignty in computing finance policy-making.

8.4.4 CBDC-Stablecoin Interoperability

Instead of considering CBDCs and stablecoins as incompatible opposites, the policy frameworks also need to consider viable models of coexistence. CBDC-backed stablecoins prove to be especially promising hybrids, balancing the stability of the business sector with the innovation of the public one. CBDCs are used in this model as wholesale settlement channel and retail users are provided by stablecoins, which can ensure the greatest innovation and stability (Arner et al., 2020).

To implement such designs, there must be technical interoperability levels that will allow a clear exchange of CBDCs with regulated stablecoins and the establishment of regulatory frameworks that will oversee the issuance of stablecoins supported by CBDCs and supervision to check on the sufficiency of reserve and operational stability. The convening power and technical assistance capability of the Commonwealth can develop pilot programs of trial of these hybrid approaches in the member states.

8.5 Open Research Challenges and Future Directions

Although significant progress has been made in the cognition of stablecoin workings and the creation of regulatory measures, there are still numerous vital questions to clarify through research.

8.5.1 Systemic Contagion Modeling

One of the immediate research agendas is developing sophisticated computational models that can model the contagion of an event of stablecoin failure across the DeFi ecosystems and into the traditional financial markets in an extremely realistic manner. These models need to offer cross-chain dependencies, liquidity interactions in times of stress, as well as feedback between crypto and traditional finance. Superior modelling would allow regulating bodies to perform stress tests and set reasonable capital buffers of those that are systemically significant issuers (Barthélémy et al., 2023).

8.5.2 Decentralized Oracle Security

Oracles represent critical infrastructure & single points of failure for decentralized stablecoins. Developing genuinely decentralized, incentive-aligned oracle mechanisms resistant to economic & governance attacks is essential for non-custodial system security. The studies should investigate cryptographic verification methods, prediction market aggregation models, and economic incentive frameworks which render oracle manipulation vehemently costly (MacDonald & Zhao, 2022).

8.5.3 Optimal CBDC-Stablecoin Institutional Arrangements

Oracles are individual critical infrastructure and single points of failure of decentralized stablecoins. The security of the non-custodial system requires the emergence of genuinely decentralized incentive-consistent oracle systems that are hostile of the economic and governance attacks. Research should be conducted on cryptographic authentication procedures, prediction market aggregation, and an economic incentive system that makes oracle manipulation very expensive (Liao and Caramichael, 2022).

9. CONCLUSION

Stablecoins represent a significant type of financial innovation that introduces efficiency and programmability provided by the blockchain technology with the security of a useful money. The fact that they are suddenly growing alongside their use as low-profile crypto markets tools into systemically significant financial infrastructure is a sign of actual demand of digital assets to function as credible money and not merely, reflect investment investments. However, this discussion suggests that stablecoins are the innovation and risk at the same time that needs careful regulatory consideration.

9.1 Key Findings

The technical, economical, and regulatory analysis has come with several very important lessons. It is proved that the stablecoin impossibility to maximize the three out of three namely the stability, decentralization and the capital efficiency is a very long phenomenon. The different designs are not risk aversion but risks reallocation. The models supported by Fiat are balanced regarding stability and economy and require central custodians. The crypto-collateral based credit systems are decentralized and they are inefficient with credit. Reiterated failures of computer algorithm tools have demonstrated that even pure code-based stability is yet unattainable.

There is a strength and weakness in the performance of the market. Big stablecoins, as per normal business operations, are strictly pegged and provide useful payment systems. Through stress, weaknesses come about. The banking system has its risks, even of the well-run fiat-backed stable coins, including USDC. Crying volatility crypto-collateralized systems divest in a spiral. Algorithms systems get involved in death spirals due to confidence crises. The stress patterns on performance above depict the need to employ tough regulations that avail reserve norms, disclosure and resolution processes.

The relationship between the use of stablecoins and the use of CBDCs is likely to shape the emergence of the digital finance to a significant degree. Rather than competition where one technology dominates another, it is likely that hybrid ecosystems will be created where CBDCs are used to provide a basic settlement infrastructure, and applications of specialization and DeFi connectivity are implemented on stablecoins. The necessity to enjoy monetary sovereignty and offer financial inclusion in the presence of such coexistence in the case of Commonwealth jurisdictions particularly, is a significant policy concern.

Among the things that were acquired during analysis is the significant contribution made by the Commonwealth in harmonizing policy responses within different economies. This Commonwealth can wind up residing in between the highly formal regulatory regimes and the emergent market realities that allow accommodative structures as in line with the institutional capabilities. This standardization besides securing the existence of consistency in the laws, is also credited with making the minor economies unattractionary to the speedy monetization into digital money, and limited supervisors.

The Commonwealth Secretariat may also provide facilitative clearing services in common supervisory infrastructures, and technical assistance schemes and cross-jurisdictional regulatory sandboxes in addition to harmonizing the policy. These would allow the lesser member states a chance to possess a standardized tool of monitoring the digital materials, supervisory education and coordinated compliance provision. This would strengthen the regulating capacity of our new economies as well as enable the interoperability and resiliency of the Commonwealth cyber-finance arena.

9.2 Policy Implications for the Commonwealth

The Commonwealth Model Law on stablecoins (2025) is a move in the right direction towards a more risk-focused, extensive regulation that meets new practices across the world. Its tiered licensing structure, reserve quality requirement and transparency requirement vehicles its fundamental defects in line with market failures and stress events. The framework attempts to trade off between the innovative and stable, managing to ban the non-proven algorithmic designs, and permitting to use the controlled fiat-backed design and crypto-collateralized design.

The priority areas of implementation should be put on the commonwealth member states. First, there is the coming of a supervisory power, which will enable the latter to control the work of stablecoins, technically, or experience in blockchains, and the life of the DeFi ecosystems. Second, encouraging coordination on the regional stage in order to discourage regulatory arbitrage besides sharing information on the emerging risks. Third, there is the prospect of creating CBDC as another piece of infrastructure that ensures monetary sovereignty, but competes against foreign currency stablecoins.

Fourth, adjusting regulatory systems to case-specific jurisdictions, particularly on remittance channels where stable coins will bring a massive efficiency improvement to diaspora populations. Fifth, active involvement in international standard-setting forums to ensure that Commonwealth opinions particularly of weaker developing economies are taken into account on international regulatory convergence.

9.3 Looking Forward

The idea of a stablecoin fundamentally altered our perception of the digital payment systems and money. They will have sufficient application in the usage of digital assets as money to a variety of applications through reasonable design. Their further evolution will significantly influence their appearance as the stable ones in the global financial system or as the technologies that will only serve as intermediaries between the CBDCs and other digital currencies that will be offered by the government.

However, regardless of the outcome, stablecoins have left indelible marks in both the theory and financial practice of money. They cause one to reexamine some of the initial assumptions: what is legitimate money in the context of trust that can be coded, algorithmic, and realised by private institutions and not necessarily directly backed by the government? What actually has to change with the emergence of programmable money that is decentralized, borderless and possibly rule by communities? Can the advantages of financial innovation come without the stability and the sovereignty of traditional monetary systems?

These reactions will be presented through continuous experimenting, regulatory formulation and also market progressions. Commonwealth, having the convening power and possessing a diverse membership of both developed and developing economies is well placed to mediate the same. The Commonwealth can facilitate positive policy debate between the policymakers, technologists, and market actors to assist in setting regulatory strategies that would not only contribute to achieving the advantages of stablecoins but also mitigate the risks.

The future of stablecoins is stablecoins eventually being money itself becoming digital first and all the possibilities and complexity of such transformation come with it. They are continuity and the timeless quest of the humanity in stable and trustworthy forms of exchange and discontinuity the type of new technologies that scatters centuries of accustomed opinions on the matter of monetary issue and management. In order to successfully negotiate the said change, one will need to find the desired equilibrium between the opposing postulations: innovation/ regulation, efficiency/ stability, interests of the entire world/ local sovereignty and power decentralization/ accountability.

The upcoming decade may prove to be the pivotal period in determining how these tensions will be managed and whether stablecoins will be mainstream financial tools or more of a financial niche. The only thing that seems to be undeniable is that the questions which digital money poses as a component of the financial infrastructure and management of money by providing stablecoins will not disappear regardless of the particular technical implementation. The quandary of policymakers particularly in the Commonwealth society is how to drawn adjusting regulatory smooth shooting in keeping pace with the technological setting without losing sight over the end objectives; financial stability, consumer protection, monetary sovereignty, and inclusive economic development.

REFERENCES

Argoz Consultants. (2025). stablecoins and CBDCs: competing for the digital economy. Argoz Consultants Blog. https://www.argozconsultants.com/blog/stablecoins-cbdcs

Arner, D. W., Auer, R., & Frost, J. (2020). stablecoins: risks, potential and regulation. BIS Working Papers, No. 905. Bank for International Settlements. https://www.bis.org/publ/work905.htm

Auer, R. (2019). Embedded supervision: how to build regulation into blockchain finance. BIS Working Papers, No. 811. Bank for International Settlements. https://www.bis.org/publ/work811.htm

Bank for International Settlements. (2024). The interplay between stablecoins and central bank digital currencies. BIS Bulletin No. 81. https://www.bis.org/publ/bisbull81.htm

Barthélémy, J., Gardin, P., & Nguyen, B. (2023). stablecoins and the financing of the real economy. Banque de France Working Paper, No. 908. https://publications.banque-france.fr/stablecoins-and-financing-real-economy

Blockchain Governance Initiative Network. (2022). stablecoins: past, present, and future (BGIN Study Report 010). https://bgin-global.org/wp-content/uploads/2022/06/BGIN_SR010_stablecoins.pdf

Commonwealth Secretariat. (2025). Draft Commonwealth model law on stablecoins (Draft as at 4 July 2025). Commonwealth Secretariat. https://thecommonwealth.org/sites/default/files/inline/Draft%20Model%20Law%20on%20stablecoins.pdf

Financial Stability Board. (2020). Regulation, supervision and oversight of "global stablecoin" arrangements. https://www.fsb.org/2020/10/regulation-supervision-and-oversight-of-global-stablecoin-arrangements/

Hafner, M., & Henriques Pereira, M. (2023). The four types of stablecoins: A comparative analysis. *LEDGER*, *8*, 44–67. DOI: 10.5195/ledger.2023.285

Harz, D., Klages-Mundt, A., Liu, J.-Y., Gudgeon, L., & Minca, A. (2020). stablecoins 2.0: economic foundations and risk-based models. arXiv. https://arxiv.org/abs/2006.12388

International Monetary Fund. (2024). Digital money, trust, and regulation. IMF Working Paper WP/24/162. https://www.imf.org/en/Publications/WP/Issues/2024/06/12/Digital-Money-Trust-Regulation-245122

Klages-Mundt, A., Harz, D., Gudgeon, L., Liu, J.-Y., & Minca, A. (2020). stablecoins 2.0: economic foundations and risk-based models. In *Proceedings of the 2nd ACM Conference on Advances in Financial Technologies* (pp. 59–79). ACM. DOI: 10.1145/3419614.3423261

Klages-Mundt, A., & Minca, A. (2022). While stability lasts: A stochastic model of noncustodial stablecoins. *Mathematical Finance*, *32*(4), 943–981. DOI: 10.1111/mafi.12357

Kochergin, D. A. (2020). Economic nature and classification of stablecoins. Finance: theory and Practice, 24(6), 140–160. DOI: 10.26794/2587-5671-2020-24-6-140-160

Kozhan, R., & Viswanath-Natraj, G. (2021). Decentralised stablecoins and collateral risk (WBS Finance Group Research Paper). Warwick Business School. https://papers.ssrn.com/sol3/papers.cfm?abstract_id=3866975

Liao, G. Y., & Caramichael, J. (2022). stablecoins: growth potential and impact on banking (International Finance Discussion Papers No. 1334). Board of Governors of the Federal Reserve System. DOI: 10.17016/ifdp.2022.1334

Lyons, R. K., & Viswanath-Natraj, G. (2023). What keeps stablecoins stable? *Journal of International Money and Finance*, *131*, 102777. DOI: 10.1016/j.jimonfin.2022.102777

MacDonald, C., & Zhao, L. (2022). stablecoins and their risks to financial stability (Staff Discussion Paper No. 2022-20). Bank of Canada. https://www.bankofcanada.ca/2022/11/staff-discussion-paper-2022-20/

Nakamoto, S. (2008). Bitcoin: a peer-to-peer electronic cash system. https://bitcoin.org/bitcoin.pdf

Sethaput, V., & Innet, S. (2023). Blockchain application for central bank digital currencies (CBDC). *Cluster Computing*, *26*(4), 2183–2197. DOI: 10.1007/s10586-022-03962-z PMID: 36686339

World Economic Forum. (2023). How are CBDCs different from cryptocurrencies and stablecoins? World Economic Forum. https://www.weforum.org/agenda/2023/02/cbdcs-different-cryptocurrencies-stablecoins/

Chapter 2
Stablecoins:
Technical Foundations, Economic Implications, and Real-World Applications

N. M. Ramu
https://orcid.org/0009-0005-1264-967X
Dayananda Sagar College of Engineering, India

M. U. Vinod Krishna
https://orcid.org/0009-0009-5150-3701
Dayananda Sagar College of Engineering, India

ABSTRACT

This chapter explores the emergence and importance of stablecoins in crypto finance, their technical construction, economic impact, and applications. It traverses the history of stablecoins as a process towards embracing blockchain efficiency and fiat money stability, theoretically challenging and charting major milestones. The three major categories—fiat-backed, crypto-collateralized, and algorithmic—are explored through the use of secondary sources and widely documented case studies. The discussion takes into account regulatory and systemic risk issues, likening the analogy to Central Bank Digital Currencies (CBDCs) and distilling lessons from success and failure. The chapter subsequently tries to de-mystify how stablecoins are transforming payments and financial infrastructure and pinning down open questions to study and policy.

DOI: 10.4018/979-8-3373-9043-7.ch002

INTRODUCTION

The global financial landscape is undergoing a rapid transformation driven by digital innovation. Among these advancements, one development stands out as particularly transformative—the emergence of the stablecoin. This form of digital currency is uniquely designed to maintain a steady value by pegging itself to a specific reference asset or a basket of assets. In essence, stablecoins merge two worlds that were once distinct: the flexibility, transparency. and technological ingenuity of blockchain-based cryptocurrencies, and the reliability, recognition, and stability of traditional fiat money. By bridging these domains, stablecoins offer what earlier cryptocurrencies like Bitcoin and Ethereum could not—practical usability in everyday transactions and integration into the broader financial system, which those earlier. more volatile assets struggled to achieve.

Stablecoins are transforming from the mere digital store of value—they are becoming a fundamental pillar of support of the future digital economy. Stablecoins drive a large number of decentralized finance (*DeFi*) use cases, facilitate instant cross-border payments, lower remittances, and even function as settlement instruments for capital markets in a few instances. What is so appealing about them is their capacity to merge the speed and low cost of transactions of blockchain networks with the price stability of the fiat currencies of the old world such as the U.S. dollar or the euro. This fusion is revolutionizing value transfer between digital and traditional financial systems, turning conventional wisdom on money, trust, and regulation on its head.

And yet, while they hold much promise, stablecoins have a set of complicated issues of their own. As their name would suggest, these tokens aspire to perform the very critical functions of fiat currency—unit of account, medium of exchange, and store of value—on semi-decentralized or decentralized systems. Such aspiration, as a matter of course, poses significant questions of transparency, reserve backing, issuer credit, and systemic risk. Stablecoins are not a homogenous category; they have many models, each with its own mechanics, risk profile, and degree of stability. Appreciation for these differences is essential in order to evaluate both their possibilities and the possible dangers they pose to the overall financial system.

As an example, fiat-backed stablecoins are collateralized by reserve assets held in traditional institutions, and their nature is centralized. Crypto-collateralized stablecoins make use of over-collateralization and smart contracts to achieve stability. Algorithmic stablecoins employ a distinct mechanism, by making use of coded protocols to adjust supply automatically, raising or lowering it as needed by the market.

This chapter explores the evolving landscape of stablecoins within the broader monetary system transformation. Stablecoins present unique roles and challenges as digital assets designed to maintain price stability and usability across various financial applications. While central banks globally are exploring digital currencies, this chapter concentrates on private stablecoins and their regulatory, technological, and market dynamics shaping the future of digital finance.

RESEARCH GAP

While stablecoins have been widely studied on the technical foundations and economic applications, with a broader gap in literature existing which integrates their technological, economic, and regulatory sides as a whole, current scholarship is extremely fragmented in that most studies focus on isolated particulars—such as blockchain architecture, monetary impacts, or policy concerns—without trying to make a broad synthesis of how the components work in relation to influencing financial stability and innovation. Also, few studies exist that provide comparative analysis of the actual performance of various stablecoin designs, especially for fiat-backed, crypto-collateralized, and algorithmic stablecoins. This chapter fills such a research gap by introducing an interdisciplinary analysis that connects technology, economics, and regulation and thus to a greater extent helps develop a comprehensive understanding of stablecoins' emerging role in the digital economy.

OBJECTIVES

1. Explain technical underpinnings of various stablecoins, for example, how various mechanisms ensure price stability.
2. Provide examples of economic effects of stablecoins, such as efficiency of payments, financial inclusion, monetary policy, and systemic stability.
3. Outline actual examples and case studies to show applications of stablecoins and lessons learned from success and failure to emphasize.
4. Analyze the regulatory challenges posed by stablecoins and prescribe potential structures for policy to encourage transparency, consumer protection, and systemic stability.
5. Identify areas of current knowledge gaps and suggest areas of future research that can further illuminate the evolving nexus of technology, finance, and regulation.

Through a systematic review of theoretical constructs and second-order sources, the chapter seeks to present readers, including researchers, policymakers, and practitioners, with a straightforward, unprejudiced picture of stablecoins' transformative power and complexity that accompanies them. The thesis seeks to highlight that stablecoins are more than technology fads but vital tools that will revolutionize the future architecture, governance, and trust networks of digital money.

METHODOLOGY

This chapter adopts a theoretical research approach grounded in the use of secondary data. It draws upon a wide range of scholarly works, institutional reports, and policy papers from well-regarded sources such as the Bank for International Settlements (BIS), the International Monetary Fund (*IMF*), and the European Central Bank (*ECB*). By reviewing and synthesizing these existing studies, the chapter examines how stablecoins emerged, how they function technically, and what their broader economic implications might be.

In addition to theoretical analysis, the discussion incorporates real-world examples—most notably USDC, DAI, and TerraUSD—to demonstrate how different models of stablecoins operate and how their stability mechanisms vary in practice. Taken together, this method provides a comprehensive view of the stablecoin ecosystem, allowing the intersection of technology, economics, and regulation to be analyzed within a unified conceptual framework.

BACKGROUND

Stablecoins are a central component of the larger confluence of money, finance, and technology. They are native assets in cryptology that have been designed to be price-stable and leverage blockchain innovation. The initial generation of cryptocurrencies, though leading the way in decentralization and cryptography, was too volatile for use in mainstream finance. Their inconsistent volatility in price left them unable to act consistently as units of account, media of exchange, or values to hold (Liberty Street Economics, 2025). Stablecoins then filled this gap.

The history of stablecoins starts with the initial attempts at uniting the effectiveness of blockchain networks with fiat stability. The first widely popular stablecoin was Tether (*USDT*), created in 2014. Tether had a stabilizing mechanism backed by centralized custodial fiat reserves, promising one-to-one redemption—each token could hypothetically be redeemed for its proportional fiat amount (Arner et al., 2020). Fiat-backed stablecoins quickly emerged as the new norm in digital economies, serving as liquidity providers, trading pairs, and payment instruments on crypto exchanges globally.

In response to centralization and reliance on trust characterizing fiat-backed designs, stablecoin designs are created. Crypto-collateralized stablecoins like

MakerDAO's DAI represent a more decentralized solution. Cryptocurrency is collateralized into smart contracts by customers, and they're issued newly minted tokens in exchange. Stability is ensured by over-collateralization, where assets locked up are valued higher than circulating tokens, and by automatic liquidation mechanisms guaranteeing solvency. Although this structure promotes transparency and decentralization, it faces difficulties in scalability, efficiency, and capital deployment (BIS, 2022).

Algorithmic stablecoins push experimentation to the next level by seeking to ensure price stability without the use of collateral. Such structures are based on automatic on-chain algorithms that manage token supply. Burning or minting tokens are used to keep a desired peg. Theoretically beautiful and capital-effective, algorithmic stablecoins were found to be very fragile in practice. The 2022 failure of TerraUSD (*UST*) is a stellar example, showing dangers of too much dependence on programmatic adjustments to the supply and leading to massive investor confidence and market value loss (Grobys, 2021).

In addition to their technology structure, stablecoins also have huge economic and financial significance. They enable new payment systems that are cheaper, quicker, and able to make almost instantaneous cross-border payments. They are therefore particularly well-suited for remittances as well as for financial inclusion of underserved populations (ECB, 2022). Stablecoins are also at the center of decentralized finance (*DeFi*), enabling borrowing, lending, trading, and yield generation without the need for traditional intermediaries.

But with stablecoins are also regulatory and operating problems. Market confidence is based on reserve transparency, sound governance mechanisms, redemption assurances, and operational stability. Some operators have been penalized for reserve overstatement or lack of disclosure, which has tainted their "stability" brands (IMF, 2025). Uncertainty in regulation is also adding to the risk since governments everywhere are still arguing whether stablecoins are securities, deposits, or new financial instruments in general (BIS, 2022).

As stablecoins become more embedded in the financial system, systemic risks related to financial stability have attracted regulatory attention. Discussions on tighter regulation, reserve requirements, and prudential measures increasingly reflect the size and interconnectedness of stablecoins in the market (IMF, 2025; ECB, 2022). Regulators continue to evaluate the regulatory frameworks necessary to manage risks associated with stablecoins to protect market integrity and consumer interests. Ongoing developments in digital currency underline the importance of stablecoins' role in future payment systems and financial innovation. (BIS, 2022).

Stablecoins are now a multi-dimensional phenomenon, which is a test of tech, a profit-making innovation, and a test of regulation. The introduction of stablecoins heralds substantial change in the design of money, the portability of money, and of the governance of money in the time of digitization. Over the coming years, while stablecoins continue to develop, it merits some historical, tech, economic, and policy context to appreciate their personalized potential through the lens of re-imaging the future of finance.

Recent developments in stablecoin regulation have been marked by significant moves toward global coordination and enhanced oversight frameworks. The European Union's Markets in Crypto-Assets Regulation (*MiCA*), effective from 2024, establishes a comprehensive legal framework aimed at ensuring consumer protection, market integrity, and financial stability across member states (European Parliament, 2025). Complementing this, the United States has proposed the Stablecoin Act draft, which outlines stringent federal supervision mechanisms, including reserve requirements and systemic risk mitigation measures targeted at safeguarding the broader financial system (U.S. Department of Treasury, 2024). Supporting these regulatory efforts, the Bank for International Settlements (*BIS*) published a 2024 report emphasizing the need for harmonized cross-border regulatory approaches to manage the unique challenges posed by stablecoins in global finance (BIS, 2024).

Market adoption trends from 2023 to 2025 demonstrate continued evolution and volatility among leading stablecoins. Major players such as USDC and DAI have maintained substantial market capitalizations, while newer entrants like PYUSD have shown rapid growth, reflecting broader user acceptance and institutional backing. These trends have been shaped in part by the fallout from the TerraUSD collapse in 2022, which underscored the systemic risks and stability challenges inherent in algorithmic stablecoins (Chainalysis, 2024).

Stablecoins are increasingly recognized for their potential to enhance financial inclusion, particularly in emerging economies. According to the OECD's 2024 report, they facilitate faster, cheaper cross-border payments and remittances, thereby expanding access to financial services for unbanked populations (OECD, 2024). Similarly, the IMF's 2025 Digital Finance Annual Report highlights the implications of stablecoins on monetary policy and banking sectors, cautioning that widespread adoption necessitates vigilant oversight to prevent disruptions in money supply and liquidity (IMF, 2025).

Technological advances have also progressed, with new research focusing on interoperability between distinct blockchain platforms, enabling seamless stablecoin transfers across networks (Blockchain Consortium, 2024). Privacy innovations, including the application of zero-knowledge proof protocols, are emerging as critical tools to balance regulatory compliance with user confidentiality (Privacy Ledger Foundation, 2025).

MAIN FOCUS OF THE CHAPTER

This chapter looks at stablecoins and how they fit into the future of digital finance. stablecoins are a type of cryptocurrency, but unlike Bitcoin or Ether, their value doesn't fluctuate wildly. Traditional cryptocurrencies can rise or fall dramatically in a short time, making them difficult to use for everyday transactions or even just for storing value safely. Stablecoins address this by pegging their value to something more predictable—usually a fiat currency like the U.S. dollar, and sometimes even commodities like gold. While there are different methods to achieve this, the core idea is to maintain price stability, positioning stablecoins somewhere between the volatility of typical cryptocurrencies and the steadiness of traditional money.

1. Technical Foundation of Stablecoins

Stablecoins are cryptocurrencies that are meant to have a fairly stable price relative to other assets, like fiat money or commodities. Stablecoins take advantage of blockchain technology' its transparency, decentralization, and programmability—without falling victim to the dizzying price volatility normally besetting cryptocurrencies like Bitcoin or Ethereum. Stablecoins really try to combine the security of traditional currency with the flexibility and innovation provided by blockchain-based assets.

There are three general technical methods that stablecoins generally take:

a. **Fiat-Backed Stablecoins:** These stablecoins are fully collateralized by classic fiat reserves—such as U.S. dollars—stored off-chain by trusted custodians. The idea is simple: for every stablecoin issued, the same amount of fiat is securely stored so that the holder can exchange his token at will. This system keeps the token value at parity with the backing currency. Examples include Tether (*USDT*) and USD Coin (*USDC*). For trust to be maintained, issuers periodically release audits or attestations of the reserves and follow pertinent regulatory guidelines. While the model is centralized in nature, it is very liquid and redeemable, and therefore is mostly relevant in digital markets.
b. **Crypto-Collateralized Stablecoins:** These stablecoins are backed by other cryptocurrencies rather than fiat, with the collateral held in on-chain smart contracts. Because, cryptocurrency prices can fluctuate widely, these systems rely on over-collateralization—meaning, for example, that $150 worth of crypto must be locked in to issue each $100 stablecoin. Liquidation systems by default rules ensure solvency even in the case of a fall in collateral value. Some tokens or bonds are occasionally issued to establish the need for rebalancing supply and preserve the peg. While more decentralized compared to fiat-backed systems, these systems are extremely reliant on trust among participants and market

confidence. The TerraUSD (*UST*) collapse in 2022 showed just how vulnerable even overcollateralized or algorithmic designs may be once trust is lost.

c. **Algorithmic Stablecoins:** Algorithmic stablecoins are not backed by any collateral. They utilize instead an algorithmic mechanism that dynamically modifies the supply to maintain price close to a desired peg. Secondary tokens or bonds are normally issued or redeemed to encourage participants to increase or decrease supply. It relies primarily on market players behaving per the protocol. TerraUSD (*UST*) is another example where loss of confidence led to a cascading fall. These models rely on on-chain automation, smart contracts, arbitrage opportunities, and economic incentives to stay stable. Traders and users rectify any price difference by selling overpriced coins or purchasing underpriced coins.
d. General Stablecoin Features
   i. Token Structure: Stablecoins are smart contract-based digital tokens that run on blockchain platforms.
   ii. Fungibility and Value: Stablecoins are usually fungible with other stablecoins or the collateralized underlying asset and hold a stable relative value.
   iii. Transferability: Stablecoins are transferable, tradable, or exchangeable for the collateralized backing asset easily.
   iv. Essentially, the technology underlying stablecoins brings together smart contract automation, cryptography, and economic incentives to ensure price stability. These aspects render stablecoins very appealing as programmable money or digital cash in blockchain-based monetary systems.

2. Economic Impacts of Stablecoins

Stablecoins are transforming global financial systems, presenting both significant opportunities and complex challenges. Research and trends up to 2025 highlight several key economic impacts:

a. **Faster, Cheaper Payments and Financial Inclusion:** Stablecoins facilitate near-instant and highly inexpensive transactions across borders and time zones. Stablecoins settle almost instantly at a fraction of the cost of current systems. Stablecoins are ideally suited for cross-border remittances, where they can significantly cut fees and delays to the advantage of millions of individuals across the globe. Further, since they are built on open blockchain platforms, stablecoins can be used to extend financial services to underbanked or unbanked populations, particularly in emerging economies with unstable domestic currencies or nascent banking infrastructures.
b. **Facilitating Decentralized Finance *(DeFi):*** Stablecoins lie at the core of decentralized finance (*DeFi*), offering stable units of account for lending, bor-

rowing, and trading, while also serving as collateral for decentralized lending and derivative platforms. They function as a dependable medium of exchange for smart contract–driven, intermediary-free financial protocols. By providing these capabilities, stablecoins expand access to financial services, foster innovation in programmable money, and enhance liquidity mechanisms across crypto markets.

c. **Monetary Policy and Financial Stability Issues:** The growth in stablecoin usage poses serious risks to both financial stability and monetary sovereignty. Stablecoins tend to be dollar-pegged and globally dispersed, and they potentially facilitate a type of stealth dollarization where foreign economies increasingly draw on dollars through stablecoins, limiting local monetary policy effects. Moreover, if stablecoins become large in size, they can replace bank deposit funding, thus impacting banks capacity to lend, leading to higher funding expenses and tighter credit terms. Modeling estimates that large growth of stablecoin holdings is capable of reducing bank deposits by 10–20%, thereby increasing lending rates and potentially constraining economic growth.

d. **Systemic Risks and Run Vulnerabilities:** Stablecoins are prone to runs, where many holders redeem en masse all at once. Such mechanisms foster fire sales of the collateral assets and liquidity shortfalls characteristic of classical banking crises. TerraUSDs failure in 2022 brutally demonstrated how loss of confidence would, at the same time, destabilize algorithmic stablecoins. Such runs could spill over into wider markets through
   i. Purposive bank runs if stablecoin issuers are themselves holders of uninsured deposits.
   ii. Treasury security or other safe assets-backed fire sales of stablecoins.
   iii. Spillovers of money market fund and financial institution contagion.

e. **Effects on Global Financial Markets:** As stablecoins are large investors in safe assets such as US Treasuries, their expanded role plays a key role in global bond markets. The evidence further indicates that expansions in the size of stablecoin markets have the potential to put downward pressure on Treasury yields, which may become more potent during periods of redemption, impacting global interest rates and capital flows. The explosion in stablecoins, particularly if permitted to earn interest, would fundamentally transform the centuries-old foundations of deposit funding, credit extension, and money transmission radically, posing policy issues for regulators.

f. **Regulatory and Policy Solutions Required:** Stablecoins offer significant benefits for financial innovation and inclusion but pose risks to consumer protection, monetary sovereignty, and financial stability. To address these, policymakers globally are developing balanced regulations focusing on transparency, reserve management, and licensing proportional to systemic risk.

Recent legislative efforts like the 2025 US Genius Act and the Draft Commonwealth Model Law exemplify comprehensive frameworks emphasizing issuer licensing, reserve asset safeguarding, risk management, and consumer protections. These laws promote innovation while ensuring market stability and consumer trust.

International coordination is critical to harmonize regulations, prevent arbitrage, and foster a resilient, transparent stablecoin ecosystem supporting the digital economy's sustainable growth.

3. Real-World Applications of Stablecoins

Stablecoins have evolved from mere experimental tokens into practical tools used daily within financial ecosystems. Their applications span several key areas, each contributing to the transformation of digital finance and generating tangible effects in the real world.

a. Stablecoins Transforming Cross-Border Remittances

Cross-border remittances have traditionally been burdened by inefficiencies including prohibitive fees, slow transaction settlement, and limited financial inclusion. Migrant workers sending money to families in countries such as the Philippines, Nigeria, India, and Brazil often face fees exceeding 6% and delays up to several days, complicating timely access to critical funds.

Fiat-backed stablecoins, exemplified by USD Coin (USDC), are disrupting this paradigm by enabling fast, secure, and cost-efficient remittance flows. USDC is fully collateralized by U.S. dollar reserves and operates on blockchain technology, allowing instant peer-to-peer transfers across borders with minimal fees. These features provide migrants with a reliable alternative to traditional remittance services.

The recipient experience is markedly improved through digital wallets and platforms like GCash (Philippines) and Chipper Cash (Africa), where funds are accessible immediately for spending or local currency exchange. This immediacy curtails cash flow disruptions and promotes economic stability at the household level.

Moreover, stablecoin transactions comply with robust regulatory frameworks including Anti-Money Laundering (AML) and Know Your Customer (KYC) protocols, enhancing transparency and guarding against financial crimes. Licensed intermediaries oversee transactions, ensuring security and consumer protection.

Beyond reducing transactional friction, stablecoins foster financial inclusion by providing digital financial services to unbanked populations who might otherwise lack access to formal banking infrastructures. This is increasingly vital in emerging economies where remittance inflows represent a significant share of GDP and are critical to social welfare.

Market trends underscore the growth and potential transformative impact of stablecoin-based remittances. Asian remittance flows alone are forecasted to surpass $250 billion by 2028. Financial innovations like stablecoins contribute not only to payment efficiency but also to broader economic resilience, supporting the digital transformation of financial ecosystems globally.

In essence, stablecoins are no longer merely speculative assets but are becoming fundamental tools for real-world economic activity, particularly in the remittance sector. Their impact extends to accelerating the modernization of global financial flows, promoting inclusivity, and enabling more equitable access to economic resources worldwide.

b. Real-World Example: USD Coin (USDC)

USD Coin (*USDC*) which was introduced in 2018 by Circle and Coinbase alongside Centre Consortium is among the most popular fiat-backed stablecoins. One token is an equivalent one-for-one to the U.S. dollar backed by reserves in regulated banks such that users can exchange tokens for cash at will, generating liquidity and trust.

What sets USDC apart from previous stablecoins such as Tether (*USDT*) is transparency and regulatory adherence. USDC is audited on a monthly basis by Grant Thornton LLP to ensure that reserves are in line with issued tokens, resolving previous allegations of concealed or inadequately managed reserves. The Financial Stability Board stresses that such transparency is critical in reducing the risk that propagates through systems and ensures public trust. In the US, USDC is governed under a system of money transmission, which aligns it with traditional financial regulation and protects users by assuring them that it's secure and responsible.

USDC has been embraced globally. It is used to settle on crypto exchanges, to provide liquidity in DeFi lending protocols, and for cheaper, faster cross-border payments. On several blockchains—Ethereum, Solana, and Polygon—it can transfer seamlessly between chains and process large transaction volumes. Regulators and institutions are praising its compliant installation, the BIS (2022) characterizing its safe coexistence with regulation and the U.S. President's Working Group on Financial Markets referencing its capacity to chart the future of digital payments.

Overall, USDC is a streamlined mashup of cutting-edge blockchain tech and old-fashioned financial sense. It's fast, it's secure, and it puts money into people's hands with the assurance it's being handled well—something regulators and cryptocurrency fans can both unite behind. It shows that stablecoins can be maintained stable and institutionally trusted as long as they are maintained backed by real-world reserves and disclosure reports. As Gorton and Zhang (2021) posit, fiat-backed stablecoins like USDC are like contemporary money- market funds liquid, safe, and regulable like wild cryptocurrencies. This model indicates that stablecoins do not necessarily have to upset existing financial infrastructures but rather enhance efficiency, trust, and transparency when designed sustainably.

c. DAI (MakerDAO) – Over-Collateralization and Decentralized Governance:

It was during March 2020 that the crypto space witnessed a crash on Black Thursday DAI (MakerDAO stablecoin) thereafter gave us a firsthand example of how decentralized stablecoins are able to stabilize. A sudden plunge in Ethereum *(ETH)* caused unprecedented volatility in the crypto market. DAI holders who had obtained DAI by putting ETH into MakerDAO Vaults saw their collateral value collapse below peg. The mechanism enforced automatic liquidations of under-collateralized vaults to always keep the DAI supply over-backed. Although some of the vaults were under-collateralized from sharp price declines, most of the system was stable, and algorithmic over- collateralization was robust.

One of the most interesting aspects of DAI is how governance is done. At the center of it are MKR token holders, and in the case of an actual crisis, MakerDAO's decentralized community acted rapidly. They cranked dials such as the stability fee and liquidation ratios to avoid a system collapse. What is simply breathtaking here is that no central bank, no individual company, could step in—yet the system self-corrected automatically, due to the community as a whole working together. DAI is a prime example of decentralized finance *(DeFi)* in action.

Yet, DAI is far from being just an emergency tool. In everyday DeFi use, it has become a go-to asset. Users can deposit DAI on platforms like Aave or Compound to earn interest, or use it as a stable collateral for other cryptocurrencies. During periods of market volatility, traders often move into DAI instead of selling their crypto holdings, using it as a safe haven. Pegged close to $1, DAI allows users to hedge their positions while maintaining full decentralization—no banks, no intermediaries, just code and community.

This case from the world illustrates both the advantages and disadvantages of DAI- inefficient, since users have to lock up more value than they take. However, DAI's actual adoption, along with its reaction to events like the Black Thursday incident, show that decentralized stablecoins can work in real life financial ecosystems, giving both algorithmic stability and community-led governance, and not depending on traditional central banks or fiat reserves.

d. Real-World Example: TerraUSD (UST) – Algorithmic Failure and Systemic Lessons

TerraUSD (*UST*) was a stablecoin issued by Terraform Labs that was designed to maintain its $1 parity without needing conventional collateral. UST did have a mint-and-burn framework on its sister token, LUNA, however. When UST was over $1, individuals were able to burn LUNA in order to generate new UST, and when UST was under $1, it was able to be burned in order to generate LUNA. The system that existed in the real world had price parity by maintaining equal supply and demand. The system operated on behalf of the investors for several months, making them trust it and achieving a market cap of over $18 billion in early 2022. Institutional and retail investors borrowed, lent, and exchanged the UST based on the algorithmic build to make it profitable.

But then came rapidly in May 2022 this abrupt LUNA price drop that triggered a calamitous chain of events. Following the drop in market value of LUNA, the mint-and-burn mechanism could not restrict UST's declining price, and the "death spiral" into which the two tokens had entered commenced. The fall of TerraUSD (*UST*) was so dramatic and revealing. UST dropped its $1 peg, and the market cap of UST and LUNA collectively went down by more than $40 billion in the space of only a few days. Overnight, retail investors made losses, confidence in algorithmic stablecoins took a massive hit, and regulators across the globe were made overnight sensations. International organizations such as the IMF and the BIS (2022) employed UST as an example of cautionary warning, quoting how susceptible confidence-based stablecoins with no or hardly any collateral are to a market shock.

Systemic risk testing in a very literal sense was the TerraUSD catastrophe for non-collateralized, algorithmic stablecoins. In contrast to DAI, collateralized by over-collateralization and decentralized governance, or USDC, collateralized by centralized reserves and regulation, UST's stability was completely ridiculously built on the balance of market confidence and speculation. The downfall was an overly bitter lesson: no matter how clever an algorithm may be, it is impossible to utilize in place of actual reserves, liquidity, and good institutional setup. Regulators worldwide reacted by calling for tighter requirements—such as reserving requirements for transparency, guarantees of redemption, and minimums in liquidity—to avert meltdowns in the future.

SYNTHESIS AND POLICY IMPLICATIONS

In light of stablecoins like USDC, DAI, and UST standing side by side, it is only an honest representation of the difference in design philosophies. DAI is overcollateralized and decentralized, USDC is centralized and regulated, and UST was unbacked and algorithmic. And it shows: even if a coin appears "stable" on paper, it doesn't always mean that it will be able to survive real-life pressure.

USDC's regulatory compliance and good governance have welcomed institutional confidence, and this has wrought real stability. DAI confirms the thesis that decentralization and transparency can be lucrative but at the expense of a more complex user interface and less capital-efficient utilization. And UST? Its collapse revealed the risks of placing confidence in nothing more than faith and sentiment in markets versus actual reserves and governance.

The teachings are in line with a growing body of evidence: stablecoin stability depends not solely on smart technology—it requires governance frameworks, institutional integrity, and adequate reserve backing (BIS, 2022; Brunnermeier & Landau, 2022). It also emphasizes the need for convergent regulation globally to deliver protection to investors as well as financial soundness in the new crypto economy.

ISSUES, CONTROVERSIES, AND PROBLEMS

1. Uncertainty of Regulators and Compliance Problem

The regulatory uncertainty is stablecoins' worst nightmare—particularly for cross-border applications. Stablecoins are viewed very differently around the world: some view them as a payment instrument, others view them as a security or even a deposit. Such heterogeneity of rules poses the issuers and the users serious issues. For stablecoin issuers, determining where which laws apply is costly and time-consuming. For users, it can present economic or even legal risk if they unintentionally violate a foreign law. To put the icing on the cake, stablecoins are in the crosshairs of anti-money laundering, anti-terrorist financing, and other ill uses. More severe AML and KYC regulations make it effectively unfeasible for certain completely decentralized stablecoins to function without experiencing challenges with compliance.

2. Cross-Border Regulation Fragmentation

The mere fact that stablecoins are usually backed by decentralized, global platforms only adds to the complexity. Various countries treat these coins in utterly disparate manners, and it is lawful gray areas for consumers as well as issuers. This fragmentation can also cause regulatory arbitrage, where stablecoin firms locate in jurisdictions that have fewer regulations, bypassing tighter worldwide rules. In short, the absence of unified standards isn't merely a frustration—it can, in fact, make regulation worldwide weaker and even add more systemic risk.

3. Good Governance-Decentralization Trade-Offs

The appropriate balance between decentralization and good governance is an issue being struggled with in stablecoin design. Decentralized stablecoins are hindered by slow decision-making and by issues of coordinating response to risk, but fiat-backed stablecoins are encumbered by single points of failure risk and censorship risk. The governance models must evolve to deliver resilience and operational efficiency, but the problem is a wide open and challenging one.

4. Challenges of Market Adoption and User Trust

Stablecoin adoption in the market in low-digital literacy or low-technology countries is an issue. Their risk, regulation, and dynamics are to confuse users and impact trust and adoption. Scalability, network fees, and compatibility also stand in the way of smooth user experience. These issues would need to be addressed by more user education and user interface.

5. Environmental Impact

The environmental concern in the energy use by blockchain networks of stablecoins, particularly PoW-consensus stablecoins like Ethereum (up to recent and complete roll-outs of Proof-of-Stake), has been a driving force behind the popular opinion and tolerance in the regulatory environment. This makes developers and platforms seek more sustainable alternatives to reduce ecological impacts.

6. Risks of Liquidity and Market Manipulation

The relatively high liquidity and ease with which stablecoins can be converted exposes markets to potential manipulation in the form of wash trading or pump-and-dump schemes. Due to concentrated issuers or holders of stablecoins, these parties may have the ability to impact market conditions, raising questions of market access and concerns about systemic risk as a result of concentrated control over stablecoin transactions.

7. Technology Fragmentation and the Lack of Standardization

The stablecoin environment suffers from a lack of one universal technical standard. Token standards that exist across blockchains are what defines interoperability across blockchains. Technical fragmentation keeps the easy transfer and use between applications out of reach, losing network effects and joint use. Convergence towards standard smart contract ones and cross-chain bridges are in progress but are faced with technology and security challenges.

8. Privacy vs. Transparency Dilemma

Transparency of blockchain nature of stablecoins promotes auditability but is incompatible with privacy needs. While regulatory regimes demand rigorous AML and KYC controls, neither can user privacy be disregarded. Finding the balance between the transparency of transactions for regulatory oversight and users' rights to privacy is a challenge constantly being pursued, with efforts on zero-knowledge proofs or permissioned privacy-enhancing tech.

9. Ethical and Governance Transparency

Questions around issuer transparency, governance fairness, and potential conflicts of interest have increased the demand for greater accountability in the stablecoin ecosystem. Centralized stablecoin issuers often face challenges in making decisions transparently, while decentralized protocols face a different hurdle: engaging token holders effectively and ensuring that governance decisions are fair, inclusive, and truly representative of the community.

SOLUTIONS AND RECOMMENDATIONS

1. Improving Transparency and Reserve Management

Trust is the foundation for all stablecoins, especially fiat-backed ones. Periodic audits and attestations guarantee each token is adequately covered by actual assets, and some sites have real-time dashboards for users and regulators. Such openness precludes fraud and mismanagement and guarantees faith in the system.

2. Good Regulatory Frameworks

Stablecoins are exposed to a complicated regulatory landscape, and therefore, straightforward and practical rules are called for. Regulators require standards that cover technicalities and financial nuances, such as direct classification—a stablecoin as a security, deposit, or payments system—and capital and liquidity requirements for issuers. Robust AML and KYC measures have to be enforced. As stablecoins can travel freely across borders, cross-border coordination is necessary in order to fill gaps, prevent regulatory arbitrage, and ensure digital money travels securely around the globe.

3. Advocating Decentralized Regulation and Risk Management

Improved governance in algorithmic and crypto-collateralized stablecoins can reduce systemic risk. Open decision-making, stronger collateral mechanisms, and regular stress tests help maintain the peg, build community consensus, and prevent broader market disruptions.

4. Industry Standards and Technological Protocols Adoption

Industry organizations are crucial for strengthening stablecoins. By establishing clear standards and promoting best practices in governance, smart contracts, auditing, and data protection, they make systems safer, more accessible, and trusted by both users and institutions.

5. Increased Consumer Education and Risk Perception

Users of stablecoins must understand the risks involved, including issuer default, regulatory changes, and price fluctuations. Education and clear guidance help them make informed decisions, manage exposure, and use the technology safely.

6. ESG, Operational, and Cyber Risks

Recent research highlights the environmental sustainability of blockchain systems, noting the shift from energy-intensive Proof-of-Work to more eco-friendly Proof-of-Stake mechanisms, such as Ethereum's 2022 upgrade, which drastically reduces energy consumption (OECD, 2024). Stablecoin issuers are increasingly adopting green initiatives, including carbon offset programs and sustainability certifications. Additionally, cybersecurity remains a significant concern, with smart contract vulnerabilities leading to notable financial losses in DeFi platforms. Strengthening security protocols and systematic audits are essential to mitigate these operational risks and protect user assets (Privacy Ledger Foundation, 2025).

7. GENIUS Act and Commonwealth Model Law.

Careful and balanced regulatory frameworks are key to managing stablecoins' risks while fostering innovation. Policymakers worldwide are enhancing transparency requirements, including more rigorous disclosures and independent audits of stablecoin reserves. Licensing regimes are being developed to ensure that only qualified entities issue stablecoins, with requirements proportionate to risk and systemic importance.

The 2025 US GENIUS Act and the Draft Commonwealth Model Law on Stablecoins exemplify leading efforts to establish comprehensive and adaptive regulatory structures. The GENIUS Act introduces tiered oversight and clear rules to encourage innovation while safeguarding market stability and consumer trust. Developed with input from multiple countries, the Commonwealth Model Law proposes a harmonized approach addressing issuer obligations, reserve asset standards, risk management, customer protection, and cross-border cooperation.

International coordination remains indispensable to align regulatory approaches, avoid fragmentation, and uphold market integrity globally. These frameworks together aim to build a resilient, transparent, and inclusive stablecoin ecosystem that supports the digital economy's growth.

FUTURE RESEARCH DIRECTIONS

1. Future-Generation Technical Innovation in Stablecoin Design

The future of stablecoins promises significant technological advancements. Developers and researchers will need to focus on frameworks that enhance stability, scalability, and security simultaneously. A solid suggestion for that is creating hybrid collateral models combining the best of fiat-backed, crypto-backed, and algorithmic stablecoins to withstand market shocks better. And while that is occurring, more interoperability between chains will be necessary so the stablecoins can travel freely between various blockchain infrastructures. When it comes to security and privacy, applications such as zero-knowledge proofs and secure multi-party computation can enable users to preserve integrity and privacy while not giving up on regulatory compliance.

2. Macro-Financial and Economic Impacts

We should also know what the big picture is. Large-scale adoption of stablecoins would have profound implications for monetary policy, inflation, and currency markets, particularly in emerging markets. For example, would stablecoins promote dollarization, or stop central banks from enforcing monetary policy? Analysis here will enable policymakers to understand the interplay of stablecoins with the broader financial system and assess the potential system risks under financial stress, enabling regulators to construct suitable frameworks for their safe use.

3. Socioeconomic Consequences and Adoption Barriers

Stablecoins are financial and technical—but are also human. Stablecoins may help facilitate financial inclusion, particularly of the unbanked in emerging economies, but take-up is uncertain. Trust, use, and domestic legislation can limit access. The subject of research into these social and behavioral challenges is at the center of designing interventions that promote extension of access but prevent issues like disinformation or digital exclusion.

4. Crisis Preparedness, Risk Management, and Resilience

Stablecoins are susceptible to risks like liquidity crises, smart contract exploits, and market manipulation. Stress testing, automatic response systems, and sound operational and legal frameworks are important to maintain risks under control and improve overall network resilience.

5. Privacy-Preserving Stablecoins

Privacy is another key concern. While users want their transactions to remain secure, regulators must still enforce AML and KYC requirements. Zero-knowledge proofs, confidential transactions, and secure multiparty computation are a few of the technologies that can assist in this balancing act. Nevertheless, there are still significant research questions that need to be solved—balancing transparency and privacy appropriately is essential if stablecoins are to be widely trusted.

6. Stablecoins and Cross-Border Payments Efficiency

Lastly, stablecoins can potentially facilitate faster, cheaper, and more efficient cross-border payments—particularly remittances in emerging economies. Additional research must measure the impact: how much does it lower the cost, how fast do they settle, and with what broader economic effects? Controlled experiments and rigorous data analysis can clarify the role these digital currencies play in financial inclusion, remittance corridor reduction, and helping solve issues of money laundering.

7. Interoperability with Legacy Financial Systems

Additional study needs to be conducted on how stablecoins can be successfully implemented within existing financial systems, like payment networks, banks, and clearinghouses. Technical as well as regulatory barriers to seamless interoperability need to be addressed to facilitate mainstream acceptance. Attempts at integration can provide best practices and lessons obtained on what not to do.

8. Ecosystem Governance Models for Stablecoins

An examination of various models of governance—centralized, decentralized, and hybrid—and security and scalability problems of the models can be used to guide future stablecoin design. Cross-case comparison of governance frameworks can identify how various methods impact resilience, responsiveness, and trust.

9. Environmental and Stability Impact of Stablecoin Networks

Investigating the carbon profile of stablecoin blockchain systems, particularly proof-of-work stablecoins, grows more urgent. One needs to research effective consensus protocols and carbon-neutral stablecoin initiatives in an effort to assist the world in reaching its sustainability goals.

CONCLUSION

Stablecoins represent a breakthrough innovation between the traditional financial system and blockchain technology. The chapter has brushed against their economic context, technological underpinning, and extensive practical applications, and hinted at revolutionizing digital finance. Through case studies and research, stablecoins have been seen to facilitate ease of payments, market access, and financial inclusion.

Still looming over them, however, are regulatory risk, systemic risk, and technology exposures. Shunning these risks will require industry-wide, regulator, and research community collaboration. Stablecoins must be aligned to have regulatory environments, increase governance, and become more transparent in a bid to reach their maximum potential in a sustainable way.

This chapter has laid a platform for understanding and set critical questions to be answered by future research, so as to enlighten the stakeholders and create an inclusive, secure, and innovative digital currency ecosystem.

REFERENCES

Arner, D. W., Auer, R., & Frost, J. (2020). Stablecoins: Risks, potential and regulation. Bank for International Settlements. https://www.bis.org/publ/othp33.pdf

Bank for International Settlements. (2022). Stablecoins and their role in the financial system. https://www.bis.org/publ/othp.pdf

Bank for International Settlements. (2024). *Stablecoin oversight framework.* https://www.bis.org

Blockchain Consortium. (2024). *Interoperability in blockchain networks: Challenges and solutions* (White paper). https://blockchainconsortium.org

Brunnermeier, M. K., & Landau, J.-P. (2022). The economics and regulation of stablecoins. *Journal of Financial Stability, 58,* 100945. DOI: 10.1016/j.jfs.2022.100945

Chainalysis. (2024). *Stablecoin market analytics report.* https://www.chainalysis.com

European Central Bank. (2022). Stablecoins and financial inclusion: Opportunities and challenges. https://www.ecb.europa.eu/pub/pdf/scpops/ecb.op281~4d5e47be30.en.pdf

European Parliament. (2025). *Markets in crypto-assets (MiCA) implementation report.* https://www.europarl.europa.eu

Gorton, G., & Zhang, J. (2021). Taming Wildcat Stablecoins. *Annual Review of Financial Economics, 13,* 279–299. DOI: 10.1146/annurev-financial-110220-070821

Grobys, K. (2021). The risks of algorithmic stablecoins: Insights from TerraUSD and beyond. *Crypto Finance Review, 3*(4), 45–60.

International Monetary Fund. (2025). The future landscape of stablecoins and CBDCs: Financial stability and innovation. https://www.imf.org/en/Publications

Liberty Street Economics. (2025). The evolution of crypto-stablecoins. Federal Reserve Bank of New York. https://libertystreeteconomics.newyorkfed.org/

Organisation for Economic Co-operation and Development. (2024). *Global stablecoin adoption and financial inclusion.* https://www.oecd.org

Privacy Ledger Foundation. (2025). *Privacy-preserving technologies in crypto compliance.*

U.S. Department of Treasury. (2024). *Stablecoin oversight framework.* https://home.treasury.gov

U.S. President's Working Group on Financial Markets. (2021). Stablecoins—Risks, regulation, and policy recommendations. https://home.treasury.gov/policy-issues/financial-markets-financial-institutions-and-fiscal-service/financial-markets/stablecoins

ADDITIONAL READINGS

Grimmelmann, J. (2021). Stablecoins: The good, the bad, and the ugly. *Yale Journal of Law & Technology*, *23*(1), 45–79.

Li, J., Shin, D., & Wu, S. (2023). Regulation and risks in stablecoin ecosystems. *Journal of Financial Regulation and Compliance*, *31*(2), 120–137. DOI: 10.1108/JFRC-11-2021-0078

Moin, A., & Lecca, P. (2022). Implications of stablecoins for central banks: An overview for policy makers. *Bank of International Settlements Papers*. https://www.bis.org/publ/bppdf/bispap120.htm

Peters, G., Panayi, E., & Chapelle, A. (2015). Trends in crypto-currencies and blockchain technologies: A monetary theory and regulation perspective. *SSRN*, *3*(3), 47–56. DOI: 10.2139/ssrn.2646618

Zohar, A., & Alasrawi, A. (2021). Algorithmic stablecoins and decentralized governance: An empirical review. *DeFi Research Journal*, *2*(1), 10–31.

ADDITIONAL READINGS

Chapter 3
From Law to Supervisory Practice:
A Toolkit for Secure, Transparent, Issuance

Silvio Andrae
https://orcid.org/0000-0002-8586-7812
Independent Researcher, Germany

ABSTRACT

Stablecoins are integral to digital payment infrastructure but may contribute to financial instability due to opaque reserves, operational risks, and regulatory arbitrage. This chapter examines how the US GENIUS Act (2025) can establish an operationally enforceable regime that ensures parity maintenance, liquidity, and transparency. A methodological approach is adopted, integrating comparative legal analysis (GENIUS, Commonwealth, MiCA, and UK) with regulatory engineering. The resulting practice-oriented toolkit aims to transform stablecoins from speculative digital assets into balance sheet- and audit-compliant payment instruments. The analysis underscores that effective stablecoin regulation requires coordinated integration of law, governance, and technology. This chapter targets regulators, supervisory authorities, and policy analysts.

INTRODUCTION

Stablecoins have emerged as a critical measure of whether digital money can achieve stability, efficiency, and inclusion. In contrast to Bitcoin, Ether, and other volatile crypto assets, which are primarily regarded as speculative investments, stablecoins are designed to maintain stable value relative to government currencies,

DOI: 10.4018/979-8-3373-9043-7.ch003

predominantly the US dollar. This stability is rooted not only in technical mechanisms but also in the underlying market and infrastructure logic. Traditional bank accounts involve three sequential steps: deposit acceptance, payment order issuance, and transaction processing through intermediaries before final posting. In contrast, stablecoins provide immediately available digital securities that can be transferred and settled without delay. Value transfer occurs through the movement of a tokenized claim on a public or consortium blockchain network, rather than as an accounting adjustment between accounts. As a result, stablecoins facilitate immediate and secure transactions, independent of business hours, clearing cycles, or correspondent bank dependencies. Settlement is typically finalized within seconds. The integration of tokenized value, instant transferability, and continuous settlement infrastructure positions stablecoins as a potentially superior vehicle for digital liquidity.

The rapid transaction speed of stablecoins is notable, as is the evolving pattern of their use. While most transactions still originate from crypto trading, businesses increasingly recognize the practical benefits of stablecoins, particularly in business-to-business treasury management and cross-border payments. Stablecoins enable instant settlement with minimal transaction costs, often less than one US cent per transfer. Financial institutions such as JPMorgan have begun processing trade and payment flows using blockchain-based stablecoin platforms, and major payment networks like Visa are incorporating stablecoins as a settlement medium. This development shifts the role of stablecoins from serving solely as a 'trading chip' in crypto markets to functioning as an efficiency-enhancing infrastructure component within the global financial system.

However, this growth is accompanied by significant risks. The occurrence of notable 'de-pegging' events, such as TerraUSD in 2022 and USDC during the collapse of Silicon Valley Bank in 2023, demonstrates that stablecoins can be as vulnerable as unsecured short-term money market instruments. 'De-pegging' occurs when a stablecoin's value ceases to be maintained relative to its underlying asset, typically the US dollar. Causes include insufficient reserves or a sudden loss of confidence. Wilmarth (2025) characterizes stablecoins as a 'time bomb,' contending that non-bank-based stablecoins are structurally susceptible to crises due to uninsured reserves, with the potential for runs to trigger systemic disruptions similar to those experienced by prime money market funds before the 2008 financial crisis. Liang (2025) further cautions that uninsured bank deposits or illiquid assets in stablecoin issuers' reserve portfolios can directly link stablecoin risk to bank risk. Empirical evidence supports these concerns: Tether and Circle maintained substantial portions of their reserves in uninsured deposits or non-high-quality liquid assets (non-HQLA) for extended periods, and the de-pegging of USDC in 2023 was only stabilized through an implicit government intervention.

Against this backdrop, the US regulatory initiative, the GENIUS Act (Guiding and Establishing National Innovation for US Stablecoins Act, 2025), marks a turning point. For the first time, there is a coherent federal legal framework that explicitly regulates payment stablecoins as a separate category of digital assets. GENIUS establishes a strict market-entry and transparency framework by allowing stablecoins to be issued exclusively by 'permitted issuers'—either regulated non-banks or subsidiaries of insured banks. The guidelines include:

- 1:1 reserves in highly liquid assets, preferably US government bonds,
- Daily or monthly disclosure of reserve composition and certifications,
- First-priority claims for token holders in the event of insolvency,
- a ban on any promises of interest or returns on stablecoin holdings.

Furthermore, the GENIUS Act mandates that supervisory authorities develop guidelines on capital and liquidity management, risk diversification, and governance, with particular emphasis on non-bank issuers. The Act also introduces a comprehensive agenda to address illicit financial activities, incorporating advanced anti-money laundering (AML) tools such as application programming interfaces (APIs), blockchain analytics, and digital identity solutions. By integrating prudential regulation—including security, liquidity, and governance—with measures to prevent illicit finance, such as AML, countering the financing of terrorism (CFT), data access, and monitoring, the GENIUS Act establishes an integrated supervisory framework for the first time.

The provisions of the GENIUS Act demonstrate that effective stablecoin regulation requires more than the establishment of standards; it depends on the interaction of three interconnected components. First, an issuer regime must ensure parity maintenance and fully liquid reserves, alongside transparent governance and robust risk management. Second, regulation must extend beyond traditional supervision to include technology-enabled supervisory infrastructure that leverages data access, automated analysis, and standardized interfaces to detect unauthorized activities and proactively monitor operational risks. Third, the regulatory framework should facilitate interoperability between stablecoins and the existing financial system, as well as across different blockchain networks, while preserving privacy and informational self-determination.

A comparison of the GENIUS Act and the Commonwealth Model Law reveals that diverse legal traditions converge on fundamental principles: parity, transparency, and liquidity are essential. The primary distinction lies in implementation. The GENIUS Act introduces a detailed, technically specific regime with stringent market-entry and disclosure requirements. In contrast, the Commonwealth model adopts a flexible approach tailored to jurisdictions with limited regulatory capacity.

This chapter synthesizes both perspectives and translates them into an operational toolkit applicable across varying levels of national development.

Recent scholarship highlights that stablecoins represent more than a technological innovation; they are integral to a strategic reconfiguration of the international monetary system. De Conti and Guttmann (2025) contend that the United States is strategically promoting private USD stablecoins through the GENIUS Act to reinforce the global dominance of the dollar, while the European Union and China prioritize central bank digital currencies (CBDCs) to assert monetary sovereignty. According to Farhat et al. (2025), stablecoins function as an 'interconnection agreement' between the dollar-based monetary system ('System 1') and Bitcoin ('System 3'), thereby expanding network reach and complicating the emergence of an alternative, BRICS-oriented currency bloc ('System 2'). Stablecoins not only enhance private-sector adoption but also facilitate the export of digital dollar liquidity, particularly in economies with capital controls or unstable currencies. Empirical evidence indicates that Tether and USDC already operate as 'digital dollars' in markets where access to USD is restricted or politically sensitive, such as Turkey, Argentina, Nigeria, and Russia. From a regulatory standpoint, this underscores that stablecoin governance must address not only financial stability but also the geopolitical implications of digital infrastructure.

Stablecoins, therefore, represent more than a novel payment instrument; they serve as a test case for digital monetary sovereignty in the twenty-first century. Their emergence compels states to approach supervision, data protection, infrastructure, and financial market stability as interconnected elements of governance. The balance between innovation and stability is determined not by the mere authorization of stablecoins, but by the specific conditions under which they are approved. In this context, the chapter develops a framework that translates regulatory standards into practical supervisory measures, encompassing reserve requirements, disclosure processes, and privacy-preserving AML systems. The objective is to establish a foundation for stable, transparent, and globally interoperable stablecoin-based monetary systems that advance financial inclusion and efficiency while safeguarding financial stability, consumer protection, and fundamental rights.

The chapter is organized into three parts. First, it analyzes the regulatory architecture of the GENIUS Act, emphasizing its significance as the first comprehensive US federal framework for payment stablecoins. This section categorizes the core regulatory elements—licensing, reserves, disclosure requirements, redemption mechanisms, and the prohibition of interest promises—and situates them within the broader context of US financial market law. The GENIUS framework is then compared with the Commonwealth Model Law on Stablecoins and with European and UK regimes (such as MiCA and e-money regulation) through a comparative legal analysis. This comparison demonstrates that, despite differing regulatory philosophies, both GENIUS and the Commonwealth Model Law uphold the same essential protection principles, though they employ distinct implementation strategies: GENIUS as a detailed 'blueprint regulation,' and the Commonwealth model as an adaptive 'minimum viable supervisory standard' for jurisdictions with limited supervisory capacity. Building on this analysis, the chapter develops an operational supervisory toolkit that translates regulatory requirements into actionable implementation measures, including a reserve codebook, disclosure workflows, governance mechanisms for smart contracts, and a privacy-by-design AML framework. The chapter's contribution lies in translating regulatory standards into verifiable supervisory practices and conceptualizing stablecoin regulation as an engineering challenge that requires integrating legal requirements, microprudential oversight, supervisory technology, and data protection. From a scholarly perspective, the chapter advances the literature on the institutional design of digital monetary systems by demonstrating how regulatory objectives—such as stability, par redemption, market integrity, and interoperability—can be operationalized through specific control instruments and how regulatory frameworks influence economic dynamics, including bank intermediation, risk allocation, and international spillovers. Ultimately, the chapter offers a framework that transcends abstract normative principles and provides a practical, adaptable toolkit for GENIUS-compatible stablecoin regulation.

The chapter unfolds in five stages. First, it contextualizes stablecoins within the evolving global payment and liquidity landscape, highlighting their increasing systemic importance. Second, it examines market structure, usage patterns, and the contribution of stablecoins to digital dollarization. Third, it assesses systemic risks associated with reserves, liquidity runs, and bank intermediation. Fourth, it develops a supervisory toolkit aligned with the GENIUS Act, translating legal requirements into operational control mechanisms. Finally, it draws strategic implications for national regulators, emerging markets, and the coexistence of stablecoins with central bank digital currencies (CBDCs).

MARKET STATUS AND SYSTEMIC RELEVANCE OF STABLECOINS

Within a few years, stablecoins have transitioned from a marginal technological phenomenon to a systemically significant component of global payment and liquidity infrastructure. Strong network effects, market fragmentation, and institutional responses to both innovation pressures and regulatory requirements characterize this evolution. Empirical data demonstrate the rapid pace of this development.

Recent data highlight the scale and concentration of stablecoin markets: (i) total outstanding stablecoin supply exceeds USD 250 billion; (ii) over 80% of circulation is concentrated in two issuers (USDT and USDC); (iii) monthly transaction volumes regularly surpass USD 1 trillion; and (iv) a majority of transfers originate from emerging and developing economies. These indicators serve as critical thresholds for assessing systemic relevance, monitoring concentration risk, and calibrating proportional regulatory responses from a supervisory perspective.

Concentration, Market Structure, and Usage Patterns

The total stablecoin market volume increased from approximately US$5 billion in 2020 to about US$260 billion in the third quarter of 2025. This growth has established stablecoins as an asset class relevant not only to the crypto market, but also to cross-border payment processes, corporate treasury functions, and, increasingly, the trading and clearing activities of conventional financial institutions. Following the passage of the GENIUS Act, the market capitalization of crypto assets reached nearly US$4 trillion by August 2025 (Chari et al., 2025).

The market is highly concentrated, with approximately 80% of the total circulating volume held by two issuers: Tether (USDT) and Circle (USDC) (Figure 1). Tether's USDT represents more than half of the total value, while Circle's USDC has experienced the fastest growth since the end of 2020 (Liang, 2025; Andrae, 2026).

Figure 1. Stablecoin supply (in billion USD)

Token	2020 Q4	2025 Q3
USDT	20.04	183.60
USDC	3.96	75.15
PYUSD		2.43
FDUSD		0.94
USDG		0.85
USDP	0.41	0.07

Source: Visa

Hutchins Center on Fiscal & Monetary Policy at BROOKINGS

Monthly transaction volumes have surpassed $1 trillion, a tenfold increase from the end of 2020 (Figure 2). Although stablecoins have the potential to reduce the cost of cross-border transfers and cash management for multinational companies, such use cases remain limited.

Figure 2. Monthly stablecoin transaction volume (billions USD, adjusted)

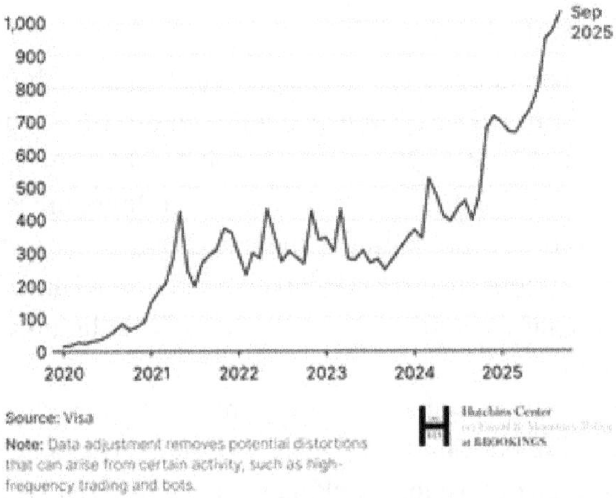

Stablecoins primarily serve as infrastructure for crypto asset transactions, with approximately 88-90% of all transfers occurring in trading and exchange contexts. However, usage patterns are shifting, as stablecoins are increasingly employed for B2B payments, cross-border transfers, and e-commerce transactions. Companies typically utilize stablecoins when traditional correspondent banking chains would result in delays and additional costs. Research indicates that cross-border stablecoin transactions can be processed in near real time, with transaction costs in some cases below one US cent (KPMG, 2025). This reduces both transaction fees and capital commitment costs, as less prefunding is required in nostro and vostro accounts.

This transformation extends beyond financial service providers. Visa and PayPal have integrated stablecoins into their settlement and merchant processes, while large retail groups are experimenting with proprietary stablecoin-issuing models to manage internal payment flows (KPMG, 2025) more efficiently. The core innovation is that stablecoins combine programming logic, such as smart contracts, with payment processing in a single medium. This integration enables technical linkage of payment terms and value transfer, a functionality not available in traditional account balances due to regulatory and technical constraints.

From a supervisory perspective, the transition from exchange-internal trading to B2B payments, treasury management, and settlement functions constitutes a qualitative threshold. When stablecoins are utilized for corporate liquidity management rather than solely for speculative trading, issues such as operational failures, reserve quality, and legal enforceability become directly relevant to the real economy.

Stablecoins as Drivers of Global Dollar Demand

The dominance of USD-denominated stablecoins reflects a structural dynamic rather than a random market occurrence. Stablecoins increasingly serve as digital proxies for the dollar in payment systems where access to traditional US banking services is limited. Approximately 99 percent of global stablecoin volume is pegged to the US dollar. This development has led to what the literature describes as the 'digital Eurodollar market,' a continuation of the Eurodollar system established in the 1960s, now operating without correspondent banks and instead utilizing blockchain infrastructures. As a result, stablecoins function as a USD liquidity layer outside the US banking system.

In many emerging markets, stablecoins are increasingly replacing local payment methods and banking products, particularly in environments characterized by high inflation, capital controls, or unstable banking systems. Regional user studies indicate that between 40 and 50 percent of users in Brazil, Nigeria, India, and Turkey utilize stablecoins to 'save in dollars.' Unlike traditional correspondent banking networks, stablecoin transfers do not require nostro or vostro accounts, significantly reducing costs and settlement times. KPMG's regulatory report highlights that banks can achieve stable value transfer without capital commitment in cross-border transactions, with settlement often occurring within seconds at near-zero cost. This function aligns with what Adrian and Mancini-Griffoli (IMF) describe as 'synthetic dollar substitution,' where market participants hold digital dollar claims rather than physical dollars.

From the user's perspective, this convergence blurs the distinctions between 'bank deposit,' 'e-money,' and 'stablecoin.' Consequently, the relationship between the form of money and trust in money changes: trust is established not by the national central bank, but by the issuer, often a US technology or payment service provider.

A study by the Deutsche Bank Research Institute contends that stablecoins reinforce the US dollar's strategic influence in the digital era by being backed by US government bonds, thereby increasing demand for US fiscal securities (Laboure & Siazon, 2025). The GENIUS Act accelerates this trend by providing regulatory clarity. The authors describe this as a 'turning point for global finance' and project that the stablecoin market could exceed $2 trillion by 2028. Economically, this creates a notable mechanism: users in emerging markets exchange local currency for stablecoins, and issuers invest the reserves in US Treasuries. The United States benefits from capital inflows into government bonds without requiring a dollar bank account, SWIFT, or a correspondent bank. Stablecoins thus generate a new form of international demand for US government securities, creating a digitized seigniorage effect that benefits the US.

While these developments are strategically advantageous for the United States, they pose significant risks for emerging and developing countries. These risks include diminished monetary policy sovereignty, challenges in controlling capital flows, and the potential displacement of local financial intermediaries. The threat of unwanted dollarization through stablecoins is increasingly recognized as a politically relevant issue in these regions. Wilmarth (2025) observes that some governments are already considering restrictions or bans on the use of USD stablecoins within their national territories, as stablecoins facilitate capital movements outside traditional control regimes and enable rapid transfers to offshore ecosystems.

Systemic Risks

The primary source of systemic risk does not stem from the stablecoin concept itself, but from its specific design features. Brookings' analysis (Liang, 2025) demonstrates that poorly calibrated reserve structures, particularly those involving uninsured bank deposits and illiquid assets, render stablecoins vulnerable to crises and establish direct feedback loops with the banking sector. The collapse of Silicon Valley Bank in March 2023 exemplifies this risk: Circle held USD 3.3 billion of USDC reserves at the bank, causing USDC to temporarily fall to USD 0.87 and triggering a significant withdrawal spiral. Parity was restored only after U.S. authorities invoked a systemic risk exception under the FDIA. This episode highlights two key points: first, stablecoins can create real demand for lender-of-last-resort mechanisms beyond the crypto market; second, such implicit public backstops introduce moral hazard when non-bank issuers depend on anticipated support measures.

Wilmarth (2025) contends that non-bank stablecoins are structurally susceptible to runs due to business models that combine three risk factors: uninsured reserves, lack of access to central bank liquidity, and frequent speculative use as leverage or arbitrage instruments. This configuration is reminiscent of the fragility observed in money market funds during the 2008 financial crisis, where short-term liabilities were considered 'quasi-safe.' Still, reserve portfolios were partially illiquid or highly volatile. When doubts emerged about asset values, even minor shocks could trigger substantial and abrupt redemptions.

Castrén and Russo (2026) address this structural vulnerability by modeling the tendency of unregulated stablecoin issuers to hold high-yield, illiquid assets in reserves, a condition identified by Wilmarth as 'run-prone.' Their model demonstrates that such reserve structures create volatility-driven value risks, prompting mass redemptions and endogenous runs. To mitigate this fragility, recent US regulations propose overcollateralization of reserves and standardized disclosure requirements. Castrén and Russo's findings indicate that these measures, by enhancing transparency and collateralization, reduce the incentives for runs by decreasing uncertainty about reserve values and lowering insolvency risks.

Bindseil (2025) extends this analysis by moving from issuer-level fragility to system-level transmission. His flow-of-funds model demonstrates that stablecoin runs can propagate through two primary channels: fire-sale contagion, when issuers liquidate securities to meet redemptions, particularly if reserves include longer-maturity or less-liquid assets; and bank liquidity pressure, when stablecoin issuers withdraw deposits from commercial banks, often concentrated among a few large institutions. Bindseil also argues that cross-border stablecoin usage introduces asymmetries, as inflows and outflows reshape bank funding structures, central bank balance sheets, and global liquidity conditions. Collectively, Bindseil's work operationalizes the run mechanisms described by Wilmarth and formalized by Castrén and Russo within a macro-financial stability framework, emphasizing the need for liquidity requirements, concentration limits, and potentially central bank access to depositors' funds for issuers.

Recent theoretical and empirical evidence indicates that stablecoins function as two-way transmission channels between the dollar system and crypto markets. A new model (Huang et al., 2025) demonstrates that the direction and magnitude of risk transmission depend on stablecoin supply dynamics and reserve composition. When stablecoin issuance expands, risk flows from dollar markets into crypto markets as reserves accumulate and token circulation increases. Conversely, when stablecoin reserves contract, such as during redemption waves or liquidity stresses, risk flows back into the dollar market, tightening funding conditions and amplifying vulnerabilities. The model predicts that this mechanism can become asymmetric: if stablecoins maintain sufficiently liquid and high-quality reserves, they can partially absorb crypto-market shocks, serving as a temporary buffer. However, if reserves fall below critical thresholds, the transmission reverses abruptly, increasing dollar-funding fragility. Copula-based CoVaR tests in the study support this asymmetric behavior, showing that extreme crypto-market movements disproportionately elevate tail risks in U.S. money markets when stablecoin reserves are low or declining.

This dynamic highlights a structural parallel to the securitization channels of the 2007-2009 global financial crisis: what initially appears as a niche segment—previously asset-backed commercial paper conduits, now dollar-backed stablecoins—can amplify systemic risks by connecting markets that operate under different regulatory regimes. Consequently, stablecoins represent not only micro-prudential technology design challenges but also meso-level intermediation nodes capable of transmitting liquidity stress across both traditional and crypto-financial systems.

However, regulatory frameworks should not be overestimated in their capacity to eliminate run dynamics. Cross-border usage, varying enforcement capabilities, and the rapidity of on-chain transactions impose structural constraints on supervisory intervention. Even robust reserve and disclosure requirements may be circumvented through regulatory arbitrage, jurisdictional fragmentation, or the migration of activities to less-regulated environments.

Stablecoins and Bank Intermediation

In addition to micro-prudential risks, stablecoins create structural incentives for capital to shift from bank deposits to stablecoins. Choi and Rhee (2025) demonstrate, through model-theoretic analysis, that stablecoins can prompt banks to engage in riskier behavior, particularly during periods when the advantages of using stablecoins increase, such as after regulatory clarity or improved interoperability. Competitive pressures may lead banks to offer higher interest rates or pursue riskier investments to retain depositors. This risk is most pronounced during transitional phases, when stablecoins are neither marginal nor dominant. This finding is critical for regulators, as it underscores the need to focus regulatory efforts not only on the steady state but also on the transition phase.

Stablecoins do not change payment transactions by simply providing a faster or cheaper transaction medium. They are changing them by:

- Integrating liquidity and execution into the same medium;
- Enabling global payment flows without intermediary chains;
- Structurally increasing demand for government debt securities, particularly US Treasuries;
- Creating interdependencies between crypto markets and the traditional banking sector.

The relevance of stablecoins cannot, therefore, be viewed solely as a technological innovation. They are a monetary theory experiment under real market conditions—with immediate consequences for financial stability, monetary sovereignty, and supervisory practice.

These findings underscore that the most significant risks emerge during transition phases, when stablecoins are neither marginal nor fully integrated. Supervisory attention should therefore address not only steady-state outcomes but also the transitional dynamics where competitive pressures and risk-taking incentives are most pronounced.

GENIUS ACT—REGULATORY ARCHITECTURE AND OBJECTIVES

The Guiding and Establishing National Innovation for US Stablecoins Act (GENIUS Act, 2025; Latham & Watkins, 2025) constitutes the first comprehensive federal regulatory framework for stablecoins in the United States. This legislation marks a significant shift by establishing a distinct legal regime for 'payment stablecoins,' separate from securities law, e-money law, and general payment transaction law. The GENIUS Act classifies stablecoins as a unique category of digital payment instrument, subject to a dedicated regulatory licensing regime, rather than as securities or deposit-taking businesses. This framework addresses prior regulatory fragmentation, in which stablecoin issuers faced inconsistent and sometimes conflicting oversight from FinCEN, the SEC, and individual states.

In addition to its technical provisions, the GENIUS Act should be analyzed within a broader political and economic context. The licensing regime alters competitive dynamics among banks, Fintech firms, and non-bank issuers, and significant industry incentives remain to influence the interpretation of permissible activities. While regulatory clarity reduces uncertainty, it does not eliminate lobbying efforts or regulatory competition across jurisdictions.

Although stablecoins appear novel, they are conceptually analogous to earlier forms of private money in US financial history. Between 1863 and 1935, 'national bank notes' functioned as private money backed by public debt. These notes were authorized by the National Banking Acts of 1863 and 1864 and issued by federally chartered commercial banks (Luck, 2025).

Licensing and Market Entry: The 'Permitted Issuer' Approach

Stablecoins are digital currencies intended to maintain a stable face value by pegging to a reference asset, such as the US dollar. They seek to integrate the technological benefits of decentralized payment systems, including digital ledgers and tokenization of traditional assets, with the convenience and familiarity of conventional money. The GENIUS Act provides a clear legal basis for fiat-backed stablecoins in the United States. Under this law, permitted payment stablecoin issuers (PPSIs), such as federally regulated banks, permitted newly licensed nonbanks, or qualified state-licensed entities (which are under the direct supervision of a federal agency), are authorized to issue stablecoins. Stablecoins under this law must be fully backed by secure, liquid assets such as US dollars, short-term Treasury securities, uninsured deposits with commercial banks, or cash equivalents. Stablecoins may therefore not constitute bank deposits, do not have access to Fed accounts, and are not subject to deposit insurance.

Issuers are prohibited from paying interest or returns on stablecoin balances, while holders are granted priority in insolvency proceedings. To enhance transparency, issuers are required to disclose their reserves publicly monthly. The primary legislative objective is to establish the stablecoin sector as a distinct, fully collateralized payment system that operates independently of deposit insurance and central bank refinancing. Additionally, the licensing regime serves as a competitive mechanism: unauthorized issuers are barred from issuing stablecoins redeemable at par, with violations subject to civil penalties of up to $1 million per day and potential criminal liability.

The GENIUS Act addresses a significant market failure: previously, unregulated issuers held a competitive advantage by offering lower-cost but riskier products, attributable to limited capital requirements and weaker transparency obligations.

Reserves, Parity, and Redemption Rights

The guiding principle of the law is that parity is an enforceable right, not a business promise. Reserves must be covered at all times by liquid assets at a ratio of at least 1:1, in particular:

- US dollar balances or
- short-term high-quality US government bonds (Treasuries) (HQLA).

The GENIUS Act mandates monthly, auditor-certified disclosures of reserve composition and grants stablecoin holders first-priority claims in insolvency scenarios. In the event of issuer insolvency, holders are treated as priority creditors and receive payments directly from reserve assets. This reverses the traditional creditor hierarchy found in bank deposits, prioritizing users over institutions.

Notably, the GENIUS Act permits uninsured bank deposits as eligible reserve assets, a provision that, according to Liang (2025), may strengthen the systemic connection between bank risk and stablecoin risk. These risks are tangible: for example, Circle previously held up to 14% of USDC reserves as uninsured bank deposits, and during the Silicon Valley Bank incident, this contributed to USDC de-pegging to $0.87. The Act addresses these concerns by empowering regulators to impose risk-adjusted capital and liquidity requirements and to mandate diversification of reserve portfolios.

Although enforceable parity and redemption rights are essential for stablecoins to serve as reliable payment instruments, they alone do not provide comprehensive consumer protection.

Governance, Supervision, and Prohibitions: 'No Returns, No Shadow Banking'

Two obligations are central to the market structure:

1. Issuers may not pay interest or income on stablecoin holdings. It is to prevent stablecoins from becoming an alternative deposit product or engaging in bank-like maturity transformation.
2. Issuers may only engage in narrowly defined business activities. They may issue and redeem stablecoins and operate the associated infrastructure, but not engage in lending or speculative transactions.

The GENIUS Act enforces stringent business restrictions on stablecoin issuers, limiting their activities to issuing and redeeming stablecoins and operating related infrastructure. Lending and speculative transactions are expressly prohibited. Nevertheless, Wilmarth (2025) contends that the Act still permits nonbanks to participate in high-risk financial activities, particularly when combined with crypto derivatives. The regulatory distinction between 'operating a stablecoin' and 'distributing financial products' remains complex, and the legislator aims to address this risk through independent business restrictions.

Even fully backed stablecoins expose users to risks that extend beyond reserve adequacy. These include (i) fraud and scams exploiting stablecoin rails; (ii) mis-selling and misleading safety claims regarding 'risk-free' digital dollars; (iii) wallet-security risks, particularly in custodial arrangements; and (iv) the absence of standardized dispute-resolution and redress mechanisms. Addressing these issues requires complementary consumer-protection rules alongside prudential safeguards.

Transparency, Auditing, and Accounting

The GENIUS Act integrates stablecoins into the established financial reporting framework, thereby removing them from the category of 'opaque digital assets.' This is accomplished through a comprehensive transparency and audit regime that exceeds prior requirements in crypto and payment law. Issuers of payment stablecoins are required to publish monthly reports detailing the size and composition of their reserves, as well as the number of stablecoins in circulation. These reports must provide both aggregated and granular data, including information on reserve instrument maturities and custodians. This requirement introduces, for the first time, standardized, verifiable, and consistent reporting for market participants and regulators, thereby enhancing confidence in the stability and reliability of stablecoin issuers.

Furthermore, the GENIUS Act mandates that external, registered auditors verify the accuracy of disclosed information. For large issuers with reserve volumes exceeding $50 billion, the reporting requirements are more stringent: audited and certified annual financial statements in accordance with recognized accounting standards must be submitted. These auditing standards align with those applied to listed capital market companies. As a result, stablecoin reserves are recognized as a distinct balance sheet item, eliminating their previous status as an internal, opaque asset of the issuer.

The regulatory implications of these transparency requirements are substantial. For the first time, a framework enables stablecoins to be classified as financial assets, rather than speculative or undefined 'digital assets,' provided they satisfy legal parity and reserve criteria. In specific cases, stablecoins may be recognized as cash equivalents if their reserves consist entirely of liquid payment instruments or short-term government bonds, and the issuer guarantees legally enforceable repayment at par value. This development marks a shift in accounting practices, moving stablecoins from the category of 'crypto assets' to that of auditable means of payment. This change is particularly significant for institutional market participants, such as treasury departments, insurance companies, and investment funds, as it allows for the integration of audit-proof payment instruments into treasury operations, thereby enhancing liquidity management and reducing settlement risks.

This repositioning clarifies that the GENIUS Act is not a 'crypto law' in the traditional sense. Instead, it establishes a distinct regulatory regime for tokenized forms of money, grounded in four core principles: full and liquid reserve backing (prohibiting fractional reserves and maturity transformation), enforceable redemption rights at par value for token holders, stringent transparency requirements including external audits, and the exclusion of yield or lending activities to prevent stablecoins from functioning as substitute deposits or shadow banking products. The law's structure intentionally mirrors the characteristics of cash: liquidity, risk-free status, immediate redeemability, and the absence of promised returns.

In summary, the GENIUS Act does not seek to create a new investment product or to foster innovation by maximizing technical flexibility. Instead, by integrating transparency, accounting, and governance measures, the legislation defines a specific role for stablecoins: they are to function as digital means of payment, not as investment vehicles. The law's structural impact arises from this interplay. Instead of merely setting standards, GENIUS establishes an operational supervisory framework that ensures verifiability through disclosure processes, reserve catalogs, stress testing, and an AML/SupTech infrastructure. While transparency reduces information asymmetries and enhances market discipline, it does not guarantee effective enforcement. The effectiveness of risk mitigation ultimately depends on supervisory capacity, cross-border cooperation, and timely intervention.

LEGAL COMPARISON

Regulatory approaches differ significantly. GENIUS offers a detailed, technically specific blueprint, whereas the Commonwealth Model Law on Stablecoins adopts an adaptive, capacity-oriented framework suitable for countries with limited supervisory infrastructure. The EU MiCA and the UK regime occupy an intermediate position: they are more standardized than the Commonwealth model but less technically detailed than GENIUS. This section examines the similarities and differences among these regimes, classifies them according to legal doctrine, and discusses the regulatory rationales underlying their divergences.

Common Core Principles

Despite divergent regulatory philosophies and implementation strategies, the GENIUS Act, the Commonwealth Model Law on Stablecoins, and the European and UK regimes (MiCA/UK) converge on three foundational principles. These globally recognized points of convergence are: full and liquid reserve coverage, enforceable redemption rights, and a commitment to transparency and disclosure.

Each regime presumes that stablecoins can serve as secure digital payment instruments only if highly liquid assets fully back them at all times. The GENIUS Act enforces this requirement stringently, mandating 1:1 backing by cash reserves or high-quality short-term government bonds and excluding fractional reserve models. MiCA adopts a similarly rigorous stance, requiring 'e-money tokens' to be fully backed by assets that can be redeemed at any time. In contrast, the Commonwealth Model Law is more flexible: it mandates full redeemability and financial security but does not specify a detailed list of permissible reserve instruments. Instead, it articulates regulatory objectives and delegates the specifics to national supervisory authorities.

Closely related to this is the second common principle: the redeemability of the stablecoin at par value as a legally enforceable relationship, not merely as a business promise. The second shared principle concerns the enforceable redeemability of stablecoins at par value, establishing a legal right rather than a mere business promise. The GENIUS Act codifies this by granting stablecoin holders a priority claim to the issuer's reserve funds in insolvency scenarios. MiCA similarly articulates the right of repayment, requiring users to redeem stablecoins at face value at any time and on demand. The Commonwealth model also mandates a payout obligation but permits greater flexibility in timing to reflect varying regulatory capacities and market infrastructures. Collectively, these regimes represent a shift from reliance on issuer promises to enforceable legal claims that provide users with direct rights: certified audits and detailed breakdowns of reserve holdings. MiCA also stipulates extensive audit and disclosure requirements, embedded in existing European supervisory structures (EBA/ESMA). The Commonwealth model pursues an approach adapted to national capacities: minimum transparency is mandatory, but the depth of disclosure can be graded depending on supervisory resources. The key point is that all regimes impose an obligation to disclose reserve quality to reduce information asymmetries and enable market participants to make their own risk assessments.

Despite varying legal traditions and implementation strategies, three elements emerge as a global normative foundation: stablecoins should be fully backed by liquid reserves, remain redeemable at par at all times, and be subject to appropriate, verifiable transparency requirements. Collectively, these principles underscore the notion that stablecoins are intended to function as digital equivalents of safe money, providing fixed rights for users and clear accountability for issuers, rather than serving as speculative financial products.

Different Regulatory Logics

While the GENIUS Act, the Commonwealth Model Law, and MiCA/UK share core principles, they diverge fundamentally in regulatory logic, granularity, and implementation philosophy. These distinctions pertain not to the objectives, but to the methods of achieving them.

The GENIUS Act adopts a blueprint approach, whereby the legislator not only sets objectives but also translates them into specific technical requirements. This applies to reserve structures, including permissible asset classes and maturity profiles, as well as to disclosure, auditing, and supervisory integration. GENIUS exemplifies regulatory engineering, treating regulation and implementation as inseparable. Its provisions are designed to prevent stablecoins from functioning as deposit products or shadow banking instruments. Consequently, GENIUS imposes strict limitations on eligible issuers and categorically prohibits promises of returns on stablecoin holdings, thereby targeting institutions with established governance and risk management capabilities.

The Commonwealth Model Law adopts a fundamentally different strategy, conceptualizing stablecoin regulation as minimum viable regulation. Its primary objective is to enable countries with limited supervisory infrastructure to authorize stablecoins without incurring systemic risks. Unlike GENIUS, which prescribes detailed technical specifications, the Commonwealth model articulates regulatory objectives—such as parity, reserve quality, and governance—while delegating implementation to national authorities. This approach acknowledges that many jurisdictions, particularly in emerging and developing economies, lack the supervisory capacity of the US or EU but still require stable digital payment solutions. Accordingly, the model is designed to be open, proportional, and interoperable.

MiCA and the UK regime represent an intermediate approach, incorporating elements of detailed regulation—such as disclosure, governance, and risk management requirements—without establishing an entirely prescriptive blueprint. In the EU, stablecoins are classified as e-money tokens or asset-referenced tokens within the existing financial market framework. At the same time, in the UK, they are regulated under the Payment Services Law. Unlike GENIUS, these regimes permit yield models, provided they do not assume the characteristics of securities or investment funds. The regulatory emphasis is placed on facilitating market entry and competition rather than imposing market restrictions.

These different logics have significant consequences for market structure and competition:

- GENIUS leads to higher barriers to entry, but to stronger institutional quality of issuers.
- The Commonwealth model promotes market entry, especially in legal systems with limited capacity.
- MiCA and the UK model enable competition between banks, Fintechs, and payment institutions.

GENIUS provides in-depth, prescriptive regulation, whereas MiCA and the Commonwealth model establish broader regulatory frameworks. In essence, GENIUS serves as a technical manual, while the others function as adaptable frameworks.

Table 1. Comparison table: Regulatory logic GENIUS — Commonwealth — MiCA, and UK

Dimension / Objective	GENIUS Act (USA)	Commonwealth Model Law	EU MiCA / UK regime
Regulatory style	Blueprint / rule-based engineering (highly granular)	Principle-based / minimum viable regulation (modular, adaptive)	Hybrid: rule-based + proportionality
Regulatory objective	Stability through full reserves, no returns, institutional quality	Enable market access even with weaker supervision	Integration into financial market regime and payment transactions
Permitted issuers	Highly limited: only 'permitted issuers' (bank-subsidiary or specially licensed non-bank)	Broader, depending on national implementation	Far-reaching: banks, e-money issuers, Fintechs

continued on following page

Table 1. Continued

Dimension / Objective	GENIUS Act (USA)	Commonwealth Model Law	EU MiCA / UK regime
Reserve requirements	Only cash and HQLA (Treasuries), strict 1:1 coverage	Full reserve principle, but implementation by national authorities	Full reserve requirement, but more flexible asset classes
Return on stablecoin holdings	Prohibited (no interest, no rewards)	Context-dependent, no explicit prohibition	Permitted as long as no securities character arises
Governance and supervision	High governance requirements, audit and reporting obligations	Governance according to capacity, focus on minimum requirements	Governance integrated into PSD2/e-money regime
Addresses market problem	Systemic risks and shadow banking behavior	Financial inclusion and connectivity	Competition, consumer protection, market integration

Source: own representation.

The three regimes do not form a regulatory continuum, but address different problems:

- GENIUS minimizes systemic risks through technological and organizational rigor.
- Commonwealth maximizes connectivity and reduces barriers to entry.
- EU MiCA and UK balances competition, consumer protection, and integration into existing structures.

These approaches do not yield a uniform, globally stablecoin model. Still, they do establish a consistent regulatory logic: stablecoins are treated as digital monetary instruments requiring operational oversight, rather than as investment products. Beyond the US, EU, and Commonwealth, supervisory practices in Asia and Africa underscore the significance of regional variation. For example, Singapore mandates fully segregated reserves and robust custody standards; Hong Kong incorporates stablecoins into its virtual-asset licensing regime; Nigeria and Kenya employ sandbox-based supervision with remittance-corridor monitoring; and South Africa's FSCA classifies stablecoins as 'digital representations of value' subject to financial-product regulations. Collectively, these examples illustrate a trend toward greater reserve transparency, segregation, and risk-based supervision.

Interoperability and Legal Conflicts

Divergent regulatory frameworks for stablecoins present significant challenges in cross-border contexts. While tokenized payment units circulate globally on public blockchain networks, regulatory and supervisory regimes remain territorially constrained. This creates a conflict between the global reach of technical execution and the national scope of legal authority. Consequently, regulation now requires not only standard-setting but also regime interoperability. The approaches of GENIUS, the Commonwealth Model Law, MiCA, and the UK illustrate that the challenge extends beyond technical interoperability to the mutual recognition of legal effects across jurisdictions.

The first line of conflict concerns which supervisory law applies when a stablecoin licensed and supervised in jurisdiction A is used en masse in jurisdiction B. GENIUS assumes that the issuer's supervision is sufficient, regardless of where the tokens are used. The Commonwealth model, on the other hand, stipulates that states need not prohibit issuance or use, but may impose a 'recognition' or 'registration' requirement if stablecoins achieve significant domestic use. MiCA or the UK pursues a third solution: it copies the concept of passporting established in payment services law. It enables issuers to operate throughout the single market under a uniform licensing system. MiCA thus addresses the problem that users are often located in a different jurisdiction than the issuer—a phenomenon that is particularly exacerbated by stablecoins' decentralized nature.

The second line of conflict concerns data access and AML/CFT monitoring. GENIUS closely links stablecoin regulation with a SupTech approach to supervision: standardized APIs, graph analysis, and address-based risk detection enable near real-time monitoring of unauthorized activities. The Commonwealth model deliberately does not provide for a technologically pre-structured supervisory infrastructure, but merely requires that supervision must be 'effective.' MiCA/UK, on the other hand, relies on existing AML and payment service regulations. This creates an asymmetrical scenario: A GENIUS stablecoin is implemented with increased monitorability, both technically and regulatorily, while a stablecoin issued under Commonwealth law may have the same technical reach but does not offer the same regulatory data access. For regulators, this creates a governance dilemma: the technical reach of the tokens exceeds the reach of regulatory powers.

A third line of conflict arises from the relationship between stablecoins and central bank digital currencies (CBDCs). The GENIUS Act does not explicitly include CBDCs, although stablecoin effects on bank intermediation and deposit migration may be similar to those of CBDCs. This is confirmed in the literature: Choi and Rhee (2025) show that competitive pressure from stablecoins can prompt banks to pursue riskier investment strategies, especially during transition phases. MiCA explicitly addresses this issue by embedding CBDCs into the regulatory framework and setting clear priorities: CBDCs are always considered 'highest-ranking money,' while stablecoins are designed for programmable use cases. The Commonwealth model goes one step further, positioning stablecoins as a complementary system—a digital interoperability bridge between local currency, CBDCs, and international payment systems.

In summary, interoperability in this context encompasses more than technical connectivity between blockchains; it also necessitates coordination among regulatory authorities. In the absence of mechanisms such as passporting or mutual recognition, parallel systems may arise in which stablecoins circulate globally but evade adequate local supervision. The widespread adoption of USD-denominated stablecoins, which in some emerging markets function as instruments of digital dollarization, intensifies this challenge. In such cases, users rely on stablecoins for value stability, yet local regulators often face uncertainty regarding the appropriate jurisdiction for addressing operational risks or AML violations.

The interplay among these regimes highlights a critical insight: in the absence of coordinated legal mechanisms—such as recognition, passporting, and joint supervisory interfaces—there is a risk of disconnecting monetary policy from regulatory oversight. Stablecoins may then evolve into supranational payment instruments beyond the effective control of any single jurisdiction, despite their widespread use. GENIUS, MiCA, and the Commonwealth model represent initial steps toward a globally interoperable regulatory system, but their effectiveness ultimately depends on the interoperability of supervisory regimes.

Emerging supervisory frameworks increasingly prioritize interoperability standards, supervisory colleges for cross-border issuers, and data-sharing protocols for reserve verification. BIS Project Mariana (2023) and IOSCO (2025) underscore the importance of global messaging standards, harmonized disclosure templates, and automated compliance attestations, highlighting the essential role of international cooperation among stakeholders.

From a supervisory standpoint, this underscores the increasing importance of cross-border coordination mechanisms, including supervisory colleges, standardized reporting, and data-exchange protocols. Without these instruments, technical interoperability may advance more rapidly than regulatory interoperability.

GENIUS, Commonwealth, and MiCA pursue the same objective—stable digital means of payment with verifiable coverage—but differ in their enforcement:

- GENIUS promotes institutional market participants and defines a precise technical target.
- Commonwealth enables market entry in jurisdictions with low regulatory capacity.
- MiCA harmonizes competition in the internal market and integrates stablecoins into existing financial market structures.

From a regulatory perspective, GENIUS should be viewed not as an 'American version of MiCA' but rather as a technical specification, whereas the Commonwealth model represents a minimum regulatory standard. Although the underlying principles are converging, enforcement remains fragmented at the national level. Mechanisms such as passporting, recognition regimes, and supervisory cooperation only partially address the reality that stablecoins circulate globally while enforcement authority is territorially bounded. These asymmetries may facilitate jurisdictional arbitrage.

NATIONAL STABLECOIN STRATEGY

Stablecoins represent not only a technical or market phenomenon but also intersect with critical aspects of national financial market policy, including monetary sovereignty, capital flow control, data access, and monetary policy autonomy. Consequently, a comprehensive national strategy is essential. Such a strategy comprises three elements: the regulated integration of existing (often foreign) stablecoins (inbound conversion), the issuance of domestically backed stablecoins (outbound issuance), and the establishment of clear guidelines for the use of public blockchain infrastructures (interoperability). This approach highlights that the central issue is not the existence of stablecoins. Still, the role national financial systems will play in this evolving ecosystem underscores the importance of a robust national strategy for stablecoin regulation.

Inbound Conversion: Control Through Routing

In many jurisdictions, users already hold or use foreign-currency-denominated stablecoins, often through international exchanges or wallet service providers. However, such activities frequently occur outside the domestic regulatory framework, lacking anti-money laundering (AML) oversight, balance sheet transparency, and the supervision of local authorities. From a monetary policy standpoint, this situation constitutes an 'uncontrolled value import.'

A national strategy should not seek to prohibit external stablecoins outright, but instead facilitate their integration into the financial system through regulated financial intermediaries. The core principle is that foreign stablecoins may be converted into the national currency exclusively via regulated entities. This requirement ensures that each conversion constitutes a financial intermediary transaction, thereby activating comprehensive know-your-customer (KYC), AML, sanctions, and supervisory obligations. As a result, national supervisors gain visibility into transaction volumes, counterparties, concentration risks, and payment flows, while still supporting innovation.

This approach offers two primary advantages. First, it enhances transparency regarding the domestic real economy's use of stablecoins. Second, it enables supervisory authorities to develop a database that will be essential for subsequent regulatory phases or potential sandbox initiatives. Inbound conversion, therefore, establishes both regulatory control and future strategic options.

Outbound Issuance: Local Stablecoins as an Instrument of Sovereignty

Whereas inbound conversion focuses on regulatory control, the second pillar emphasizes proactive design. States may authorize or initiate the issuance of locally denominated stablecoins, provided these comply with the reserve and governance parameters defined as GENIUS-compatible in Section 6. The objective is not to supplant banks, but to establish an additional, fully backed payment layer that achieves two key outcomes:

- Demand for government debt securities: Holding reserves in HQLA or government bonds creates structural demand for domestic bond markets.
- Mitigation of offshore dollarization: Users have a stable digital alternative in local currency, reducing the need to migrate to USD stablecoins.

In countries experiencing high inflation or diminished confidence in the banking sector, empirical evidence indicates that users adopt stablecoins primarily as a hedge against currency devaluation rather than for their innovative features. Outbound issuance enables the currency zone to become digitally compatible while maintaining oversight of payment flows. However, the local stablecoin mustn't function as a shadow banking product; it must not offer returns, maturity transformation, or lending. Only under these conditions will the stablecoin remain a medium of payment rather than compete for deposits.

Interoperability and Public Blockchains: Use Yes, Loss of Control No

Stablecoins can realize their innovative potential only when operating on open, globally accessible infrastructure. A complete ban on public blockchains would result in the loss of both innovative capacity and competitive advantage, while permitting unregulated use would undermine regulatory control. Therefore, a national strategy must establish a balanced approach that enables usage while implementing appropriate safeguards.

This includes four elements:

1. **Policy-as-code**: Rules for issuance, redemption, or blocking must be technically anchored, not just contractually.
2. **Smart contract governance**: Upgrades must be controlled, key management documented, and emergency mechanisms (freeze/kill switch) in place.
3. **Oracle redundancy**: If a stablecoin requires external price data, that data must be validated multiple times (a redundant oracle setup).
4. **Risk allocation**: The use of public chains is not technically 'outsourcing' in the regulatory sense; issuers remain responsible.

Interoperability should be regarded as a matter of governance rather than solely a technical requirement. The central issue is not the permissibility of public blockchains, but the specific conditions under which their use is allowed.

A national stablecoin strategy integrates stability, innovation, and sovereignty by establishing a clear regulatory framework:

- External stablecoins are made visible via inbound routing.
- Independent, locally denominated stablecoins strengthen sovereignty.
- Public blockchains may be used, but only with governance and control mechanisms.

This approach shifts the perspective from a reactive stance focused on risk prevention to a proactive strategy that leverages stablecoins to achieve national objectives. The state assumes the role of architect, rather than spectator, in the global stablecoin economy, thereby facilitating the attainment of national goals.

PHASED IMPLEMENTATION PATH FOR EMDE COUNTRIES

Recent empirical evidence demonstrates the growing significance of stablecoins in emerging markets, reflecting broader trends in global finance. Chainalysis (2024) estimates that over 60% of stablecoin transfers originate in emerging and developing economies, with Nigeria, Turkey, and Argentina among the top ten user jurisdictions. The World Bank (2024) reports that stablecoin-based remittance rails account for 2–5% of transfers in selected Africa–EU and LatAm–US corridors, particularly where remittance fees exceed 6% (Feyen et al., 2024).

These developments present regulators with observable indicators, including rising transaction volumes in remittance corridors, increased household use of stablecoins as stores of value, and expanding corporate settlement volumes. Such indicators can inform threshold-based supervision and phased regulatory escalation, rather than binary approval or prohibition.

Corporate adoption of stablecoins is also expanding. According to Circle data (2024), USDC settlement volumes for B2B payments doubled year-on-year, driven by e-commerce and cross-border trade among SMEs. These trends underscore the increasing role of stablecoins in corporate finance and reinforce regulatory concerns regarding digital dollarisation and user dependence, particularly in jurisdictions with volatile exchange rates, high inflation, or weak local banking infrastructure.

In many emerging and developing economies (EMDEs), the regulation of stablecoins has become an immediate concern. Users are already heavily reliant on USD-denominated stablecoins for various financial activities, resulting in digital dollarization. This reliance is occurring without adequate transparency, anti-money laundering (AML) integration, or oversight from national regulators. Regulation is therefore a current necessity to address existing use, while avoiding stifling innovation or overburdening local regulatory structures.

The implementation path proposed in this chapter is a carefully planned, risk-adaptive approach. It follows a sequential model compatible with the Commonwealth Model Law and the GENIUS concept. This approach is intended to avoid cliff effects that could force issuers or users out of the regulated sector due to excessive requirements. Simultaneously, it establishes sustainable governance structures that balance risk management with innovation.

Phase 1: Creating Visibility

In the first phase, the focus shifts from issuance to controlling existing stablecoin inflows. Users may continue to use external stablecoins, but only through regulated intermediaries such as banks, payment service providers, or licensed digital asset brokers. These entities serve as regulatory gatekeepers.

The operational logic is straightforward: stablecoin conversions into local currency must occur through supervised institutions. Consequently, transactions are subject to AML/KYC and sanctions screening. This process enables the state to obtain transparency regarding transaction volumes, origins, counterparties, and risk profiles.

This phase does not inhibit innovation; instead, it shifts the locus of supervision—unregulated use transitions to controlled use. Concurrently, a structural database is established, which serves as a critical success factor for subsequent issuance decisions.

Phase 2: Pilot Issuance

The second phase commences only after successful stabilization of inbound conversion, involving a controlled and narrowly limited issuance of a locally denominated stablecoin. The objective is not to replace the banking system, but to establish a digital payment layer that is:

- is fully backed (cash/HQLA),
- can be redeemed at any time,
- is transparent and auditable,
- does not allow returns on stablecoin holdings.

This approach creates both a local payment medium and an instrument of monetary sovereignty. Users are no longer dependent on USD stablecoins for stability; instead, they can utilize programmable liquidity in their own currency, thereby enhancing financial independence and control.

The pilot phase should be limited to specifically defined use cases, such as:

- government transfers to citizens (e.g., subsidy payments),
- B2B payments in export/import,
- selected remittance corridors.

This 'sandbox approach' protects against systemic risks and enables iterative learning. Simultaneously, supervisory authorities develop operational routines and address governance issues, including key management, vendor management, Oracle risks, and emergency processes, such as freeze and kill-switch mechanisms.

Phase 3: Scaling

Scaling only takes place once phase 2 is functioning stably. There are two main objectives here:

1. Interoperability with international stablecoin clearing systems to reduce correspondent banking costs and enable 24/7 settlement.
2. Exit/clawback rules that allow an issuer to withdraw a product from the market in an orderly manner without jeopardizing users or financial stability.

A key mechanism is the establishment of an interoperability corridor between local stablecoins and international payment systems, with defined rules for maintaining parity and settlement processing. This creates a networked payment infrastructure that enables digital forms of money to remain convertible while preventing regulatory arbitrage. User acceptance remains stable during the pilot phase. This allows undesirable developments to be identified and corrected on a small scale.

The sequential implementation path has three structural advantages:

1. Reduced systemic risks: No abrupt market opening, but relatively gradual operationalization of governance and supervision.

2. Sovereignty through data and control: Supervision first gains transparency and then design authority.
3. Financial inclusion without shadow banking effects: Users gain access to stable digital payment methods without deposit migration or maturity transformation.

These usage patterns offer empirical support for assertions of digital dollarization and user dependency. Stablecoins are increasingly held not solely for transactional convenience, but as substitutes for local bank deposits and savings instruments in jurisdictions characterized by high inflation, capital controls, or weak banking systems.

STABLECOINS AND CBDCS: COMPLEMENTARITY INSTEAD OF SUBSTITUTION

The prevailing discourse on digital currencies frequently presents a binary choice between central bank digital currencies (CBDCs) and stablecoins. This comparison is inadequate, as it assumes both instruments serve identical functions and are therefore direct competitors. Empirical evidence challenges this assumption. Stablecoins originate through bottom-up processes within open networks, addressing programmable payment logic, interoperability, and global applicability. In contrast, CBDCs are implemented through top-down approaches, emphasizing state and infrastructure sovereignty as well as the controllability of monetary policy. These systems facilitate digital value transfer at different levels. Consequently, complementary coexistence is more probable than outright substitution.

Distinct Value Propositions: Settlement Layer vs. Interface Layer

CBDCs and stablecoins operate in separate domains, each fulfilling a specific role. CBDCs act as the settlement layer for sovereign currency, issued by central banks to provide finality for large-value payments and transaction-critical processes. In contrast, stablecoins serve as interface layers within open, programmable ecosystems, enabling payment terms to be integrated with smart contracts, decentralized applications, or tokenized assets. Recognizing this distinction is essential for a comprehensive understanding of digital currencies.

In practical terms, this distinction implies the following:

- CBDCs answer the question 'Is the payment legitimate and final?'
- Stablecoins answer the question 'Can the payment be linked to an event in terms of programmability?'

In software-enabled processes, including automated supply chains, machine-to-machine payments, and tokenized securities transfers, the programmability provided by stablecoins is essential. Numerous central banks acknowledge that CBDCs can only partially address this functional domain. The Bank of England explicitly notes that stablecoins and CBDCs serve distinct market segments, and both are required to facilitate 'digital value chains.'

Intermediation Effects

Despite their functional distinctions, CBDCs and stablecoins exert comparable effects on bank intermediation. Choi and Rhee (2025), employing a model-theoretical framework, demonstrate that two primary effects emerge, particularly during transitional periods when digital forms of money are neither marginal nor dominant. First, users may withdraw deposits to maintain liquidity in a digital form. Second, banks respond to this competitive environment by adopting more aggressive investment or interest rate strategies. These effects occur regardless of whether stablecoins or CBDCs are involved; the critical factor is the introduction of an alternative for users to hold balances outside the traditional banking system.

Dollar-denominated stablecoins create demand for the US dollar through network externalities rather than central bank policy. Farhat et al. (2025) demonstrate that stablecoins exhibit 'demand-side economies of scope,' whereby increased usage enhances the network's value. This dynamic enables countries such as the United States to maintain currency dominance within private digital networks, an outcome unattainable through CBDCs alone.

The GENIUS framework, which outlines principles for stablecoin design, addresses these challenges through three restrictive mechanisms: issuers are prohibited from paying interest, reserves must remain fully liquid at all times, and issuers are barred from engaging in maturity transformation. These measures result in a digital payment claim that does not resemble a deposit transaction. Conversely, CBDCs mitigate intermediation effects by implementing limited quotas, tiered interest rates, or non-interest-bearing deposits.

Both systems address the same underlying issue, albeit through distinct mechanisms.

- Stablecoins limit the issuer.
- CBDCs limit the user.

Ensuring Sovereignty via Convertibility

The central issue for national authorities is not which instrument will prevail, but instead how to guarantee convertibility between CBDCs and stablecoins.

Erosion of monetary sovereignty does not result from the existence of stablecoins alone, but from the absence of parity. Digital dollarization occurs when residents of emerging markets hold USD stablecoins because there is no stable local alternative. Proper currency connectivity is achieved only when a local, fully backed stablecoin can be converted at face value into CBDC or bank money at any time.

The GENIUS toolkit approach provides structural stability in this context by implementing the following measures:

- Parity is not a business promise, but a legal right.
- Reserves must be liquid at all times.
- Issuers may not generate additional income from customer funds.

CBDCs and GENIUS-compliant stablecoins can therefore function within a division of labor as follows:

- CBDCs provide government-end customer accounts and the legal value anchor.
- Stablecoins act as an interface for innovation and use in open networks.

The system operates in a complementary manner once legal and technical parity is established. Competition arises when parity is either implicitly or economically unstable.

Digital Money Architecture as a Layered Model

An integrated digital monetary system is achieved not by substituting one instrument for another, but by layering multiple instruments.

Table 2. Layer architecture

Level (layer)	Function	Primary actor
Settlement layer	Finality, legal enforceability, sovereignty	**CBDC / Central bank**
Interface layer	Programmability, interoperability, innovation	**Stablecoins (GENIUS-compatible)**

Source: own representation.

A 'winner-takes-all' outcome does not characterize the future of digital currencies. Instead, it presents an architectural challenge: CBDCs provide sovereignty, while stablecoins facilitate connectivity.

FROM LEGAL FRAMEWORK TO SUPERVISORY PRACTICE: THE TOOLKIT APPROACH

The GENIUS Act is distinguished by its emphasis on operational supervisory capability in addition to establishing regulatory standards. Stablecoins must be not only regulated but also verifiable, monitorable, and capable of integration into existing supervisory frameworks. This approach reframes regulation as a regulatory engineering challenge rather than solely a legal matter. The following section demonstrates how specific operational control mechanisms can be derived from the GENIUS regime, which comprises three interconnected control levels: the reserve and liquidity regime, the transparency and disclosure workflow, and the technology-enabled supervisory and anti-money laundering (AML) stack.

Reserve Codebook and Liquidity Discipline

The GENIUS Act formalizes a principle long regarded as essential for stability in monetary and banking systems, yet previously unimplemented for privately issued digital payment instruments: no maturity, risk, or liquidity transformation. Stablecoin issuers are prohibited from reallocating customer funds into longer-term or riskier assets to seek returns. Every digital unit issued must be fully backed by an equivalent, highly liquid reserve that remains accessible at all times and can be realized without loss of value. This requirement fundamentally distinguishes the stablecoin business model from that of traditional financial intermediaries. Rather than accepting deposits and reallocating them into loans or securities, liquidity is immobilized and tokenized. Value is derived from programmable availability rather than lending or investment performance.

This regulatory approach results in a significant shift in governance. Whereas banks traditionally distribute and transform risk, the GENIUS Act compels stablecoin issuers to avoid risk entirely. The legislation effectively establishes a 'reserve codebook,' permitting only assets that can be liquidated without causing market disruption during crises. Specifically, eligible assets are limited to cash and short-term US government bonds with minimal interest rate and default risk. Other investment vehicles, such as money market funds, commercial paper, structured products, or cryptocurrencies, are excluded regardless of their potential returns. The legislative framework intentionally accepts the economic opportunity cost: since reserves cannot earn interest, issuers lack incentives to assume risk or offer returns. The intent is for stablecoins to function as digital equivalents of sovereign money, not as components of the shadow banking sector.

Governance structures vary significantly among stablecoin issuers. Clarifying these distinctions enhances understanding of the regulatory landscape, particularly because fiat-backed stablecoins such as USDC or PYUSD operate under centralized corporate governance. In contrast, decentralized autonomous organisation (DAO)-based models, such as MakerDAO, face distinct challenges. Understanding these differences is critical for effective compliance and enforcement.

The regulatory logic goes even further: reserves must not only be secure, but also usable under stress — without discounts, without delays, without dependence on secondary markets. GENIUS thus follows a monetary theory clarification: a stablecoin that can only be liquidated with haircuts in times of stress is not a stable means of payment, but a credit-like product. In the GENIUS regime, the liquidity of the reserve system is therefore a systemic protection goal. The technical design of the reserve portfolios is not based on optimizing returns, but on three priorities: (1) immediate liquidity, (2) value retention even in times of market stress, (3) convertibility at par value ('par redemption') within a defined time window (T+0/T+1).

In practice, this requirement increasingly causes stablecoin reserve portfolios to resemble miniature central bank balance sheets. These portfolios comprise only risk-free, highly liquid assets with negligible price fluctuations, enabling settlement under any market conditions. This structure ensures that users' rights to repayment are enforceable both legally and operationally. Full reserve coverage is necessary for tokens to function as cash equivalents. The GENIUS regime addresses issues highlighted by the Terra USD crisis and other leading stablecoin issuers, demonstrating that transparency alone is insufficient; only high-quality reserves can render transparency a stabilizing force.

Notably, the GENIUS Act treats stablecoins similarly to how central banks approach digital central bank money: as infrastructural liquidity media rather than financial products. Returns on reserves are allocated to cover issuer costs and guarantee parity redemption, rather than being distributed to users. This approach de-commercializes stablecoins, positioning their economic value in settlement functionality rather than financial performance. Consequently, governance is essential not only for regulatory approval but also for the economic viability of the model. Any issuer that breaches liquidity discipline risks undermining both their product and broader trust in digital payment instruments.

Consequently, the GENIUS Act reorients stablecoins from credit-like products with implicit risk to tokenized cash whose value is anchored in legally enforceable, externally audited reserves rather than trust.

Transparency, Disclosure, and Certification

Transparency constitutes the second structural pillar of the GENIUS regime. While the reserve codebook secures the material stability of stablecoins, the disclosure workflow ensures that this stability is continuously verifiable through ongoing supervision, not merely ex post. Rather than imposing a simple reporting requirement, the GENIUS Act establishes a procedural transparency system with technically, temporally, and institutionally differentiated control points. The objective is to enable continuous verification of reserve and liquidity status, ensuring that par value redemption is both legally guaranteed and enforceable by supervisory authorities.

The workflow initiates at the level of issuers' internal systems. Issuers are required to determine and document internal liquidity and portfolio metrics daily. These metrics encompass not only the amount and composition of reserves, but also their maturities, custody locations, concentration risks, and all transactions that impact the reserve ratio. This daily internal assessment compels issuers to monitor solvency continuously and mitigates the accumulation of risks between audit intervals.

The next stage of the disclosure regime operates at the public level. Issuers are required to disclose the composition of their reserves monthly, providing a look-through perspective so that users and market participants can assess both the quantity and nature of reserves. Disclosures must be sufficiently granular to enable evaluation of the quality and liquidity of reserve instruments. GENIUS thereby transitions transparency from aggregate statements ('100% covered') to verifiable details ('79% in treasury bills under 30 days; held at custodian bank X').

The subsequent control point involves quarterly external audits (attestations). Registered auditors are required to verify that published information is materially accurate and that reserve holdings comply with legal standards. This requirement surpasses current MiCA or FinCEN guidelines by establishing transparency as an auditable fact rather than mere self-disclosure. For large issuers (reserves exceeding USD 50 billion), the framework is further strengthened. In addition to annual financial statements audited in accordance with recognized accounting standards, these statements must also be submitted for regulatory review. As a result, stablecoin reserves transition from voluntary reporting to compliance with audit and accounting law enforceable under capital market regulations.

The disclosure workflow operates as an 'attestation pipeline,' establishing transparency as a continuous, functional state rather than an ad hoc occurrence. Each stage—internal daily measurement, monthly reporting, quarterly audits, and annual financial statements—produces data points that are systematically linked and traceable for supervisors and auditors. This pipeline creates an auditable trail throughout the lifecycle of each stablecoin, enabling regulators to identify risks during market stress and to pinpoint their origin and timing within specific portfolio segments. Transparency thereby becomes a technical prerequisite for financial stability.

In stress scenarios, this structure serves a secondary function by making par redemption claims enforceable. Since the assets backing stablecoins are continuously documented, users or regulators can promptly access reserve pools in the event of insolvency. These reserves are segregated and cannot be included in the issuer's general liabilities. Governance and insolvency protection are thus closely linked: assets that cannot be accounted for cannot be redeemed, and instruments that cannot be redeemed do not qualify as stablecoins under the law.

In summary, the disclosure workflow converts stablecoins from 'trust products' into verifiable financial instruments. The statutory transparency obligation is implemented through technical and auditable control mechanisms. The GENIUS regime thereby introduces a new control model for digital assets, making transparency an institutionally enforced requirement on a daily, monthly, quarterly, and annual basis.

SupTech, Data Access, and AML/CFT

The third component of the toolkit addresses the prevention of illicit financial activities. The GENIUS Act directly links stablecoin regulation to regulators' technical capabilities to evaluate transactions. This approach responds to empirical evidence indicating that a substantial share of illegal cryptocurrency transactions involve stablecoins. The US Treasury is mandated to establish a framework for advanced AML methods that explicitly incorporates technologies such as graph analysis, cluster identification, address-based risk profiling, and API-based access to transaction data. The objective is to develop a supervisory infrastructure capable of operating not only retrospectively but also in near real time, thereby shifting the focus from form-based reporting to data-driven risk scoring.

A notable feature of the GENIUS Act is its allowance for the use of public blockchains without categorizing them as regulatory outsourcing. This results in a hybrid architecture in which issuance is supervised, while token transfers occur on open networks. To maintain control, the Act mandates ongoing governance of keys and smart contracts, including access controls, multi-signature mechanisms, change management, and emergency measures such as freeze or kill switches. These governance mechanisms are designed to prevent unchecked errors in smart contracts or compromised keys from impacting the system.

Simultaneously, this model necessitates privacy-by-design. The GENIUS Act stipulates that AML monitoring and data protection are complementary rather than opposing functions. Accordingly, the law requires risk-based procedures and restricts data collection to what is necessary for supervision. The Treasury's request for comment (RFC) specifically mandates pseudonymization, data minimization, and access control.

The GENIUS toolkit approach operationalizes regulation through defined procedures. Legislators establish not only regulatory standards but also the enforcement process logic. For jurisdictions and supervisory authorities adopting the Commonwealth model or MiCA, this framework offers significant impetus: regulatory objectives must be translatable into actionable, controllable processes. Consequently, stablecoin regulation is not solely a legal undertaking but a governance challenge addressed through architectural solutions such as liquidity discipline, disclosure pipelines, and technology-enabled supervision.

To implement the toolkit concept, the following elements should be regarded as modular control instruments rather than abstract principles. Each component—reserves, disclosure, and SupTech-enabled AML—can be translated intospecifice supervisory checks, reporting templates, and escalation triggers, as demonstrated in the accompanying tables and workflow.

CONCLUSION

Stablecoins have evolved beyond a niche product within digital assets and are becoming a foundational component of international payment infrastructure. They now serve as a benchmark for assessing whether digital forms of money can achieve stability, transparency, and innovation. Analysis of the GENIUS Act demonstrates that regulatory quality is determined not by the proliferation of rules, but by the capacity to operationalize issuer- and technology-related risks. GENIUS departs from the traditional regulatory approach of merely articulating objectives. Instead, it specifies processes, measurement criteria, and governance requirements: liquidity discipline is maintained through a reserve codebook, transparency is ensured via certified disclosure workflows, supervisory oversight is achieved through SupTech/AML architectures, and smart contracts and key governance structures support operational resilience. Consequently, parity is transformed from an issuer's promise into a legally enforceable right for users.

The comparative law analysis reveals that GENIUS, the Commonwealth Model Law, and MiCA/UK share the same normative objective: establishing stablecoins as digital means of payment with immediate repayment claims. However, each framework adopts a distinct approach. GENIUS employs a blueprint regulatory framework characterized by high technical specificity and a restricted group of issuers. The Commonwealth Model Law advocates for minimum viable regulation, tailored for jurisdictions with limited supervisory capacity. MiCA/UK adopts a hybrid model that balances competition with the management of systemic risks. As a result, the global regulatory landscape is fragmented not by differing protection principles, but by varying implementation strategies. Convergence occurs at the core principles level: full reserve, parity, and transparency.

This chapter contributes by translating foundational principles into supervisory practice. Stablecoin regulation is framed as a challenge of regulatory engineering. The analysis demonstrates that stability is not achieved through abstract standard setting, but through system architectures that eliminate misaligned incentives: prohibiting maturity transformation, disallowing returns on stablecoin holdings, ensuring transparent reserves, and clarifying responsibilities. Regulation thus becomes performative, directly shaping issuers' business models. The operational toolkit presented in this chapter renders the design logic both visible and actionable: reserves are systematically cataloged, disclosure processes are organized sequentially, AML/SupTech functions are integrated into modular pipelines, and smart contract governance is established in a verifiable format. This toolkit equips policymakers with transferable instruments that operationalize national strategies at both the application and process-control levels.

The chapter further demonstrates that stablecoin strategies and central bank digital currency (CBDC) initiatives are complementary rather than mutually exclusive. In contemporary payment architectures, CBDCs maintain state sovereignty within the settlement layer, whereas stablecoins facilitate programmable use cases at the interface layer. The coexistence of both instruments is essential for fostering an innovative and resilient digital monetary system.

The essential insight is that stability is not an inherent property of the token itself, but rather a function of the underlying system architecture.

Stablecoins attain viability as a form of money when legal frameworks, market structures, and technological implementations are coherently aligned. This is particularly relevant for emerging and developing countries, for which the chapter proposes a risk-adapted introduction pathway: initial inbound conversion to enhance transparency, followed by pilot issuance of domestic stablecoins, and subsequently, scaling and interoperability. In this context, digital currency innovation is positioned not as a regulatory challenge but as a tool for enhancing sovereignty.

From an academic standpoint, this chapter offers three key contributions to the literature:

1. It demonstrates that stablecoins constitute a distinct category of tokenized payment infrastructure, separate from money market funds and e-money.
2. It translates regulatory principles into verifiable supervisory practices, thereby advancing research from regulatory theory to regulatory engineering.

3. It develops a model of state sovereignty suited to a context in which payments are organized on a network-based, global scale rather than a purely national basis.

The future of digital money systems will not be determined by the identity of the issuer, whether state or private sector, but by the prevailing governance logic. GENIUS-compatible stablecoins exemplify a regulatory framework that enforces stability, encourages innovation, and safeguards sovereignty. Within this model, regulation serves as an enabler of secure, equitable, and accessible digital money rather than an impediment.

It is essential to recognize the limitations of regulation. No legal framework can eliminate incentives for risk-taking, circumvention, or market-driven innovation. Consequently, effective stablecoin governance relies not only on established rules but also on adaptive supervision, international coordination, and ongoing learning.

From an environmental, social, and governance (ESG) perspective, stablecoin ecosystems inherit the energy and ecological footprints of their underlying settlement infrastructures. Although modern Layer 1 networks increasingly employ low-energy proof-of-stake consensus mechanisms, several global stablecoins continue to operate primarily on high-energy networks, such as Ethereum, before their transition. Regulatory bodies, including the OECD (2022), recommend integrating sustainability metrics—such as energy efficiency per transaction, node distribution, and environmental disclosure—into supervisory frameworks.

REFERENCES

Andrae, S. (2026). U.S. strategy to dominate the Dollar with stablecoins: Geopolitical and economic implications. In Akhtar, S., Khan, M., Almaqtari, F. A G., Selvam, V., & Bahl, S. (Eds.), *Policy Implications on International Financial Economics and Banking* (pp. 195–236). IGI Global Publishing., DOI: 10.4018/979-8-3373-3725-8.ch007

Bindseil, U. (2025). Regulatory responses to the financial stability implications of stablecoins. DOI: 10.2139/ssrn.5710762

BIS (Bank for International Settlements). (2023). Cross-border exchange of wholesale CBDCs using automated market-makers. https://www.banque-france.fr/system/files/2023-09/20230928%20Mariana%20final%20report.pdf

Castrén, O., & Russo, R. (2026). Runs, transparency and regulation: On the optimal design of stablecoin frameworks. *Economics Letters*, *258*, 112720. DOI: 10.1016/j.econlet.2025.112720

Chainalysis (2024). The 2024 geography of crypto report. https://www.chainalysis.com/wp-content/uploads/2024/10/the-2024-geography-of-crypto-report-release.pdf

Chari, A., Converse, N., Mehl, A., Milesi-Ferretti, G. M., & Vansteenkiste, I. (2025). Geopolitical tensions and international financial fragmentation Evidence and implications. Geneva Reports on the World Economy 28. https://cepr.org/system/files/publication-files/271360-geneva_28_geopolitical_tensions_and_international_fragmentation_evidence_and_implications.pdf

Choi, K. J., & Rhee, K. (2025) From the fringe to the core: Stablecoins and the future of banking stability. DOI: 10.2139/ssrn.5374790

Circle (2024). USDC as a platform for global prosperity. https://6778953.fs1.hubspotusercontent-na1.net/hubfs/6778953/Davos%202025/USDC-report-2025-Digital_AW.pdf

De Conti, B., & Guttmann, R. (2025). Digital money: Fragmentation of the monetary regime. *Review of Political Economy*, 1–22. Advance online publication. DOI: 10.1080/09538259.2025.2573356

Farhat, K., Mueller, M., & Srivastava, V. (2025). Interconnection and rivalry in global monetary networks. IGP White Paper 13, February 2025. https://www.internetgovernance.org/wp-content/uploads/Networks_of_money_research_paper-1-1.pdf

Feyen, E., Klingebiel, D., & Ruiz, M. (2024). Can crypto-assets play a role in foreign reserve portfolios? Not today, and likely not in the near future. https://documents1.worldbank.org/curated/en/099553102232444409/pdf/IDU1c16366af173fa148931a28b189e8eca412f3.pdf

Huang, Y., Ji, Y., Lin, J., Su, D., & Wang, P. (2025). The crumbling wall between crypto and non-crypto markets: Risk transmission through stablecoins. *Journal of Financial Markets, 101043*, 101043. Advance online publication. DOI: 10.1016/j.finmar.2025.101043

IOSCO (International Organization of Securities Commissions). (2025). Tokenization of financial assets. https://www.iosco.org/library/pubdocs/pdf/IOSCOPD809.pdf

KPMG. (2025). Stablecoins: The bridge between traditional finance and digital assets. https://kpmg.com/kpmg-us/content/dam/kpmg/pdf/2025/stablecoins-kpmg.pdf

Laboure, M., & Siazon, C. (2025). Stablecoins: How the GENIUS Act strengthens US geopolitical dominance. Deutsche Bank Research Institute. https://www.dbresearch.com/PROD/RI-PROD/PDFVIEWER.calias?pdfViewerPdfUrl=PROD0000000000603306

Latham & Watkins. (2025). The GENIUS Act of 2025: Stablecoin legislation adopted in the US. https://www.lw.com/en/insights/the-genius-act-of-2025-stablecoinlegislation-adopted-in-the-us

Liang, N. (2025). Stablecoins: Issues for regulators as they implement GENIUS Act. October 21, 2025. https://www.brookings.edu/articles/stablecoins-issues-for-regulators-as-they-implement-genius-act/

Luck, S., (2025). A historical perspective on stablecoins. Federal Reserve Bank of New York Liberty Street Economics, October 1, 2025. DOI: 10.59576/lse.20251001

OECD. (2022). Environmental impact of digital assets: Crypto-asset mining and DLT consensus mechanisms, OECD Business and Finance Policy Papers, OECD Publishing. DOI: 10.1787/bf84ff64-en

Wilmarth, A. E. (2025). Time bomb: How uninsured stablecoins and crypto derivatives threaten financial and economic stability. October 6, 2025. https://www.ineteconomics.org/perspectives/blog/time-bomb-how-uninsured-stablecoins-and-crypto-derivatives-threaten-financial-and-economic-stability

KEY TERMS AND DEFINTIONS

DAO Governance: DAO governance refers to decisions about protocol rules, parameters, and risk management of a decentralized organization, typically through token-based voting. For algorithmically controlled stablecoins or collateral management systems, DAO governance can create systemic risks, such as coordinated manipulation or low participation rates. From a regulatory perspective, liability, accountability, and sanctions enforcement remain unresolved.

Digital Dollarization: Digital dollarization refers to the use of USD stablecoins as an everyday means of payment or store of value in countries with unstable currencies. Empirically, this is particularly evident in Nigeria, Argentina, Turkey, and Venezuela, with growing corridor remittances via USDC/USDT. It changes the monetary sovereignty of these countries and creates dependencies on offshore intermediaries.

Interoperability (Technical & Regulatory): Recognizing interoperability's role in cross-border stability can inspire the audience to value international cooperation and the need for unified standards to mitigate systemic risks.

Programmable Settlement: Programmable settlement refers to settlement processes (e.g., payments, FX conversions) that are executed automatically, simultaneously, and conditionally by smart contracts. Projects such as BIS Project Mariana use programmable AMMs to settle cross-border CBDC transactions atomically. It creates new systemic hubs and interoperability requirements for stablecoins.

Redemption Risk: Redemption risk is the risk that a stablecoin issuer cannot meet redemptions at par value at any time, for example, because reserves are illiquid or impaired. It is closely linked to liquidity and market risks. Regulation (e.g., MiCAR Art. 36 ff.) addresses this risk through requirements on reserve quality and daily liquidity profiles.

Reserve Segregation: Reserve segregation involves separating customer funds from other assets, ensuring insolvency assets are protected, and preventing misuse, which is crucial to avoid classic bank runs or FTX-like failures, as mandated by regulations like GENIUS Act and the MiCAR.

Stablecoin Run: A stablecoin run can spark widespread concern about financial stability, underscoring the need for the audience to understand its systemic effects and the importance of risk mitigation.

Supervisory Colleges (for Stablecoins): Supervisory colleges are multilateral supervisory bodies in which national regulators exchange information and make joint supervisory decisions for cross-border financial structures. Such colleges are increasingly being considered for globally used stablecoins to consistently monitor risks related to reserve composition, liquidity profiles, and AML risks. IOSCO and FSB explicitly recommend such structures for systemic stablecoins.

Chapter 4
Financial Stability and Systemic Risk in Stablecoins:
When Does Digital Currency Infrastructure Become "Too Big to Fail"?

Ameya Anil Patil
https://orcid.org/0000-0002-4920-7630
Dr. Vishwanath Karad MIT World Peace University, India

ABSTRACT

The rapid growth of stablecoins has introduced novel forms of systemic risk to the global financial system, fundamentally challenging traditional notions of financial stability. This perspective paper examines the conditions under which stablecoins may become "too big to fail" and analyzes the unique risks posed by algorithmic and decentralized autonomous organization (DAO)-based models. Through comprehensive examination of the Terra Luna/TerraUSD (UST) collapse, Silicon Valley Bank's impact on USDC, and other significant stablecoin failures, we identify critical thresholds for systemic importance and propose an enhanced framework for assessing systemic risk in digital currency ecosystems. Our analysis reveals that traditional metrics of systemic importance inadequately capture the interconnectedness, velocity-driven risks, and reflexive mechanisms inherent in algorithmic stablecoin systems .

DOI: 10.4018/979-8-3373-9043-7.ch004

1. INTRODUCTION

The emergence of stablecoins as critical infrastructure within the cryptocurrency ecosystem has fundamentally altered the landscape of digital finance, creating new vectors for systemic risk transmission that extend far beyond traditional financial boundaries (Schär, 2021). These digital assets, designed to maintain stable value relative to reference assets such as the US dollar, have experienced exponential growth from a niche experiment to a market exceeding $130 billion in total capitalization as of mid-2024. However, the spectacular collapse of TerraUSD (UST) and its associated Luna token in May 2022, which wiped out over $60 billion in market value within days, alongside the March 2023 USDC depeg following Silicon Valley Bank's failure, has highlighted the potential for stablecoins to generate systemic risks that cascade through both digital and traditional financial systems (Gudgeon et al., 2020).

The concept of "too big to fail" (TBTF) has traditionally been applied to financial institutions whose failure would pose unacceptable risks to the broader financial system and economy (Stern & Feldman, 2004). In the context of stablecoins, this framework requires substantial modification to account for the unique characteristics of decentralized digital assets, including their algorithmic governance mechanisms, cross-protocol dependencies, the velocity at which distress can propagate through interconnected networks, and their increasing integration with traditional financial institutions.

1.1 Research Objectives and Contributions

This paper contributes to the growing literature on cryptocurrency systemic risk by developing a comprehensive, multi-dimensional framework for assessing when stablecoins become systemically important (Auer & Tercero-Lucas, 2022). We examine four primary research questions: what factors determine systemic importance in stablecoin markets, and how these differ from traditional financial institutions; how algorithmic and DAO-based governance models amplify systemic risk through reflexive mechanisms and coordination failures; what are the transmission channels through which stablecoin distress propagates to the broader financial system; and what regulatory and policy responses are necessary to mitigate these risks while preserving beneficial innovation in digital finance.

Our analysis draws on established theories of financial stability while incorporating novel considerations specific to decentralized digital assets (Catalini & de Gortari, 2022). We argue that traditional size-based metrics inadequately capture the systemic importance of stablecoins, necessitating new frameworks that account for network effects, algorithmic dependencies, velocity characteristics of digital asset markets, and real-time risk transmission mechanisms.

1.2 Methodological Approach

This study employs a multi-method approach combining theoretical framework development, empirical case study analysis, and policy evaluation. We utilize both quantitative metrics such as market capitalization, transaction volumes, and network centrality measures, alongside qualitative assessments including governance structures, algorithmic mechanisms, and regulatory compliance to develop a comprehensive risk assessment framework (Harvey et al., 2021).

Our analysis incorporates real-time data from multiple blockchain networks, traditional financial market indicators, and regulatory developments across major jurisdictions to provide a holistic view of stablecoin systemic risk evolution.

2. LITERATURE REVIEW AND THEORETICAL FRAMEWORK

2.1 Systemic Risk in Traditional Finance: Foundations and Evolution

The literature on systemic risk in traditional finance provides essential groundwork for understanding when financial institutions become "too big to fail," though these concepts require significant adaptation for digital assets (Kaufman & Scott, 2003). Kaufman and Scott (2003) define systemic risk as the risk that financial system instability will severely disrupt the flow of credit and payment services, potentially causing substantial losses in economic output. This definition remains relevant for stablecoins, which increasingly serve as critical payment and settlement infrastructure.

The Basel Committee on Banking Supervision (2013) has identified five key indicators of systemic importance: size, interconnectedness, substitutability, complexity, and cross-jurisdictional activity. While these metrics provide a starting point, they require substantial modification for stablecoins due to their unique operational characteristics and risk profiles.

De Bandt and Hartmann (2000) distinguish between two types of systemic risk: contagion effects, where problems spread from one institution to others, and common shocks that affect multiple institutions simultaneously. Both mechanisms are relevant to stablecoin ecosystems, though they manifest through novel channels including smart contract interactions, algorithmic trading mechanisms, and cross-chain bridge protocols.

2.1.1 Evolution of TBTF Doctrine

The "too big to fail" doctrine has evolved significantly since its formal recognition following the Continental Illinois crisis in 1984. Stern and Feldman (2004) argue that TBTF creates moral hazard by encouraging excessive risk-taking, as institutions and their creditors expect government bailouts during crises. This moral hazard concern is particularly acute for stablecoins, where the absence of traditional deposit insurance or lender-of-last-resort facilities may create perverse incentives.

Recent developments in traditional finance, including the designation of Global Systemically Important Banks (G-SIBs) and the development of resolution frameworks, provide lessons for stablecoin regulation. However, the decentralized nature of many stablecoin systems challenges traditional resolution approaches, requiring novel regulatory tools and intervention mechanisms.

2.2 Stablecoin Mechanics and Evolution

2.2.1 Classification and Stabilization Mechanisms

Stablecoins can be classified into increasingly complex categories based on their stabilization mechanisms (Lyons & Viswanath-Natraj, 2023). Fiat-collateralized stablecoins such as Tether (USDT) and USD Coin (USDC) maintain reserves of traditional assets backing the digital tokens. While conceptually simple, these systems face risks related to custodial arrangements, reserve composition, and regulatory compliance. The March 2023 USDC depeg following Silicon Valley Bank's failure demonstrated how traditional banking sector stress can propagate to stablecoins.

Crypto-collateralized stablecoins use cryptocurrency assets as collateral, typically over-collateralized to account for volatility. MakerDAO's DAI represents the most sophisticated example, employing multiple collateral types and complex liquidation mechanisms (Gudgeon et al., 2023). These systems face risks from collateral volatility, liquidation cascades, and governance attacks.

Algorithmic stablecoins attempt to maintain stability through market mechanisms and protocol incentives without direct asset backing. The failure of TerraUSD demonstrated the fundamental limitations of purely algorithmic approaches, particularly during extreme market stress (Kwon & Platias, 2019). Hybrid models combine elements from multiple categories, such as Frax Finance's fractional-algorithmic approach or newer designs incorporating real-world assets (RWAs) alongside crypto collateral.

2.2.2 Advanced Algorithmic Mechanisms

Klages-Mundt et al. (2020) take a close look at how algorithmic stablecoins actually work, and their conclusion isn't especially comforting. They argue that when markets come under serious stress, these systems run into fundamental roadblocks. In fact, they borrow the idea of an "impossible trinity" from international economics to explain the dilemma: you can have stability, capital efficiency, or decentralization—but not all three at once.

Recent innovations in algorithmic stablecoin design include elastic supply mechanisms where protocols automatically adjust token supply based on demand, protocol-controlled value (PCV) systems where the protocol directly owns and manages backing assets, multi-token ecosystems with complex systems featuring multiple interdependent tokens serving different functions, and cross-chain stability mechanisms that maintain pegs across multiple blockchain networks.

2.3 Network Effects and Ecosystem Dynamics

2.3.1 Network Topology and Risk Propagation

The DeFi ecosystem exhibits characteristics of complex network systems, where stablecoins serve as critical nodes connecting diverse protocols and applications (Jensen et al., 2021). Network analysis reveals that stablecoins often occupy central positions in the DeFi graph, making them critical for overall system stability.

Aramonte et al. (2021) from the Bank for International Settlements highlight how stablecoins' role as "plumbing" in DeFi creates dependencies that can amplify systemic risk. When a major stablecoin experiences distress, effects cascade through lending protocols, decentralized exchanges, automated market makers, and yield farming platforms that rely on the stablecoin for liquidity and pricing.

2.3.2 Velocity and Liquidity Dynamics

Unlike traditional financial assets, stablecoins exhibit extremely high velocity, with some tokens turning over their entire supply multiple times per day (Baur et al., 2018). This high velocity creates unique risks including rapid confidence loss where negative sentiment can propagate faster than in traditional markets, liquidity evaporation where secondary market liquidity can disappear within minutes during stress, and reflexive mechanisms where price movements can trigger algorithmic responses that amplify volatility.

2.4 Governance Structures and Institutional Risk

2.4.1 DAO Governance Challenges

The governance structures of stablecoins, particularly those managed by DAOs, introduce novel forms of systemic risk that have no direct analogue in traditional finance (Zetzsche et al., 2020). While DAOs promise decentralized decision-making, they may suffer from coordination problems including difficulty reaching consensus during rapidly evolving crises, governance attacks where malicious actors acquire voting power to destabilize the system, plutocracy issues where large token holders exercise disproportionate influence, and technical vulnerabilities such as smart contract bugs in governance systems. The governance challenges facing decentralized systems are exacerbated by the absence of clear legal structures and accountability mechanisms, thereby creating unique risks for stakeholders.

2.4.2 Hybrid Governance Models

Recent developments in stablecoin governance include hybrid models that balance decentralization with operational efficiency. These include guardian systems where emergency powers are granted to trusted entities during crises, timelocks and delays that serve as mechanisms to prevent rapid governance changes, multi-signature arrangements requiring multiple parties to authorize critical decisions, and legal wrappers consisting of traditional legal entities controlling key protocol functions.

3. ENHANCED CASE STUDY ANALYSIS

3.1 Terra Luna/UST: Anatomy of an Algorithmic Collapse

3.1.1 System Architecture and Incentive Mechanisms

The Terra ecosystem represented the most ambitious attempt to create a scalable algorithmic stablecoin system, with TerraUSD (UST) maintaining its dollar peg through a sophisticated dual-token mechanism involving Luna, the ecosystem's native governance and staking token (Kwon & Platias, 2019). The system relied on arbitrage incentives: when UST traded above $1, users could mint new UST by burning $1 worth of Luna tokens, capturing the spread. Conversely, when UST traded below $1, users could burn UST to mint $1 worth of Luna tokens.

At its peak in April 2022, the Terra ecosystem had achieved remarkable scale with UST market capitalization reaching $18.7 billion, Luna market capitalization at

$26.2 billion, Anchor Protocol total value locked (TVL) at $14.2 billion, and over 100 integrated protocols and applications.

3.1.2 The Anchor Protocol Concentration Risk

Approximately 75% of UST supply was deposited in Anchor Protocol, which offered unsustainably high yields of 19.5% APY on UST deposits. This concentration created a single point of failure that amplified withdrawal pressure during the crisis. The protocol's yield was subsidized by Luna Foundation Guard (LFG) reserves, creating an unsustainable feedback loop.

The Anchor mechanism worked through borrower incentives where users borrowed UST against bLuna collateral while receiving ANC token rewards, a yield reserve funded by LFG and protocol revenues, and liquidation mechanisms where undercollateralized positions were liquidated to protect lenders.

3.1.3 Detailed Collapse Timeline and Mechanisms

The UST collapse unfolded with unprecedented speed due to the algorithmic nature of the system and high-velocity trading environment. On May 7, 2022, during the initial pressure phase, large UST redemptions began totaling approximately $2 billion, UST briefly depegged to $0.985 triggering arbitrage mechanisms, and the Curve 3pool experienced imbalanced withdrawals.

May 8, 2022 marked the acceleration phase when UST fell to $0.91 breaking critical psychological support, Luna Foundation Guard began Bitcoin sales to defend the peg, and Anchor Protocol experienced massive withdrawal requests. The death spiral initiation occurred on May 9, 2022, as UST reached $0.67 triggering massive Luna minting, Luna supply increased from 725 million to over 1.4 billion tokens, and secondary market liquidity evaporated across major exchanges.

The system collapse phase lasted from May 10-12, 2022, when UST fell to $0.12 while Luna approached zero, Terraform Labs halted the blockchain to prevent further damage, and over $60 billion in combined market value was destroyed.

3.1.4 Systemic Impact Analysis and Contagion Channels

The Terra collapse's systemic impact extended through multiple transmission channels (Gudgeon et al., 2020). Direct institutional exposure affected Three Arrows Capital with estimated $200+ million direct losses, Celsius Network with significant exposure leading to liquidity crisis, Jump Trading with major losses from market making activities, and multiple smaller funds and family offices.

Market contagion mechanisms included correlation spikes across cryptocurrency markets, Bitcoin declining 30% in the immediate aftermath, Ethereum and other major tokens experiencing significant volatility, and DeFi TVL declining by over 40% in the following months.

Infrastructure disruption occurred as projects built on Terra blockchain faced operational challenges, cross-chain bridges experienced liquidity shortages, stablecoin confidence broadly declined across the sector, and regulatory acceleration followed with South Korean authorities launching criminal investigations, the U.S. Treasury accelerating stablecoin regulatory proposals, the European Union expediting MiCA implementation, and multiple jurisdictions implementing emergency measures.

3.2 USDC and the Silicon Valley Bank Crisis: Traditional-Digital Risk Transmission

3.2.1 The SVB Exposure and Confidence Crisis

The March 2023 Silicon Valley Bank failure demonstrated how traditional banking sector stress can propagate to stablecoins, even those considered among the safest. Circle, USDC's issuer, held approximately $3.3 billion in reserves at SVB, representing roughly 8% of USDC's total backing.

The crisis unfolded differently from algorithmic stablecoin failures through several mechanisms. The disclosure impact occurred when Circle's transparency about SVB exposure initially increased panic, weekend uncertainty arose as the bank closure over the weekend prevented immediate resolution, and institutional response emerged as major exchanges and protocols quickly adjusted to maintain operations.

3.2.2 Market Response and Recovery Mechanisms

USDC's temporary depeg to approximately $0.87 demonstrated both the vulnerability of fiat-backed stablecoins and the resilience provided by robust reserve management. The immediate market response included massive redemption requests totaling over $10 billion, flight to USDT and other stablecoin alternatives, and DeFi protocols experiencing liquidity stress.

Recovery factors included FDIC guarantee coverage for SVB deposits below $250,000, Circle's diversified reserve structure which limited exposure, quick regulatory response that restored confidence, and strong institutional support from major exchanges.

3.2.3 Lessons for Systemic Risk Assessment

The USDC incident revealed several critical insights: traditional financial sector stress can rapidly transmit to digital assets, transparency while generally positive can amplify short-term volatility, diversified reserve structures provide resilience during crises, and regulatory backing such as FDIC insurance remains crucial for confidence.

3.3 Comparative Analysis: Additional Case Studies

3.3.1 Iron Finance TITAN/IRON (June 2021): Early Warning System

The collapse of Iron Finance provided crucial early insights into algorithmic stablecoin vulnerabilities that would later manifest more dramatically in Terra. The IRON stablecoin used a fractional reserve model with 75% backing by USDC and 25% backing by TITAN tokens, along with automated rebalancing mechanisms.

The system failed when large redemptions depleted USDC reserves, increased reliance on TITAN backing created reflexivity, TITAN price decline triggered a death spiral, and Mark Cuban's public criticism accelerated panic. Key lessons included the dangers of partial algorithmic backing and celebrity endorsement risks.

3.3.2 Tether (USDT): The Systemic Importance of Market Dominance

Tether's periodic scrutiny demonstrates how even well-capitalized stablecoins can generate systemic risk through their market position. Reserve composition concerns arose from commercial paper holdings creating credit risk exposure, lack of real-time attestations reducing transparency, and regulatory investigations creating periodic stress.

Market impact events included brief depeg to $0.95 in May 2022 during the Terra crisis, multiple depegs in 2021 during regulatory pressure, and ongoing basis risk in derivative markets. Systemic implications encompass the $80+ billion market cap creating systemic importance, extensive use across cryptocurrency exchanges, critical role for Bitcoin and altcoin trading pairs, and primary liquidity source for many emerging markets.

3.3.3 MakerDAO DAI: Evolution Under Pressure

MakerDAO's DAI stablecoin has experienced multiple stress events that illuminate the evolution of crypto-collateralized systems. Black Thursday on March 12, 2020, involved rapid ETH price decline triggering liquidation cascade, network congestion preventing efficient liquidations, DAI trading significantly above peg due to supply shortage, and the system requiring emergency governance intervention.

Centralization pressures include increasing reliance on USDC backing currently exceeding 50%, real-world asset integration introducing traditional risks, governance centralization around large holders, and regulatory compliance requirements. Innovation responses encompassed implementation of the Peg Stability Module (PSM), Direct Deposit DAI Module (D3M) for yield optimization, enhanced liquidation mechanisms, and emergency governance procedures.

4. ADVANCED FRAMEWORK FOR SYSTEMIC RISK ASSESSMENT

4.1 Multi-Dimensional Risk Taxonomy

Building upon our case study analysis, we propose a comprehensive framework that categorizes stablecoin systemic risk across multiple dimensions (Basel Committee on Banking Supervision, 2013).

4.1.1 Quantitative Metrics (Enhanced)

Tier 1 Systemically Critical stablecoins requiring enhanced supervision are characterized by market capitalization exceeding $50 billion or representing more than 15% of the total stablecoin market, daily transaction volume exceeding $5 billion, integration with more than 100 DeFi protocols, and cross-chain presence on more than five major blockchains.

Tier 2 Systemically Important stablecoins requiring regulatory oversight exhibit market capitalization between $10-50 billion or representing 3-15% of the total stablecoin market, daily transaction volume between $1-5 billion, integration with 25-100 DeFi protocols, and cross-chain presence on 2-5 blockchains.

Tier 3 Systemically Relevant stablecoins requiring monitoring demonstrate market capitalization between $1-10 billion or representing 0.5-3% of the total stablecoin market, daily transaction volume between $100 million and $1 billion, integration with 10-25 DeFi protocols, and single or limited multi-chain deployment.

Additional quantitative metrics include network centrality measures such as eigenvector centrality in DeFi protocol graphs, betweenness centrality for liquidity flows, and PageRank importance in transaction networks. Velocity and liquidity indicators encompass average transaction size and frequency, order book depth across major exchanges, cross-exchange arbitrage efficiency, and time-to-liquidity during stress events. Concentration risk metrics involve Gini coefficient for holder distribution, percentage held by top 10/100/1000 addresses, protocol concentration where single protocol exposure exceeds 25%, and geographic concentration of nodes/validators.

4.1.2 Qualitative Risk Factors (Expanded)

Stabilization mechanism risk assessment varies by system type (Bullmann et al., 2019). For fiat-collateralized systems, considerations include reserve diversification and custody arrangements, regulatory compliance and oversight quality, redemption mechanism efficiency and accessibility, and transparency and attestation frequency.

Crypto-collateralized systems require evaluation of collateralization ratios and volatility buffers, liquidation mechanism robustness, oracle security and manipulation resistance, and multi-collateral diversification. Algorithmic systems demand assessment of mechanism sustainability during stress, reflexivity and death spiral resistance, confidence-dependency and market psychology, and emergency intervention capabilities.

Governance structure assessment differs between centralized control systems and DAO governance models (Prasad, 2021). Centralized control evaluation includes single points of failure and key person risk, regulatory compliance and legal structure, crisis response capabilities and track record, and succession planning and operational continuity. DAO governance assessment encompasses token distribution and voting power concentration, governance participation rates and effectiveness, emergency decision-making procedures, and legal recognition and enforceability. Hybrid models require evaluation of balance between decentralization and efficiency, emergency powers and guardian systems, upgrade mechanisms and security procedures, and stakeholder alignment and incentive structures.

4.2 Dynamic Risk Assessment Framework

4.2.1 Real-Time Monitoring Systems

Early warning indicators include peg stability metrics such as standard deviation of price from peg over rolling periods, maximum intraday deviation frequency, recovery time from depeg events, and cross-exchange basis risk levels. Flow and sentiment indicators encompass net redemption/minting flows, social sentiment analysis from multiple sources, Google Trends and search volume analysis, and options market implied volatility.

Network health metrics involve transaction confirmation times and fees, node/validator participation rates, smart contract interaction success rates, and cross-chain bridge operational status.

4.2.2 Stress Testing Methodologies

Scenario-based stress tests include confidence crisis simulation involving gradual and sudden loss of confidence scenarios, social media-driven panic simulations, celebrity/influencer negative sentiment impact, and regulatory announcement sensitivity analysis. Market stress integration encompasses correlation with traditional market stress, cryptocurrency market crash scenarios, interest rate shock transmission, and foreign exchange volatility impact. Operational stress testing involves network congestion and high gas fee scenarios, smart contract bug and exploit simulations, oracle failure and manipulation events, and cross-chain bridge failure impact.

Agent-based modeling incorporates multi-agent simulations of user behavior, institutional versus retail user differentiation, arbitrageur behavior and market efficiency analysis, and governance token holder decision-making processes.

4.3 Cross-Protocol Risk Assessment

4.3.1 Interconnectedness Mapping

Protocol dependency analysis includes direct integration counting and weighting, indirect dependency through shared infrastructure, circular dependency identification, and critical path analysis for liquidity flows. Contagion channel identification encompasses smart contract interaction risk, shared collateral and liquidity pools, governance token cross-holdings, and developer and infrastructure dependencies.

4.3.2 Systemic Risk Amplification Mechanisms

Network effect amplifiers include Metcalfe's law application to stablecoin adoption, platform competition and winner-take-all dynamics, switching cost analysis and lock-in effects, and interoperability benefits and risks. Algorithmic amplification involves high-frequency trading bot interactions, arbitrage mechanism efficiency and limits, automated liquidation cascade risks, and MEV (Maximum Extractable Value) manipulation.

5. REGULATORY FRAMEWORK AND POLICY IMPLICATIONS

5.1 Current Regulatory Landscape Analysis

5.1.1 Jurisdiction-by-Jurisdiction Assessment

The United States has pursued a fragmented approach across multiple agencies. The Treasury/OCC focuses on banking regulations for stablecoin issuers, the SEC applies securities law to governance tokens, the CFTC handles commodity regulation for certain stablecoin activities, the Federal Reserve oversees payment systems and conducts CBDC research, while Congressional proposals suggest various comprehensive frameworks. Key regulatory gaps include lack of clear authority, inconsistent treatment across agencies, and limited international coordination.

The European Union's MiCA (Markets in Crypto-Assets) provides the most comprehensive stablecoin regulatory framework with clear authorization requirements for stablecoin issuers, reserve requirements and segregation rules, operational and governance standards, and cross-border supervision mechanisms. Implementation challenges include technical complexity, coordination across member states, and adaptation to rapidly evolving technology.

The Asia-Pacific Region demonstrates diverse approaches reflecting different regulatory philosophies. Singapore's comprehensive Payment Services Act provides coverage, Japan integrates with existing financial regulations, Hong Kong implements licensing regimes for stablecoin activities, while China maintains a prohibition approach with CBDC focus.

5.1.2 International Coordination Efforts

The Financial Stability Board (FSB) provides global stablecoin recommendations for G20, international standards for regulation and supervision, cross-border cooperation frameworks, and systemic risk assessment methodologies. The Bank for International Settlements (BIS) conducts research on stablecoin risks and opportunities, develops central bank digital currency design principles, analyzes international settlement system implications, and studies monetary policy transmission effects.

5.2 Proposed Enhanced Regulatory Framework

5.2.1 Systemic Importance Designation Process

The multi-stage assessment process begins with Stage 1 quantitative screening involving automated monitoring of market cap and volume thresholds, real-time assessment of network centrality metrics, cross-border flow analysis and impact assessment, and integration scoring across DeFi protocols.

Stage 2 qualitative analysis includes detailed review of stabilization mechanisms, governance structure and crisis management assessment, operational resilience and cybersecurity evaluation, and regulatory compliance and legal structure review.

Stage 3 systemic impact modeling encompasses stress testing under various scenarios, contagion analysis and spillover effects, economic impact assessment for different failure modes, and international coordination and cross-border effects analysis.

Dynamic re-assessment involves quarterly reviews for Tier 1 stablecoins, semi-annual reviews for Tier 2 stablecoins, annual comprehensive assessments for all tiers, and event-triggered reassessments following major incidents.

5.2.2 Regulatory Requirements by Tier

Tier 1 Systemically Critical Stablecoins require enhanced capital and liquidity requirements including 110% backing requirement with high-quality liquid assets, diversified reserve composition limits, real-time reserve monitoring and reporting, and liquidity stress testing and buffer requirements.

Operational standards mandate 24/7 operations centers with crisis management protocols, redundant technical infrastructure across multiple jurisdictions, cybersecurity standards equivalent to systemically important banks, and regular penetration testing and security audits.

Governance and risk management requirements include independent board oversight with regulatory representation, Chief Risk Officer with direct regulatory reporting, regular stress testing and scenario planning, and recovery and resolution planning with regulatory approval.

Disclosure and transparency obligations encompass real-time reserve composition reporting, monthly detailed financial statements, immediate disclosure of material risks or incidents, and public API for key operational metrics.

Tier 2 Systemically Important Stablecoins must meet reserve and backing requirements including 105% backing requirement with approved asset classes, limited exposure to commercial paper and corporate debt, monthly reserve attestations by approved auditors, and segregated customer asset protection.

Risk management standards include comprehensive risk management framework, regular stress testing and contingency planning, incident response and business continuity plans, and regular regulatory reporting and supervision.

Tier 3 Systemically Relevant Stablecoins must satisfy basic requirements including 100% backing with transparent asset composition, quarterly audited reserve reports, basic operational standards and security measures, and registration and regulatory notification requirements.

5.2.3 Algorithmic Stablecoin Restrictions

The prohibition framework includes absolute prohibition for Tier 1 systemic importance, enhanced restrictions for Tier 2 with mandatory stress testing, disclosure requirements for Tier 3 with clear risk warnings, and grandfathering provisions for existing systems with transition periods.

Alternative innovation pathways encompass regulatory sandbox programs for new algorithmic designs, limited-scale testing environments with participant protection, academic and research exemptions for non-commercial experiments, and international coordination for innovation-friendly jurisdictions.

5.3 Cross-Border and International Considerations

5.3.1 Global Coordination Mechanisms

A proposed International Stablecoin Authority would serve as a joint oversight body for systemically important global stablecoins, develop harmonized standards and best practices, coordinate crisis management protocols, and facilitate information sharing and supervisory cooperation.

Mutual recognition frameworks would include equivalence determinations for compatible regulatory regimes, cross-border supervision agreements, joint inspections and enforcement actions, and coordinated crisis response mechanisms.

5.3.2 Enforcement and Compliance

Technology-enabled supervision involves real-time blockchain monitoring and analysis, automated compliance checking and reporting, AI-powered risk assessment and early warning systems, and RegTech integration for efficient supervision.

Sanctions and penalties include graduated enforcement approach based on violation severity, operating license suspension and revocation powers, financial penalties scaled to systemic importance, and personal accountability for key management personnel.

6. TECHNOLOGICAL AND INNOVATION CONSIDERATIONS

6.1 Emerging Stablecoin Technologies

6.1.1 Next-Generation Stabilization Mechanisms

AI-powered monetary policy represents recent developments in stablecoins that employ artificial intelligence and machine learning to optimize their stabilization mechanisms. These include dynamic collateral ratios based on market conditions, predictive analytics for demand fluctuation management, real-time sentiment analysis integration, and automated crisis response protocols (Ante, 2023).

Cross-chain native designs feature new architectures designed from the ground up for multi-chain operation, including omnichain stablecoins using LayerZero or similar protocols, unified liquidity across multiple blockchain networks, cross-chain arbitrage mechanisms for peg maintenance, and interoperability-first security models.

Real-world asset integration involves sophisticated hybrid models incorporating traditional financial assets such as tokenized government bonds and treasury bills, corporate debt and commercial paper tokenization, real estate and commodity-backed variants, and integration with traditional banking and payment systems.

6.1.2 Programmable Compliance and Regulation

Smart contract-based compliance includes automated reserve requirement enforcement, real-time regulatory reporting through oracles, programmable circuit breakers and emergency stops, and compliance-by-design architecture.

Privacy-preserving regulatory technology encompasses zero-knowledge proofs for reserve verification, selective disclosure mechanisms for regulatory reporting, privacy-preserving transaction monitoring, and compliance without compromising user privacy.

6.2 Central Bank Digital Currencies (CBDCs) Impact

6.2.1 Competitive Dynamics

CBDC versus stablecoin positioning involves wholesale versus retail CBDC impact on different stablecoin categories, interoperability opportunities and competitive threats, public-private partnership models, and innovation space preservation.

Cross-border payment evolution includes CBDC corridors reducing stablecoin demand, enhanced cross-border settlement efficiency, regulatory arbitrage and jurisdiction shopping, and monetary sovereignty preservation.

6.2.2 Coexistence Models

Complementary ecosystems feature stablecoins for DeFi applications while CBDCs serve government functions, specialized use cases and market segmentation, technology sharing and standard development, and regulatory harmony and coordination.

7. FUTURE RESEARCH DIRECTIONS AND EMERGING CHALLENGES

7.1 Advanced Risk Modeling

7.1.1 Network Science Applications

Graph neural networks for risk assessment involve deep learning models for network topology analysis, dynamic risk propagation modeling, anomaly detection in transaction patterns, and predictive modeling for systemic events.

Complex systems analysis includes phase transition modeling for market confidence, tipping point identification and early warning, emergence theory application to DeFi ecosystems, and behavioral economics integration.

7.1.2 Quantum Computing Implications

Cryptographic security evolution encompasses post-quantum cryptography for stablecoin security, quantum-resistant signature schemes, distributed ledger quantum vulnerability assessment, and migration strategies for quantum-safe systems.

7.2 Socioeconomic Impact Research

7.2.1 Financial Inclusion and Accessibility

Developing market integration involves stablecoin adoption in emerging economies, financial inclusion impact measurement, remittance corridor optimization, and monetary policy transmission in dollarized economies.

Social and economic externalities include impact on traditional banking sector employment, digital divide considerations and accessibility barriers, environmental sustainability of different stablecoin architectures, and wealth distribution effects and inequality implications.

7.2.2 Behavioral Economics and User Psychology

Confidence and trust dynamics encompass psychological factors in stablecoin adoption and abandonment, social proof and network effects in user behavior, crisis psychology and panic propagation mechanisms, and cultural differences in stablecoin acceptance and usage.

Decision-making under uncertainty involves bounded rationality in stablecoin investment decisions, herding behavior during market stress, information processing and cognitive biases, and risk perception calibration across different user segments.

7.3 Environmental and Sustainability Considerations

7.3.1 Energy Efficiency and Carbon Impact

Blockchain energy consumption analysis includes comparative energy usage across different blockchain platforms, proof-of-stake versus proof-of-work environmental implications, carbon footprint of major stablecoin operations, and sustainable blockchain technology development.

Green finance integration encompasses Environmental, Social, and Governance (ESG) criteria for stablecoins, carbon-neutral stablecoin design principles, integration with green bond and sustainable finance markets, and climate risk assessment for stablecoin reserves.

7.3.2 Circular Economy Applications

Resource optimization involves stablecoins for circular economy token systems, waste reduction and resource sharing applications, supply chain sustainability tracking, and carbon credit and environmental impact tokenization.

8. CASE STUDIES IN REGULATORY INNOVATION

8.1 Sandbox Programs and Regulatory Experimentation

8.1.1 Singapore's Approach to Stablecoin Innovation

Singapore's Monetary Authority (MAS) has pioneered a balanced approach to stablecoin regulation through its regulatory sandbox program. The Project Guardian Initiative involves industry collaboration for institutional DeFi, stablecoin integration with traditional finance, cross-border payment corridor development, and risk management framework testing.

Key lessons include that controlled environments enable innovation while managing risk, industry-regulator collaboration improves policy effectiveness, real-world testing reveals implementation challenges, and international coordination enhances cross-border efficiency.

8.1.2 European Central Bank's Digital Euro Exploration

The ECB's digital euro project provides insights into CBDC-stablecoin coexistence. Design considerations include privacy versus regulatory compliance balance, offline payment capability requirements, integration with existing payment infrastructure, and international interoperability standards.

Stablecoin implications encompass potential displacement of euro-pegged stablecoins, complementary use cases identification, regulatory harmonization opportunities, and innovation space preservation strategies.

8.2 Crisis Management and Resolution

8.2.1 Emergency Intervention Mechanisms

Circuit breaker systems involve development of automated systems to prevent systemic collapse including smart contract-based trading halts during extreme volatility, automatic redemption rate limiting during stress, emergency governance activation protocols, and coordinated cross-protocol intervention mechanisms.

Lender of last resort analogues explore mechanisms to provide emergency liquidity including central bank digital currency lending facilities, industry-funded stabilization mechanisms, cross-protocol mutual insurance systems, and international coordination for global stablecoins.

8.2.2 Resolution Planning for Decentralized Systems

Living wills for DAOs include predetermined liquidation procedures, asset distribution mechanisms during wind-down, governance token holder protection, and cross-border coordination for international operations.

Recovery mechanisms encompass automatic recapitalization triggers, emergency governance procedures, stakeholder bail-in mechanisms, and operational continuity planning.

9. ECONOMIC THEORY AND STABLECOIN EVOLUTION

9.1 Monetary Theory Applications

9.1.1 Quantity Theory and Velocity Considerations

Modern quantity theory application shows that traditional monetary theory requires adaptation for stablecoin ecosystems including velocity measurement in 24/7 digital markets, money demand functions for programmable money, transmission mechanisms for algorithmic monetary policy, and international spillover effects of private digital currencies.

Empirical velocity analysis reveals stablecoin velocity patterns distinct from traditional money including intraday velocity spikes during market stress, seasonal patterns in DeFi yield farming cycles, cross-chain velocity variations and arbitrage effects, and institutional versus retail velocity differences.

9.1.2 Seigniorage and Value Capture

Digital seigniorage models include revenue generation through float investment, transaction fee-based models, governance token value capture mechanisms, and protocol-owned liquidity strategies.

Competitive dynamics involve race-to-zero in transaction fees, innovation-based differentiation strategies, network effect sustainability, and multi-sided platform economics.

9.2 Game Theory and Strategic Interactions

9.2.1 Coordination Games and Multiple Equilibria

Bank run dynamics in digital systems encompass self-fulfilling prophecy mechanisms in algorithmic stablecoins, coordination failure in DAO governance, strategic complementarities in adoption decisions, and information cascade effects in crisis situations.

Mechanism design for stability includes incentive-compatible stability mechanisms, auction theory for collateral liquidations, voting mechanisms for governance decisions, and fee structures for sustainable operations.

9.2.2 Multi-Player Strategic Interactions

Ecosystem competition involves platform competition between blockchain networks, stablecoin substitutability and switching costs, strategic alliances and protocol partnerships, and regulatory arbitrage and jurisdiction competition.

10. TECHNICAL ARCHITECTURE AND SECURITY CONSIDERATIONS

10.1 Smart Contract Security and Formal Verification

10.1.1 Advanced Security Frameworks

Formal verification methods include mathematical proof systems for critical smart contracts, property-based testing for complex interactions, invariant checking for system stability properties, and compositional verification for modular systems.

Runtime security monitoring encompasses real-time anomaly detection systems, behavioral analysis of contract interactions, economic security monitoring and alerting, and automated response to detected threats.

10.1.2 Upgrade Mechanisms and Governance Security

Secure upgrade patterns include timelock delays for critical changes, multi-signature requirements for upgrades, community governance for major modifications, and emergency upgrade procedures with safeguards.

Governance attack prevention involves quadratic voting and other resistance mechanisms, delegate voting systems with accountability, reputation-based governance weighting, and anti-manipulation measures and detection.

10.2 Scalability and Performance Optimization

10.2.1 Layer 2 Solutions and Sidechains

Scaling architecture patterns include optimistic rollups for Ethereum-based stablecoins, zero-knowledge rollups for privacy-preserving transactions, state channels for high-frequency trading, and hybrid approaches combining multiple scaling solutions.

Interoperability and bridge security encompass cross-chain communication protocol security, bridge contract audit and monitoring, economic security models for cross-chain transfers, and recovery mechanisms for bridge failures.

10.2.2 Performance Optimization Strategies

Transaction throughput enhancement includes batch processing and aggregation techniques, parallel execution and sharding approaches, off-chain computation with on-chain verification, and lazy evaluation and deferred settlement.

Gas optimization involves contract bytecode optimization techniques, storage layout efficiency improvements, proxy patterns for upgradeable contracts, and meta-transaction support for user experience.

11. MACROECONOMIC IMPLICATIONS AND POLICY COORDINATION

11.1 Monetary Policy Transmission

11.1.1 Central Bank Policy Effectiveness

Traditional transmission channels require analysis of how stablecoins affect established monetary policy transmission through interest rate channel modifications, credit channel bypass mechanisms, exchange rate channel complications, and asset price channel amplification or dampening.

Quantitative impact assessment includes econometric models incorporating stablecoin adoption, impulse response functions for policy shocks, regional variations in transmission effectiveness, and time-varying parameter analysis for evolving markets.

11.1.2 International Spillover Effects

Cross-border capital flow implications encompass stablecoin-mediated capital flow volatility, bypass of traditional capital controls, exchange rate regime sustainability, and balance of payments accounting challenges.

Currency substitution dynamics involve digital dollarization in emerging markets, local currency displacement risks, monetary sovereignty preservation strategies, and international cooperation requirements.

11.2 Financial System Integration

11.2.1 Banking Sector Interface

Bank-stablecoin ecosystem integration includes correspondent banking for stablecoin issuers, reserve management and custody services, payment rail integration and interoperability, and risk management for bank-stablecoin exposure.

Disintermediation risks and opportunities encompass traditional payment system bypass, new intermediation models and revenue sources, cost reduction and efficiency gains, and financial inclusion expansion possibilities.

11.2.2 Capital Market Integration

Bond market integration includes stablecoin-denominated debt instruments, government bond tokenization and trading, corporate financing through stablecoin markets, and secondary market liquidity enhancement.

Derivatives and risk management involve stablecoin futures and options markets, hedging instruments for stablecoin exposure, risk transfer mechanisms and insurance products, and market maker incentive structures.

12. SOCIAL IMPACT AND DISTRIBUTIONAL EFFECTS

12.1 Financial Inclusion and Access

12.1.1 Democratization of Financial Services

Barrier reduction analysis includes cost reduction for cross-border remittances, 24/7 availability and geographic accessibility, minimal account balance requirements, and smartphone-based financial service access.

Empirical impact studies encompass adoption patterns in underbanked populations, economic impact measurement methodologies, case studies from developing market implementations, and long-term sustainability assessment.

12.1.2 Digital Divide Considerations

Technology access requirements involve internet connectivity and smartphone penetration needs, digital literacy requirements and training programs, language localization and cultural adaptation, and accessibility for disabled users and elderly populations.

Equity and fairness concerns include wealth concentration effects in early adoption, geographic disparities in access and benefits, gender and demographic inclusion analysis, and policy interventions for equitable access.

12.2 Labor Market and Economic Structure Impacts

12.2.1 Employment and Skill Transformation

Financial sector employment effects encompass traditional banking job displacement analysis, new job category creation in crypto/DeFi sectors, skill retraining and education requirements, and geographic concentration and dispersion effects.

Gig economy and micropayments involve enabling new business models and payment structures, reduced transaction costs for small payments, real-time settlement for service providers, and cross-border freelancing facilitation.

12.2.2 Small Business and Entrepreneurship Impact

Access to capital and markets includes DeFi lending for small business financing, global market access through stablecoin payments, reduced foreign exchange risk and costs, and streamlined international commerce.

Innovation ecosystem development encompasses startup ecosystem support through programmable money, venture capital and tokenized investment models, open-source development incentive structures, and community-driven project funding mechanisms.

13. CONCLUSION AND STRATEGIC RECOMMENDATIONS

13.1 Key Findings and Synthesis

The comprehensive analysis presented in this paper reveals that stablecoins have evolved far beyond their original conception as simple digital representations of fiat currency (Gorton & Zhang, 2023). They now constitute critical financial infrastructure that exhibits unique systemic risk characteristics requiring fundamentally new approaches to regulation and supervision.

13.1.1 Systemic Risk Evolution

Our research demonstrates that stablecoin systemic risk manifests through novel channels that traditional financial risk frameworks inadequately capture. Velocity-amplified contagion occurs due to the 24/7, high-velocity nature of digital asset markets enabling risk transmission at unprecedented speeds, as demonstrated by the Terra UST collapse where $60 billion in value was destroyed within days.

Network effect dependencies show that unlike traditional financial institutions, stablecoins derive their systemic importance not just from size but from their position in interconnected DeFi ecosystems, creating unique vulnerabilities to confidence-driven failures. Algorithmic reflexivity demonstrates that algorithmic stabilization mechanisms can amplify rather than dampen shocks, creating death spiral dynamics that have no analogue in traditional finance. Cross-domain risk transmission, as illustrated by the USDC-Silicon Valley Bank incident, shows how traditional financial sector stress can rapidly propagate to digital assets, and vice versa, creating bidirectional contagion channels.

13.1.2 Regulatory Framework Inadequacy

Current regulatory approaches, focusing primarily on reserve requirements and transparency, prove insufficient for managing the systemic risks posed by large-scale stablecoin operations. Size-based metrics limitation shows that traditional TBTF metrics inadequately capture the systemic importance of stablecoins, requiring new frameworks incorporating network effects, velocity characteristics, and algorithmic dependencies.

Jurisdictional challenges arise from the global, decentralized nature of many stablecoin systems creating regulatory gaps and coordination challenges that existing frameworks struggle to address. Innovation-regulation balance considerations show that overly restrictive approaches risk stifling beneficial innovation, while inadequate regulation creates unacceptable systemic risks, requiring nuanced, technology-aware approaches.

13.2 Strategic Policy Recommendations

13.2.1 Immediate Action Items (0-12 months)

Enhanced monitoring infrastructure should implement real-time blockchain monitoring systems across major regulators, establish automated early warning systems for systemic risk indicators, create cross-jurisdictional information sharing protocols, and develop standardized risk assessment methodologies.

Emergency preparedness requires establishing crisis management protocols for major stablecoin failures, creating inter-agency coordination mechanisms for rapid response, developing templates for emergency intervention authorities, and designing public communication strategies for crisis situations.

Industry engagement involves launching regulatory sandboxes for stablecoin innovation, establishing regular industry-regulator dialogue forums, creating technical working groups for standard development, and implementing graduated compliance approaches for different risk tiers.

13.2.2 Medium-Term Objectives (1-3 years)

Comprehensive regulatory framework implementation should include tiered supervision based on systemic importance, clear authorization requirements for stablecoin issuers, enhanced capital and liquidity standards, and resolution and recovery planning requirements.

International coordination involves negotiating bilateral and multilateral supervision agreements, harmonizing standards across major jurisdictions, establishing dispute resolution mechanisms, and creating joint oversight bodies for global stablecoins.

Technology integration encompasses deploying AI-powered risk assessment tools, implementing programmable compliance mechanisms, developing quantum-resistant security standards, and creating interoperability standards for regulatory reporting.

13.2.3 Long-Term Vision (3-10 years)

Ecosystem maturation aims to achieve stable coexistence between stablecoins and CBDCs, establish mature risk management practices across the industry, create sustainable innovation incentive structures, and develop comprehensive consumer protection frameworks.

Global financial integration involves integrating stablecoins into international payment systems, establishing cross-border regulatory mutual recognition, creating global standards for digital asset supervision, and developing coordinated crisis management capabilities.

13.3 Research Priorities and Future Directions

13.3.1 Critical Knowledge Gaps

Empirical research needs include long-term impact studies on financial stability and monetary policy, quantitative analysis of network effects and systemic risk amplification, cross-jurisdictional comparative studies of regulatory effectiveness, and behavioral economics research on user adoption and crisis response.

Technical research priorities encompass advanced modeling techniques for complex DeFi ecosystems, formal verification methods for critical financial infrastructure, quantum-resistant cryptographic implementations, and privacy-preserving regulatory compliance mechanisms.

Policy research areas involve optimal regulatory design for innovation preservation, international coordination mechanisms and governance structures, economic impact assessment methodologies, and social equity and inclusion policy frameworks.

13.3.2 Interdisciplinary Collaboration Needs

Academic-industry-government partnerships should include joint research initiatives on systemic risk modeling, shared datasets and benchmarking standards, cross-sectoral talent exchange programs, and collaborative crisis simulation exercises.

International academic networks require global research consortiums for stablecoin studies, standardized methodology development, cross-cultural adoption pattern analysis, and comparative regulatory effectiveness studies.

13.4 Final Reflections

The emergence of stablecoins as systemically important financial infrastructure represents a profound shift in the global financial landscape. Unlike previous financial innovations that operated within existing institutional frameworks, stablecoins challenge fundamental assumptions about money, payment systems, and regulatory authority.

The path ahead will require an unusual degree of coordination among domains that have historically operated in silos. Expertise from computer science and finance must be integrated with regulatory oversight that spans jurisdictions, while public institutions, private sector actors, and academic researchers will need to establish more consistent channels of engagement. Such cooperation is admittedly difficult to achieve, yet the alternative is stark: an absence of coherent frameworks for addressing stablecoin-related risks could amplify vulnerabilities in the global financial system, whereas excessively restrictive regulation risks suppressing mechanisms that may enhance efficiency, inclusion, and access to financial services.

Recent shocks have underscored the importance of resilience and adaptability in financial infrastructure. The COVID-19 pandemic revealed how quickly stress can propagate through interconnected systems, while climate change and persistent geopolitical tensions add further layers of uncertainty. Within this context, stablecoins if appropriately regulated, could plausibly contribute to both systemic stability and incremental financial innovation. Realizing such potential, however, requires more than initial regulatory intervention; it demands ongoing vigilance and adaptive governance capable of responding to new risks as they emerge.

The trajectory of stablecoins is unlikely to plateau. Advances in distributed ledger technologies, shifting consumer expectations, and evolving regulatory responses suggest that their development will accelerate in the coming years. Decisions made in the present will thus shape not only the contours of stablecoin markets but also the broader evolution of digital finance. Regulatory frameworks must therefore balance two imperatives: they must be sufficiently stringent to contain systemic risk, while remaining flexible enough to accommodate continued technological and market innovation.

The transition from traditional financial architecture to digital infrastructure is best understood not as a question of possibility, but of timing and design. By adopting proactive approaches to supervision, grounded in careful monitoring, adaptive regulation, and international coordination, policymakers can increase the likelihood that this transition reinforces, rather than undermines, global financial stability and prosperity.

REFERENCES

Ante, L. (2023). The non-fungible token (NFT) market and its relationship with Bitcoin and Ethereum. *FinTech*, *2*(1), 216–224.

Aramonte, S., Huang, W., & Schrimpf, A. (2021). DeFi risks and the decentralisation illusion. *BIS Quarterly Review*, (December), 21–36.

Auer, R., & Tercero-Lucas, P. (2022). Distrust or speculation? The socioeconomic drivers of U.S. cryptocurrency investments. *Journal of Financial Stability*, *62*, 101066. DOI: 10.1016/j.jfs.2022.101066

Basel Committee on Banking Supervision. (2013). *Global systemically important banks: Updated assessment methodology and the higher loss absorbency requirement*. Bank for International Settlements.

Baur, D. G., Hong, K., & Lee, A. D. (2018). Bitcoin: Medium of exchange or speculative assets? *Journal of International Financial Markets, Institutions and Money*, *54*, 177–189. DOI: 10.1016/j.intfin.2017.12.004

Bullmann, D., Klemm, J., & Pinna, A. (2019). *In search for stability in crypto-assets: Are stablecoins the solution?* European Central Bank Occasional Paper Series No. 230.

Catalini, C., & de Gortari, A. (2022). On the economic design of stablecoins. *Management Science*, *68*(2), 949–977.

De Bandt, O., & Hartmann, P. (2000). Systemic risk: A survey. *ECB Working Paper Series*, No. 35.

Gorton, G., & Zhang, J. (2023). Taming wildcat stablecoins. *University of Pennsylvania Law Review*, *171*(4), 1125–1187.

Gudgeon, L., Perez, D., Harz, D., Livshits, B., & Gervais, A. (2020). The decentralized financial crisis. *Proceedings of the 2020 Crypto Valley Conference on Blockchain Technology*, 1-15.

Gudgeon, L., Werner, S., Perez, D., & Knottenbelt, W. J. (2023). DeFi protocols for loanable funds: Interest rates, liquidity and market efficiency. *ACM Computing Surveys*, *55*(13s), 1–48.

Harvey, C. R., Ramachandran, A., & Santoro, J. (2021). *DeFi and the future of finance*. John Wiley & Sons.

Jensen, J. R., von Wachter, V., & Ross, O. (2021). An introduction to decentralized finance (DeFi). *Complex Systems Informatics and Modeling Quarterly*, *26*(26), 46–54. DOI: 10.7250/csimq.2021-26.03

Kaufman, G. G., & Scott, K. E. (2003). What is systemic risk, and do bank regulators retard or contribute to it? *The Independent Review*, 7(3), 371-391.

Klages-Mundt, A., Harz, D., Gudgeon, L., Liu, J. Y., & Minca, A. (2020). Stablecoins 2.0: Economic foundations and risk-based models. *Proceedings of the 2nd ACM Conference on Advances in Financial Technologies*, 59-79. DOI: 10.1145/3419614.3423261

Kwon, D., & Platias, N. (2019). *Terra money: Stability and adoption*. Terra White Paper.

Lyons, R. K., & Viswanath-Natraj, G. (2023). What keeps stablecoins stable? *Journal of International Money and Finance*, *131*, 102777. DOI: 10.1016/j.jimonfin.2022.102777

Prasad, E. S. (2021). *The future of money: How the digital revolution is transforming currencies and finance*. Harvard University Press.

Schär, F. (2021). Decentralized finance: On blockchain-and smart contract-based financial markets. *Review - Federal Reserve Bank of St. Louis*, *103*(2), 153–174.

Stern, G. H., & Feldman, R. J. (2004). *Too big to fail: The hazards of bank bailouts*. Brookings Institution Press.

Zetzsche, D. A., Buckley, R. P., Arner, D. W., & Föhr, L. (2020). The ICO gold rush: It's a scam, it's a bubble, it's a super challenge for regulators. *Harvard International Law Journal*, *60*(2), 267–315.

Chapter 5
Stablecoins as Public Good:
Remittances, Humanitarian Aid, and Digital ID

Oumaima Abouzaid
https://orcid.org/0009-0007-8002-6110
Chouaib Doukkali University, Morocco

Faouzi Boussedra
Chouaib Doukkali University, Morocco

ABSTRACT

Stablecoins—digital assets designed to maintain price stability by pegging to fiat currencies or collateralized reserves—have often been examined through the lens of private finance, focusing on market speculation, systemic risk, and regulatory arbitrage. This article reframes stablecoins as potential public goods, investigating their role in advancing financial inclusion, humanitarian effectiveness, and digital identity infrastructures. Drawing on recent data from the World Bank, the World Food Programme (WFP), and case studies across the Global South, the analysis adopts a comparative methodology, triangulating case study evidence with theoretical modeling. It applies transaction cost economics (Coase's theorem) to remittances, graph theory (max-flow/min-cut) to humanitarian aid distribution, set-theoretical analysis (via Venn modeling) to digital ID integration, and game theory to governance risks between states and private issuers.

DOI: 10.4018/979-8-3373-9043-7.ch005

I. INTRODUCTION

Stablecoins, defined as digital assets designed to maintain price stability by pegging their value to fiat currencies, commodities, or collateralized reserves, represent one of the most significant innovations in the cryptocurrency ecosystem. Unlike volatile assets such as Bitcoin or Ether, stablecoins offer a hybrid form of money—anchored in traditional finance yet transferable across decentralized infrastructures. This duality makes them both an extension of existing monetary practices and a potential disruption to traditional intermediaries.

To date, much of the scholarly and policy debate has treated stablecoins primarily as private financial instruments, situating them within frameworks of systemic risk, regulatory arbitrage, and their interaction with central bank digital currencies (CBDCs) (Guseva et al., 2025). This perspective, while valuable for prudential regulation, risks narrowing the debate to stability concerns and overlooking broader socio-economic implications. Stablecoins can also be conceptualized as infrastructural public goods—protocols and networks that, once deployed, generate non-rivalrous and potentially non-excludable benefits. In environments where traditional financial systems are costly, slow, or inaccessible, they may enable alternative models of financial inclusion, humanitarian effectiveness, and digital empowerment.

The relevance of such infrastructures is underscored by persistent global inequalities. The World Bank (2023) reports that global remittances exceeded USD 860 billion in 2022, surpassing official development assistance. Yet, nearly 1 billion people remain without legal identity (World Bank, 2018), while humanitarian crises increasingly strain the capacity of aid delivery mechanisms (UNOCHA, 2024). In this context, the deployment of stablecoins—sometimes experimental and ad hoc—offers insights into both their potential and their limitations.

For example, the World Food Programme's Building Blocks Project in Jordan disbursed aid to over 500,000 Syrian refugees using a private Ethereum-based blockchain, reducing administrative costs by 98% and improving transparency in resource allocation (WFP Innovation, 2025). In Venezuela, NGOs experimented with distributing Tether (USDT) to households in order to mitigate the effects of hyperinflationary collapse. Similarly, in the Philippines, fintech startups piloted stablecoin-based remittances, successfully cutting transaction costs by more than half (Kulkarni et al., 2019). These cases illustrate both the promise of stablecoins as infrastructures of resilience and the fragility of such systems, which remain dependent on governance models, trust in issuers, and integration with existing financial ecosystems.

The objective of this paper is therefore to reframe stablecoins not only as financial instruments, but as candidate public goods. We identify three domains where their application may yield significant social value:

1. Remittances: Lowering transaction costs could release billions of dollars in household income annually, particularly benefitting low-income families reliant on cross-border transfers.
2. Humanitarian aid: Efficiency, transparency, and accountability gains could transform crisis response, reducing leakage, delays, and corruption in aid distribution.
3. Digital identity integration: Stablecoins could support the development of inclusive infrastructures, but also raise risks related to exclusion, surveillance, and data sovereignty.

Methodologically, the paper employs a multi-pronged analytical framework:

- Transaction cost economics (Coase's theorem) to model efficiency gains from reducing intermediation.
- Graph theory (max-flow min-cut) to simulate flows in remittance and aid networks under different infrastructural designs.
- Probabilistic risk modeling to assess systemic vulnerabilities, such as issuer default or de-pegging events.
- Game theory to capture governance dilemmas between private issuers, regulators, and users in global networks.

By bridging economic theory with real-world case studies, this research contributes to a growing body of literature situating stablecoins within debates on financial inclusion, digital sovereignty, and humanitarian innovation (Allen & Carletti, 2022; Jutel, 2021). Beyond their financial utility, stablecoins can thus be examined as *institutional technologies*—tools capable of reshaping governance, rights, and access in digital economies.

The rest of the paper is structured as follows. Section 2 reviews the existing literature on stablecoins and public goods. Section 3 outlines the methodological framework, including mathematical models and case study selection. Section 4 presents results across remittances, humanitarian aid, and digital identity integration. Section 5 discusses the broader implications for governance and regulation, particularly regarding transparency, accountability, and human rights. Section 6 concludes with recommendations for aligning stablecoin development with inclusive, transparent, and rights-respecting infrastructures.

II. LITERATURE REVIEW

2.1 Stablecoins and Financial Inclusion

The potential of stablecoins to advance financial inclusion has emerged as a central theme in recent debates on digital finance. Financial inclusion, understood as the ability of individuals and businesses to access affordable and useful financial services, remains a global challenge, with the World Bank estimating that over 1.4 billion adults remain unbanked, particularly in low- and middle-income countries (Demirgüç-Kunt et al., 2018). Conventional banking systems often exclude marginalized populations due to geographic inaccessibility, high compliance costs, and the lack of formal identification. In this context, stablecoins are increasingly framed as a technological innovation capable of bridging these systemic gaps.

Empirical studies highlight two main advantages. First, they substantially reduce remittance costs. Kulkarni et al. (2019) demonstrated that blockchain-based remittance channels could cut average transaction fees by more than half, particularly in high-cost corridors where fees can exceed eight percent of the transaction value (Kulkarni et al., 2019). Jegerson and Mertzanis (2025) reached similar conclusions, noting that stablecoins provide reliability and trust advantages compared to volatile cryptocurrencies, while outperforming legacy providers such as Western Union or MoneyGram, which rely on costly agent networks (Jegerson & Mertzanis, 2025). By lowering transaction costs and enabling faster settlement, stablecoins can increase the share of remittances received by households, thereby releasing resources that could be redirected into education, healthcare, or local investment.

Beyond cost considerations, scholars also emphasize the functional capacities, or "affordances," enabled by stablecoins. Gaudreau (2024) identifies three dimensions that distinguish them from traditional financial instruments: programmability, which allows transfers to include built-in conditions; instant settlement, which reduces temporal delays in cross-border transfers; and borderless reach, which bypasses jurisdictional barriers (Gaudreau, 2024). These affordances are particularly salient for marginalized communities that operate outside of formal banking ecosystems and whose livelihoods depend on the ability to transact quickly and securely across borders.

The literature further situates stablecoins within the broader rise of decentralized finance (DeFi). Ali, Butt, and Senturk (2025) argue that DeFi applications—enabled by stablecoins and smart contracts—reduce entry barriers to participation in financial markets, allowing individuals without credit histories or access to bank accounts to engage in saving, lending, and investment activities (Ali et al., 2025). This is especially relevant in Sub-Saharan Africa, where mobile money adoption is already widespread, as seen with M-Pesa in Kenya. Stablecoins could extend the functionality of these systems by anchoring value in globally stable currencies, thereby protecting users from local currency volatility.

At the same time, scholars urge caution against overly celebratory narratives. Vasselin (2024) points out that blockchain-based financial inclusion may expose migrants and low-income users to new risks of data exploitation, surveillance, and dependency on opaque infrastructures (Vasselin, 2024). Zwitter et al. (2021) similarly warn of "crypto-colonialism," arguing that the introduction of stablecoin-based systems, often controlled by actors in the Global North, risks replicating historical patterns of asymmetry and dependency under the guise of empowerment (Zwitter et al., 2021).

Taken together, the literature on stablecoins and financial inclusion illustrates a dual reality. On the one hand, stablecoins hold significant potential to reduce costs, expand accessibility, and provide functional capacities that empower marginalized communities. On the other hand, these same mechanisms carry risks of dependency, surveillance, and inequity if not embedded within inclusive governance frameworks. The debate therefore shifts from whether stablecoins can advance financial inclusion to the more complex question of under what institutional and regulatory conditions they can be harnessed as genuine public goods.

2.2 Stablecoins in Humanitarian Aid

The integration of stablecoins into humanitarian aid has been widely discussed as crises increasingly expose the weaknesses of conventional delivery mechanisms. Traditional disbursement methods, such as bank transfers, cash distributions, or voucher systems, are often constrained by delays, high administrative costs, corruption risks, and limited accessibility in fragile contexts. Against this background, stablecoins appear as a technological innovation with the potential to transform humanitarian operations by enhancing efficiency, transparency, and accountability.

Several emblematic case studies illustrate this trend. The most frequently cited is the World Food Programme's Building Blocks project in Jordan's Azraq refugee camp. Launched in 2017, it used a private Ethereum blockchain to deliver food assistance to more than half a million Syrian refugees. Instead of relying on bank accounts, beneficiaries authenticated transactions through biometric scans, while every transfer was immutably recorded on the blockchain. Evaluations indicate that this approach reduced administrative costs by up to 98 percent, while simultaneously strengthening traceability and donor confidence (Idris, 2024).

Other humanitarian settings have seen similar initiatives. In Venezuela, where hyperinflation rendered the bolivar nearly worthless, NGOs experimented with distributing Tether (USDT) to households. This allowed recipients to preserve value in a U.S. dollar–pegged token and circumvent collapsing banking institutions. Mannan

(2024) conceptualizes these experiments as forms of "crypto-humanitarianism," in which NGOs and multilateral organizations increasingly turn to blockchain to bypass state repression and market failure. Likewise, during the outbreak of the war in Ukraine in 2022, humanitarian organizations and volunteer networks raised and distributed millions of dollars in stablecoins such as USDC and DAI within days. These transfers provided urgently needed liquidity in an environment where banking systems were disrupted, demonstrating the agility and responsiveness of digital assets in times of acute crisis (Howson, 2021).

Across these cases, scholars consistently highlight three key advantages: speed, transparency, and accountability. Stablecoin transfers settle within minutes rather than days, which is critical in rapidly deteriorating crises. Every transaction is recorded on-chain, providing unprecedented levels of transparency that reduce the risk of diversion and corruption, while increasing donor trust. Moreover, the programmability of stablecoins allows aid to be disbursed with restrictions, ensuring that funds are used for specific goods or services. This resonates with Boiardi and Stout's (2021) emphasis on the broader governance capacities of blockchain in development cooperation.

At the same time, literature underscores critical risks. Even collateralized stablecoins such as USDT or USDC remain dependent on the credibility of private issuers, raising concerns about reserve adequacy and long-term stability. Access barriers persist, as recipients must possess smartphones and reliable internet connectivity, which risks excluding precisely those most vulnerable. Furthermore, in politically sensitive contexts, governments may perceive stablecoin-based transfers as an intrusion on sovereignty, potentially leading to surveillance, repression, or outright prohibition. Jutel (2021) warns of what he terms "crypto-colonialism," where Western-backed humanitarian organizations deploy technological infrastructures that reinforce North–South dependency rather than empowering local communities. Idris (2024) echoes this concern by stressing that digital transfers must be carefully designed to respect humanitarian principles of neutrality, impartiality, and inclusivity.

In sum, the literature presents stablecoins in humanitarian aid as a double-edged innovation. Evidence from Jordan, Venezuela, and Ukraine demonstrates tangible efficiency and accountability gains, but these are accompanied by risks related to volatility, access, and political legitimacy. The scholarly consensus increasingly suggests that the success of stablecoins in humanitarian contexts depends not only on their technical capabilities but also on the governance frameworks and ethical safeguards that regulate their deployment.

2.3 Stablecoins, Digital Identity, and Self-Sovereignty

The intersection of stablecoins and digital identity represents one of the most promising yet contested areas in the literature on digital finance. Nearly one billion people worldwide still lack legal identity, according to the World Bank's ID4D Initiative (World Bank, 2018), limiting their access to basic services such as healthcare, education, and finance. Digital identity programs, ranging from India's Aadhaar to emerging self-sovereign identity (SSI) systems, have been proposed as a solution to this exclusion. In this context, stablecoins are increasingly viewed not only as payment instruments but also as complementary infrastructures that can integrate with identity systems to promote inclusion.

Scholars such as Wang and De Filippi (2020) argue that when stablecoins are paired with SSI frameworks, individuals are empowered to control their personal data and simultaneously gain access to financial services that were previously out of reach (Wang & De Filippi, 2020). By enabling identity-linked wallets, refugees or undocumented migrants could access humanitarian transfers or remittances securely, without needing to rely on fragile or hostile state systems. Laatikainen et al. (2021) highlight how self-sovereign identity ecosystems can provide verifiable credentials and enhance access to financial services for marginalized populations, bypassing exclusionary formal banking structures (Laatikainen et al., 2021).

The Global South has become an important testing ground for such initiatives. In Africa, for example, the African Union has supported proposals for a continental digital identity system that could, in theory, be interoperable with blockchain-based financial services. Scholars like Vasselin (2024) highlight the emancipatory potential of such systems, framing them as tools of "self-sovereign empowerment" where individuals—not states or corporations—hold authority over their identities and financial data (Vasselin, 2024). Stablecoins, in this vision, serve as the transactional layer of an inclusive digital infrastructure, capable of anchoring value in stable units while interoperating with identity verification systems.

At the same time, literature underscores significant risks associated with coupling stablecoins and digital identity. The most pressing concern relates to exclusion by design. Digital identity programs such as India's Aadhaar have faced criticism for inadvertently excluding individuals who lack biometric data, technological literacy, or consistent access to digital devices. Sindhu (2025) notes that women in developing economies, while benefiting from the financial autonomy enabled by digital identity and stablecoin integration, are also disproportionately exposed to exclusion risks due to structural inequalities in digital access (Sindhu, 2025). In humanitarian settings, refugees who cannot obtain formal identity credentials may find themselves doubly excluded—from both state systems and blockchain-based aid programs.

Surveillance is another central theme in the critical literature. Linking stablecoin transactions to digital IDs risks creating unprecedented opportunities for financial monitoring by states and private actors. Sezer and Prinz (2022) echo this concern, showing that combining digital currencies with self-sovereign identity frameworks could enable programmable money but also create risks of centralization and control (Sezer & Prinz, 2022). This aligns with broader concerns raised by Laatikainen et al. (2021), who caution that the governance of self-sovereign identity ecosystems will determine whether they empower users or entrench dependency (Laatikainen et al., 2021).

Taken together, the literature on stablecoins and digital identity reveals a paradox. On one side, integration with self-sovereign and interoperable ID systems offers transformative opportunities for inclusion, empowerment, and the creation of digital infrastructures as public goods. On the other side, the risks of exclusion, surveillance, and dependency underscore the fragility of such arrangements. Scholars increasingly argue that the outcome depends not on the technology itself but on the governance frameworks that regulate its design and implementation. Open standards, transparent protocols, and strong privacy safeguards emerge as recurring recommendations to ensure that the coupling of stablecoins and digital identity fosters genuine empowerment rather than new forms of control.

2.4 Risks and Governance Concerns

While the literature highlights the potential of stablecoins to enhance remittances, humanitarian aid, and digital identity systems, scholars consistently emphasize that their promise is inseparable from the risks and governance challenges they pose. Central to this debate is the tension between inclusion and dependency. On the one hand, stablecoins offer unprecedented opportunities for financial access and efficiency; on the other, they risk entrenching reliance on infrastructures controlled by private issuers, particularly in the Global North. Guseva et al. (2025) warn that the dominance of a handful of issuers such as USDT and USDC—together accounting for more than 80 percent of the market—may undermine national monetary sovereignty and expose vulnerable economies to foreign corporate control.

Another governance concern relates to compliance with international norms on anti-money laundering and countering the financing of terrorism (AML/CFT). A recent analysis highlights that the pseudonymous nature of stablecoin transactions complicates regulatory oversight, prompting legislators in the United States to propose the STABLE Act and other measures to extend Bank Secrecy Act obligations to stablecoin issuers (Reuters, 2025). Without hybrid solutions that combine compliance mechanisms with digital identity safeguards, stablecoins could exacerbate the very risks they seek to address.

The coupling of stablecoins with digital identity infrastructures intensifies these risks. While identity-linked transfers may improve accountability, they also create opportunities for surveillance and exclusion. Jutel (2021) cautions that authoritarian regimes could weaponize blockchain-based ID systems to monitor and control populations, transforming instruments of empowerment into tools of repression. Beyond technical and political risks, critical perspectives also address questions of legitimacy and power asymmetry. Jutel (2021) frames the proliferation of blockchain-based humanitarian and financial systems as a form of "crypto-colonialism," in which Western-backed technologies impose new forms of dependency under the guise of innovation.

Other scholars stress that structural inequalities—particularly gender gaps in digital access—can lead to systematic exclusion, even in systems designed to promote inclusion. Research on gender and digital finance shows that women often face barriers such as lower digital literacy, limited device ownership, and weaker connectivity, which restrict their ability to benefit from blockchain-based systems (Horky, 2024).

These critiques underscore the broader lesson that stablecoins cannot be understood purely as technical instruments. Their role as potential public goods is shaped by the governance regimes that regulate their use, the transparency of their issuers, and the inclusivity of their design. In sum, the literature converges on a cautious but forward-looking consensus. Stablecoins hold significant potential to act as infrastructures of inclusion and resilience, but only if embedded within governance frameworks that prioritize transparency, accountability, interoperability, and rights protection. Without these safeguards, they risk exacerbating inequalities, undermining sovereignty, and entrenching new forms of dependency.

III. METHODOLOGY

This research adopts a comparative and multi-method approach, combining theoretical modeling with empirical case studies, to evaluate the potential of stablecoins as public goods in three domains: remittances, humanitarian aid, and digital identity. The methodology integrates tools from transaction cost economics, network analysis, governance theory, and risk assessment.

3.1 Transaction Cost Economics (Remittances)

Building on Coase's (1937) concept of transaction costs, this section examines how fees reduce the value that recipients actually receive from cross-border transfers. For clarity, the analysis compares the total amount received under two systems —

traditional remittances versus stablecoin transfers — highlighting the efficiency gains when intermediaries are reduced.

By comparing f across traditional remittance services (≈6% on average globally, World Bank 2023) and stablecoin-based transfers (≈1%), we can quantify potential household-level and aggregate savings. This model will be applied in the *Results* to corridors such as the U.S.–Philippines and intra-African transfers.

3.2 Network Analysis (Humanitarian Aid)

Humanitarian aid distribution is modeled as a flow network G(V,E), where nodes (V) represent donors, intermediaries, and beneficiaries, and edges (E) represent transfer channels with capacity constraints. The efficiency of aid distribution is constrained by the max-flow min-cut theorem:

where f(s,t) is the maximum feasible flow from source sss (donor) to sink t (beneficiary), and c(u,v) are the capacities of edges across a cut set C.

In conventional systems, multiple intermediaries reduce flow efficiency and increase leakages. By contrast, stablecoin transfers reduce the size of C, creating quasi-direct donor–beneficiary channels. This formalization will support the case study analysis of WFP's *Building Blocks* project, where efficiency gains exceeded 90%.

The distribution of humanitarian aid can be compared to a network of connected actors — donors, intermediaries, and beneficiaries — through which resources must flow. Each intermediary adds friction or cost to the system. Stablecoins, by enabling more direct transfers, streamline this flow and reduce leakages, as illustrated in the case of WFP's *Building Blocks* project.

3.3 Governance Modeling (Game Theory)

The interaction between regulators (states) and stablecoin issuers (private entities) is analyzed using game-theoretical frameworks. A simplified two-player payoff matrix illustrates cooperative versus non-cooperative strategies.

- State strategies: Cooperative (enable regulated adoption) vs Non-Cooperative (restrict or ban).
- Issuer strategies: Cooperative (transparency, compliance) vs Non-Cooperative (opacity, regulatory arbitrage).

Payoffs are expressed qualitatively as:

	Issuer Cooperative	Issuer Non-Cooperative
State Cooperative	(+3, +3)	(+1, +2)
State Non-Cooperative	(+2, +1)	(0, 0)

This model will be applied in the *Results* to evaluate the conditions under which stablecoins can evolve from private assets into public goods through regulatory cooperation.

3.4 Qualitative Risk Assessment

Beyond efficiency, the study incorporates a qualitative risk framework to evaluate challenges such as volatility, issuer concentration, exclusion risks in digital ID integration, and potential surveillance. These risks are contextualized using case studies from Venezuela, Jordan, and India, supported by academic literature (Korkmaz, 2023; Holloway, Al Masri & Yahia, 2021; Mathews, 2017; Feldstein, 2021; Kılıç & Bodur, 2024).

3.5 Data Sources

The analysis draws on multiple datasets and case studies:

- Remittances: World Bank's *Remittance Prices Worldwide* database (2023).
- Humanitarian Aid: WFP reports on *Building Blocks*, NGO pilots in Venezuela, and crypto-donations in Ukraine.
- Digital Identity: World Bank *ID4D* dataset, Aadhaar program reports, and African Union proposals.
- Governance: Regulatory papers, FATF guidelines, and academic assessments of stablecoin governance.

3.6 Limitations

Three methodological limitations are acknowledged. First, the empirical evidence discussed throughout this study is primarily derived from pilot-scale initiatives, such as the WFP's Building Blocks or NGO-led stablecoin transfers in Venezuela. While these pilots offer valuable insights into feasibility and efficiency, they cannot yet be generalized to national or systemic adoption without longitudinal evaluation. Second, the analytical models applied—transaction cost economics, network flow, and game theory—simplify complex socio-technical systems; their outputs are therefore illustrative rather than predictive. Third, the study relies heavily on secondary data and institutional reports, which may embed biases linked to funding or implementation agendas. Recognizing these constraints is essential for situating the findings: they reveal the potential of stablecoins as public goods, but not their guaranteed outcomes at scale.

IV. RESULTS

4.1 Remittances: Cost Savings and Household Impacts

Building on the transaction cost framework developed in Section 3.1, this analysis quantifies the comparative efficiency of stablecoin-based remittance channels relative to traditional intermediated systems. The application of transaction cost economics confirms the significant efficiency gains associated with stablecoin-based remittances. Using the model R=T×(1−f)R = T \times (1 - f)R=T×(1−f), where fff represents transaction fees, the analysis shows that a USD 300 transfer via traditional services (average fee 6%) results in only USD 282 reaching the recipient, while the same transfer via stablecoins (1% fee) yields USD 297. This difference of USD 15 per transfer scales to USD 180 per year for households receiving monthly remittances.

At the macro level, these savings become substantial. Figure 1 illustrates the potential aggregate benefits in the U.S.–Philippines corridor, which processes USD 20 billion annually. With full adoption, stablecoins could generate USD 4.8 billion in savings—comparable to the national social protection budgets of several low-income countries.

Figure 1. Comparison of remittance efficiency between traditional services and stablecoin transfers in the U.S.–Philippines corridor.

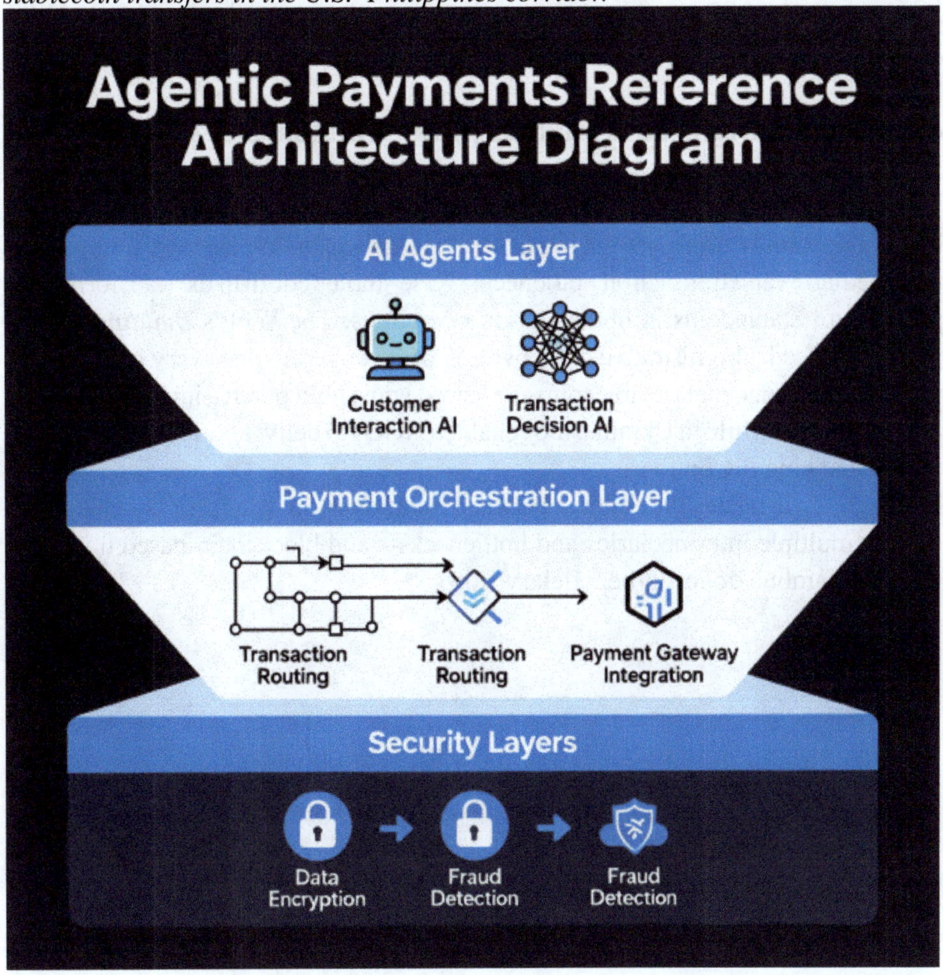

The figure illustrates how reducing average transaction fees from 6% to 1% could generate up to USD 4.8 billion in household savings annually.

Table 1. Average remittance costs by region (World Bank, 2023)

Region	Average Cost (%)	Most Expensive Corridor	Least Expensive Corridor
Sub-Saharan Africa	8.2	Nigeria–Cameroon	Kenya–Uganda
South Asia	4.5	Pakistan–Afghanistan	India–Nepal
Latin America	6.1	USA–Cuba	USA–Mexico
Global Average	6.0	—	—

These results underscore the redistributive potential of stablecoins, particularly in Sub-Saharan Africa, where average fees exceed 8%. By reducing transaction costs, stablecoins could redirect billions into household consumption and local economic development.

4.2 Humanitarian Aid: Efficiency and Transparency Gains

Applying the network flow model outlined in Section 3.2, this section evaluates how stablecoins reconfigure the humanitarian aid distribution chain by minimizing intermediaries and transaction bottlenecks. Case studies confirm the transformative potential of stablecoins in humanitarian operations. The WFP's *Building Blocks* project reduced administrative costs by 98% while ensuring that every transfer was verifiable. In Venezuela, stablecoins preserved household purchasing power amidst hyperinflation, while in Ukraine, they enabled NGOs to deliver liquidity within days despite banking disruptions.

Figure 2 visualizes the contrast between traditional aid distribution—characterized by multiple intermediaries and bottlenecks—and blockchain-based transfers, which streamline donor-to-beneficiary flows.

Figure 2. Conceptual comparison of humanitarian aid delivery networks

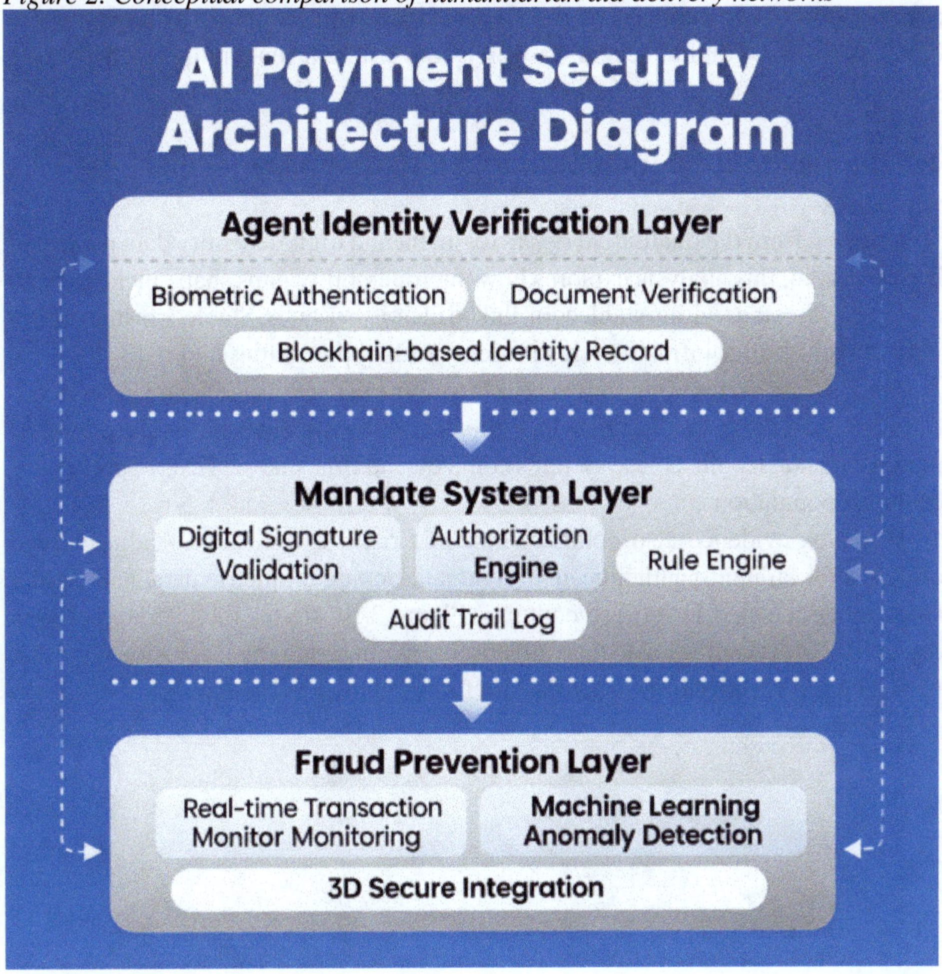

The left side represents traditional multi-intermediary systems prone to cost leakage, while the right side shows blockchain-based stablecoin transfers that enable near-direct donor–beneficiary flows with greater transparency.

Table 2. Stablecoin humanitarian case studies (Jordan, Venezuela, Ukraine)

Case	Mechanism	Main Benefit	Main Risk
WFP - Jordan	Private Ethereum blockchain	98% cost reduction	Biometric exclusion
Venezuela NGOs	Tether (USDT) distribution	Value preservation	Issuer dependency
Ukraine Conflict	USDC/DAI transfers	Rapid liquidity delivery	Regulatory uncertainty

These findings confirm the literature's emphasis on speed, transparency, and accountability. Yet they also highlight the risks of exclusion in contexts where beneficiaries lack digital access, as well as the political sensitivities of bypassing state-controlled financial systems.

4.3 Digital Identity: Inclusion and Exclusion Dynamics

Drawing from the qualitative risk assessment and digital identity data presented in Section 3.4, this analysis explores how interoperability gaps shape inclusion and exclusion outcomes within stablecoin-linked identity systems. Stablecoin integration with digital identity infrastructures presents both opportunities and risks. In India, Aadhaar-linked systems facilitated access to subsidies, while African Union initiatives envision continental digital IDs interoperable with financial systems. When paired with stablecoins, these systems could extend financial services to previously excluded populations.

However, evidence also points to systemic risks of exclusion. Aadhaar faced criticism for failing to authenticate individuals lacking biometric data, and similar risks are anticipated in refugee contexts. Figure 3 illustrates the overlap between digital ID holders and stablecoin wallet users, emphasizing the "inclusion gap" that persists when identity infrastructures are fragmented or exclusionary.

Figure 3. Overlap between populations with digital identity credentials and those using stablecoin wallets

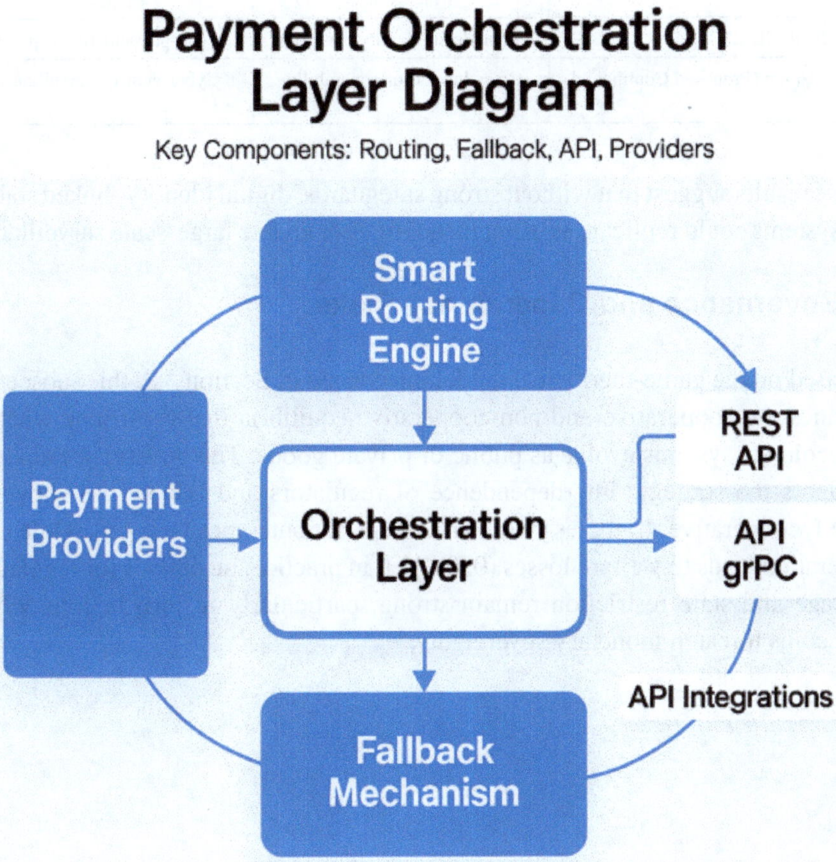

The shaded area illustrates the "inclusion gap" — individuals who possess one but not both, highlighting persistent access inequalities

Table 3. Interoperability challenges and exclusion risks

Case	Opportunities	Risks
India (Aadhaar)	Subsidy access, financial inclusion	Authentication failures, exclusion
World Bank (ID4D)	Global legal identity campaign	Implementation gaps
African Union (Proposed Continental ID)	Cross-border interoperability	Cybersecurity, surveillance

The results suggest that without strong safeguards, digital identity–linked stablecoin systems could replicate existing inequalities or enable large-scale surveillance.

4.4 Governance and Dependency Risks

Based on the game-theoretical model introduced in Section 3.3, this subsection examines the cooperative and non-cooperative equilibria that determine whether stablecoin ecosystems evolve as public or private goods. The governance analysis highlights the strategic interdependence of regulators and issuers. As shown in Table 1, cooperative strategies yield Pareto-superior outcomes (+3, +3), while non-cooperation leads to welfare losses (0, 0). Yet, in practice, incentives for regulatory arbitrage and state restriction remain strong, particularly in jurisdictions where stablecoins threaten monetary sovereignty.

Figure 4. Game-theoretical representation of strategic interactions between state regulators and private issuers

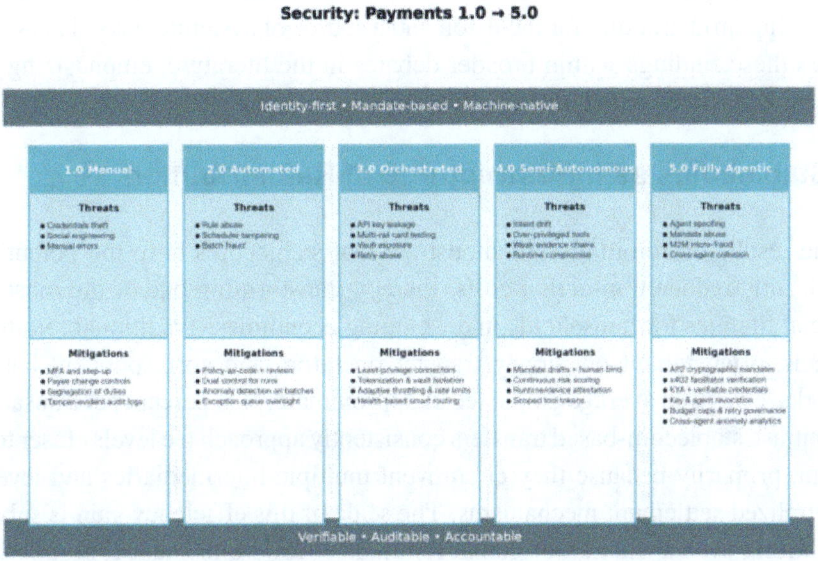

Cooperative strategies yield Pareto-superior outcomes (+3, +3), while non-cooperation results in collective welfare loss (0, 0).

Table 4. Governance challenges: AML/CFT, issuer concentration, sovereignty risks

Risk	Description	Potential Solution
AML/CFT compliance	Difficulty monitoring pseudonymous flows	Hybrid on/off-ramp KYC + digital IDs
Issuer concentration	USDT/USDC dominate >80% of market	Support open-source, diversified stablecoins
Sovereignty loss	Dependence on private actors from Global North	Develop regional public–private frameworks

The results confirm Cantú et al. (2025)'s warning that dependence on a few private issuers could compromise sovereignty, while Pocher (2025) stresses the difficulties of ensuring AML/CFT compliance in fragile states. Together, these findings underscore that stablecoins cannot be sustainable public goods without inclusive governance frameworks and transparent reserve management.

V. DISCUSSION

The results presented in Section 4 confirm the dual nature of stablecoins as both a promising infrastructure for inclusion and a source of systemic risks. This section situates these findings within broader debates in the literature, emphasizing their policy, governance, and ethical implications.

5.1 Stablecoins as Infrastructures of Redistribution

The results on remittances demonstrate that stablecoins have the potential to significantly reduce transaction costs, thereby transforming one of the most vital financial lifelines for households in developing economies. Traditional remittance channels, often reliant on money transfer operators and correspondent banking networks, charge an average global fee of approximately six percent per transaction. By contrast, stablecoin-based transfers consistently approach fee levels closer to one percent, primarily because they circumvent multiple intermediaries and leverage decentralized settlement mechanisms. The scale of this efficiency gain is substantial: shifting even a fraction of global remittance flows into stablecoin rails could return billions of dollars annually to migrant households. These findings reinforce earlier scholarship by Kulkarni et al. (2019) and Jegerson & Mertzanis (2025), both of whom argue that cost reduction is the most immediate and quantifiable benefit of blockchain-based remittances. Beyond the arithmetic of transaction savings, the redistribution of these resources has macroeconomic and developmental implications. In countries where remittances account for more than 10% of GDP, cumulative savings could amount to the scale of national welfare budgets. Redirected into local economies, these resources could strengthen household resilience and stimulate multiplier effects in education, healthcare, and small enterprise growth, thereby amplifying the broader developmental impact of migration. However, these benefits are not automatic, as they remain highly contingent upon three interrelated factors. First, adoption levels: the widespread use of stablecoin-based remittances depends on user trust, financial literacy, and access to digital wallets, without which adoption risks reproducing existing inequalities by privileging digitally connected groups. Second, interoperability with local financial systems: stablecoin rails must integrate seamlessly with banks, mobile money platforms, and regulatory frameworks; otherwise, remittances risk remaining "trapped" in digital form, limiting their utility in cash-based economies. Third, stable value maintenance: the efficiency promise collapses if stablecoins fail to maintain their peg or face liquidity shortages, since price instability or issuer default could erase the very gains remittances are supposed to generate. Taken together, the results underscore that stablecoins hold promise not only as instruments of financial efficiency but also as redistributive infrastructures with profound implications for development and equity. Yet, their transformative capacity depends on scaling responsibly—balancing innovation with safeguards that ensure stability, accessibility, and trust.

5.2 Humanitarian Innovation and the Risk of Dependency

Evidence from humanitarian pilots reinforces the potential of stablecoins to enhance efficiency and transparency in crisis response. As shown in earlier analyses (see Section 2.2), initiatives such as the World Food Programme's Building Blocks project in Jordan, NGO-led Tether distributions in Venezuela, and emergency liquidity transfers in Ukraine demonstrate measurable reductions in administrative costs and fraud risk—up to 98% in some cases. These findings validate the theoretical expectations of reduced intermediation and improved traceability highlighted in the methodological framework. Rather than reiterating case-specific details, this section focuses on synthesizing their broader implications: stablecoin-based systems, when deployed under transparent and cooperative governance structures, can act as infrastructural accelerators of humanitarian efficiency. However, their experimental and pilot-scale nature underscores the need for cautious extrapolation when envisioning adoption at scale.

Yet, while stablecoins can accelerate aid delivery and strengthen accountability through traceable transfers, their deployment also raises significant risks. Chief among them is the danger of deepening dependency on private infrastructures: many stablecoin solutions are issued and governed by private entities whose operational models may not align with humanitarian principles of neutrality and impartiality. Similarly, reliance on digital rails presupposes access to smartphones, internet connectivity, and basic digital literacy—resources often unavailable to the most vulnerable populations, including displaced persons, the elderly, and those in rural or conflict-isolated areas. In such cases, technological acceleration risks reinforcing exclusion rather than alleviating it.

The promise of speed and transparency must therefore be balanced with ethical safeguards. As Ekshian (2025) argues, humanitarian adoption of blockchain and stablecoins should be guided by principles of neutrality, impartiality, and inclusivity to ensure that innovation does not come at the expense of humanitarian legitimacy or equity. Designing governance frameworks that embed rights-based protections, ensure open access where possible, and limit concentration of power among private issuers will be critical to aligning stablecoin infrastructures with humanitarian mandates. In this sense, stablecoins represent not only a technical tool for aid delivery but also a governance challenge—requiring careful coordination between humanitarian organizations, regulators, and technology providers to preserve trust, protect beneficiaries, and secure the public-good dimension of humanitarian assistance.

5.3 Digital Identity: Empowerment or Exclusion?

The overlap between digital identity systems and stablecoin wallets highlights both unprecedented opportunities and significant risks. On the opportunity side, the results suggest that linking stablecoins to self-sovereign or interoperable digital ID frameworks could dramatically expand access to financial services, particularly for populations currently underserved by traditional banking. Such integration would allow individuals to authenticate themselves across borders, access remittance channels, and store value securely without relying on fragile state infrastructures. This vision resonates with Wang & De Filippi's (2020) articulation of *identity-linked digital empowerment*, in which portable and cryptographically verifiable identities serve as a foundation for inclusive participation in digital economies.

However, the exclusion gap highlighted in Figure 3 points to persistent vulnerabilities. Nearly one billion people worldwide still lack any form of legal identification, while many more remain without reliable internet or smartphone access. These individuals risk being excluded from both state-managed identity systems and blockchain-based alternatives, reinforcing cycles of marginalization. Sindhu's (2025) gendered critique is especially pertinent: structural inequalities—such as lower rates of mobile phone ownership among women, or cultural restrictions on formal registration—translate directly into new forms of digital exclusion when identity-linked financial systems are introduced. Stablecoins, far from being neutral infrastructures, may thus reproduce or even exacerbate pre-existing inequalities if adoption strategies are not explicitly inclusive.

Moreover, the convergence of stablecoins and digital IDs raises deep concerns about surveillance and control. Jutel (2021) warns that systems designed to empower users with financial and identity autonomy could be weaponized by states or private actors, shifting from tools of inclusion to instruments of monitoring and discipline. The traceability of blockchain transactions, when combined with identity-linked data, could create infrastructures of financial visibility that undermine privacy and civil liberties. In fragile democracies or authoritarian regimes, such infrastructures risk transforming empowerment into control, where access to financial services becomes contingent on political loyalty or behavioral conformity.

Beyond the individual-level risks of exclusion and surveillance, stablecoin-based digital identity systems also reproduce structural asymmetries of power between actors in the Global North and beneficiaries in the Global South. Most pilot infrastructures—whether humanitarian or financial—are designed, coded, and governed by institutions headquartered in technologically dominant economies. This concentration of control shapes not only the technical architecture but also the flow of value, data, and decision-making authority. As Jutel (2021) and Zwitter et al. (2021) argue, this dynamic reflects forms of "crypto-colonialism," where blockchain-based solutions, under the guise of empowerment, entrench historical dependencies through new digital means. Addressing these asymmetries requires a governance reorientation: fostering regional ownership, open-source standards, and South–South collaboration to ensure that digital infrastructures serve as instruments of emancipation rather than digital subordination.

Taken together, these findings underscore a paradox: the integration of digital ID frameworks with stablecoin infrastructures can enable greater financial inclusion and resilience, but only if accompanied by robust safeguards around governance, equity, and rights protection. Without such safeguards, the promise of empowerment may give way to exclusion and surveillance, undermining the very goals these innovations seek to achieve.

5.4 Governance, Sovereignty, and the Dilemma of Cooperation

The governance matrix confirms the strategic interdependence between regulators and private issuers in shaping the future of stablecoin infrastructures. At one level, cooperative equilibria—in which states facilitate adoption through enabling regulation while issuers commit to transparency and accountability—produce outcomes that are *Pareto-superior*. In such scenarios, regulatory certainty fosters innovation, issuers gain legitimacy, and users benefit from trust and stability. However, the persistence of divergent incentives means that cooperative outcomes cannot be taken for granted.

On the state side, governments may choose to restrict or even ban stablecoins in order to protect monetary sovereignty, safeguard capital controls, or accelerate the development of central bank digital currencies (CBDCs). On the issuer side, private actors have strong motivations to preserve opacity, whether by minimizing disclosure on reserves or concentrating market power to maximize profits. These conflicting incentives generate equilibria where mistrust prevails, fragmenting markets and undermining the potential of stablecoins to operate as global infrastructures.

These dynamics echo the concerns raised by Wen, Li and Zhang (2025) and Agama (2024), who warn that the market concentration of leading stablecoins such as USDT and USDC represents a direct threat to monetary sovereignty in the Global South. In contexts where dollar-denominated stablecoins dominate cross-border transactions, states risk ceding control over monetary policy and payment infrastructures to private corporations headquartered abroad. At the same time, the findings resonate with Owen, Dawson and Walker (2025) and South (2024), who highlight the acute regulatory difficulties in enforcing anti-money laundering (AML) and counter-terrorist financing (CFT) standards across decentralized networks. The absence of harmonized oversight mechanisms allows illicit actors to exploit stablecoin rails, while overregulation risks stifling legitimate financial innovation.

Ultimately, these results suggest that stablecoins can only evolve into public good infrastructures under governance frameworks that balance innovation with accountability. Such frameworks must reconcile the tension between global interoperability and local sovereignty, ensuring that private issuers operate transparently while states avoid excessively restrictive measures that could undermine financial inclusion. Governance, in this sense, is not merely a matter of regulatory compliance but a structural determinant of whether stablecoins remain private instruments of profit or develop into infrastructures that deliver collective benefits.

5.5 Beyond Technology: Conditions for Stablecoins as Public Goods

The discussion suggests that the benefits of stablecoins are neither automatic nor evenly distributed. Their potential to act as public goods depends on at least three conditions:

1. Transparent and diversified issuance to reduce dependency on private actors.
2. Interoperable and inclusive digital identity systems that avoid exclusion.
3. Regulatory cooperation that integrates stablecoins into hybrid financial infrastructures, ensuring AML/CFT compliance without undermining access.

Absent these conditions, stablecoins risk reinforcing inequalities, entrenching dependency, and enabling surveillance. In other words, the technology itself is neutral; it is the governance context that determines whether stablecoins evolve into infrastructures of justice or instruments of control.

VI. CONCLUSION

This article has examined the potential of stablecoins to function as public goods in three critical domains: remittances, humanitarian aid, and digital identity. By combining theoretical models with empirical case studies and visual data analysis, the study highlights both the transformative potential and the systemic risks of stablecoin adoption.

The results on remittances demonstrate that stablecoins can significantly reduce transaction costs, yielding billions of dollars in annual household savings. In humanitarian contexts, blockchain-based aid distribution illustrates how stablecoins can enhance speed, transparency, and accountability, while also exposing new dependencies on private infrastructures and digital access. Digital identity integration emerges as a double-edged sword: while it can broaden financial inclusion, it also risks deepening exclusion and enabling surveillance. Governance analysis further shows that the long-term sustainability of stablecoins as public goods depends on cooperative frameworks between regulators and issuers, diversification of supply, and transparent reserve management.

The findings underscore that technology alone cannot guarantee inclusion or justice. Stablecoins can act as infrastructures of redistribution only under specific governance conditions: (1) transparent and diversified issuance, (2) interoperable and inclusive identity frameworks, and (3) regulatory cooperation balancing AML/CFT compliance with access. Absent these safeguards, stablecoins risk entrenching inequalities, undermining sovereignty, and amplifying surveillance.

This study contributes to ongoing debates by reframing stablecoins not merely as private financial instruments but as contested infrastructures of global public value. However, the analysis is constrained by the limited availability of longitudinal adoption data and the still-nascent nature of pilot projects. Future research should explore stablecoin adoption dynamics at scale, particularly in low-income countries, and examine comparative governance models that balance innovation with accountability.

Ultimately, whether stablecoins evolve into public goods or instruments of private control will depend less on their technological design than on the political choices and institutional frameworks that govern their deployment.

Policy Implications

The findings presented throughout this chapter underscore that realizing the public-good potential of stablecoins requires not only technological innovation but also deliberate institutional design. To this end, several policy implications emerge:

1. Transparent and diversified issuance frameworks. Policymakers should encourage the creation of regional or consortium-based stablecoins backed by verifiable reserves to reduce dependency on a handful of private issuers from the Global North.
2. Inclusive digital infrastructure development. Governments and humanitarian organizations must prioritize equitable access to digital identity systems, mobile connectivity, and financial literacy initiatives, ensuring that the most vulnerable populations are not excluded from blockchain-based services.
3. Ethical and rights-based governance. Regulatory frameworks should integrate human rights, privacy, and data protection principles to prevent surveillance and discrimination in stablecoin and digital ID ecosystems.

4. South–South and multilateral cooperation. Building collaborative research and policy platforms across the Global South can mitigate structural asymmetries and foster technological sovereignty in digital finance experimentation.
5. Hybrid regulatory innovation. A balanced approach that combines AML/CFT compliance with open-access design will be essential to integrate stablecoins responsibly into national financial systems.

These policy dimensions emphasize that stablecoins cannot evolve into inclusive public infrastructures through market forces alone. Coordinated action among regulators, development agencies, and civil society actors is indispensable to ensure that digital financial transformation aligns with social justice, transparency, and sovereignty.

REFERENCES

Agama, D. E. (2024) *Stablecoins and National Security: Implications for Nigeria's Regulatory Landscape. SSRN.* Available at: https://papers.ssrn.com/sol3/papers.cfm?abstract_id=5098084

Ali, A., Butt, M. H., & Senturk, I. (2025) 'Decentralised Finance as a Catalyst for Financial Inclusion: Evidence from Emerging Economies', *Policy Journal of Social Sciences and Research.* Available at: https://policyjssr.com/index.php/PJSSR/article/view/399

Allen, F., & Carletti, E. (2022). Some simple economics of stablecoins. *Annual Review of Financial Economics, 14*(1), 195–214. DOI: 10.1146/annurev-financial-111621-101151

AlOkaily, A. (2024) *Exploring Blockchain Technology for Humanitarian Aid in Conflict Zones: A Syrian Case Study.* Available at: https://peacerep.org/wp-content/uploads/2024/10/Exploring-Blockchain-Technology-for-Humanitarian-Aid-in-Conflict-Zones-DIGITAL.pdf

Boiardi, P., & Stout, E. (2021) *To what extent can blockchain help development co-operation actors meet the 2030 Agenda?* OECD. Available at: https://www.oecd.org/content/dam/oecd/en/publications/reports/2021/05/to-what-extent-can-blockchain-help-development-co-operation-actors-meet-the-2030-agenda_14630965/11857cb5-en.pdf

Cantú, C., Frost, J., & Noone, T. (2025) 'Some Perspectives on the Regulation of Stablecoins', *Law and Contemporary Problems.* Available at: https://scholarship.law.duke.edu/cgi/viewcontent.cgi?article=5161&context=lcp

Demirgüç-Kunt, A., Klapper, L., Singer, D., Ansar, S., & Hess, J. (2018). *The Global Findex Database 2017: Measuring Financial Inclusion and the Fintech Revolution.* World Bank., Available at https://documents1.worldbank.org/curated/en/491271624538346557/pdf/The-Global-Findex-Database-2017-Measuring-Financial-Inclusion-and-Opportunities-to-Expand-Access-to-and-Use-of-Financial-Services.pdf DOI: 10.1596/978-1-4648-1259-0

Ekshian, E. (2025) *Stablecoins and the Future of Remittances.* FGVEurope Research Study. Available at: https://www.fgveurope.de/wp-content/uploads/2025/02/Research-Study-Emily-Ekshian.pdf

Feldstein, S. (2021). *The rise of digital repression: How technology is reshaping power, politics, and resistance*. Oxford University Press., Available at https://books.google.com/books?hl=en&lr=&id=W3QjEAAAQBAJ DOI: 10.1093/oso/9780190057497.001.0001

Gaudreau, D. (2024) *Analyzing Crypto's Potential to Expand Financial Inclusion in EMDEs*. Theseus. Available at: https://www.theseus.fi/handle/10024/872077

Guseva, A., Pistor, K., & Riles, A. (2025). On innovation and the coexistence of stablecoins and central bank digital currencies. *Law and Contemporary Problems, 87*(2), 89–117. https://scholarship.law.duke.edu/lcp/vol87/iss2/5/

Holloway, K., Al Masri, R., & Yahia, A. A. (2021) *Digital identity, biometrics and inclusion in humanitarian responses to refugee crises*. The CALP Network. Available at: https://www.calpnetwork.org/wp-content/uploads/2021/10/Digital_IP_Biometrics_case_study_web.pdf

Horky, N. (2024) *Stablecoins and their implications in emerging markets with gender disparities*. Medium, 17 October. Available at: https://medium.com/@hrknsinst/stablecoins-and-their-implications-in-emerging-markets-with-gender-disparities-8cbf2ecce50e

Howson, P. (2021). Crypto-giving and surveillance philanthropy: Exploring the trade-offs in blockchain innovation for nonprofits. *Nonprofit Management & Leadership, 32*(4), 509–530. DOI: 10.1002/nml.21452

Idris, I. (2024) *Humanitarian Digital Transfers in Challenging Contexts*. Institute of Development Studies. Available at: https://opendocs.ids.ac.uk/articles/report/Humanitarian_Digital_Transfers_in_Challenging_Contexts/26379823

Jegerson, D., & Mertzanis, C. (2025) 'Deciphering the role of cryptocurrencies in global remittances: a comprehensive literature review', *Journal of Money Laundering Control*. Emerald Insight. Available at: https://www.emerald.com/insight/content/doi/10.1108/msar-12-2023-0061/full/html

Jutel, O. (2021). Blockchain humanitarianism and crypto-colonialism. *Patterns (New York, N.Y.), 2*(12), 100422. DOI: 10.1016/j.patter.2021.100422 PMID: 35079720

Kılıç, M. A., & Bodur, M. Y. (2024) 'Between empowerment and surveillance: Forced migration and information and communication technologies', *DergiPark*. Available at: https://dergipark.org.tr/en/download/article-file/3526318

Korkmaz, E. E. (2023). *Digital Identity and Surveillance Capitalism*. Bristol University Press., Available at https://bristoluniversitypressdigital.com/monochap/book/9781529233520/ch004.xml

Kulkarni, R., Schintler, L., Koizumi, N., & Olds, J. (2019) *Cryptocurrency, Stablecoins and Blockchain: Exploring digital money solutions for remittances and inclusive economies. SSRN.* Available at: https://papers.ssrn.com/sol3/papers.cfm?abstract_id=3524988 DOI: 10.2139/ssrn.3511139

Laatikainen, G., Kolehmainen, T., & Abrahamsson, P. (2021). Self-sovereign identity ecosystems: Benefits and challenges. *Information and Organization, 31*(2), 105–117. https://jyx.jyu.fi/bitstreams/8d5377a9-ab2c-45a9-a5de-e9d8324bc545/download

Laatikainen, G., Kolehmainen, T., Li, M., & Hautala, M. (2021) *Towards a trustful digital world: exploring self-sovereign identity ecosystems.* arXiv. Available at: https://arxiv.org/pdf/2105.15131

Mannan, M. (2024) 'From Digital Humanitarianism to Crypto-Humanitarianism', *International Trade and Business Law Annual*, 24. Available at: https://heinonline.org/hol-cgi-bin/get_pdf.cgi?handle=hein.journals/itbla24&section=11

Mathews, R. (2017). Interrogating "privacy" in a world brimming with high political entanglements, surveillance, interdependence & interconnections. *Health and Technology*, *7*(4), 373–381. https://link.springer.com/article/10.1007/s12553-017-0211-5. DOI: 10.1007/s12553-017-0211-5

Owen, A., Dawson, G., & Walker, J. (2025) *The Role of Stablecoins in Money Laundering and Financial Crime*. ResearchGate. Available at: https://www.researchgate.net/profile/Antony-Owen/publication/394787347_The_Role_of_Stablecoins_in_Money_Laundering_and_Financial_Crime/links/68a649ef7984e374acea2dd0/The-Role-of-Stablecoins-in-Money-Laundering-and-Financial-Crime.pdf

Pocher, N. (2025). AML/CFT and Crypto-Assets: EU Law and Global Standards. In *Crypto-Asset Ecosystems and the EU Anti-Money Laundering Framework.* Springer., Available at https://link.springer.com/chapter/10.1007/978-3-031-94698-1_5 DOI: 10.1007/978-3-031-94698-1_5

Reuters (2025) *Keeping crypto clean: Risk-based controls for stablecoins.* Reuters Legal Industry News, 24 June. Available at: https://www.reuters.com/legal/legalindustry/keeping-crypto-clean-risk-based-controls-stablecoins-2025-06-24

Sindhu, S. (2025) *Blockchain-Enabled Decentralized Identity and Finance: Advancing Women's Socioeconomic Empowerment in Developing Economies. Journal of Women in Information Technology and Engineering*. Available at: https://aasrresearch.com/index.php/jwite/article/view/5

South, S. N. (2024) *Towards a Stablecoin Regulatory Framework in India*. Esya Centre. Available at: https://www.esyacentre.org/s/Esya-Centre-Report-045-Towards-a-Stablecoin-Regulatory-Framework-in-India.pdf

United Nations Office for the Coordination of Humanitarian Affairs (UNOCHA). (2024) *Global Humanitarian Overview 2024*. Geneva: UNOCHA. Available at: https://www.unocha.org/publications/report/world/global-humanitarian-overview-2024-enarfres

Vasselin, F. (2024) *Blockchain for Migrants: Promoting Self-Sovereign Identity and Financial Inclusion*. HAL Open Science. Available at: https://hal.science/hal-04815373/.

Wang, F., & De Filippi, P. (2020). Self-sovereign identity in a globalized world: Credentials-based identity systems as a driver for economic inclusion. *Frontiers in Blockchain*, *3*(28), 28. https://www.frontiersin.org/journals/blockchain/articles/10.3389/fbloc.2019.00028/full. DOI: 10.3389/fbloc.2019.00028

Wen, H., Li, S., & Zhang, J. (2025) *Hybrid Monetary Ecosystems: Integrating Stablecoins and Fiat in the Future of Currency Systems*. arXiv. doi: /arXiv.2505.10997. Available at: https://arxiv.org/abs/2505.10997DOI: 10.48550

World Bank. (2018) *ID4D Annual Report 2018*. Washington, DC: World Bank. Available at: https://id4d.worldbank.org/sites/id4d.worldbank.org/files/2018_ID4D_Annual_Report.pdf

World Bank. (2023) *Migration and remittances: Overview*. Washington, DC: World Bank. Available at: https://www.worldbank.org/en/topic/migration/overview

World Food Programme (WFP) Innovation. (2025) *Building Blocks Project*. Rome: WFP. Available at: https://innovation.wfp.org/project/building-blocks

Zwitter, A., Boisse-Despiaux, M., Karpouzoglou, T., & Rabé, J. (2021). Blockchain humanitarianism and crypto-colonialism. *Patterns (New York, N.Y.)*, *2*(12), 100385. https://www.cell.com/patterns/pdf/S2666-3899%2821%2900305-6.pdf

Chapter 6
Designing Trust in Digital Money:
Interdisciplinary Approaches to Stablecoin Governance

David López Jiménez
https://orcid.org/0000-0002-7013-9556
Universidad de Sevilla, Spain

Eduardo Carlos Dittmar
https://orcid.org/0000-0002-8087-2444
Universidad Rey Juan Carlos, Spain

Jenny Patricia Vargas Portillo
https://orcid.org/0000-0002-0226-3053
Universidad de Sevilla, Spain

ABSTRACT

Stablecoins have emerged as a transformative yet controversial development in digital finance, promising stability while posing novel regulatory and systemic risks. Their growing role in payments, decentralized finance, and remittances raises questions about monetary sovereignty, consumer protection, and financial integrity. This chapter examines the governance of stablecoins through comparative and interdisciplinary perspectives, focusing on the evolving relationship between self-regulation, soft law, and hard law. Special attention is given to the Commonwealth Model Law on Stablecoins (2025), which provides a harmonised legislative framework designed to balance innovation with financial stability and inclusion. By comparing this model law with international approaches such as the EU's Markets in Crypto-Assets

DOI: 10.4018/979-8-3373-9043-7.ch006

Regulation (MiCA) and voluntary standards from global standard-setting bodies, the chapter highlights how model laws can bridge the gap between flexibility and enforceability in the governance of digital money.

INTRODUCTION

The rise of stablecoins represents one of the most striking paradoxes in modern finance: digital assets designed to deliver stability through technology that was originally built to challenge state-backed money. Stablecoins promise to mitigate the volatility of cryptocurrencies, facilitating digital payments and financial inclusion, yet they have also exposed weaknesses in financial oversight, reserve management, and legal classification. As the failures of projects such as TerraUSD have shown, trust and transparency-not algorithms alone-determine whether stablecoins can function as credible components of the financial system.

Globally, regulators are struggling to define coherent approaches to these hybrid instruments that blur the boundaries between currencies, commodities, and securities. While initiatives such as the EU's Markets in Crypto-Assets Regulation (MiCA, 2023) and industry-led principles by the Global Digital Finance (GDF) group offer partial responses, they reveal persistent gaps between voluntary guidance and enforceable legal frameworks. To address this, the Commonwealth Secretariat has introduced the Commonwealth Model Law on Stablecoins (2025), a legislative template enabling member states-particularly developing economies-to implement robust, interoperable, and technology-neutral regulation.

This chapter explores how such model laws can operationalise global standards while respecting national sovereignty. It compares the Commonwealth Model Law with other regulatory approaches to argue that model legislation offers a practical bridge between soft law flexibility and hard law enforceability. By examining this through interdisciplinary lenses-law, economics, and technology-it contributes to the broader debate on how trust can be institutionally designed into digital money systems.

THE RISE OF STABLECOINS IN THE WORLDWIDE FINANCIAL ECOSYSTEM

From Cryptocurrencies to Stable Digital Assets

The emergence of stablecoins marks a decisive step in the evolution of digital assets. Early cryptocurrencies such as Bitcoin and Ethereum were designed to operate independently of states and financial intermediaries, but their volatility prevented them from serving as reliable means of payment or stores of value. In response, innovators introduced stablecoins-digital tokens designed to maintain a stable price, usually by linking their value to fiat currencies or other assets.

Stablecoins generally fall into three categories: fiat-backed, crypto-collateralised, and algorithmic. Fiat-backed tokens such as USD Coin (USDC) or Tether (USDT) promise one-to-one redemption with underlying reserves; crypto-collateralised tokens like DAI rely on excess digital collateral; and algorithmic models attempt to stabilise prices through automated supply adjustments. Although differing in design, all share a common goal-to make digital value behave like traditional money while retaining the efficiency and programmability of blockchain systems.

Their rapid growth has turned stablecoins from niche crypto instruments into critical infrastructure for digital transactions. By 2024, they represented hundreds of billions of dollars in circulation, underpinning both centralized payment platforms and decentralized finance. This transformation has intensified the need for robust governance frameworks capable of addressing their legal, economic, and technological complexities.

As stablecoins evolved from experiments in digital currency to foundational elements of global finance, their regulation became an urgent priority. The next sections therefore shift from technical foundations to the question of governance - how different jurisdictions, and particularly the Commonwealth, are designing trust through law.

Use Cases: Payments, Remittances, and DeFi

Stablecoins today serve diverse functions across the financial ecosystem. In retail and cross-border payments, they enable faster and cheaper transfers compared with traditional banking channels. For remittances, they offer a lifeline to workers sending funds across borders, often at a fraction of conventional costs. In decentralized finance (DeFi), stablecoins operate as the unit of account that sustains lending, trading, and liquidity protocols.

These use cases demonstrate both the potential and the risks of stablecoins. Their efficiency and accessibility can support financial inclusion, particularly in regions with underdeveloped banking infrastructure. Yet, their borderless nature and partial anonymity also create opportunities for regulatory evasion, money laundering, and illicit financial flows. Moreover, heavy reliance on privately issued tokens can threaten monetary sovereignty in emerging markets, where dollar-linked stablecoins may displace local currencies.

These practical applications highlight why stablecoins now sit at the intersection of finance, technology, and regulation. Their growing role has prompted policymakers to design comprehensive frameworks - most notably the Commonwealth Model Law on Stablecoins (2025)-to ensure that innovation proceeds within clear boundaries of trust and accountability.

Emerging Risks: Volatility, Trust, and Exposure

Although stablecoins seek to eliminate the price swings of traditional cryptocurrencies, they introduce new forms of vulnerability. Their apparent stability depends not on technology alone but on credible governance-transparent reserve management, sound legal rights for users, and effective oversight of issuers. When these safeguards are weak, confidence can evaporate quickly, as shown by the collapse of TerraUSD in 2022.

Legal uncertainty remains another major challenge. Many stablecoin users lack enforceable redemption rights or clarity on whether tokens constitute securities, e-money, or a new asset class. This ambiguity allows issuers to exploit gaps between jurisdictions, creating regulatory arbitrage and undermining consumer protection.

At a systemic level, the expansion of stablecoins can expose financial markets to liquidity and contagion risks. If issuers hold large quantities of short-term debt or commercial paper to back their reserves, sudden redemption runs could transmit shocks to traditional money markets. In developing economies, widespread adoption of dollar-pegged stablecoins can intensify dollarisation, limiting domestic monetary control.

Finally, the anonymity and programmability of stablecoins raise concerns about their potential use in illicit finance, including money laundering, terrorist financing, and sanctions evasion. Without binding regulation and international cooperation, these risks could undermine the very stability that stablecoins promise.

These vulnerabilities underline a central lesson: stability in stablecoins is not inherent-it must be legally and institutionally constructed. Voluntary principles and self-regulation have proved inadequate to ensure transparency or accountability. Consequently, policymakers are turning toward binding, harmonised frameworks-exemplified by the Commonwealth Model Law on Stablecoins (2025)-which seek to embed trust, financial integrity, and systemic stability directly into law (Franceschi et al., 2025).

REGULATORY APPROACHES AND THE GLOBAL SEARCH FOR FRAMEWORKS

The vulnerabilities and systemic exposures outlined above have accelerated the global search for effective regulatory responses to stablecoins. Policymakers now face the challenge of designing rules that preserve innovation while ensuring financial stability and consumer protection. As a result, several distinct governance models have emerged-ranging from industry-led soft law and voluntary standards, to comprehensive legislative regimes such as the EU's MiCA Regulation, and most recently, the Commonwealth Model Law on Stablecoins (2025). This section examines these evolving approaches, underlining how they differ in scope, enforceability, and international coordination.

Soft Law and Self-Regulation: Industry Codes and Principles

The regulation of stablecoins has not evolved exclusively through statutory law or formal binding mechanisms. Instead, a significant part of the early governance of this phenomenon came up in the form of soft law instruments and self-regulatory codes developed by industry groups, consortia, and transnational organizations. Soft law is particularly relevant in areas where technological innovation outpaces the ability of legislators to design complete legal responses. By providing voluntary guidelines, codes of conduct, and best practice frameworks, these instruments seek to fill the regulatory vacuum while fostering trust among users, developers, and regulators.

One of the earliest and most cited examples in this field is the set of Principles for Stablecoin Issuers published by GDF in 2019. These principles sought to establish a common baseline of transparency, reserve management, and governance for stablecoin projects at a time when regulators were only beginning to recognize the potential risks associated with digital assets (GDF, 2019). The GDF code emphasized the importance of disclosing information about reserve assets, redemption mechanisms, and audit procedures, aiming to build confidence among both retail and institutional users. While entirely voluntary, the framework provided a reference point for evaluating the seriousness of different projects and was, in many ways, an attempt by the industry to demonstrate its capacity for self-regulation before stricter governmental intervention became inevitable.

Other industry-led initiatives have followed similar logics. The International Organization of Securities Commissions (IOSCO), although not producing binding law, issued several reports analyzing how stablecoins might fall within the perimeter of securities regulation (IOSCO, 2020). These documents do not create enforceable obligations but guide national regulators in interpreting their own frameworks in light of new technological realities. Similarly, the FSB has provided recommendations on global stablecoins, urging jurisdictions to develop proportionate and risk-based approaches (FSB, 2020). Such recommendations are not binding but exert a normative influence: financial authorities take them into account to correspond their policies with international expectations, thereby avoiding regulatory fragmentation.

From an analytical perspective, these soft law instruments perform three key functions. First, they reduce uncertainty by signaling how market participants should behave in order to gain legitimacy. Second, they foster a minimum degree of worldwide convergence in a field where full harmonization is elusive. And third, they offer regulators a testing ground to evaluate the effectiveness of different practices without imposing immediate legal obligations. Scholars have pointed out that this combination of flexibility and persuasion is typical of transnational private regulation in finance, where industry groups often seek to preempt harsher state intervention by proving their own capacity to enforce norms (Zetzsche et al., 2021).

Yet the limits of self-regulation are evident. Stablecoin projects such as TerraUSD, which collapsed dramatically in 2022, demonstrated that voluntary principles alone are insufficient to prevent failures. In practice, many issuers selectively adopt best practices, while others disregard them altogether. Unlike statutory law, soft law lacks binding enforcement mechanisms, meaning that compliance depends largely on reputational incentives. While these incentives can be strong in highly scrutinized markets, they may prove ineffective in jurisdictions with weaker oversight or in projects that target less sophisticated investors.

Despite these shortcomings, soft law continues to play a vital role in shaping the regulatory environment of stablecoins. It provides a foundation upon which statutory frameworks can later be built and offers regulators a repertoire of concepts and techniques that can be incorporated into formal law. For instance, the stress on transparency and reserve audits in the GDF Principles was later echoed in legislative initiatives such as MiCA and in proposals by the U.S. President's Working Group on Financial Markets. This cross-pollination between voluntary codes and binding law illustrates the interaction between private ordering and public regulation in the governance of digital assets.

In this sense, self-regulation and soft law should not be seen as substitutes for statutory frameworks but as complementary mechanisms. They operate in the regulatory interstices where law is still in formation, providing guidance and structure to markets that would otherwise mature in a vacuum. As the global community moves toward more entire and coordinated approaches, these early instruments remain relevant for their normative content and for their role in demonstrating the possibilities and limitations of self-regulation in a fast-evolving technological landscape.

Regional Strategies: EU, US, and Asia-Pacific Contrasts

The regulatory landscape for stablecoins is marked by profound regional divergences that reflect distinct legal traditions, market priorities, and political economies. While the European Union has opted for a complete and codified approach through MiCA, the United States continues to rely on a fragmented and sectoral framework rooted in its legacy financial infrastructure. By contrast, jurisdictions in the Asia-Pacific region have adopted pragmatic, often experimental, strategies that balance innovation with financial stability, thereby offering valuable lessons for emerging economies.

In Europe, MiCA represents the most ambitious attempt so far to bring stablecoins under a unified legal umbrella. Adopted in 2023, this regulation introduces clear requirements for reserve management, transparency, and consumer protection, establishing a licensing regime for issuers of "asset-referenced tokens" and "e-money tokens." Crucially, MiCA situates stablecoins within the broader logic of financial market regulation, aligning them with the EU's emphasis on harmonization and risk prevention. The regulation reflects the EU's traditional preference for codification and legal certainty, as well as its geopolitical ambition to shape GDF standards. Its extraterritorial impact is already visible: issuers seeking access to the European market must adapt their operations to MiCA's stringent provisions, thereby extending the EU's normative influence beyond its borders.

The United States has followed a very different trajectory. Rather than creating a single federal statute, regulatory oversight is dispersed across agencies such as the Securities and Exchange Commission (SEC), the Commodity Futures Trading Commission (CFTC), and the Office of the Comptroller of the Currency (OCC). This overlapping jurisdiction has generated uncertainty for stablecoin issuers, many of whom face the risk of being categorized simultaneously as securities, commodities, or banking products. The President's Working Group on Financial Markets, together with the Federal Deposit Insurance Corporation (FDIC) and the OCC, published a seminal report in 2021 stressing the need for stablecoin issuers to operate within insured depository institutions. Yet, progress towards federal legislation has stalled amid partisan divisions, leaving state-level initiatives, such as New York's BitLicense regime, as key regulatory anchors. This patchwork reflects both the dynamism and the unpredictability of U.S. financial regulation, where enforcement actions often substitute for comprehensive rulemaking.

Asia-Pacific jurisdictions present an equally diverse but often more experimental panorama. Japan stands out as the first major economy to enact binding legislation specifically targeting stablecoins, with amendments to its Payment Services Act coming into force in 2023. Under this framework, only licensed banks, trust companies, and registered money transfer agents can issue stablecoins, and issuers must back tokens with legal tender. This model prioritizes consumer safety and financial stability while granting stablecoins a legitimate role in Japan's payments ecosystem. Singapore has taken a different path, benefiting from its Payment Services Act and subsequent amendments to build a flexible licensing system that accommodates innovation while maintaining strong anti-money laundering and counter-terrorism financing standards. In doing so, Singapore has positioned itself as a hub for digital finance experimentation in Asia.

China, by contrast, has opted to ban private stablecoins altogether, channeling innovation into its central bank digital currency, the digital yuan. This decision underscores a strategic choice: instead of competing with privately issued digital money, China seeks to monopolize the future of digital payments through a state-led model. Other jurisdictions in Asia, such as South Korea and Hong Kong, have adopted intermediate strategies, allowing stablecoin experimentation within regulatory sandboxes while maintaining close supervisory scrutiny (Zetzsche et al., 2020).

When viewed together, these regional approaches reveal the tensions inherent in regulating an innovation that transcends borders. Europe's codification provides certainty but may constrain flexibility. The United States' fragmented oversight fosters innovation but creates ambiguity. Asia's pragmatic strategies demonstrate how jurisdictions can experiment with different balances between innovation and control, often being consistent with their broader monetary and geopolitical strategies. For emerging economies in Africa and Latin America, these models offer diverse pathways: from adopting EU-style harmonized frameworks to experimenting with flexible sandbox regimes that prioritize financial inclusion.

Ultimately, the worldwide regulatory mosaic for stablecoins is unlikely to converge on a single model. Instead, regional strategies will continue to progress in dialogue with each other, influenced by cross-border coordination through bodies such as the FSB and the International Monetary Fund (IMF). The interplay between these regional trajectories underscores the importance of comparative perspectives in understanding how stablecoins are reshaping the financial ecosystem and why international cooperation remains indispensable. Table 1 provides a comparative overview of regulatory approaches to stablecoins across key jurisdictions.

Table 1. Comparative overview of regulatory approaches

Jurisdiction	Licensing requirements	Reserve rules	Redemption rights	Extraterritorial scope
EU (MiCA)	Authorisation as ART/EMT issuer	High-quality liquid assets, segregated custody	Legal right to redeem at par	Applies to issuers offering in the single market
US	Fragmented: state licensing + proposed federal oversight	Proposal for bank-level reserves	Varies by state/federal regime	Issuers with US customers must comply
Japan	Registration with FSA as issuer	Yen reserves held in banks	Immediate redemption in yen	Applies to issuers offering in Japan
Singapore	Licence as "major payment institution"	High-quality liquid assets	Immediate redemption mechanisms	Strict on cross-border activities
China	Ban on private stablecoins; promotion of e-CNY	Not applicable	Not applicable	External issuers restricted

Source: Authors

The Limits of Soft Law and the Push Toward Binding Frameworks

While soft law and self-regulation have played a vital role in shaping the early governance of stablecoins, their limitations have become increasingly evident as the sector has matured and its relevance has grown. Voluntary codes of conduct, industry principles, and international recommendations provide guidance and legitimacy, but they lack the enforcement mechanisms necessary to ensure consistent compliance. The dramatic collapse of TerraUSD in 2022, which wiped out billions of dollars in market value and destabilized the wider crypto ecosystem, offered a stark reminder that reputational incentives alone cannot safeguard financial stability.

The weakness of soft law lies in its non-binding nature and in its reliance on uneven implementation. Some projects, particularly those with global ambitions or institutional backers, adopt best practices in transparency and auditing to gain legitimacy. Others exploit regulatory arbitrage, locating their operations in jurisdictions with minimal oversight while marketing their tokens globally. This uneven playing field undermines the credibility of self-regulation and erodes trust among users, who cannot reliably distinguish between responsible and opportunistic issuers. As Zetzsche et al. (2020) have noted, voluntary norms in digital finance often serve as transitional instruments, valuable in the short term but ultimately insufficient to address risks.

The limits of soft law have prompted international organizations and national regulators to push for binding frameworks. The FSB (2020) has explicitly warned that global stablecoin arrangements could threaten monetary sovereignty and financial stability if left unchecked. Similarly, the IMF (2021) has underlined the potential spillover effects of stablecoins on emerging markets, where dollar-linked tokens could accelerate unofficial dollarization. These concerns underscore why policymakers increasingly view binding regulation not as an obstacle to innovation but as a prerequisite for sustainable market expansion.

MiCA illustrates this shift from voluntary to binding law. Many of MiCA's provisions echo earlier industry principles, particularly those of GDF, but the regulation transforms them into enforceable obligations backed by supervisory authorities. Transparency about reserve assets, governance structures, and redemption mechanisms is no longer a matter of best practice but of legal compliance, with sanctions for non-adherence. This evolution demonstrates how soft law can act as a laboratory for ideas that later crystallize into statutory frameworks.

In the United States, the same logic has fueled ongoing debates in Congress about whether stablecoin issuers should be required to operate as insured depository institutions. While federal legislation remains elusive, the insistence on bank-like safeguards reflects a recognition that voluntary adherence to prudential standards is inadequate. Even in jurisdictions with strong industry-led frameworks, such as Singapore, regulators have moved toward embedding key soft law principles into statutory requirements.

This worldwide trend highlights an important theoretical point: soft law is most effective when it operates in tandem with hard law, not in isolation. In the case of stablecoins, self-regulatory codes have been instrumental in building early market discipline, shaping discourse, and guiding regulatory imagination. Yet their inability to prevent crises has accelerated the demand for formal legal frameworks. The transition reflects a broader pattern in financial regulation: innovation initially governed by norms of flexibility and persuasion eventually demands codification as risks become more apparent.

Ultimately, the limits of soft law do not invalidate its relevance but rather redefine its role. Instead of being the final stage of regulation, it serves as a bridge between market experimentation and legal formalization. Stablecoin governance thus exemplifies the dialectic between voluntary principles and binding law, where each stage draws upon and reshapes the other. As worldwide coordination efforts intensify, this dialectic is likely to remain a defining feature of the evolving regulatory architecture.

The movement from voluntary standards toward binding frameworks has recently taken a new form within the Commonwealth context. In 2025, the Commonwealth Secretariat introduced the Commonwealth Model Law on Stablecoins, a legislative blueprint that translates international best practices into adaptable, enforceable provisions. Unlike soft-law instruments or industry codes, this model law is designed for direct adoption by member states, combining the legitimacy of formal legislation with the flexibility of principle-based drafting. The following section examines its structure, objectives, and potential to harmonise stablecoin regulation across diverse jurisdictions.

The Commonwealth Model Law on Stablecoins: A Harmonised Framework for Digital Trust

The Commonwealth Model Law on Stablecoins, adopted in 2025, represents one of the most ambitious attempts to create a harmonised yet flexible legal framework for the governance of digital money. Developed by the Commonwealth Secretariat as an extension of the 2022 Model Law on Virtual Assets, it seeks to provide member states with a legislative template that translates global principles into enforceable domestic provisions. The Model Law responds to a growing consensus that voluntary standards and fragmented national rules are inadequate to address the cross-border nature and systemic relevance of stablecoins. Its stated purpose is to promote trust, transparency and financial integrity while enabling innovation and financial inclusion throughout the Commonwealth.

The background to the Model Law is the recognition that stablecoins have become essential infrastructure for digital transactions but remain subject to inconsistent regulation. Many jurisdictions, particularly in the developing world, face the dual challenge of facilitating digital transformation while safeguarding consumers and monetary sovereignty. The Commonwealth Secretariat therefore aimed to design an instrument that would both harmonise key regulatory principles and respect the sovereignty of member states. The Model Law draws heavily on international standards developed by the Financial Action Task Force, the International Organization of Securities Commissions and the Financial Stability Board, but converts their broad recommendations into specific legal obligations. Its methodology rests on three guiding ideas: harmonisation, flexibility and enforceability. Harmonisation provides a common baseline for member states; flexibility allows local adaptation; and enforceability ensures that principles become binding law once enacted nationally.

The structure of the Model Law reflects this philosophy. It begins with broad definitions and interpretative principles intended to ensure technological neutrality and future adaptability. It then establishes a comprehensive licensing regime for stablecoin issuers and service providers. The law distinguishes between small-scale issuers and those whose activities are systemically significant, applying a proportional approach to authorisation and supervision. Larger issuers are required to meet stricter prudential standards, maintain minimum capital, and demonstrate effective governance and risk management arrangements. This tiered model recognises the diversity of the Commonwealth's financial systems while ensuring that oversight increases with potential impact.

A central element of the framework is the regulation of reserves and transparency obligations. The Model Law requires all issuers to maintain High-Quality Liquid Assets equivalent to the value of stablecoins in circulation, to hold those assets in segregated accounts with regulated custodians, and to submit to regular independent audits. Issuers must publish clear and verifiable disclosures of the composition and valuation of their reserves. These provisions aim to prevent the opacity and under-collateralisation that have undermined confidence in several global stablecoin projects. By linking legal authorisation to continuous disclosure and auditing, the Model Law seeks to institutionalise transparency as a condition for trust.

Financial integrity and consumer protection constitute two further pillars of the legislation. The Model Law integrates anti-money-laundering and counter-terrorism-financing requirements in line with FATF Recommendations 15 and 16. Issuers and service providers must perform customer due diligence, monitor transactions and report suspicious activities. They are also required to implement risk-based compliance programmes and cooperate with domestic and international authorities. On the consumer side, the law establishes the right of redemption at par value, mandating that users be able to convert stablecoins into fiat currency on demand. It also requires clear contractual terms, complaint procedures and redress mechanisms to strengthen market confidence.

Supervision and enforcement mechanisms give practical effect to these obligations. Competent authorities are empowered to issue, suspend or revoke licences, conduct inspections and impose administrative sanctions for breaches. The Model Law also envisages cross-border cooperation among Commonwealth regulators, encouraging information sharing and mutual recognition of supervisory decisions. This approach reflects the increasingly international character of stablecoin activity and the need for coordinated oversight to prevent regulatory arbitrage. The inclusion of interoperability provisions further supports cross-jurisdictional consistency and integration within the Commonwealth digital economy.

The design of the Commonwealth Model Law is notable for its principle-based rather than prescriptive character. Instead of imposing a uniform regulatory template, it articulates broad standards-proportionality, technology neutrality and risk sensitivity-that can be implemented according to national circumstances. Once a member state adopts the Model Law, however, its provisions acquire full legal force within that jurisdiction. This hybrid structure allows it to operate as a bridge between soft coordination and hard harmonisation. It moves beyond voluntary codes, which rely on reputational compliance, without replicating the rigidity of highly centralised regimes such as the European Union's Markets in Crypto-Assets Regulation. In doing so, it introduces a middle path for transnational financial governance: adaptable yet enforceable.

Compared with other global approaches, the Commonwealth Model Law demonstrates a distinctive balance of scope and flexibility. Regional initiatives such as MiCA provide comprehensive but geographically limited regulation; industry codes such as the Global Digital Finance Principles promote ethical conduct but lack legal enforceability. The Model Law integrates the strengths of both approaches. It provides legislative clarity, but its modular drafting allows for incremental adoption by jurisdictions with differing institutional capacities. In this respect it serves as both a template for immediate implementation and a reference model for future convergence between national regimes.

An important contribution of the Model Law lies in its treatment of illicit finance and high-risk instruments. Recognising the lessons of algorithmic stablecoin failures, it subjects such projects to enhanced prudential and disclosure requirements. The explicit incorporation of AML/CFT obligations ensures that financial integrity is built into the regulatory framework rather than added as an afterthought. This feature is particularly significant for smaller Commonwealth members, where limited supervisory resources make clear statutory duties essential for enforcement.

Beyond its technical content, the Model Law carries broader implications for global governance. It illustrates how model legislation can operationalise international norms while maintaining domestic autonomy. By providing ready-to-adopt text, it reduces the cost and complexity of legislative development and promotes interoperability among diverse legal systems. The law's stress on proportionality and cooperation also reflects an effort to align financial regulation with the developmental priorities of the Commonwealth, including inclusion, innovation and sustainable growth.

In essence, the Commonwealth Model Law on Stablecoins demonstrates that stability in digital money depends on reserves and algorithms and on credible legal and institutional design. It shows that trust can be engineered through law as effectively as through code. By embedding transparency, accountability and financial integrity into a coherent regulatory framework, the Model Law offers a pragmatic pathway toward safer and more inclusive digital finance. It stands as an example of how transnational collaboration can convert global standards into actionable national regulation and thus represents a significant milestone in the evolving architecture of digital monetary governance.

THE EMERGENCE OF MODEL LAW APPROACHES

Objectives, Scope, and Guiding Principles

The idea of a model law in the field of financial innovation arises from the need to respond to the rapid, borderless expansion of digital assets, particularly stablecoins. Unlike national statutes, which are bound to local legal traditions and domestic political negotiations, a model law operates as a flexible template. Its objective is not to impose uniformity but to provide countries with a coherent structure that can be adapted to their regulatory systems while maintaining a degree of global consistency (Buckley et al., 2020). In the specific case of stablecoins, this approach has become increasingly relevant as these instruments circulate across jurisdictions, creating potential regulatory arbitrage if left uncoordinated.

The scope of such an initiative reflects the multiple layers of the stablecoin phenomenon. On one level, it addresses the purely financial dimension: the issuance, backing, and redemption of tokens that claim to preserve a stable value. On another, it encompasses the technological underpinnings-blockchain architecture, smart contracts, and custody mechanisms-that determine how these assets function in practice. Beyond these technical elements, the scope also extends to social implications, including financial stability, consumer protection, market integrity, and the prevention of criminal misuse. By articulating these layers together, a model law aims to avoid the fragmented treatment that has characterized much of the early regulatory experimentation.

The guiding principles of a model law for stablecoins are typically grounded in proportionality, risk sensitivity and flexibility. Proportionality ensures that regulatory burdens are commensurate with the risks posed by different types of issuers and tokens. For instance, a consortium managing a multi-billion-dollar stablecoin should not face the same requirements as a start-up testing a limited-scope payment token. Risk sensitivity reflects the recognition that not all stablecoins are equal: fiat-backed tokens, algorithmic models, and crypto-collateralized variants present distinct vulnerabilities and require differentiated oversight (Zetzsche et al., 2021). Flexibility, meanwhile, acknowledges the fast pace of technological innovation. Regulations that are overly prescriptive risk becoming obsolete; a model law must therefore be drafted in a technology-neutral way that can endure future developments.

Underlying these principles is the recognition that stablecoins straddle both public and private spheres. Their potential for financial inclusion, cheaper cross-border payments, and efficiency in settlement systems makes them attractive from a policy perspective. At the same time, their capacity to destabilize monetary policy or undermine traditional banking structures demands caution (Gorton & Zhang, 2023). The challenge for a model law is to reconcile these opposing forces: enabling innovation while ensuring that such innovation does not compromise the resilience of the financial system.

Equally important is the integration of safeguards for users. Stablecoins are often marketed to unbanked or underbanked populations as tools of empowerment. Yet without clear redemption rights, reserve audits, or transparent governance, users may face risks that are opaque and severe. Principles of fairness, transparency, and accountability thus permeate the model law framework. These strengthen consumer trust and help level the playing field between private issuers and state-backed digital initiatives such as central bank digital currencies (CBDCs).

Finally, the global orientation of a model law reflects an ambition to build bridges across jurisdictions. Stablecoins cannot be effectively regulated through purely national approaches, given their transnational circulation. A model law signals the possibility of harmonization without imposing a one-size-fits-all regime. By aligning key concepts-such as definitions, licensing tiers, reserve requirements, and supervisory powers-it provides a common grammar through which regulators, policymakers, and industry actors can communicate. This cooperative foundation is essential if stablecoins are to mature from fragmented experiments into reliable instruments embedded within the worldwide financial architecture.

Comparative Lessons From Other Model Laws

The model law as a regulatory technique has a long pedigree in international economic governance. Its strength lies in the balance between standardization and flexibility: it offers countries a well-structured draft while allowing adaptation to diverse legal systems. One of the most frequently cited precedents is the United Nations Commission on International Trade Law (UNCITRAL) Model Law on International Commercial Arbitration (1985, amended in 2006), which has been adopted in over one hundred jurisdictions. The success of this instrument demonstrates that when carefully designed, a model law can provide certainty to global actors while respecting domestic particularities (UNCITRAL, 2017). This is particularly relevant to stablecoins, where cross-border consistency is indispensable, yet national sovereignty over monetary and financial matters must be preserved.

Another instructive case is the UNCITRAL Model Law on Electronic Commerce (1996) and its subsequent expansion into electronic signatures. These instruments paved the way for the legal recognition of digital transactions, building trust in an area where technological innovation had outpaced traditional legislation (Schmitz, 2019). By articulating principles of functional equivalence and non-discrimination between paper-based and digital processes, the law enabled interoperability and commercial certainty. The stablecoin debate resembles this challenge: states must recognize new digital instruments without undermining their financial order.

Comparisons can also be drawn with the Basel Core Principles for Effective Banking Supervision, while not a model law in the strict sense, they function as soft law benchmarks guiding domestic regulatory reforms. Their widespread influence demonstrates how globally accepted standards can shape national frameworks and promote convergence. For stablecoins, similar benchmarks-whether on capital adequacy, reserve transparency, or operational resilience-can ensure that minimum safeguards are observed worldwide, mitigating the risk of a "race to the bottom" in regulatory competition (Zetzsche et al., 2021).

In the realm of consumer protection, the UN Guidelines for Consumer Protection (2016 revision) serve as another point of comparison. While not binding, they have informed national legal reforms across regions by stressing fairness, redress mechanisms, and transparency. Stablecoin regulation could benefit from embedding such principles explicitly within its design. In practice, this would mean mandating clear disclosure of redemption rights, ensuring that reserve audits are accessible to users, and guaranteeing channels of recourse in cases of fraud or mismanagement.

However, not all model law experiments have been unqualified successes. The UNCITRAL Model Law on Secured Transactions (2017) illustrates some of the difficulties. Despite offering modernized provisions for asset-based lending, its adoption has been uneven, especially in jurisdictions where secured credit systems were already deeply entrenched. This underlines the risk of legal transplantation: a model law may provide elegant solutions on paper, but without domestic buy-in, institutional capacity, and contextual adjustment, implementation can falter. For stablecoins, this lesson is critical. Countries differ vastly in financial infrastructure, central bank independence, and public trust in digital currencies. Any model law must anticipate resistance and provide pathways for gradual implementation, technical assistance, and adaptation.

The comparative analysis reveals several overarching lessons. First, successful model laws tend to focus on clear, technology-neutral definitions, avoiding excessive detail that might become obsolete. Second, they incorporate tiered approaches, recognizing that not all actors present the same risk profile-a lesson particularly relevant for distinguishing between local payment tokens and globally stablecoins. Third, they succeed when coupled with international coordination, often through regional organizations or multilateral bodies that encourage convergence and mutual recognition. Finally, effective model laws combine legal certainty with flexibility, balancing the need for harmonization with the reality of diverse domestic conditions.

Applied to stablecoins, these lessons suggest that the path forward lies not in replicating existing financial regulation wholesale, but in crafting a purpose-built framework inspired by prior successes in international economic law. The model law strategy can offer regulators a structured yet adaptable blueprint, fostering both innovation and stability in an arena that increasingly defines the future of money.

Political Economy of Model Laws in the Digital Era

The creation and diffusion of model laws are never purely technical exercises. They unfold in a political economy context shaped by the interests of states, private corporations, and multilateral organizations. In the case of stablecoins, this dynamic is particularly visible, since the regulatory decisions surrounding digital money implicate both sovereign monetary power and the market incentives of worldwide technology and financial actors.

From the perspective of states, the appeal of a model law is twofold. For advanced economies, such as members of the European Union or the United States, a global benchmark can help prevent regulatory arbitrage by ensuring that stablecoin issuers cannot simply relocate to jurisdictions with laxer oversight (Arner et al., 2020). For developing countries, a model law offers access to a ready-made regulatory template, reducing the cost of policy design and bolstering credibility in international financial markets. Yet, this same relationship creates asymmetries: countries with limited bargaining power may adopt frameworks heavily influenced by the priorities of dominant economies, even if these do not fully reflect their domestic needs.

Private actors also play a decisive role. Large stablecoin issuers, particularly those backed by worldwide firms, have strong incentives to shape the contours of regulation in ways that facilitate market expansion while minimizing compliance burdens. Industry associations such as the GDF initiative, with its "Principles for Stablecoin Issuers" (2019), illustrate how private sector guidelines often prefigure or compete with public regulation. While such principles promote transparency and accountability, they are also strategic tools: by proposing self-regulation, issuers seek to forestall heavier state intervention (Zetzsche et al., 2021). The interplay between self-regulation and formal law thus becomes a negotiation of legitimacy, where industry codes can either complement or dilute public oversight.

Multilateral institutions occupy a mediating space. Organizations like the FSB and the Bank for International Settlements (BIS) frame stablecoins within the broader agenda of global financial stability, highlighting risks and advocating for cross-border coordination. Their influence is considerable, as their reports often inform both national policy debates and the drafting of model frameworks. Yet, their recommendations reflect the consensus of member states, which may privilege the concerns of important economies. For smaller jurisdictions, this raises the question of ownership: to what extent can they adapt a worldwide model to safeguard local interests, such as financial inclusion or developmental priorities, without undermining adherence to international standards?

The digital era intensifies these tensions. Unlike earlier model laws on arbitration or commerce, stablecoins sit at the intersection of finance and technology, domains that are both highly globalized and highly concentrated. The dominance of a few technology firms in providing infrastructure-cloud computing, blockchain platforms, payment networks-creates a scenario where regulatory design may indirectly reinforce existing market power. Critics warn that without careful checks, a model law could inadvertently entrench "digital oligopolies" under the guise of legal harmonization (Ringe & Ruof, 2020).

Moreover, geopolitics cannot be overlooked. Competing approaches between the United States, the European Union, and China reflect deeper struggles over the future architecture of global finance. China's promotion of the digital yuan illustrates a state-led alternative to privately issued stablecoins, stressing sovereignty and control. In contrast, U.S. policy debates often revolve around integrating stablecoins into the banking system while harnessing private sector innovation. These divergent models complicate the search for a single global template. Any model law must therefore navigate technical and legal challenges and strategic rivalries between major powers.

At the same time, the political economy of stablecoin regulation holds opportunities. By embedding developmental objectives-such as promoting financial inclusion, reducing remittance costs, or enhancing regional payment integration-a model law can go beyond risk mitigation to serve broader social purposes. For example, in

Africa and Southeast Asia, where mobile money already plays a transformative role, a tailored version of a model law could legitimize stablecoins as a complementary tool for expanding access to financial services. Such an approach would allow the Commonwealth and other international bodies to position the model law not as a top-down imposition, but as an enabler of local innovation.

In sum, the political economy lens underscores that the viability of a stablecoin model law depends less on the elegance of its provisions than on its ability to balance competing interests. States seek to protect sovereignty and stability, firms seek market opportunities, and multilateral bodies seek coherence. Navigating this triangular relationship requires a design that is technically robust and politically legitimate. The digital era, with its new forms of concentration and competition, raises the stakes. Yet it also creates the possibility of reframing financial regulation as a global public good, where harmonization serves efficiency, inclusion and resilience.

LICENSING AND SUPERVISION IN PRACTICE

Tiered Licensing and Proportionality

The debate on licensing stablecoin issuers has increasingly gravitated toward the principle of proportionality. Unlike banks or securities firms, which fit relatively neatly into established categories, stablecoin issuers present diverse profiles. Some operate as large-scale entities with systemic implications-backing billions of dollars' worth of tokens with complex reserve structures-while others are small start-ups experimenting with limited-purpose tokens in niche markets. Applying a uniform licensing regime to this spectrum of actors risks either overregulation, which stifles innovation, or underregulation, which leaves significant vulnerabilities unaddressed.

Regulators in several jurisdictions have therefore begun to embrace tiered licensing frameworks, in which requirements scale with the size, reach and importance of the issuer. MiCA distinguishes between issuers of asset-referenced tokens and e-money tokens, imposing heightened obligations on entities whose operations could affect financial stability or monetary sovereignty (European Securities and Markets Authority, 2025). Similarly, in Singapore, the Payment Services Act of 2019 establishes licensing categories ranging from standard payment institution licenses to major payment institution licenses, with criteria linked to transaction volumes and risk exposure.

The proportional approach reflects broader trends in financial regulation. The FSB (2020) has argued that a one-size-fits-all model is ill-suited for digital assets, where business models advance rapidly. Instead, it advocates risk-based licensing, grounded in the potential impact on consumers and markets. Academic literature reinforces this point: Zetzsche et al. (2020) point out that proportionality is not merely a matter of regulatory efficiency but a prerequisite for achieving a balance between innovation and safety.

Proportional licensing also addresses the asymmetry between large and small issuers. While worldwide players like Circle or Tether may be expected to maintain robust governance and auditing mechanisms, smaller actors can be brought under lighter regimes that focus on transparency and consumer safeguards without imposing prohibitive costs. This tiered approach, however, is not without critics. Some scholars caution that lighter regimes may inadvertently create "regulatory enclaves" where smaller but riskier projects escape adequate oversight, potentially leading to contagion effects if their models fail (Carapella, 2025).

The tiered system has the added benefit of enhancing regulatory adaptability. As the market grows, issuers can migrate from one category to another, supporting obligations with their evolving risk profile. This model echoes practices in banking supervision, where capital requirements and oversight intensity scale with the institution's size and interconnectedness. It also resonates with the philosophy behind Basel Committee's proportionality principle, which has influenced stablecoin discussions by stressing that the regulatory burden should correspond to the risk posed.

In this way, licensing regimes for stablecoins are not merely administrative tools; they are critical levers in shaping market behavior. By embedding proportionality into their design, regulators signal that innovation is welcome, but responsibility scales with ambition. This philosophy, already visible in Europe and Asia, is increasingly being discussed in the United States, where debates on whether stablecoin issuers should hold banking charters reflect the tension between safeguards and space for experimentation.

Supervisory Challenges in a Cross-Border Environment

Stablecoins, by design, do not respect national boundaries. A token issued in New York or Singapore can circulate seamlessly among users in Nairobi, São Paulo, or Frankfurt, often without the issuer being directly aware of the jurisdictions where its product is most actively used. This borderless character creates acute supervisory challenges. Unlike banks, which usually operate through identifiable branches or subsidiaries, stablecoin networks distribute risk and exposure across chains, wallets, and exchanges that transcend the control of any single national regulator.

The FATF has repeatedly pointed out this cross-border dimension, particularly in its guidance on virtual assets and virtual asset service providers (VASPs). FATF notes that the speed and anonymity with which stablecoins can be transferred magnifies the risk of regulatory arbitrage: issuers and intermediaries may choose to establish operations in jurisdictions with lighter oversight, thereby undermining coordinated worldwide standards (FATF, 2021). This concern is echoed by the Bank for International Settlements (BIS), which has argued that fragmented approaches to supervision create vulnerabilities, as gaps in one jurisdiction may ripple globally.

MiCA again offers a telling example of how regional blocs are trying to address this problem. MiCA requires that any stablecoin accessible within the EU comply with its framework, regardless of the issuer's origin, in effect creating an "extra-territorial" supervisory reach (European Securities and Markets Authority, 2025). Yet such approaches risk clashes with sovereignty principles. Non-EU issuers may argue that subjecting them to European oversight without local presence violates jurisdictional norms. Similar tensions are visible in the United States, where congressional proposals for stablecoin regulation have raised questions about how to regulate offshore issuers whose tokens are nonetheless widely used by American consumers.

Supervisory cooperation mechanisms have been proposed to mitigate these tensions. The FSB's 2020 report called for "global supervisory colleges" for stablecoin issuers of importance, modeled on those used in banking and insurance. These colleges would enable regulators from different jurisdictions to share information, coordinate audits, and harmonize enforcement actions. Scholars such as Zetzsche (2020) argue that without such cooperative frameworks, national supervisors will remain reactive and fragmented, struggling to keep pace with the speed of innovation.

A further challenge arises from the technical architecture of stablecoins. Many rely on smart contracts deployed on public blockchains. Supervisors may lack the tools or authority to access the data needed to assess compliance, particularly when transactions are pseudonymous. Some regulators have begun experimenting with regulatory technology (RegTech) solutions, such as blockchain analytics tools, to trace flows of funds and monitor reserve backing. Yet this raises questions about data privacy, proportionality, and the allocation of supervisory costs between issuers and the state.

The cross-border nature of supervision also underscores the interplay between soft law and binding regulation. Industry-led initiatives, such as the GDF principles for stablecoin issuers (2019), attempt to set voluntary worldwide standards on disclosure, reserves, and governance. While these frameworks lack legal enforceability, they can serve as reference points for national supervisors, providing a degree of convergence while formal regulation catches up. Still, without binding commitments, their effectiveness depends on market incentives and reputational pressures.

Ultimately, supervisory challenges in the cross-border context underline the paradox of stablecoins: their appeal lies in seamless global circulation, but their safety depends on fragmented national regimes that often move at different speeds. Bridging this gap remains one of the central tasks for regulators and scholars alike.

Lessons From Traditional Finance and Payment Systems

Stablecoin regulation is not unfolding in a vacuum. Policymakers and supervisors can draw on decades of experience in regulating banks, payment systems, and e-money institutions to design frameworks that balance innovation with stability. Indeed, many of the supervisory dilemmas faced today-ensuring sufficient reserves, protecting consumers, and maintaining stability-are not new but rather reappear in digital form.

The regulation of e-money in the European Union under the E-Money Directive provides a striking precedent. E-money issuers are required to safeguard customer funds through segregated accounts and are subject to prudential oversight, albeit with lighter capital requirements compared to banks. Several scholars note that these rules, developed to govern prepaid cards and digital wallets, could serve as a blueprint for stablecoin regimes, particularly those backed one-to-one by fiat reserves (Buckley et al., 2020). The lesson here is that proportionality is essential: overregulation risks stifling innovation, while underregulation exposes consumers and financial systems to undue risks.

Banking regulation also offers valuable parallels. The Basel III framework, with its stress on liquidity coverage ratios and high-quality liquid assets (HQLA), echoes many of the debates around reserve management for stablecoins. Just as banks must maintain adequate liquidity buffers to withstand shocks, stablecoin issuers may be required to hold transparent, verifiable reserves to guarantee redemption at par value. The collapse of TerraUSD demonstrated the consequences of failing to apply these prudential lessons: algorithmic models without sufficient backing can unravel quickly, with contagion effects across worldwide markets.

Payment system oversight also sheds light on supervisory strategies. Central banks worldwide operate under the principle that payment infrastructures are critical public goods, demanding oversight to ensure resilience, efficiency, and trust. The Committee on Payments and Market Infrastructures - International Organization of Securities Commissions (CPMI-IOSCO) Principles for Financial Market Infrastructures (PFMI), although not designed for crypto-assets, set out standards on governance, operational risk, and settlement finality that can be adapted to stablecoin ecosystems (CPMI-IOSCO, 2012). Applying such principles could ensure that important stablecoins adhere to risk-management norms comparable to traditional clearinghouses and settlement systems (Arner et al., 2020).

Furthermore, the "too big to fail" problem in banking provides an instructive analogy. When stablecoins grow to systemic proportions-processing billions in daily transactions-they may become indispensable to the functioning of global markets. Supervisors may then face the same dilemma as with banks: whether to allow market discipline to prevail at the risk of contagion, or to step in with backstops that could create moral hazard. Scholars such as Schwarcz (2016) warn that replicating bank-style bailouts in the digital realm could distort incentives and entrench private actors with quasi-public roles.

Another lesson comes from the history of international regulatory coordination. Banking crises of the late 20th century pushed regulators toward cross-border cooperation, culminating in the Basel Committee's global standards. A similar trajectory may arise for stablecoins, with model laws, supervisory colleges, and memoranda of understanding functioning as tools for gradual convergence. The difference, however, lies in the speed of digital innovation: whereas banking standards took decades to crystallize, stablecoin regulation must evolve within years to keep pace with technological adoption.

These analogies highlight both opportunities and limits. Stablecoins cannot be simply folded into existing categories, but nor are they wholly unprecedented. Supervisors can avoid repeating past mistakes by adapting tried-and-tested principles, particularly around prudential requirements, governance and oversight. Yet, as stablecoins blur the boundaries between private money and public monetary systems, regulators must recognize that the stakes extend beyond technical compliance: they implicate the very trust that underpins modern finance.

KEEPING RESERVES SAFE

What Backs a Stablecoin?

The credibility of a stablecoin rests on its capacity to maintain a consistent value against a reference asset. This stability depends primarily on the reserves backing the token, which determine whether it can effectively function as a medium of exchange, store of value, and unit of account. Fiat-backed stablecoins, such as USDC or Paxos Standard, rely on bank deposits and short-term government securities, offering a relatively secure form of collateralization that anchors digital innovation in the stability of the traditional financial system (Buckley et al., 2020). By contrast, crypto-collateralized stablecoins like DAI employ overcollateralization mechanisms using volatile digital assets such as Ether. This design requires excess collateral to absorb price shocks, but it still faces the risk of liquidation cascades during episodes of market stress.

A more experimental model-algorithmic stablecoins-attempts to sustain value through endogenous mechanisms such as seigniorage shares or governance tokens. TerraUSD (UST) epitomized this design, promising price stability through arbitrage incentives with its sister token, LUNA. However, the collapse of UST in May 2022 demonstrated the fragility of purely algorithmic stabilization, leading to billions of dollars in losses and undermining confidence in such models (Arner et al., 2020). The episode underlined that algorithmic designs are highly vulnerable to coordinated market pressure and lack the external anchor that reserves provide.

Thus, the question of "what backs a stablecoin" is not merely technical but a matter of trust. As international organizations such as the FSB (2020) stress, the nature and sufficiency of reserves must be transparent, independently verified, and legally enforceable to prevent risks of instability and contagion. Stablecoins without credible reserves effectively become speculative instruments, diverging from their intended role as safe digital money.

High-Quality Liquid Assets and Transparency

The debate over stablecoin reserves is inseparable from the question of asset quality. To ensure that tokens can be redeemed at par, issuers must hold instruments that are both safe and liquid, capable of being converted into cash quickly without significant loss of value. The Bank for International Settlements (2022) points out that HQLA, such as short-term government bonds or central bank deposits, are the cornerstone of credibility. These instruments provide resilience during market stress, when demand for redemptions may surge and issuers must meet obligations without delay.

However, not all issuers have adhered to these standards. Tether (USDT), for instance, has faced persistent scrutiny regarding the composition of its reserves. Reports revealed that a substantial portion of its backing once included commercial paper of uncertain quality, raising concerns over whether such assets could withstand a liquidity crisis (Lyons & Viswanath-Natraj, 2023). This opacity not only threatened user confidence but also risked creating contagion, as redemptions could force fire sales in broader financial markets.

Transparency is therefore as important as asset quality. Regulatory frameworks increasingly require issuers to publish frequent, independently audited attestations of their reserves. MiCA goes a step further, mandating disclosure of the nature, maturity, and concentration of assets held. This approach seeks to prevent the kind of uncertainty that plagued the commercial paper market during the 2008 financial crisis and, more recently, during the stress induced by the COVID-19 pandemic (European Securities and Markets Authority, 2023).

Yet transparency alone does not guarantee stability. Even if issuers disclose the composition of reserves, questions remain about the enforceability of redemption rights, the jurisdiction of custodians, and the legal segregation of assets from the issuer's balance sheet. These issues underline that transparency must be combined with strong supervisory oversight and enforceable legal safeguards. Otherwise, disclosure becomes little more than a public relations exercise, insufficient to ensure that a stablecoin can weather a shock.

In this sense, the insistence on HQLA and transparency is not only a regulatory preference but a matter of public interest. Stablecoins, if widely adopted, could underpin payment systems, savings mechanisms, and cross-border remittances. Their failure, as the collapse of TerraUSD demonstrated, can inflict losses on millions of users, disproportionately affecting those in emerging economies where financial alternatives are scarce. Ensuring that reserves are both of high quality and transparently reported is therefore a prerequisite for integrating stablecoins into the worldwide financial system safely.

Redemption Rights and Audits

A defining feature of a credible stablecoin regime is the assurance that tokens can be redeemed at par, on demand, and without undue friction. Redemption rights are the foundation of trust: without them, the promise of stability becomes illusory, and users are left with an asset that may track fiat only under favorable conditions. As Arner et al. (2020) point out, a failure to enforce redemption rights transforms stablecoins into speculative instruments rather than reliable payment tools.

The collapse of TerraUSD revealed the dangers of weak or absent redemption mechanisms. Its algorithmic model promised parity with the US dollar, but lacked enforceable legal guarantees or asset backing. When market sentiment shifted, redemption spirals accelerated collapse, causing billions in losses and undermining faith in the broader digital asset ecosystem. In contrast, asset-backed stablecoins such as USDC and Paxos have explicitly framed redemption at one dollar as a legal obligation, coupled with defined timelines for processing withdrawals. These commitments, although operationally costly, signal resilience and help to prevent destabilizing runs.

Regulation is moving toward embedding redemption rights into law. MiCA in the European Union requires issuers of "asset-referenced tokens" to honor redemption requests without delay and at no additional cost to the holder (European Securities and Markets Authority, 2023). Similarly, the U.S. President's Working Group on Financial Markets et al. (2021) underscored that stablecoin arrangements should guarantee redemption into fiat currency, ideally through bank-regulated custodians. These legal frameworks converge on a principle: user protection depends on reserve adequacy and on enforceable rights to reclaim value.

Audits are the parallel safeguard to redemption rights. Independent verification of reserves ensures that redemption promises are not hollow. While attestations from accounting firms have become common, critics argue that only full audits-conducted according to established international standards-can uncover discrepancies in asset composition, custodial risks, or overstatement of liquidity. The controversy around Tether's delayed and partial disclosures illustrates how limited assurance erodes confidence and invites regulatory scrutiny (Lyons & Viswanath-Natraj, 2023).

Beyond traditional audits, regulators are considering real-time or continuous verification mechanisms, benefiting from blockchain's transparency and automated reporting. Such innovations could mitigate time lags inherent in quarterly reviews and provide users with higher confidence in the issuer's solvency. Still, these tools require technical capacity and governance safeguards to ensure that data integrity and audit independence are not compromised.

Ultimately, redemption rights and audits serve as two sides of the same coin. Redemption without credible audits risks unsustainable liabilities, while audits without legally enforceable redemption rights render disclosures toothless. A robust regulatory regime must therefore link both obligations, creating a cycle of accountability that reinforces public trust and stability.

CONSUMER PROTECTION IN A DIGITAL AGE

Redress Mechanisms

The rise of stablecoins has blurred the boundaries between traditional finance and the digital economy, exposing consumers to risks for which existing remedies are often insufficient. In conventional banking, redress frameworks are anchored in deposit insurance schemes, ombudsman services, and supervisory mechanisms that ensure swift dispute resolution. By contrast, many stablecoin users operate in environments where such protections are absent or ambiguous. When issuers freeze withdrawals, exchanges suspend operations, or tokens de-peg from their reference currency, consumers frequently face long delays or find themselves with no avenue for compensation (Zetzsche et al., 2021).

Recent regulatory responses reflect a recognition of this gap. MiCA obliges stablecoin issuers to establish complaint-handling systems that are clear, accessible, and free of charge (European Securities and Markets Authority, 2023). This represents a shift toward corresponding digital asset protections with those of mainstream finance, signaling that consumer complaints are not peripheral but central to market integrity. Similarly, policy discussions in the United States and the United Kingdom have stressed the need for arbitration mechanisms that can adapt to the transnational and digital nature of stablecoin disputes (President's Working Group on Financial Markets et al., 2021).

Yet the problem is not simply the absence of regulation-it is also the challenge of decentralization. Stablecoins issued or governed by decentralized autonomous organizations (DAOs) distribute authority among token holders, making it unclear who bears responsibility for resolving user grievances. In such contexts, traditional legal avenues may falter, as there is no central counterparty to hold accountable. Scholars have proposed hybrid solutions in which decentralized governance retains operational control, while external, centralized entities-such as ombudsman-style panels-handle consumer complaints (Allen et al., 2022). This dual model could help reconcile the ethos of decentralization with the demands of legal accountability.

Redress mechanisms also intersect with the question of trust. When users believe they have access to effective remedies, they are more willing to adopt stablecoins for payments, remittances, and savings. Conversely, the absence of credible redress undermines consumer confidence and magnifies risks, as sudden loss of trust can trigger large-scale withdrawals and destabilize whole systems. The history of financial crises suggests that consumer protection is not an afterthought but a cornerstone of resilience.

Preventing Fraud and Financial Loss

Fraud has long been a persistent threat in financial systems, but the digital nature of stablecoins amplifies the scale and complexity of abusive practices. Unlike traditional bank deposits, which are subject to strict know-your-customer (KYC) and anti-money laundering (AML) safeguards, many stablecoin platforms still operate in lightly regulated environments. This gap has allowed fraudulent schemes-ranging from Ponzi structures to fake wallet applications-to proliferate, often targeting vulnerable users with limited financial literacy (Zetsche et al., 2020). The collapse of TerraUSD (UST) in 2022, while not a case of outright fraud, highlighted how opaque governance and inadequate disclosure can expose users to devastating losses, blurring the line between intentional misconduct and structural negligence (Aramonte et al., 2021).

Regulatory responses have increasingly prioritized proactive risk disclosure as a deterrent against fraud. MiCA requires issuers to publish whitepapers with detailed information on the design, risks, and governance of stablecoins (European Securities and Markets Authority, 2023). This measure is intended to counteract the asymmetry of information between issuers and users, reducing opportunities for misrepresentation. Similarly, in Asia, the Monetary Authority of Singapore (MAS) has advanced guidelines that emphasize operational transparency and security audits as preconditions for licensing stablecoin issuers. These safeguards help correspond digital finance with consumer expectations formed in the traditional financial sector.

Yet fraud prevention extends beyond regulatory compliance. Technological safeguards such as multi-signature wallets, hardware-based authentication, and AI-driven fraud detection systems are increasingly being deployed to protect stablecoin users. For example, fraud detection algorithms can flag unusual transaction patterns in real time, preventing malicious actors from exploiting vulnerabilities. However, these mechanisms are only as effective as the governance structures that enforce them. Without credible accountability, even the most advanced security tools risk being underutilized or circumvented.

The social dimension is equally critical. Populations with limited access to financial education are particularly susceptible to fraud, as they may be unable to distinguish between legitimate stablecoin projects and opportunistic scams. In emerging markets where stablecoins are promoted as tools for inclusion and remittances, the failure to prevent fraud can erode trust in specific projects and in the broader promise of digital finance. Therefore, protecting consumers from fraud and financial loss is not simply about maintaining fairness at the micro level-it is about safeguarding the legitimacy of stablecoins as instruments of transformation.

Why This Matters for the Unbanked

The significance of consumer protection in the context of stablecoins becomes even more pronounced when considering the world's unbanked and underbanked populations. According to the World Bank (Ansar et al., 2022), nearly 1.4 billion adults still lack access to formal financial services, with the majority concentrated in developing regions of Africa, Asia, and Latin America. Stablecoins have been hailed as potential tools to bridge this gap by offering low-cost, borderless access to payments, remittances, and savings mechanisms. Yet without adequate protection, these very groups-who stand to benefit the most-may instead be exposed to disproportionate risks.

The unbanked often rely on informal financial channels, such as cash-based remittances or community savings groups, where trust is localized and personal. By contrast, stablecoin platforms operate within digital ecosystems that require a baseline of technological literacy, access to secure devices, and reliable internet connectivity. This asymmetry introduces new vulnerabilities: phishing scams, counterfeit wallets, and predatory intermediaries who exploit knowledge gaps. If early experiences with stablecoins lead to significant financial loss, unbanked users may retreat to informal systems, reinforcing cycles of exclusion instead of breaking them (Allen et al., 2021).

Moreover, unbanked users typically lack access to legal recourse when financial harm occurs. In traditional banking, consumers can appeal to regulators, ombudsmen, or deposit insurance schemes. In contrast, when stablecoin systems collapse or fraudulent actors abscond with funds, recourse is often limited, especially if the issuer is based in another jurisdiction. This makes cross-border regulatory coordination essential to ensure that vulnerable populations are not left unprotected in globalized digital markets (Brummer & Yadav, 2019).

Protecting the unbanked in the context of stablecoins also intersects with broader development goals. If regulators succeed in establishing robust safeguards-such as mandatory disclosure of risks, guaranteed redemption rights, and stringent cybersecurity audits-stablecoins could serve as credible substitutes for unreliable or inaccessible banking systems. In this scenario, digital assets may promote financial inclusion and encourage economic empowerment, enabling participation in e-commerce, access to microloans, or even integration into government welfare programs. Conversely, a lack of protection risks turning stablecoins into tools of exploitation that entrench as opposed to alleviate financial inequality.

Ultimately, the challenge is not just to regulate stablecoins for advanced economies, but to ensure that their governance frameworks account for the unique vulnerabilities of unbanked populations. In doing so, stablecoins can fulfill their promise as instruments of inclusion, rather than becoming yet another frontier for exclusion and harm.

TECHNOLOGY, SECURITY, AND CYBER RISKS

Secure Wallets and Custody Solutions

The design of custody arrangements for stablecoins is not merely a technical matter but a fundamental issue of trust and market integrity. Stablecoin users interact with the technology through digital wallets, which can be custodial-managed by regulated intermediaries-or non-custodial, where users retain direct control over their private keys. Each model carries distinct risks. Custodial wallets may expose users to mismanagement, insolvency, or fraud by the provider, while non-custodial wallets shift the burden of security entirely onto individuals, who may lack the knowledge or tools to protect their assets adequately (Arner et al., 2020).

From a regulatory perspective, secure custody requires both technological safeguards and institutional accountability. Encryption, multi-signature mechanisms, and hardware wallets provide technical protection against theft or hacking. However, no technical measure can compensate for the absence of governance standards, especially regarding segregation of customer funds, clear terms of service, and recourse in cases of loss.

Recent cases have demonstrated that vulnerabilities in wallet infrastructure can have implications. Hacks targeting decentralized finance protocols-such as the 2022 Wormhole exploit that drained over $300 million-highlight how weaknesses in custody arrangements reverberate across ecosystems (Bank for International Settlements,

2022). These events underscore the need for a layered approach, combining robust cybersecurity requirements with consumer protection rules. Importantly, regulators must also ensure that wallet providers adopt transparent disclosure practices about the risks borne by end users, particularly in jurisdictions with low financial literacy.

In this sense, custody solutions for stablecoins sit at the intersection of private innovation and public oversight. Secure wallets are not only about safeguarding digital tokens but also about reinforcing confidence in the broader financial system where stablecoins increasingly operate.

Smart Contracts and Oracles

Stablecoins frequently rely on smart contracts to manage issuance, redemption, and collateralization, especially in decentralized models. These self-executing codes promise efficiency and transparency by automating financial logic without intermediaries. However, they also introduce a new layer of operational and legal risk, since vulnerabilities in coding or governance can directly translate into financial instability. Unlike traditional contracts, smart contracts are immutable once deployed, meaning that an error in design-or malicious manipulation-can result in irreversible losses (Schär, 2021).

A central concern lies in the use of oracles, mechanisms that feed off-chain data-such as exchange rates or collateral prices-into the blockchain. Oracles act as the bridge between digital code and the real economy, but they are also potential points of failure. If an oracle is compromised, whether through data manipulation or collusion, the entire system of a stablecoin can be undermined. The 2020 bZx attack, where faulty oracle data enabled massive exploitation, remains one of the most cited examples of this risk.

From a regulatory standpoint, the question becomes: how do you supervise code? IOSCO (2022) has suggested that governance frameworks for smart contracts must incorporate accountability mechanisms, such as designated responsible parties, even in decentralized settings. Without identifiable entities, users and regulators are left with no clear path for dispute resolution or enforcement in case of failures.

In practice, hybrid governance models are emerging. Some projects combine decentralized execution with centralized oversight mechanisms, allowing upgrades or interventions if unforeseen bugs threaten stability. While purists criticize such approaches as undermining decentralization, regulators increasingly see them as pragmatic compromises that balance innovation with resilience (Zetzsche et al., 2020).

The reliability of smart contracts and oracles is therefore not only a technical matter but also a legal and ethical one. They reshape questions of liability, risk allocation, and consumer trust in ways that traditional regulation was not designed to address. For stablecoins to play a role in payments and finance, supervisory authorities will need to establish standards for code audits, third-party oracle verification, and contingency mechanisms to handle failures without triggering contagion.

Ultimately, smart contracts and oracles exemplify the paradox of stablecoins: the very tools that enable efficiency and disintermediation also create new vectors of fragility, requiring fresh regulatory thinking that bridges technology and law.

Human Error, AI and Vulnerabilities

While discussions on stablecoin regulation often stress technical failures such as hacks or oracle manipulation, a more subtle but equally dangerous risk arises from human error and the increasing reliance on artificial intelligence (AI) within digital financial infrastructures. In complex ecosystems where code, collateral, and governance are intertwined, a single miscalculation by a developer, a mistaken parameter in an algorithm, or even a lapse in monitoring procedures can cascade into systemic crises. The collapse of TerraUSD in 2022 illustrates how overconfidence in algorithmic design, combined with insufficient stress testing and human misjudgments, can bring down projects with billions in market capitalization (Aramonte et al., 2021).

The integration of AI into financial systems further complicates this picture. AI-driven risk management tools and automated decision-making engines are increasingly used to adjust collateral ratios, detect anomalies, or even forecast user behavior. While these tools promise efficiency and predictive accuracy, they also create opaque black boxes where the logic of decisions cannot be easily audited or explained. Regulators face a dilemma: requiring explainability may slow down innovation, but ignoring it leaves both users and supervisors blind to vulnerabilities.

Moreover, human operators interacting with AI-based systems may overestimate their reliability, a phenomenon known as automation bias. This cognitive tendency can lead to insufficient oversight of automated processes, reinforcing vulnerabilities instead of mitigating them (Parasuraman & Riley, 1997). In the context of stablecoins, such misplaced trust can delay responses to market stress, amplifying contagion effects across platforms.

To address these risks, international bodies like the FSB (2023) have begun pointing out the need for operational resilience frameworks that integrate both human and technological factors. These frameworks encourage regular audits of code and governance procedures, training for operators, and protocols for intervention in case of unexpected AI malfunctions. In practice, some regulators are already considering requiring that AI systems in financial infrastructure be accompanied by human-in-the-loop mechanisms, ensuring that critical decisions-such as suspending redemptions or altering collateral parameters-cannot be left solely to automated processes.

What becomes evident is that stablecoins, despite their technological sophistication, remain embedded in a socio-technical context where human judgment and machine intelligence interact in unpredictable ways. Ignoring the role of human error or the limits of AI would be a profound regulatory oversight. On the contrary, recognizing these vulnerabilities allows for the design of layered safeguards-combining code audits, explainable AI, operator accountability, and crisis protocols-that can help ensure resilience in an environment where digital assets increasingly intersect with financial stability.

RISKS, REGULATION, AND THE FUTURE OF STABLECOINS

Financial Stability and Challenges

The rise of stablecoins has reshaped debates on financial stability in ways that echo the risk concerns traditionally associated with banks and payment systems. Unlike early cryptocurrencies, whose volatility restricted them largely to speculative trading, stablecoins aspire to function as everyday money. Their integration into payment infrastructures, remittances, and decentralized finance creates new pathways for risk transmission across markets. If a widely used stablecoin loses credibility, the effects can spread far beyond the crypto sector, undermining trust in digital assets more broadly and potentially spilling over into the traditional financial system.

The collapse of TerraUSD (UST) in May 2022 stressed the dangers of algorithmic designs that lack robust backing mechanisms (Aramonte et al., 2021). The event wiped out billions in market value and revealed how fragile confidence-based systems can be when they scale. Scholars such as Carapella (2025) argue that once stablecoins reach significant adoption, their failure could resemble a "digital bank run," with sudden mass redemptions destabilizing broader markets. This potential for contagion is particularly concerning when stablecoins are linked to lending protocols in decentralized finance (DeFi), where leverage and interconnectedness magnify shocks.

Some jurisdictions have responded by embedding stablecoin oversight into broader digital finance frameworks. The MiCA sets out capital and reserve requirements designed to prevent destabilizing failures (European Parliament & Council, 2023). In contrast, the United States has debated several legislative proposals, but regulatory clarity remains partial, creating uncertainty for both issuers and users. Emerging economies face a different dilemma: while stablecoins promise cheaper remittances and financial inclusion, their volatility and reliance on foreign reserves could undermine domestic monetary policy (Kosse & Mattei, 2022).

Ultimately, the risk question surrounding stablecoins is not simply whether they can maintain their pegs under stress, but how their interconnectedness with financial infrastructures amplifies vulnerabilities. The test for regulators is to design frameworks that prevent destabilization while not suffocating innovation.

Global Regulatory Coordination and AML/CFT Concerns

Stablecoins also present a governance challenge that transcends national borders. Because issuers and users operate across multiple jurisdictions, the effectiveness of any regulatory framework depends on domestic and international correspondence. A stablecoin issued in one country may circulate globally within minutes, rendering unilateral rules insufficient. This raises the stakes for cross-border cooperation and highlights the limits of fragmented oversight.

The FSB (2020) has stressed that worldwide stablecoins require a coordinated approach, warning that regulatory gaps could be exploited for arbitrage. The challenge is compounded by the diversity of legal traditions and policy priorities. For instance, while MiCA advances a full supervisory regime, many Asian and African jurisdictions rely on a patchwork of guidelines or remain in early stages of consultation (Arner et al., 2020). The absence of harmonized standards can encourage issuers to base operations in lenient jurisdictions, creating a "race to the bottom" in regulatory compliance.

Beyond prudential risks, stablecoins raise acute concerns related to money laundering, terrorist financing, and sanctions evasion. Their global reach and relative anonymity make them attractive tools for illicit flows. The FATF (2021) has updated its guidance to require virtual asset service providers to comply with the "travel rule," obligating the sharing of customer information across borders. Yet implementation has been uneven, with some states lacking the infrastructure or political will to enforce these standards. This inconsistency undermines worldwide trust and creates vulnerabilities that criminal actors can exploit.

At the same time, private sector initiatives have sought to fill gaps where regulators lag. The GDF (2019) principles for stablecoin issuers outline voluntary commitments on transparency, governance, and anti-money laundering standards. Although these self-regulatory codes lack enforcement power, they illustrate how industry actors can contribute to responsible practice. However, as Schwarcz (2023) notes, the effectiveness of soft law depends on market incentives: without credible sanctions for non-compliance, voluntary regimes risk being ignored by profit-driven issuers.

The broader geopolitical context adds another layer of complexity. Stablecoins denominated in U.S. dollars, such as Tether (USDT) and USD Coin (USDC), reinforce the global dominance of the dollar, which may trigger strategic responses from other economies seeking to reduce dependency. This monetary dimension blurs the line between financial regulation and international relations, further complicating cooperative approaches (Brummer, 2020).

In sum, stablecoins operate in a transnational arena that strains traditional regulatory boundaries. Effective oversight requires technical solutions, such as interoperable compliance systems, and political commitment to reflect divergent interests. Without such coordination, the risks of regulatory arbitrage, illicit finance, and disruption remain significant.

Stablecoins, CBDCs and Inclusive Futures

The debate on stablecoins cannot be isolated from broader transformations in digital money, particularly the rise of central bank digital currencies (CBDCs). While stablecoins arose as a private-sector innovation designed to overcome the volatility of cryptocurrencies, CBDCs reflect a public-sector response to the same demand for efficient, programmable, and borderless payments. Their coexistence raises critical questions about competition, complementarity, and the role of money in promoting the public good.

For many policymakers, stablecoins represent both a threat and an opportunity. On the one hand, privately issued tokens can undermine monetary sovereignty if they achieve widespread adoption without regulatory safeguards. The experience of dollar-pegged stablecoins circulating in emerging economies shows how they may substitute local currencies, limiting central banks' ability to control inflation or implement countercyclical policies (Kosse & Mattei, 2022). On the other hand, stablecoins have demonstrated how digital tokens can deliver cheaper cross-border transfers and improve financial access, particularly for migrants and unbanked populations. In this sense, they can serve as laboratories for innovation that informs the design of CBDCs.

Several central banks have acknowledged this dual dynamic. The People's Bank of China, through its digital yuan pilot, has sought to pre-empt the spread of foreign-denominated stablecoins while experimenting with programmable features that mirror the flexibility of private tokens (Arner et al., 2020). In contrast, the Federal Reserve has adopted a cautious stance, exploring the risks and benefits of a digital dollar while monitoring how stablecoins mature in practice. In Africa and Latin America, where remittances play a relevant economic role, the attraction of stablecoins lies precisely in their ability to reduce costs compared to traditional intermediaries. For these regions, the question is less about replacing domestic currencies and more about integrating digital assets into strategies for financial inclusion (Allen et al., 2022).

The future trajectory of stablecoins and CBDCs may not be adversarial but symbiotic.

Stablecoins can complement CBDCs by offering specialized services, such as programmable financial contracts in decentralized finance, while CBDCs provide the trust anchor of sovereign backing. A pluralistic ecosystem, in which public and private digital monies coexist under clear regulatory frameworks, may harness innovation without sacrificing stability. The challenge lies in ensuring that this coexistence does not entrench inequalities-for example, by giving technologically advanced economies disproportionate advantages in setting worldwide standards.

From a broader perspective, the evolution of stablecoins illustrates a fundamental tension between market-driven innovation and state-centered monetary authority. How this tension is resolved will shape the future of payments and the distribution of financial power globally. A balanced approach, grounded in international cooperation and inclusive design, may allow stablecoins and CBDCs together to advance goals of efficiency, trust, and access in the digital era.

CONCLUSIONS

The trajectory of stablecoins reveals both the promises and perils of a rapidly evolving financial innovation. Initially framed as a technical response to the volatility of cryptocurrencies, stablecoins have grown into instruments with global implications for payments, remittances, and financial inclusion. Their expansion underscores the ingenuity of private actors and the need for coherent frameworks that can safeguard users, ensure stability, and encourage trust.

The regulatory conversation cannot be confined to one jurisdiction or one approach. Instead, the governance of stablecoins is shaped by a continuum that spans from soft-law mechanisms and industry-driven self-regulation to binding statutory frameworks such as MiCA. The emergence of model laws, such as those currently being debated within the Commonwealth, illustrates the effort to harmonize principles while leaving flexibility for domestic adaptation. This balance between convergence and sovereignty remains one of the greatest challenges for the future.

An interdisciplinary perspective is essential. Lawyers, economists, computer scientists, and policymakers must work together to address the multidimensional risks associated with stablecoins, including fragility, consumer protection, and the prevention of financial crime. Experiences from Asia, Africa, Europe, and the Americas demonstrate that context matters: while stablecoins may be engines of inclusion in emerging markets, in advanced economies they are often evaluated through the lens of risk and monetary sovereignty. A comparative and integrated approach is therefore the only path forward.

Ultimately, the evolution from voluntary soft-law standards to binding model legislation marks a decisive step in institutionalizing trust in digital money. The Commonwealth Model Law on Stablecoins (2025) shows that cooperative legal design can translate abstract principles of transparency, proportionality, and inclusion into enforceable obligations across diverse jurisdictions. Its approach bridges the gap between innovation and stability, allowing member states to adapt global norms without surrendering regulatory autonomy. As digital assets continue to blur the boundaries between private and public money, the capacity to embed trust through law will determine their legitimacy and sustainability. The future of stablecoins, therefore, depends on technological soundness or reserve quality and on the creation of interoperable, principle-based, and enforceable frameworks. The Commonwealth initiative demonstrates that trust in digital money is not a by-product of markets-it is a collective achievement of law, governance, and cooperation.

Looking ahead, the debate will not center solely on whether stablecoins should exist, but on how they coexist with central bank digital currencies, how resilience can be ensured without stifling innovation, and how global standards can be reconciled with local needs. In this sense, regulation is not an obstacle but a necessary enabler: it can provide the clarity, accountability, and legitimacy that allow innovation to thrive in the service of the public good.

The future of money is not merely digital-it is also normative, interdisciplinary, and deeply political. Stablecoins sit at the heart of this transformation, embodying the tension between technological disruption and institutional continuity. Ensuring that this transformation results in systems that are fair, transparent, and inclusive is one of the defining governance tasks of our time.

REFERENCES

Allen, F., Gu, X., & Jagtiani, J. (2021). A survey of fintech research and policy discussion. *Review of Corporate Finance, 1*(3-4), 259–339. DOI: 10.1561/114.00000007

Allen, F., Gu, X., & Jagtiani, J. (2022). Fintech, cryptocurrencies, and CBDCs: Financial Structural Transformation in China. *Journal of International Money and Finance, 124*, 102625. DOI: 10.1016/j.jimonfin.2022.102625

Ansar, S., Demirguc-Kunt, A., Klapper, L., & Singer, D. (2022). *The Global Findex Database 2021: Financial Inclusion, Digital Payments, and Resilience in the Age of COVID-19*. World Bank Group. Retrieved from: https://documents.worldbank.org/curated/en/099818107072234182

Aramonte, S., Huang, W., & Schrimpf, A. (2021). *DeFi risks and the decentralisation illusion*. BIS Quarterly Review. Retrieved from: https://www.bis.org/publ/qtrpdf/r_qt2112b.htm

Arner, D. W., Auer, R., & Frost, J. (2020). Stablecoins: Risks, potential and regulation. *SSRN*, Working paper N° 905. DOI: 10.2139/ssrn.3979495

Bank for International Settlements. (2022). The future monetary system. In *BIS Annual Economic Report 2022*. Retrieved from: https://www.bis.org/publ/arpdf/ar2022e3.pdf

Brummer, C. (2020). *Fintech law in a nutshell*. West Academic Publishing.

Brummer, C., & Yadav, Y. (2019). Fintech and the innovation trilemma. *The Georgetown Law Journal, 107*(2), 235–307. https://scholarship.law.vanderbilt.edu/faculty-publications/1084

Buckley, R. P., Arner, D., Veidt, R., & Zetzsche, D. (2020). Building Fintech Ecosystems: Regulatory Sandboxes, Innovation Hubs and Beyond. *Washington University Journal of Law and Policy, 61*(1), 55–98. https://openscholarship.wustl.edu/law_journal_law_policy/vol61/iss1/10

Carapella, F. (2025). Stablecoin Self-Regulation. *SSRN*. DOI: 10.2139/ssrn.5133007

Committee on Payments and Market Infrastructures & International Organization of Securities Commissions. (2012). *Principles for financial market infrastructures*. Retrieved from: https://www.bis.org/cpmi/publ/d101a.pdf

Commonwealth Secretariat (2025). Draft Commonwealth Model Law on Stablecoins. Retrieved from Commonwealth Secretariat consultation document, July 2025.

European Securities and Markets Authority. (2025). *Markets in Crypto-Assets Regulation (MiCA).* Retrieved from: https://www.esma.europa.eu/esmas-activities/digital-finance-and-innovation/markets-crypto-assets-regulation-mica

Financial Action Task Force. (2021). *Updated Guidance for a Risk-Based Approach to Virtual Assets and Virtual Asset Service Providers.* Retrieved from: https://www.fatf-gafi.org/en/publications/Fatfrecommendations/Guidance-rba-virtual-assets-2021.html

Financial Stability Board. (2020). *Regulation, Supervision and Oversight of "Global Stablecoin" Arrangements.* Retrieved from: https://www.fsb.org/uploads/P131020-3.pdf

Financial Stability Board. (2022). *Assessment of Risks to Financial Stability from Crypto-assets.* Retrieved from: https://www.fsb.org/uploads/P160222.pdf

Financial Stability Board. (2023). *High-level Recommendations for the Regulation, Supervision and Oversight of Global Stablecoin Arrangements.* Retrieved from: https://www.fsb.org/uploads/P170723-3.pdf

Franceschi, L. G., Macharia, E., Binns, M. L., Jarvis, S., & Joseph, L. (2025). *Commonwealth Model Law on Stablecoins: Regulatory framework for emerging economies.* Commonwealth Secretariat.

Global Digital Finance. (2019). *Principles for stablecoin issuers.* Retrieved from: https://www.gdf.io/wp-content/uploads/2019/03/0010_GDF_VI-Principles-for-Stablecoin-Issuers_Digital_161019.pdf

Gorton, G. B., & Zhang, J. I. (2023). Taming Wildcat Stablecoins. *SSRN, 90,* 909–971. DOI: 10.2139/ssrn.3888752

International Organization of Securities Commissions. (2020). Global Stablecoin Initiatives. Retrieved from: https://www.iosco.org/library/pubdocs/pdf/IOSCOPD650.pdf

Kosse, A., & Mattei, I. (2022). *Gaining momentum-Results of the 2021 BIS survey on central bank digital currencies.* Bank for International Settlements. Retrieved from: https://www.bis.org/publ/bppdf/bispap125.pdf

Lyons, R. K., & Viswanath-Natraj, G. (2023). What keeps stablecoins stable? *Journal of International Money and Finance, 131,* 102777. DOI: 10.1016/j.jimonfin.2022.102777

Parasuraman, R., & Riley, V. (1997). Humans and automation: Use, misuse, disuse, abuse. *Human Factors, 39*(2), 230–253. DOI: 10.1518/001872097778543886

President's Working Group on Financial Markets. Federal Deposit Insurance Corporation, & Office of the Comptroller of the Currency (2021). *Report on Stablecoins*. U.S. Department of the Treasury. Retrieved from: https://home.treasury.gov/system/files/136/StableCoinReport_Nov1_508.pdf

Schär, F. (2021). Decentralized Finance: On Blockchain- and Smart Contract-Based Financial Markets. *Review - Federal Reserve Bank of St. Louis*, *103*(2), 153–174. DOI: 10.20955/r.103.153-74

Schwarcz, S. L. (2016). Regulating financial change: A functional approach. *SSRN*, *100*, 1441–1494. DOI: 10.2139/ssrn.2469467

Schwarcz, S. L. (2023). Regulating Global Stablecoins: A Model-Law Strategy. *Vanderbilt Law Review*, *75*(6), 1729–1785.

United Nations Commission on International Trade Law. (1996). *UNCITRAL Model Law on Electronic Commerce*. Retrieved from: https://uncitral.un.org/en/texts/ecommerce/modellaw/electronic_commerce

United Nations Commission on International Trade Law. (2017). *UNCITRAL Model Law on Electronic Transferable Records*. Retrieved from: https://uncitral.un.org/en/texts/ecommerce/modellaw/electronic_transferable_records

Zetzsche, D. A., Birdthistle, W. A., Arner, D. W., & Buckley, R. P. (2020). Digital finance platforms: Toward a new regulatory paradigm. *University of Pennsylvania Journal of Business Law, 23*(1), 273-339. Retrieved from: https://scholarship.law.upenn.edu/jbl/vol23/iss1/6

Zetzsche, D. A., Buckley, R. P., & Arner, D. W. (2021). Regulating Libra. *Oxford Journal of Legal Studies*, *41*(1), 80–113. DOI: 10.1093/ojls/gqaa036 PMID: 33762888

Chapter 7
Payments 1.0 to 5.0: Pathways to Agentic Autonomy

A. V. Senthil Kumar
https://orcid.org/0000-0002-8587-7017
Nehru Institute of Information Technology and Management, India

Mohan Sankaran
https://orcid.org/0009-0005-2058-2946
PayPal Inc., USA

Nagaraju Jooluri
https://orcid.org/0009-0009-6694-020X
Incode Technologies, USA

Amit Chaudhary
https://orcid.org/0009-0007-7658-6684
Coupa Software, USA

ABSTRACT

This chapter traces the evolution from Payments 1.0 (cash) through 2.0 (cards), 3.0 (e-commerce and wallets), and 4.0 (real-time rails with machine learning) to Payments 5.0 agentic autonomy. Agentic payments are intelligent, intent-driven systems where software agents understand user goals, plan execution across risk assessment, authentication, funding and rewards, then act within safety guardrails while providing clear explanations. This chapter presents the architecture with five components: intent capture, tool-augmented planning, policy, safety, action and verification with dry-runs and cryptographic trails, and privacy-preserving learning . Key metrics include approval rates, fraud detection precision and recall, payment

DOI: 10.4018/979-8-3373-9043-7.ch007

speed, and explanation quality. Use cases include proactive bill pay, agentic wallets and dispute resolution. The chapter analyzes threats such as prompt injection and tool abuse, proposing mitigations like least-privilege access and rate limiting.

INTRODUCTION

The payments industry has historically mirrored the evolution of commerce itself, reflecting society's broader shifts in technology, trust, and economic organization. From the earliest exchange of coins and notes to the emergence of global card networks, online wallets, and instant digital transfers, each generation of payments has been defined by innovations that not only altered how money moved but also reshaped relationships between consumers, merchants, and institutions. Today, the industry stands at the threshold of a fifth evolutionary phase: Payments 5.0, marked by the rise of intelligent, autonomous payment agents capable of interpreting user intent, planning execution strategies, and acting safely within well-defined parameters.

Whereas previous phases emphasized digitization, efficiency, and speed, Payments 5.0 introduces a more profound transformation - agentic autonomy. In this model, software agents equipped with natural language understanding, reasoning capabilities, and integration with financial infrastructure can manage complex financial tasks proactively on behalf of users. Instead of issuing a direct instruction such as "transfer $100," a user might express a goal - "ensure my bills are paid on time while minimizing fees" - and the agent would design and execute a multi-step plan, considering variables like cash flow, regulatory compliance, rewards optimization, and fraud risk. Such a paradigm moves the payments industry beyond mere automation toward adaptive, explainable systems that blend intelligence, safety, and user empowerment (Cambridge Centre for Alternative Finance, 2025; Ghosh & Sanyal, 2024).

Evolutionary Trajectory Toward Autonomy

To understand the magnitude of this shift, it is useful to trace the industry's prior evolutionary stages. Payments 1.0, rooted in physical currency, established the fundamental notions of value exchange, verification, and trust. Payments 2.0 brought about card-based systems in the mid-twentieth century, extending commerce across geographies and enabling standardized digital settlement. The rise of Payments 3.0, coinciding with e-commerce in the 1990s and 2000s, introduced digital wallets, stored value, and tokenization - paving the way for mobile-first payment ecosystems (Benson et al., 2017). Payments 4.0, beginning in the 2010s, leveraged real-time rails, artificial intelligence, and machine learning for fraud detection and instant settlement, creating a globally interconnected payment environment (Oliver & Warfe, 2020).

Each stage built upon its predecessor: cash created trust, cards scaled commerce, wallets expanded accessibility, and real-time systems delivered speed. Payments 5.0 now layers intelligence and autonomy on top of these foundations, transforming payments from a mechanical task into a dynamic, goal-driven interaction between human intent and machine agency.

Drivers of the Transition

Several converging factors are accelerating the transition to Payments 5.0.

1. **Technological Progress**. Advances in natural language processing, large language models (LLMs), and autonomous agent frameworks now enable systems to interpret unstructured human input, reason across multiple constraints, and interact with external APIs for execution. Capco (2025) highlights the role of agentic AI in cash management, where systems can dynamically route payments across multiple rails, balancing fees, FX rates, and settlement speeds. Similarly, AWS (2025) reports that financial institutions are experimenting with AI-driven agents that manage tasks such as dispute resolution and account optimization.
2. **User Experience Demands**. Modern consumers expect seamless, intuitive, and personalized financial services. Friction-heavy processes such as manually scheduling bill payments or reconciling cross-border transfer fees are increasingly out of step with digital lifestyles. By leveraging agentic systems, users can delegate these burdens, achieving outcomes like optimized payment timing, minimized fees, or automated dispute resolution (Zhu et al., 2024).
3. **Regulatory and Compliance Pressures**. Financial services operate under strict oversight, requiring transparency, auditability, and adherence to evolving regulatory frameworks. Payments 5.0 incorporates built-in compliance monitoring and explainability features, ensuring that every autonomous decision is both interpretable and traceable. Academic research stresses that trustworthy AI in finance must prioritize fairness, accountability, and transparency to align with regulatory expectations and avoid systemic risk (Ghosh & Sanyal, 2024).
4. **Security Imperatives.** With increasing autonomy comes new risks, including adversarial manipulation, tool abuse, and prompt injection attacks. Researchers emphasize integrating explainable AI with privacy-preserving techniques such as federated learning to maintain security without sacrificing user data sovereignty (Aljunaid, Alamoudi, & Alkahtani, 2025). Payments 5.0 systems must therefore balance autonomy with stringent guardrails, ensuring resilience in the face of novel threats.

Toward an Agentic Framework

What distinguishes Payments 5.0 from earlier paradigms is its framework for autonomy. At its core, this involves four interdependent capabilities: intent understanding, autonomous planning, tool integration, and safety with explainability. Together, these capabilities create a system in which agents not only act but also justify their actions. For example, an agent that delays a bill payment by two days must be able to explain that the decision avoids overdraft fees while still meeting due dates. Such transparency fosters trust, which is essential for widespread adoption (Capco, 2025; FXCintel, 2025).

The framework also highlights interoperability. Payments 5.0 agents are not standalone entities but rather orchestrators of complex ecosystems, integrating across legacy payment rails, digital wallets, fraud detection systems, compliance databases, and loyalty programs. This interoperability ensures that the transition to autonomy builds on, rather than replaces, existing financial infrastructure.

Implications for Industry Stakeholders

For banks, fintechs, and regulators, the rise of Payments 5.0 presents both opportunity and challenge. Financial institutions that adopt agentic frameworks may unlock new revenue streams through personalized services and efficiency gains. Merchants may benefit from faster settlement and lower transaction costs, while consumers gain greater convenience and security. Regulators, however, will need to adapt oversight mechanisms to address autonomous decision-making and ensure accountability in cases of error or abuse (Zhu et al., 2024).

Ultimately, Payments 5.0 represents more than a technological milestone - it is a systemic redefinition of payments as intent-driven, autonomous, and explainable interactions. By blending intelligence with compliance and user trust, this new paradigm promises to make payments not just faster or cheaper, but smarter and safer. The remainder of this chapter develops a detailed reference architecture, explores use cases from bill pay to cross-border transactions, and proposes pathways for secure deployment of agentic payment systems.

BACKGROUND

Evolution of Payment Systems

Payments 1.0: The Physical Currency Era (Pre-1950s)

The story of payments begins with the widespread use of physical currency, which became the bedrock of global commerce. Coins and notes not only represented value but also embodied the concepts of trust, verification, and exchange, which continue to underpin all subsequent payment innovations (Oliver & Warfe, 2020). This period, often referred to as Payments 1.0, enabled standardized trade by providing tangible, universally recognized mediums of exchange.

Cash established the foundation of transactional trust, supported by centralized authorities such as governments and central banks. The physical form of money also embedded inherent controls: once exchanged, ownership was final, and double spending was nearly impossible. However, this model faced significant limitations, including geographic restrictions, risk of theft or loss, and the absence of digital traceability (Knodell, 2016). These limitations gradually drove the demand for more scalable, secure, and efficient forms of payment.

Despite its shortcomings, cash remains deeply relevant in many economies today, particularly in regions where digital penetration is low or trust in financial intermediaries is limited (Lietaer, 2001). The legacy of Payments 1.0 thus persists, shaping perceptions of money as both a social contract and a trusted store of value.

Payments 2.0: Card-Based Systems (1950s–1990s)

The mid-twentieth century ushered in Payments 2.0, defined by the introduction of credit and debit cards. The launch of the Diners Club card in 1950, followed by Visa and Mastercard networks, marked a pivotal shift from physical money to digital payment rails. These systems standardized authorization, clearing, and settlement processes across merchants and financial institutions, creating the infrastructure for global commerce (Benson et al., 2017).

Card-based systems revolutionized consumer behavior by embedding convenience, credit availability, and global acceptance. They also introduced early concepts of interoperability and network effects: a larger base of merchants accepting cards incentivized more consumers to use them, reinforcing growth. By the 1970s, card schemes had scaled internationally, allowing cross-border transactions in ways physical cash could not.

However, Payments 2.0 also exposed systemic vulnerabilities. Fraud, chargebacks, and identity theft became major challenges as the industry struggled with balancing consumer protection and merchant risk (Schwartz, 2010). These challenges gave rise to mechanisms like the magnetic stripe, CVV codes, and later, EMV chip standards, which enhanced security. Importantly, the era institutionalized intermediated trust, where banks and networks guaranteed transaction validity - a key departure from the direct trust model of cash.

Payments 3.0: Digital Commerce and Mobile Wallets (1990s–2010s)

The emergence of the internet and mobile technology catalyzed Payments 3.0, an era characterized by e-commerce platforms, mobile wallets, and digital stored value. Companies like Alipay, and Apple Pay introduced new paradigms in digital payments, allowing consumers to transact online without directly exposing card details (Benson et al., 2017).

Central to Payments 3.0 was the concept of tokenization, which replaced sensitive payment credentials with secure tokens, reducing fraud risk while enabling seamless checkout experiences. Digital wallets also consolidated multiple funding sources - credit cards, bank accounts, stored value balances - into unified interfaces, dramatically simplifying consumer interaction.

This era also witnessed the rise of multi-party orchestration, where payments became intertwined with marketplaces, subscriptions, and peer-to-peer transfers. Platforms like eBay and later, Venmo or WeChat Pay, embedded payment services into social and commercial ecosystems, blurring the line between commerce and communication (Schwartz, 2010).

Nonetheless, Payments 3.0 faced challenges around fragmentation, interoperability, and regulatory oversight. Many systems operated within siloed ecosystems, making global standardization difficult. Furthermore, as e-commerce grew, so did the sophistication of cyberattacks, pushing the industry to invest in PCI-DSS standards, encryption, and fraud detection systems (Chen, 2021).

Payments 4.0: Real-Time Rails with Machine Learning (2010s–Present)

The current phase, Payments 4.0, builds on digital foundations by introducing instant settlement, advanced risk management, and machine learning-driven fraud detection. The development of real-time payment networks such as the U.K.'s Faster Payments Service, India's Unified Payments Interface (UPI), and the U.S. RTP system reflects the industry's shift toward immediacy.

Machine learning has become central to fraud prevention, analyzing vast volumes of data in real time to identify anomalies and prevent unauthorized transactions.

These systems use pattern recognition, behavioral analytics, and adaptive algorithms to continuously refine their models, achieving higher precision and recall than traditional rule-based systems (Chen, 2021).

Beyond fraud, Payments 4.0 also emphasizes global interoperability. Cross-border corridors are increasingly optimized through intelligent routing, while APIs allow fintechs and banks to integrate seamlessly. The role of open banking frameworks has further expanded, enabling consumer-controlled data sharing and fostering innovation across financial ecosystems (Oliver & Warfe, 2020).

Despite these advances, challenges persist. Instant payments raise new forms of liquidity, compliance, and operational risks, particularly for institutions operating across multiple jurisdictions (Chen, 2021). Moreover, the speed of settlement leaves little room for error resolution, demanding more robust dispute resolution frameworks.

Conclusion

The trajectory from Payments 1.0 to 4.0 demonstrates a clear progression: from tangible trust in cash, to network-driven interoperability, to digital convenience, and finally to real-time, intelligence-enabled systems. Each phase not only addressed the limitations of its predecessor but also introduced new challenges in security, regulation, and scalability.

This historical progression provides the necessary foundation for understanding Payments 5.0: agentic autonomy. Unlike earlier phases, which digitized or optimized existing processes, Payments 5.0 introduces a paradigm shift - where intelligent agents proactively interpret user intent, plan execution strategies, and act autonomously under strict guardrails. As the next section will show, this marks a redefinition of payments as goal-driven, explainable, and autonomous systems, setting the stage for the future of financial technology.

Foundations of Agentic Systems

Agentic payment systems build upon advances in artificial intelligence, specifically large language models and autonomous agent frameworks. These systems demonstrate the ability to understand natural language instructions, reason about complex payment scenarios, and execute multi-step plans while adhering to safety constraints.

Research in autonomous agents has shown promising results in domains requiring planning, tool use, and safety compliance. The application of these techniques to payments presents unique opportunities for improving user experience while addressing the complexity of modern financial ecosystems.

The emergence of agentic payment systems represents the convergence of advances in artificial intelligence (AI), large language models (LLMs), and autonomous agent frameworks. Unlike earlier automation tools that relied on rigid, rule-based execution, agentic systems possess the ability to understand natural language instructions, reason about complex payment scenarios, and carry out multi-step actions under safety guardrails. This combination of interpretability, adaptability, and explainability lays the foundation for Payments 5.0, where intent-driven autonomy becomes central to the user experience.

Large Language Models as Cognitive Engines

At the core of modern agentic systems are large language models. LLMs provide the natural language understanding (NLU) and reasoning capabilities that allow payment agents to interpret user intent. For example, when a user says, "Make sure my bills are paid on time without overdrawing my account," the system must parse goals (timely bill payment), constraints (account balance), and preferences (avoiding overdraft fees). LLMs, trained on vast corpora, excel at capturing these nuances and translating them into structured plans (Brown et al., 2020).

What distinguishes LLMs from traditional natural language systems is their ability to generalize across domains and contexts. In payments, this flexibility is critical, as users express financial intent in varied and often ambiguous ways. Furthermore, advancements in fine-tuning, prompt engineering, and reinforcement learning from human feedback (RLHF) have enhanced the ability of LLMs to provide contextually accurate, safe, and personalized responses (OpenAI, 2023). This adaptability positions LLMs as the "cognitive engines" of agentic payments, bridging the gap between unstructured human input and structured financial execution.

Autonomous Agent Frameworks

While LLMs provide linguistic and reasoning capability, autonomous agent frameworks supply the infrastructure for planning, tool use, and environment interaction. These frameworks allow systems to go beyond simple question answering to execute multi-step workflows, such as verifying account balances, selecting optimal payment rails, conducting fraud checks, and completing transactions.

Frameworks like LangChain and AutoGPT have demonstrated how agents can orchestrate complex tasks by chaining reasoning steps with external tool calls (Qian et al., 2023). In the payments context, this means that an agent can dynamically route transactions through different providers, optimize for fees or rewards, and comply with regulatory checks - all without explicit user intervention. By integrating APIs, fraud detection modules, and compliance databases, autonomous agent frameworks ensure seamless interaction with the broader financial ecosystem (Capco, 2025).

Importantly, these frameworks are designed to support tool-augmented intelligence. Agents can call external services - such as exchange rate APIs, identity verification systems, or blockchain explorers - when additional data is required. This capacity for adaptive tool use is essential for handling cross-border transactions, high-value payments, and dispute resolution, where multiple systems must work in concert to ensure security and efficiency.

Safety, Compliance, and Guardrails

A defining characteristic of agentic systems is their capacity to operate within safety and compliance boundaries. Unlike rule-based payment systems, autonomous agents must contend with the risk of hallucination, prompt injection, and misuse of tools. Research in AI safety emphasizes the necessity of guardrails, least-privilege access, and real-time monitoring to ensure that agent behavior remains aligned with regulatory and institutional policies (Jaipuria et al., 2025).

For payments, this involves embedding safeguards such as:

- Dry-run simulations, where agents test transactions in a controlled environment before execution.
- Cryptographic audit trails, which provide verifiable records of agent decisions.
- Human-in-the-loop oversight for high-risk or anomalous cases.
- Differential privacy and federated learning, which allow systems to learn from aggregate behavior without compromising individual user data (Aljunaid, Alamoudi, & Alkahtani, 2025).

These mechanisms ensure that even as agents gain autonomy, their operations remain transparent, explainable, and legally compliant.

Cross-Domain Lessons for Payments

The application of agentic systems in payments benefits from cross-domain research in robotics, healthcare, and cybersecurity. In robotics, for example, autonomous planning frameworks have shown how agents can manage sequential tasks under uncertainty while respecting safety constraints (Sutton & Barto, 2018). Similarly, in healthcare, AI-driven clinical agents are required to balance autonomy with ethical oversight, offering a blueprint for integrating compliance and accountability into agentic systems (Ghosh & Sanyal, 2024).

These lessons transfer directly to financial ecosystems, where trust is paramount. Users must not only believe that payments will be executed correctly but also understand the reasoning behind agentic decisions. The inclusion of explainability features - such as natural language justifications of why one payment method was chosen over another - can enhance user trust and regulatory acceptance (Linklaters, 2025).

Opportunities for Payments 5.0

By combining LLM-based reasoning, autonomous frameworks, and robust safety layers, agentic systems offer transformative opportunities in financial services. They can:

- Automate routine payment tasks such as recurring bill pay while optimizing timing for cash flow.
- Enable cross-border optimization by dynamically choosing the most cost-effective rails.
- Enhance fraud detection through real-time behavioral analysis.
- Provide personalized financial advice, integrating spending, rewards, and risk considerations.

In short, agentic foundations position Payments 5.0 as a paradigm where intelligence, autonomy, and safety intersect, reshaping how individuals and businesses experience financial transactions. The shift is not merely technological but also behavioral and institutional, requiring industry-wide collaboration between banks, fintechs, regulators, and consumers.

MAIN FOCUS OF THE CHAPTER

Defining Payments 5.0: Agentic Autonomy

Payments 5.0 is not merely an incremental upgrade; it represents a systemic redefinition of the relationship between humans, money, and machines. As intelligent agents become central to the payments landscape, their success will depend on the seamless interplay of understanding, planning, integration, and safety, ensuring that autonomy enhances - not undermines - the reliability and inclusivity of global financial systems.

Payments 5.0 marks a profound transformation in the way financial transactions are conceptualized and executed. Unlike earlier phases of payment evolution - where innovation largely digitized existing processes or improved settlement speeds - Payments 5.0 introduces agentic autonomy, a model in which intelligent software agents act on behalf of users to interpret goals, design optimal strategies, and execute transactions safely. This shift is not just technological but also philosophical: it reflects a movement from reactive payment tools toward proactive, autonomous systems that blend artificial intelligence, compliance, and human oversight (Cambridge Centre for Alternative Finance, 2025; Ghosh & Sanyal, 2024).

At the heart of Payments 5.0 are four core capabilities: intent understanding, autonomous planning, tool integration, and safety with explainability. Together, these dimensions establish the foundation for trustworthy, efficient, and user-centric payment ecosystems.

Intent Understanding

The defining feature of agentic payments is the ability of systems to interpret user intent. Unlike traditional systems that require structured inputs - such as account numbers or pre-selected payment methods - agentic agents employ natural language processing (NLP) and contextual awareness to infer what the user wants. A customer might simply say, “Pay my bills in the most cost-effective way this week,” and the agent will translate that vague request into a set of precise actions: identifying which bills are due, prioritizing based on due dates, aligning with cash-flow forecasts, and selecting payment rails that minimize fees.

Recent industry analyses highlight this trend. For example, AWS and Forrester note that financial institutions are already deploying agentic AI to interpret customer queries and align them with financial workflows, including dispute resolution and account optimization (Amazon Web Services [AWS], 2025). This capability expands financial accessibility by allowing users to communicate in plain language rather than navigating rigid interfaces.

Autonomous Planning

Once intent is captured, agents must reason across multiple dimensions to design a payment plan. This involves balancing factors such as risk assessment, regulatory compliance, cost optimization, funding source selection, and even loyalty reward maximization. Unlike rule-based automation, autonomous planning employs multi-step reasoning algorithms capable of evaluating trade-offs in real time.

Capco (2025) emphasizes that such systems excel in areas like cash management and cross-border routing, where they dynamically select rails based on fees, FX rates, and settlement times. Similarly, FXCintel (2025) reports that agentic AI is being applied to cross-border payments to continuously monitor corridors, optimize routing, and adapt to fluctuating regulations. These examples illustrate how autonomous planning can transform complex financial decisions into seamless user experiences, while maintaining efficiency and compliance.

Tool Integration

A payment agent cannot function in isolation. To operationalize plans, it must integrate seamlessly with the surrounding ecosystem: payment networks, banking APIs, fraud detection platforms, compliance databases, and third-party financial services. Tool-augmented agents effectively act as conductors, orchestrating interactions among diverse systems to execute user intent.

Capco (2025) identifies tool integration as one of the most impactful uses of agentic AI, highlighting how agents are already combining data from risk engines, transaction monitoring systems, and payment gateways to streamline workflows. This interoperability ensures that Payments 5.0 does not require reinventing the financial infrastructure; rather, it leverages existing rails and augments them with intelligence (Zhu et al., 2024).

Safety and Explainability

The autonomy of Payments 5.0 would be untenable without robust safety mechanisms and explainability. Users and regulators must be confident that agentic systems are not only effective but also trustworthy. Safety encompasses measures such as least-privilege access, multi-factor authentication, transaction velocity controls, and anomaly detection. Explainability ensures that when an agent decides to delay a bill payment, reroute a transaction, or freeze a suspicious account, the rationale is clear and auditable.

Aljunaid, Alamoudi, and Alkahtani (2025) demonstrate how federated learning combined with explainable AI (e.g., SHAP and LIME models) can achieve both privacy protection and transparency in fraud detection. Likewise, the Cambridge Centre for Alternative Finance (2025) stresses governance, fairness, and oversight as essential to sustaining trust in autonomous systems. By embedding these safeguards, Payments 5.0 differentiates itself from opaque "black-box" AI systems and aligns with the compliance-driven nature of financial services [Ghosh & Sanyal, 2024].

Toward a Unified Paradigm

Collectively, these four capabilities establish Payments 5.0 as a unified paradigm for intent-driven, autonomous, and explainable financial transactions. The promise of this model lies not only in efficiency - faster payments, optimized routes, reduced costs - but also in trust: users remain in control of intent, while agents transparently manage the complexity of execution.

Payments 5.0 is not merely an incremental upgrade; it represents a systemic redefinition of the relationship between humans, money, and machines. As intelligent agents become central to the payments landscape, their success will depend on the seamless interplay of understanding, planning, integration, and safety, ensuring that autonomy enhances - not undermines - the reliability and inclusivity of global financial systems.

REFERENCE ARCHITECTURE FOR AGENTIC PAYMENTS

An innovative paradigm change in financial transactions is represented by agentic payments, in which artificial intelligence agents function as independent economic players that start and finish transactions without direct human supervision. This new technology calls into question established payment systems and necessitates the development of completely new security, identity verification, and transaction processing frameworks.

By adding AI agents as a fifth crucial actor, the reference architecture for agentic payments revolutionizes the conventional four-party payment model. Agentic payment systems must support multi-agent coordination, autonomous decision-making, and continuous operation, in contrast to traditional systems built around human interaction patterns.

Core Architectural Layers

Agent Layer: This foundational layer manages AI entities that initiate transactions and interact with payment systems. Each agent requires registration, authentication, and authorization to perform specific transaction types within defined parameters. Agents must declare their capabilities, including authorized transaction types, merchant interactions, and approved payment methods.

Payment Orchestration Layer: Serving as the central intelligence hub, this layer coordinates between agents, payment providers, and merchants while abstracting complexity behind a unified interface. The orchestration layer implements smart routing algorithms that determine optimal transaction paths based on cost, speed, reliability, and success rates.

Security and Identity Management Layer: This critical component addresses the unique challenge of establishing trust for entities lacking traditional identity markers such as biometric data or government-issued identification. The system implements sophisticated multi-factor authentication combining device verification, behavioral analysis, and contextual verification.

Agent Authentication and Identity Framework (Security Architecture)

Security architecture for AI agent payment authentication and fraud prevention

Digital Identity Verification

AI agent identity management relies on verifiable credentials and cryptographic signatures to establish trust and accountability. Each agent possesses unique cryptographic key pairs for transaction signing and communication authentication. The system maintains clear ownership chains linking agents to their human or organizational controllers, essential for regulatory compliance and dispute resolution.

Agent Registration Process: The registration establishes agent identity, ownership, and operational scope through digital credentials linking agents to their owners. This process involves creating comprehensive agent profiles that include operational parameters, transaction history, and security credentials.

Mandate System: A crucial innovation in agentic payments, mandates provide frameworks for users to delegate specific payment authorities while maintaining control. These digital contracts define authorization scope including transaction limits, allowed merchants, payment methods, and time-based restrictions. The system supports dynamic permission adjustment based on changing circumstances or risk factors.

Multi-Factor Authentication

Agentic payment systems implement sophisticated authentication beyond traditional credentials. Device authentication verifies execution environments to ensure agents operate in secure, uncompromised systems. Behavioral analysis uses machine learning to detect anomalies indicating potential compromise or unauthorized use.

PAYMENT ORCHESTRATION AND PROCESSING

The diagram "Payment Orchestration Layer Diagram" illustrates how a payment orchestration system operates by linking merchants to several payment providers through an orchestration layer in between. Such an arrangement improves efficiency, resilience, and flexibility for online transactions. The orchestration layer is the command center that manages routing logic, fallback functionality, and API integrations.

Key Components

1. Payment Providers
   - These are third-party services that process payments.
   - The Payment Providers box is intentionally extended, indicating the ability to support multiple providers instead of being locked into just one.
   - This diversification reduces dependency on a single provider and enables businesses to optimize transaction success rates and costs.
2. Smart Routing Engine
   - The routing engine applies business logic and rules to determine which payment provider should handle each transaction.
   - Factors influencing routing decisions include:
     - Transaction type (credit card, ACH, digital wallet, etc.)
     - Cost optimization (choosing providers with lower transaction fees)
     - Geographic relevance (selecting providers strongest in a customer's region)
     - Provider performance (latency, uptime, and past success rates).
   - This ensures **higher success rates** and **reduced transaction failures**.
3. Orchestration Layer
   - Serves as the **core control unit** that connects smart routing, payment providers, APIs, and fallback mechanisms.
   - Main responsibilities include:
     - Unifying integrations with multiple providers.
     - Exposing a **single integration point** to merchants, simplifying complexity.
     - Enforcing security standards such as **tokenization, fraud detection hooks, and PCI compliance**.
     - Ensuring observability with logging, monitoring, and analytics.
4. Fallback Mechanism
   - Acts as a backup system in case a primary provider or route fails.
   - For example:

    - If Provider A is unavailable due to downtime, the orchestration layer reroutes the payment to Provider B automatically.
    - This prevents lost transactions and improves customer trust.
  - Key for ensuring business continuity and reliability.
5. API Integrations
  - Located on the right side of the diagram.
  - The orchestration layer exposes APIs (REST API, gRPC, etc.) for integration into merchant platforms, mobile apps, or backend systems.
  - APIs allow developers to:
    - Initiate payments.
    - Query transaction statuses.
    - Trigger refunds or chargebacks.
  - Using standardized APIs reduces integration costs and makes the system scalable.

Smart Routing Engine

The payment orchestration layer implements intelligent routing that analyzes real-time data to optimize transaction paths. Dynamic provider selection maintains performance metrics for all connected payment providers, including success rates, processing times, and costs. When primary payment paths fail, automatic fallback mechanisms attempt alternative routes without agent intervention.

Transaction Lifecycle Management: The system manages complete transaction lifecycles through sophisticated state management and coordination. Pre-transaction validation checks agent authorization, account balances, and applies risk assessment rules before submitting to payment providers. Real-time monitoring tracks progress across all involved parties, providing status updates and enabling rapid issue response.

Provider Integration Framework

The integration framework ensures consistent behavior while accommodating unique provider requirements. A unified API layer standardizes access to all payment providers, normalizing requests and responses. Protocol translation handles differences in data formats, authentication methods, and communication protocols between providers.

Security and Fraud Prevention Architecture

Advanced Fraud Detection

Agentic payment systems require multiple security layers addressing unique risks from autonomous AI agents. Behavioral analytics continuously learn normal agent patterns, creating baseline profiles enabling detection of anomalous activities. Cross-agent analysis identifies coordinated attacks or suspicious coordination between agents indicating broader security breaches.

Real-Time Risk Scoring: Each transaction receives fraud risk scores based on agent history, transaction characteristics, merchant reputation, and threat intelligence. High-risk transactions undergo additional verification or blocking. Dynamic risk assessment continuously recalculates based on changing factors including transaction patterns, agent behavior, and market conditions.

Zero-Trust Security Model

The architecture implements zero-trust principles requiring authentication and authorization for every access request. End-to-end encryption protects all communications between system components. Secure enclaves provide hardware-level protection for critical operations such as key management and transaction authorization.

Integration Standards and Protocols

Emerging Protocol Standards

- Agent2Agent (A2A) Protocol: This open communication standard enables interoperability between AI agents from different providers. The protocol defines agent discovery, service negotiation, and complex transaction coordination.
- Agent Payments Protocol (AP2): Google's comprehensive framework extends A2A with payment capabilities, supporting multiple payment types from traditional rails to stablecoin transactions. AP2 includes over 60 industry partners including Mastercard, and Coinbase.
- x402 Integration: Coinbase's x402 protocol leverages HTTP 402 status codes for instant stablecoin payments, enabling automatic payment and retry mechanisms. The integration allows agents to transact using USDC and other stablecoins with instant settlement and lower fees.

Scalability and Performance

Agentic payment systems must handle massive transaction volumes as AI agents operate continuously at speeds exceeding human capabilities. Horizontal scaling across multiple servers and data centers maintains performance under increasing loads. Microservices architecture enables independent component scaling based on demand patterns.

Performance Optimization: Multi-level caching systems store frequently accessed data close to processing components. Geographic distribution through content delivery networks reduces latency by bringing processing closer to agents and users.

Operational Management

Comprehensive monitoring systems track performance, success rates, and agent behavior in real-time. Automated operations handle routine tasks including scaling, failover, and optimization while escalating complex issues with complete context.

FUTURE OUTLOOK AND EVOLUTION

Regulatory Development

As agentic payments proliferate, regulatory frameworks will evolve to address unique challenges. Banks must validate AI agent identities as these entities become customers themselves. Agent licensing requirements may emerge similar to current financial advisor regulations.

Agentic Wallets / Digital Wallets Managed by Agents

Smart wallets merge AI with financial optimization by dynamically managing funds across checking, savings, credit, and investment accounts. Agents automatically rebalance allocations, anticipate spending needs, and choose the most cost-effective payment method for each transaction. More sophisticated strategies include tax-loss harvesting, dollar-cost averaging, and asset allocation based on market volatility. Agents prevent overdraft fees by shifting funds, tap credit lines strategically, and negotiate better terms with institutions based on user behavior. These wallets act like personalized wealth managers—providing complex financial strategies to everyday users—offering optimized returns, cost savings, and alignment with life changes or market conditions while remaining secure and compliant.

Regulatory, Compliance & Legal Use Cases KYC/AML

Compliance in financial services requires constant vigilance, and agentic systems automate much of this workload. They perform Know Your Customer (KYC) and Anti–Money Laundering (AML) checks by verifying identities against databases, detecting suspicious actions, and maintaining full audit trails. These systems automatically update to reflect new regulatory requirements, flag risks proactively, and generate detailed, explainable audit trails for regulators. Beyond compliance, they support legal risk management by automating contract review, regulatory filings, and monitoring obligations. Privacy compliance is also strengthened, with automated consent management, data retention policies, and cross-border transfer safeguards. By transforming compliance from a reactive, manual process into a proactive, intelligent one, agentic systems allow institutions to confidently operate across jurisdictions while minimizing risks and maintaining transparency.

USE CASES AND APPLICATIONS

Institutional Use Case Example

Agentic programmable payments increasingly enable asset tokenization at scale. Global banks and asset managers now tokenize large blocks of equities and real estate, allowing instant, automated settlement via smart contracts. For instance, a commercial real estate transaction using tokenized shares on a distributed ledger can execute transfer of ownership and programmable settlement of escrow, fees, and taxes within seconds—dramatically reducing counterparty risk and process overhead. Likewise, the bond tokenization pilot by major European institutions demonstrates how programmable coupon payments and real-time agentic audits lower operational risk and increase transparency, with compliance controls embedded in each transaction (World Economic Forum, 2025; Capco, 2025).

Proactive Bill Payment Management

Intelligent billing systems modernize how payment providers manage users' financial obligations by pairing automation with predictive analytics. These systems continuously track recurring costs- utilities, subscriptions, loans—and learn each user's cash-flow patterns, spending habits, and goals. Using machine learning, they determine optimal payment timing based on account balances, upcoming deposits, and reward cycles. Advanced capabilities include negotiating bill due dates, switching funding sources to maximize rewards or minimize fees, consolidating payments to cut costs, and sequencing transactions to maintain healthy credit-utilization while avoiding late fees. For example, an agent may align a utility payment with the user's payday to prevent overdrafts, or stagger credit-card payments across the month to preserve credit scores. They also run predictive cash-flow models that surface potential shortfalls well in advance, triggering alerts and recommending budget adjustments or revised payment terms before pressure builds.

Intelligent Dispute Resolution

Agentic dispute resolution systems streamline transaction dispute handling by using pattern recognition across spending behavior and merchant reputation to flag fraudulent or erroneous charges. Once triggered, agents automatically assemble evidence - transaction logs, merchant communications, and supporting documents - then open negotiations with merchants through automated channels. Routine cases are closed in the first stage with automation alone; human analysts are rarely needed. For card disputes, the agent files chargebacks complete with evidence, monitors case status, pushes real-time updates to users, and preserves a secure, end-to-end audit trail. Beyond remediation, these systems add prevention: they surface suspicious behavior before customers complain, prompt users when risky actions occur, and, in high-risk scenarios, temporarily freeze accounts or transactions pending verification to curb losses and bolster trust. The approach blends partial automation (rapid detection and evidence collection), full automation (preliminary negotiations and information exchange), and proactive controls into a single workflow that speeds resolution, reduces operational cost, and strengthens user protection - while maintaining the accuracy, transparency, and traceability regulators and institutions require.

Agentic Wallets / Digital Wallets Managed by Agents

Smart wallet management applies AI to personal finance, with autonomous agents interpreting spending patterns, income timing, and market conditions to decide how funds move across checking, savings, cards, and investment accounts. Agents allocate and rebalance continuously, shifting cash between high-yield savings and transaction accounts based on forecasted needs, and selecting the optimal payment method per transaction to maximize rewards or minimize fees. Sophisticated wallets orchestrate institution-grade strategies - tax-loss harvesting, automated dollar-cost averaging, and volatility-aware asset allocation - while honoring minimum-balance rules. They preempt overdrafts by sweeping funds, choose low-cost credit lines before selling assets, and can negotiate preferred rates or perks with providers using relationship data. Always-on optimization turns money management from manual tasks into proactive execution aimed at higher returns, lower costs, and consistent goal progress. The model delivers personalized wealth management to everyday users - even without deep financial expertise - by adapting plans to shifting markets, spending trends, and life events. Throughout, operations remain secure and compliant through guardrails like least-privilege access, audit trails, and policy-driven controls.

Regulatory, Compliance & Legal Use Cases KYC/AML

Agentic systems shift compliance from manual, retrospective checks to proactive, always-on oversight. They automate KYC/AML by verifying identities across multiple data sources, assessing risk, and spotting anomalous behaviors - while preserving complete, time-stamped audit trails. Continuously updated rule libraries ingest regulatory changes across jurisdictions, auto-flag impacts, recommend control updates, and alert teams before breaches occur. Beyond screening, agents mitigate legal risk by parsing contracts, preparing regulatory filings, tracking obligations, and embedding explainability so every decision is traceable for auditors and supervisors. Privacy is enforced by design through consent management, purpose limitation, retention schedules, and governed cross-border data transfers. Real-time monitoring and adaptive controls - velocity limits, step-up verification, and least-privilege access - adjust to emerging risks without adding unnecessary friction. The result is a virtuous cycle: continuous surveillance enables early intervention; interventions generate robust evidence; evidence strengthens oversight and trust; and trusted, up-to-date controls let institutions operate confidently across markets. In short, agentic compliance unifies detection, prevention, documentation, and transparency - reducing operational burden while improving accuracy, accountability, and resilience.

SECURITY AND RISK MANAGEMENT

Threat Analysis

Prompt Injection and Manipulation Attacks

Agentic payment systems are vulnerable to prompt injection attacks that exploit natural language processing. Attackers insert deceptive instructions into valid-looking inputs to bypass fraud detection and authorization, tricking agents into executing unauthorized transactions or leaking sensitive data. Indirect attacks occur when poisoned content in external sources (e.g., merchant descriptions, memos) is ingested, making detection difficult. Because agents adapt through subtle linguistic shifts and multi-turn dialogues, they are highly susceptible to social engineering. The autonomous nature of these systems amplifies risks, as a compromised agent can process many fraudulent transactions before discovery, exposing multiple points of failure.

Tool Abuse and Privilege Escalation

Agentic systems interact with diverse financial tools and APIs, creating wide attack surfaces for misuse. Attackers exploit legitimate functionality- such as refund systems, payment routing, or timing adjustments - by chaining valid requests in harmful ways. Examples include high-frequency microtransactions designed to evade detection thresholds, exploiting float periods, or biasing market data to trigger favorable conversions. Since these abuses mimic normal operations, they are hard to detect. More advanced threats manipulate probabilistic AI decision-making by skewing input data, tampering with training feedback, or exploiting edge cases. Because operations are autonomous, a single compromise can cascade across thousands of transactions while appearing normal.

Adversarial Algorithm Manipulation

The algorithms driving agentic planning and decision-making are sensitive to adversarial interference. Attackers may poison training data, embed backdoors, or manipulate inputs at inference time to bias decisions. Subtle probability shifts or incremental behavioral changes can spread across transactions unnoticed, while still yielding attacker benefits. These attacks are dangerous because once malicious logic is embedded in decision flows, agents amplify harmful outcomes autonomously. They can influence routing, timing, and authorization without detection, all while maintaining a façade of normalcy. Such risks highlight the need for specialized defenses designed for the unique vulnerabilities of autonomous AI-driven financial systems.

Comprehensive Mitigation Strategies

Advanced Access Control and Privilege Management

Defense requires enforcing least-privilege models through dynamic policy engines. Fine-grained permission matrices restrict agent access to tools, transaction types, and data depending on contextual factors such as transaction value, recipient status, or behavioral history. Capability sandboxing isolates agents in controlled execution environments, preventing unauthorized API calls. Adaptive role-based access control (RBAC) adjusts permissions in real time - escalating for verified safe actions or reducing when risks increase. These intelligent frameworks replace static models with adaptive controls, ensuring agents remain functional but constrained, balancing operational efficiency with strong security.

Intelligent Rate Limiting and Behavioral Controls

Rate limiting evolves from simple action caps to behavior-aware throttling. Machine learning continuously monitors transaction patterns to detect anomalies, enabling dynamic limits based on history, behavior, activity type, and risk context. Controls span transaction size, frequency, destinations, and timing. Advanced models detect subtle coordinated attacks or bot-like patterns, gradually imposing stricter restrictions as risks emerge. This adaptive throttling reduces false positives while preventing sophisticated exploitation of system thresholds.

Enhanced Authentication and Verification Frameworks

Agentic systems require risk-based, adaptive authentication. Multi-factor authentication scales dynamically: routine transactions remain frictionless, while high-value or unusual actions trigger additional checks. Strong measures include biometrics, cryptographic transaction signing, and hardware security modules. Next-generation methods emphasize continuous authentication, using behavioral biometrics such as typing patterns, navigation, and decision-making traits to verify user identity. This persistent validation thwarts account takeovers while minimizing user disruption.

Continuous Monitoring and Anomaly Detection

Multi-layered monitoring powered by machine learning builds behavioral baselines for each agent. Systems analyze transaction streams, API calls, decision processes, and communications to detect anomalies. Real-time alerts flag deviations from normal profiles, enabling early intervention. Integration with global threat intelligence enhances detection of both known and emerging attack patterns. This proactive approach supports rapid response, preventing small compromises from escalating into systemic failures.

Performance Metrics and Evaluation

Technical Performance Indicators

1. Transaction Processing Excellence

Transaction approval rates reflect system dependability across domestic transfers, international remittances, merchant, and P2P payments. Analytics break down performance by transaction type, value, and corridor to identify optimization opportunities. Processing speed is tracked as total round-trip time - from user initiation to verification - covering decision cycles, rail selection, and settlement.

2. Fraud Detection and Security Metrics

Fraud detection balances security with user experience through precision, recall, and false-positive rates. Key measures include discovery rates (how quickly threats are identified) and response times (how effectively systems adapt to new fraud patterns). These indicators reveal the maturity of machine learning models in handling evolving risks.

3. System Reliability and Availability

Reliability is assessed via uptime across all components - payment engines, decision algorithms, and APIs - under normal and peak conditions. Standard measures such as Mean Time Between Failures (MTBF) and Mean Time to Recovery (MTTR) gauge stability, while safeguards against cascading failures and external disruptions ensure continuous service availability.

User Experience Metrics

1. Natural Language Understanding and Interaction Quality

Metrics track how accurately agents interpret diverse user intents, resolve ambiguities, and maintain coherent multi-turn dialogues in complex financial contexts.

2. User Satisfaction and Task Completion

Task completion rates, segmented by transaction complexity and demographics, measure system usability. Broader satisfaction indicators include transaction speed, accuracy, trust, and Net Promoter Scores (NPS) that reveal engagement and loyalty trends.

3. Explanation and Transparency Effectiveness

Metrics evaluate how clearly agents explain decisions (e.g., fraud alerts, routing choices), user comprehension of those explanations, and the efficiency of error recovery. Clear, trust-building communication ensures transparency and confidence in the system.

EVOLUTION OF PAYMENT SECURITY MODELS

The provided image provides a comprehensive overview of the evolution in payment security models from Payments 1.0 (Manual) to Payments 5.0 (Fully Agentic), focusing on the pathways to agentic autonomy. The analysis below details the structure, key concepts, threats, and mitigations for each payment maturity stage presented in the diagram.

Overarching Themes

- Identity-first, Mandate-based, Machine-native: Security approaches evolve alongside payments technology, emphasizing identity, policy mandates, and deep integration with machine processes.
- Verifiable, Auditable, Accountable: These foundational principles anchor the security frameworks at every stage.

Stage-by-Stage Breakdown

1.0 Manual

- Threats: This early stage features classic threats such as credentials theft, social engineering, and manual errors. The human-centric processes make these systems especially vulnerable to traditional attack vectors.
- Mitigations: Controls at this level focus on more rigorous identity checks (multi-factor authentication, "step-up" verification), segregation of duties, and tamper-evident audit trails.

2.0 Automated

- Threats: Automation introduces new threats including rule abuse, schedule tampering, and batch fraud—primarily due to the centralized nature of automated process controls.
- Mitigations: Mitigations evolve towards policy formalization (policy-as-code), dual control over critical runs, anomaly detection within batch operations, and dedicated management of exception queues.

3.0 Orchestrated

- Threats: Systems become more interconnected, introducing threats like API key leakage, multi-rail card testing, exposure in vault systems, and retry logic abuse.
- Mitigations: Security measures advance to include least-privilege architectural patterns, tokenization, vault isolation, adaptive throttling at orchestrated layers, and intelligent routing based on system health.

4.0 Semi-Autonomous

- Threats: Semi-autonomous payments expand the threat surface to include intent drift, over-privileged tools, weak evidence chains, and runtime compromise. These are consequences of systems that blend human oversight with significant machine autonomy.
- Mitigations: Counter-measures span mandate drafts with explicit human binding, continuous risk assessment, attestation of runtime/device integrity, and tightly scoped tool authorizations.

5.0 Fully Agentic

- Threats: At this frontier, systems confront advanced threats such as agent spoofing, abuse of mandate constructs, micro-fraud between M2M transfers, and collusion among autonomous agents.
- Mitigations: Security matures into cryptographic mandates (AP2), facilitator verification (xA02), strong identity credentials (KYA: Know Your Agent), revocation of keys/agents on demand, budget and retry governance, and system-wide anomaly analytics.

Key Insights

- Security maturity in payments shifts from human-centric to agent-centric, requiring adaptive, layered mitigations that address both policy and technology risks.
- Each stage builds on previous controls, integrating new mechanisms for auditability, oversight, and interoperability as autonomy increases.
- The final goal is machine-native, agentic systems that remain verifiable, auditable, and accountable through formal mandates and persistent oversight.

This detailed pathway visualizes the technological and organizational journey required for secure agentic autonomy in payments, highlighting how new forms of threats and countermeasures emerge in step with automation and intelligence sophistication.

SOLUTIONS AND RECOMMENDATIONS

A practical roadmap to evolve from Payments 1.0 (manual) to Payments 5.0 (autonomous, agent-based) using open protocols. Integrates AP2 for verifiable intent, x402 for machine micropayments, and orchestration with fraud/risk safeguards for safe scale.

Implementation Framework

Adopt a staged approach: start with low-risk use cases, expand as confidence grows. Use AP2 mandates, orchestration best practices, and fraud controls to progress from basic automation to full autonomy.

Phase 1: Foundations

Build intent capture and routine automation under human oversight. Deploy orchestration to unify providers via a single API, enabling smart routing, cost control, and policy-based flows (e.g., bills, subscriptions). Adopt AP2-style intent capture, agent identity verification, and baseline fraud tools. Pilot x402 machine-to-machine micropayments in sandbox with stablecoins. Add compliance guardrails, auditable logs, and monitor KPIs such as authorization lift, reduced reviews, and lower latency.

Phase 2: Autonomous Operations

Enable autonomous execution in deterministic scenarios with orchestration-based failover and AP2 mandates for non-repudiable audit trails. Use strong guardrails (caps, whitelists, time windows) for human-not-present flows. Infuse identity, credentials, and step-up authentication. Advance fraud detection with behavioral baselines and merchant reputation. Run targeted agent trials with networks (e.g., Mastercard Agent Pay, Worldpay), expand x402 adoption for microtransactions, and enforce mandate-linked forensics for disputes.

Phase 3: High-End Intelligence

Deploy multi-agent optimization: bundling, contextual routing, and contingent purchasing via AP2 mandate chains. Use MCP interfaces for secure agent collaboration and governed execution. Expand x402 and on-chain rails for micro-settlements and cross-border flows. Standardize products so payments become embedded, with consent, identity, and accountability verifiable by open protocols.

Recommendations

- Embrace AP2 for consent and accountability.
- Use x402 for autonomous micropayments.
- Employ orchestration for resilience.
- Align identity, fraud, and law with non-human actors from the start.

- Collaborate with Visa, Mastercard, Worldpay to accelerate merchant acceptance and reduce custom integrations.

Intent Domain Specific Language (DSL)

An Intent DSL harmonized across providers, merchants, and agents enables consistent representation and verification of payment intent, aligning with AP2's Intent Mandate and Cart Mandate abstractions. The DSL must remain human-readable, machine-verifiable, and schema-versioned to preserve interoperability as standards evolve.

Canonical Structure

INTENT: pay_bills

PARAMETERS: recipients [electricity, internet, phone], optimization minimize_fees, timing before_due_date, funding_source checking_account

CONSTRAINTS: max_total $500, require_confirmation high_value_only

In AP2 mapping, Intent + Parameters define purpose, optimization, timing, and funding, while Constraints impose guardrails such as caps, categories, and confirmation policies. The Cart Mandate links items, values, and totals to non-repudiable signatures. To support machine-to-machine monetization, the DSL may specify per-call budgets, rate limits, and x402-based fallbacks. Core design principles include schema versioning, cryptographic credential binding, and AP2 compatibility. Validation pipelines must enforce semantic integrity, constraint satisfiability, and agent authenticity, enabling auditable, bank-grade, autonomous execution.

PAY-Bench Simulation Suite

A full test model enables secure development and verification of payment systems based on agency in virtualized environments that simulate real-life payment scenarios, regulator constraints, and user behavior patterns. PAY-Bench should provide modular building blocks for merchants, PSPs, issuers, networks, identity providers, and attackers, including end-to-end simulation of AP2 mandates, x402 flows, orchestration routing, and fraud interventions under various business and risk scenarios.

Core Capability 1

Protocol conformance and mandate integrity tests. Scenarios should verify that Intent and Cart mandates are properly constructed, signed, and authenticated between parties, with tamper tests, replay defenses, and non-repudiation checks in human-present and delegated flows. Negative tests should introduce invalid cart data, stale signatures, or mandate scope errors to ensure that merchants, PSPs, and networks reject transactions and produce actionable diagnostics to facilitate remediation.

Core Capability 2

Orchestration, routing, and resilience training. Simulations need to emulate multi-rail routing, provider latency spike, partial outage, and currency or fee change, ensuring smart routing policy for cost, speed, and reliability trade-offs when volumes are agent-influenced. Benchmarks need to track authorization uplift, failover success ratio, and end-to-end latency impact when agent throughput is scaled, ensuring continuity of operation readiness.

Core Capability 3

Adversarial risk and fraud lab. PAY-Bench should have synthetic agent personas, device fingerprints, and behavioral baselines to mimic detection of drift, agent collusion, merchant spoofing, and step-up triggers for high-risk transactions. KPI outputs should be able to quantify false positive and negative rates, time-to-detection, and downstream loss prevention in scenarios blending new agent behavior with proven fraud typologies.

Engineering Harness and Metrics

PAY-Bench should provide reproducible scenario specifications, seedable randomness for comparability, and golden datasets for regression, as well as dashboards mapping protocol events to business and risk KPIs. Standard outputs should cover protocol pass/fail, orchestration KPIs, fraud metrics, identity/consent coverage, and economic metrics like fees per success, cost per failover, and time to settle for on-chain flows. Integration with CI pipelines can block agent feature promotion on mandate integrity limits, acceptance rates, and loss boundaries, allowing for secure iteration toward autonomy.

Recommendations

Adopt AP2 reference implementations for mandate validation, use x402 facilitator sandboxes for synthetic M2M traffic, and obtain realistic fraud corpora and merchant response curves to avoid overfitting to idealized scenarios. Engage with networks and leading processors to obtain anonymized acceptance and risk signals that mimic production behavior for agent-originated transactions to accelerate readiness for live deployment at Payments 5.0 scale.

Together, this staged roadmap, Intent DSL standardization, and PAY-Bench simulation toolset provide a real-world path from first-level automation right out to dependable agentic autonomy, grounded in open protocols, orchestration discipline, and verifiable accountability across the payments stack. By implementing on AP2, leveraging x402 for micropayments natively available to machines, and honing controls by simulation, organizations can realize the "invisible payments" potential of Payments 5.0 without sacrificing safety, compliance, or merchant acceptance

TECHNICAL ARCHITECTURE

The provided technical architecture diagram represents a staged pathway for progressing from basic competency to full agentic autonomy, which can be mapped to Payments 1.0 to 5.0 transformation for agentic and autonomous payment system evolution. Each phase builds upon the previous, integrating core payment functionalities with adaptive, learning, and autonomous agentic capabilities.

Phase 1: Core Competency Development

This initial phase focuses on establishing foundational skills relevant to payment processing, including basic transaction modules, security protocols, and interoperability capabilities. For Payments 1.0, this involves simple, rule-based transaction execution and integration of basic modules such as authorization, authentication, and payment posting.

- Data Flow: Skill Acquisition
- Core elements: Basic Skill, Modules

Phase 2: Autonomous Decision-Making

Here, payment systems start employing algorithmic frameworks for decision-making, such as automated risk assessment, dynamic transaction routing, and rule-based approval processes. This aligns with the transition from Payments 2.0 (basic automation and conditional logic) towards Payments 3.0, introducing elements like contextual payment routing and feedback-based optimizations.

- Data Flow: Decision Feedback
- Core elements: Decision Algorithm Framework, Algorithm Framework

Phase 3: Environmental Adaptation

Payment systems incorporate sensor data and environmental context (e.g., transaction histories, real-time fraud indicators, behavioral analytics) to adapt payment strategies in response to changing market, regulatory, or user scenarios. This enables adaptive payment flows characteristic of Payments 3.0-4.0, leveraging environmental integration for dynamic adjustment of parameters.

- Data Flow: Adaptation
- Core elements: Sensor Data, Integration

Phase 4: Goal Optimization

The system introduces reward mechanisms (for positive outcomes such as successful transactions, minimized fraud, or optimized fees) and fine-tuning algorithms that continuously optimize goal achievement. This phase marks the evolution towards self-improving, learning-enabled Payments 4.0 systems, where adaptation metrics and reward-driven learning facilitate ongoing optimization.

- Data Flow: Adaptation Metrics
- Core elements: Reward System, Tuning
- Integration point: Learning Algorithm Update

Phase 5: Full Autonomy

At this advanced stage, the payment architecture executes dynamic strategy adjustments autonomously, leveraging previous adaptation and optimization steps. Payments 5.0 systems operate with minimal human oversight, optimizing strategies in real-time based on environmental models and threshold criteria for true agentic autonomy.

- Core elements: Dynamic Strategy Adjustment (multiple types)
- Integration Points: Environmental Model Sync, Autonomy Threshold Adjustment

Systemic Data Flows & Integration Points

- Skill acquisition feeds initial modules.
- Decision feedback loops inform ongoing improvements.

- Adaptation outcomes and optimization outputs are continuously fed back into system learning and environmental syncing.
- Integration points synchronize with learning algorithms and environmental models to adjust autonomy thresholds and ensure robust, scalable evolution.

Application to Payments 1.0 to 5.0 Pathway

- Payments 1.0: Manual, basic digital transactions performed by rule-based systems.
- Payments 2.0: Introduction of automation and conditional logic for enhanced transaction flows.
- Payments 3.0: Adaptive systems using feedback and environment data to refine processes.
- Payments 4.0: Optimization through ML-based learning, reward systems, and continuous adaptation.
- Payments 5.0: Completely agentic payment systems capable of autonomous decision-making, dynamic environmental response, and threshold adjustment for self-regulated operation.

This architecture is designed to ensure secure, efficient, and autonomous payment processes as systems mature from basic digitized operations to fully agentic, AI-driven financial transactions.

FUTURE RESEARCH DIRECTIONS

The evolution toward Payments 5.0 represents a paradigm shift from traditional transaction processing to intelligent, autonomous financial ecosystems. This transformation opens unprecedented research opportunities that span artificial intelligence, distributed systems, regulatory technology, and advanced cryptography. As we advance toward more sophisticated agentic payment infrastructures, several critical research domains emerge that will shape the future of global financial transactions.

Multi-Agent Payment Ecosystems

The design of multi-agent payment ecosystems is one of the most fertile topics and challenges in this area, involving complex coordination mechanisms with multiple autonomous agents that co-operate, compete and negotiate through complex financial settings and landscapes with a wide variety of stakeholders, institutions, regulatory contexts. Studies in this area concentrate on the design of consensus algorithms that can make agents converge to optimal payment solutions, which attempt to balance competing interests among groups of different parties and advanced game theory may play an important role for modeling agent behaviors where multiple institutions compete for transaction routing but need to cooperate at the same time for obtaining satisfactory results. Some of the prominent research challenges are in designing reputation systems for agents network, devising mechanisms for fair value distribution in collaborative payment processing and trust models that lay out secure inter agent communication without any centralised control.

Regulatory Technology Integration

The successful AI-ization of regulatory compliance means a paradigm shift from reactive checking of adherence to proactive adjustment in regulations with efforts being focused on the development of AIs that are able to read and understand natural language regulation, predict changes in them and adjust itself accordingly in order to be compliant in multiple jurisdictions at once. These future research directions also involve developing transparent AI systems for decisions based on regulation, setting up automatic regulatory impact assessments and devising guidelines for real-time compliance monitoring with the challenge to create systems that can manage accurate interpretation of laws whilst remaining flexible enough to accommodate different emerging legislative paradigms in fast moving fintech worlds.

There is also a research opportunity in designing standardised protocols that allow agentic payment systems to operate consistently across regulatory jurisdictions while complying with local regulations such as the exploration of automated means for regulatory mapping which find equivalent regulation among different areas or the design of generic compliance interfaces that map jurisdiction-specific compliance demands into standard agent behaviour. By pursuing this cross-jurisdiction harmonization, one of the desired goals is to develop sets of standardized compliance requirements that minimize operational burden and meet local regulatory expectations with the intent that global payment agents will operate consistently no matter where they are subject to regulation.

Emerging Research Frontiers

Agricultural e-payments must be studied with an eye towards the development of new generation payment agents, considering embedded behavioral economics in agent modelling and designing how to enable payment agents to recognize and cope with personal users' behavior patterns, preferences or biases (e.g., personalized optimization algorithms can be developed in order that they are able to balance financial efficiency against user comfort levels; adaptive user interfaces should evolve based on individual behavior). There are also research opportunities in developing eco-friendly payment routing algorithms at more than network level, carbon offset mechanisms for forging payment processing or sustainable metrics of agentic payment systems that can optimize environmental sustainability without degrading the financial processes.

The convergence of these research strands is likely to produce payment systems that are not only more efficient and secure, but also adaptive, sustainable and aligned with human values and societal needs – such an approach reflects a comprehensive understanding of the evolution in payment systems where psychological, environmental and social dimensions complement traditional criteria focused on technical optimisation as well as financial ones. This overarching research perspective ensures that future agentic payment systems are delivered as responsible technological solutions addressing user experience and positively impacting environmental sustainability and broader societal well-being.

CONCLUSION

Payments 5.0 represents a fundamental evolution in how financial transactions are conceived, planned, and executed, marking a paradigm shift from reactive transaction processing to proactive, intelligent financial orchestration. By leveraging advances in artificial intelligence and autonomous agent technology, agentic payment systems promise to deliver unprecedented levels of optimization, security, and user experience while maintaining the trust and reliability required for financial infrastructure. This transformation extends beyond mere technological advancement to encompass a complete reimagining of the relationship between users, institutions, and financial systems.

The Intelligence Revolution in Financial Services

Transitioning to agentic payment systems heralds the era of financial intelligence, in which self-determining agents are constantly monitoring market conditions, user needs, regulatory policies and security adversities to reach optimal decisions on when's best for payments to be made. These systems go beyond standard rule-based automation, leveraging machine learning, natural language processing and predictive analytics to understand complex financial contexts and tailor nuanced decisions that evolve with dynamic circumstances. The result is a digital payment ecosystem that works with human-like problem-solving, but possesses the speed, accuracy and sheer size that only physical systems can offer.

This revolution in intelligence allows payment systems to predict the needs of users, proactively optimize transaction flows, and smoothly handle the wide array of complex financial situations that once required substantial human intervention. That ranges from automatically concatenating the best currency conversion rate with a real-time payment in remotely-vindicated currencies, to finding the most optimal payment routes between multiple parallel providers and of course ensuring these patterns are routable efficiently based on information as recent as milliseconds ago and offering more such optimizations possibly packed with some groundbreaking Machine Learning algorithms that would encapsulate seamless Money Transfer Optimization irrespective of even knowing what is SWIFT.

Transformative User Experience and Accessibility

Agentic payment services change how users can interact with financial services by building applications people can chat to in natural language, which then translate a request into richer financial actions. It enables users to talk about payment intent in natural language, and smart agents deal with everything related to payment routing, compliance checks and optimizations. This democratization of financial savvy means that advanced payment capabilities, once reserved for institutional clients, will be readily available to consumers and small businesses.

The customization abilities of such systems make for unique value propositions to each segment. For businesses it provides automated expense management, smart credit optimization and streamlined integrations into their current financial workflows. Consumers themselves have easy bill monitoring, automatic savings optimization and proactive financial advice that just works better to help them reach their financial goals.

Strategic Implementation Considerations

When driving these payments, Agent based though this model also expected that the due adherence to risk and compliance, technology platform and innovation is made considering the user acceptance. Enterprises must have a strong security framework for the specific weaknesses that are present in robotic or autonomous systems and also meet changing regulatory requirements across jurisdictions. This breaks down into features such as comprehensive audit trails, "explainable AI" type mechanisms and clear accountability frameworks around agent actions.

User acceptance is still the key for extensive use: organizations need clear arguments and at the same time they have to remain transparent regarding system capacities and drawbacks. Establishing user trust requires incremental deployment strategies that provide users with the benefits of agentic systems while securing control over important financial decisions. Educational activities and user-friendly interfaces are crucial to the transition to these new systems.

Industry Leadership and Competitive Advantage

Those that invest in developing them will be leading the next wave of financial services innovation, with an edge from operational efficiencies, better customer experiences and lower costs. Quick adoption of agent payment technologies helps firms acquire in-house skills, form strategic partnership and trigger network externalities that reinforce the position as incumbents.

"Artificial intelligence; blockchain technology and regulatory innovation solutions combined with outstanding payment experiences, unique service propositions and superior security features offer a real chance for any company to stand out." Success in this new era comes from having the vision, investing in technology and a strong responsible innovation focus where user safety is at least as important as business aims.

The evolution to Payments 5.0 isn't just technological – it's a holistic revolution toward increasingly intelligent, agile, human-centered financial systems that will sculpt the new contours of global finance for generations to come.

ACKNOWLEDGMENT

This research received no specific grant from any funding agency in the public, commercial, or not-for-profit sectors.

REFERENCES

x402 Working Group (Coinbase). (2025, May 5). x402: An HTTP-native protocol for paid API access (Whitepaper). x402.org. https://www.x402.org/x402-whitepaper.pdf

Aljunaid, A. M., Alamoudi, A., & Alkahtani, M. (2025). Explainable artificial intelligence-driven federated learning model for financial fraud detection. *Journal of Risk and Financial Management, 18*(4), 179. DOI: 10.3390/jrfm18040179

AWS. (2025, September 4). Agentic AI solutions in financial services. AWS Marketplace Blog. https://aws.amazon.com/blogs/awsmarketplace/agentic-ai-solutions-in-financial-services/

Benson, C. C., Loftesness, S., & Jones, R. (2017). *Payment systems in the U.S* (3rd ed.). Glenbrook Press., https://books.google.com/books/about/Payments_Systems_in_the_U_S.html?id=IGmhcQAACAAJ

Brown, T. B., Mann, B., Ryder, N., Subbiah, M., Kaplan, J., Dhariwal, P., & Amodei, D. (2020). Language models are few-shot learners. *Advances in Neural Information Processing Systems, 33*, 1877–1901. DOI: 10.48550/arXiv.2005.14165

Cambridge Centre for Alternative Finance. (2025, June 12). From automation to autonomy: The agentic AI era of financial services. Cambridge Judge Business School. https://www.jbs.cam.ac.uk/2025/from-automation-to-autonomy-the-agentic-ai-era-of-financial-services/

Capco. (2025, June 30). Agentic AI: Transforming payments & cash management. Capco Intelligence. https://www.capco.com/intelligence/capco-intelligence/agentic-ai-transforming-payments-and-cash-management

Chen, H. (Ed.). (2021). *Regulation, emerging risk, and ethics in FinTech and AI*. IGI Global., https://books.google.com/books/about/Regulation_Emerging_Risk_and_Ethics_in_F.html?id=TAl-EQAAQBAJ

FXCintel. (2025, September 3). Agentic AI and efficiency drive recent developments in cross-border payments. FXCintel Research. https://www.fxcintel.com/research/analysis/agentic-ai-cross-border-payments-sep-2025

Ghosh, A., & Sanyal, S. (2024). Trustworthy AI in financial services: A framework for explainability, fairness, and accountability. *AI and Ethics*, *4*(2), 233–246. https://www.sciencedirect.com/science/article/pii/S0045790624003379

Jaipuria, N., Gatto, L., Kan, Z., Poddar, S., Cheung, B., Bansal, D., Balakrishnan, R., Suri, A., & Estevez, J. (2025). CASE: An agentic AI framework for enhancing scam intelligence in digital payments. arXiv. https://doi.org//arXiv.2508.19932DOI: 10.48550

Knodell, J. (2016). The anatomy of global banking: 1781–2013. Routledge. https://www.routledge.com/The-Second-Bank-of-the-United-States-Central-banker-in-an-era-of-nation-building-18161836/Knodell/p/book/9780367870225

Lietaer, B. (2001). The future of money: Beyond greed and scarcity. Random House. https://www.penguin.com.au/books/the-future-of-money-9781448149933

Linklaters. (2025, August 20). Agentic payments: What are they, what are the legal risks … Linklaters FinTechLinks. https://www.linklaters.com

Mastercard. (2025, September 9). Mastercard unveils Agent Pay, pioneering agentic payments technology to power commerce in the age of AI. Mastercard Newsroom. https://www.mastercard.com/global/en/news-and-trends/press/2025/april/mastercard-unveils-agent-pay-pioneering-agentic-payments-technology-to-power-commerce-in-the-age-of-ai.html

Oliver, R., & Warfe, G. (2020). The story of payments: How the industrialization of trust created the modern payment system. Glenbrook Partners. https://www.barnesandnoble.com/w/payment-systems-in-the-us-carol-coye-benson/1144602923

Open, A. I. (2023). GPT-4 technical report. arXiv. https://doi.org//arXiv.2303.08774DOI: 10.48550

Qian, C., Zhang, Y., Liu, H., & Yu, L. (2023). AutoGPT and beyond: Toward general-purpose autonomous agents. arXiv preprint arXiv:2305.01210. https://arxiv.org/abs/2305.01210

Schwartz, G. (2010). The impulse economy: Understanding mobile shoppers and what makes them buy. Simon & Schuster. https://www.simonandschuster.com/books/The-Impulse-Economy/Gary-Schwartz/9781451671872

Sutton, R. S., & Barto, A. G. (2018). *Reinforcement learning: An introduction* (2nd ed.). MIT Press., https://mitpress.mit.edu/9780262039246/reinforcement-learning-second-edition

Zhu, J., He, W., & Liu, Y. (2024). Implementing artificial intelligence-empowered financial services: Design principles and regulatory considerations. *Journal of Business Research*, *168*, 114–127. DOI: 10.1016/j.jbusres.2023.113959

Chapter 8
Stablecoins and the Future of Financial Regulation:
Nigeria's Experience and Global Lessons

Oluseyi Ishola C. Oladapo
Newcross Exploration and Production Limited, Nigeria

Obinna Chukwunonso Ezeala
https://orcid.org/0009-0009-7232-8789
Lagos Business School, Nigeria

ABSTRACT

Stablecoins are reshaping global finance, enabling low-cost payments, remittances, and inclusion, but also raising risks for sovereignty, consumer protection, and stability. This chapter examines regulatory challenges with a focus on Nigeria, drawing lessons from the EU's MiCA, the fragmented U.S. model, and Singapore's balanced approach. It pursues four aims: (i) review global and regional responses; (ii) position Nigeria as a test case for emerging economies; (iii) assess the Commonwealth Model Law as a harmonizable framework; and (iv) explore how regulation can mitigate risks while fostering inclusion. Using a qualitative, desk-based design combining doctrinal and comparative analysis, the study finds Nigeria's stance to be restrictive yet experimental: a banking ban excluded stablecoins, while the SEC and eNaira signaled cautious innovation. The Model Law's tiered, risk-based framework offers a path to balance sovereignty, stability, and innovation, making Nigeria a microcosm of Global South dilemmas.

DOI: 10.4018/979-8-3373-9043-7.ch008

1. INTRODUCTION

Money, long dominated by state-backed fiat currencies and intermediated by banks, is undergoing a profound transformation. The emergence of digital tokens—programmable, borderless, and fast—represents one of the most disruptive innovations in the history of finance (Auer & Böhme, 2021). Among these innovations, stablecoins have attracted particular attention. Unlike volatile cryptocurrencies such as Bitcoin and Ether, stablecoins are designed to maintain a stable value, typically pegged to a fiat currency like the US dollar, euro, or naira. This stability makes them attractive for payments, remittances, savings, and as a building block of decentralized finance (DeFi) (Arner et al., 2020).

Stablecoins have surged in circulation and relevance since 2017, with global market capitalization at times exceeding US$180 billion (CoinGecko, 2022). Tokens such as USD Coin (USDC), Tether (USDT), and Dai (DAI) are now widely integrated into global payment rails, crypto exchanges, and lending markets. They promise to reduce frictions in cross-border remittances—an especially critical use case for emerging markets like Nigeria, where remittances exceed US$20 billion annually (World Bank, 2021). For millions of unbanked or underbanked households, stablecoins could provide access to digital finance without dependence on costly intermediaries.

Yet, the promise of stablecoins is shadowed by profound risks. They raise urgent questions over monetary sovereignty, financial stability, consumer protection, and systemic resilience. Policymakers worry about "dollarization 2.0," where privately issued dollar-pegged tokens undermine domestic currencies (Brunnermeier et al., 2021). Events such as the collapse of TerraUSD in 2022—which erased over US$40 billion in market value—demonstrate that algorithmic stablecoins can unravel rapidly, threatening users and broader market confidence (Financial Stability Board, 2022). Even fiat-backed stablecoins, if poorly managed, may suffer from inadequate reserves, opacity, or liquidity mismatches that expose users to losses.

There is growing consensus that stablecoins are no longer a niche innovation but a systemically relevant financial instrument. Regulators across the globe—from the Financial Stability Board (FSB) to the Bank for International Settlements (BIS)—acknowledge their potential to reshape cross-border payments and financial inclusion while also amplifying systemic risks (Bank for International Settlements, 2022; Financial Stability Board, 2020). In advanced economies, regulatory frameworks are emerging: the European Union's Markets in Crypto-Assets Regulation (MiCA) (2023) provides the most comprehensive regime to date, while the United States is debating bespoke legislation for stablecoin issuance. In Asia, Singapore has integrated stablecoins under its Payment Services Act, requiring issuers to hold high-quality liquid reserves and comply with consumer protection rules.

Regulation in Africa is not even. South Africa is incorporating crypto-assets into its financial system on a prudential and conduct basis. Kenya is an early adopter of mobile currency but M-Pesa heavily depends on it, and is starting to consider a stablecoin oversight. Nigeria, on the contrary, is a promise and a paradise. Nigeria has been restrictive, despite being the host of one of the most vibrant fintech ecosystems in Africa, which include international players like Flutterwave, Paystack, and ChipperCash. In 2021, the Central Bank of Nigeria (CBN) prohibited banks to service crypto-related businesses i.e. due to its perceived risks to the financial system. In the meantime, in 2022, the Securities and Exchange Commission (SEC) introduced Rules on Issuance, Offering Platforms, and Custody of Digital Assets and did not deny the existence of digital tokens but restricted their application. The launch of the eNaira in 2021 made Nigeria the first African country to introduce a central bank digital currency (CBDC). Yet uptake has been sluggish, and many Nigerians continue to rely on informal crypto and stablecoin channels for remittances and savings (International Monetary Fund, 2024).

Despite these developments, significant gaps remain. First, there is no globally harmonized regulatory framework for stablecoins. Diverging approaches—between permissive innovation hubs like Singapore, comprehensive regimes like the EU, and restrictive jurisdictions like Nigeria—create opportunities for regulatory arbitrage. Stablecoins, by nature, flow across borders, making fragmented oversight inadequate (Zetzsche et al., 2020). Second, the interaction between CBDCs and stablecoins is poorly understood. Can they coexist as complementary instruments, or will state-issued CBDCs crowd out private tokens? For Nigeria, where the eNaira competes with dollar-pegged stablecoins used by its diaspora, this is a pressing concern. Third, consumer protection remains underdeveloped. Most stablecoin users in Nigeria operate outside formal regulation, exposing them to fraud, loss, and volatility without legal recourse. Finally, systemic implications are uncertain. If stablecoins become widely used for trade settlement or government transactions in emerging economies, they may destabilize monetary policy transmission and weaken sovereignty.

The stakes surrounding stablecoin regulation are particularly high for Nigeria and, more broadly, for the Global South. In such settings, the problem is not just about the issues of financial technology in an abstract sense; it applies directly to the livelihoods, financial sovereignty, and financial system resilience of countries. The regulation of stablecoins is urgent and strategically important because of several dimensions which are demonstrated.

To begin with, the stablecoins offer a genuine chance to improve the financial inclusion rate and decrease the price of remittances. Nigeria has the highest amount of remittances in Sub-Saharan Africa and the inflows amount to over USD 20 billion every year (World Bank, 2021). These transfers are a lifeline to many families as they are sometimes spent on education, healthcare and day to day living. Stablecoins have the potential to also greatly decrease transaction costs, making the use of expensive middlemen unnecessary and offering faster, borderless settlement (Arner et al., 2020). However, unless they have strong protections in place, this may become a potential danger: families that use remittances as a source of income based on the stablecoins might fall victims to fraud, hacks, or systemic failures like the one of the TerraUSD (Brunnermeier et al., 2021).

Second, the adoption of stablecoins raises profound questions of sovereignty and monetary stability. Nigeria's domestic currency, the naira, has faced chronic depreciation pressures, eroding public trust and driving demand for dollar substitutes (International Monetary Fund, 2024). The widespread circulation of dollar-pegged stablecoins could intensify this trend, accelerating capital flight and diminishing the Central Bank of Nigeria's ability to steer monetary policy (Zetzsche et al., 2020). Conversely, an excessively restrictive regulatory approach risks stifling innovation and driving stablecoin use into unregulated, underground markets (Auer & Böhme, 2021). This tension underscores the delicate balance Nigeria must strike: enabling innovation while preserving monetary sovereignty.

Third, stablecoins pose systemic risks that demand careful attention to consumer protection. The collapse of TerraUSD in 2022 revealed how quickly confidence in even widely used digital assets can evaporate, erasing tens of billions of dollars in value in a matter of days (G7 Working Group on Stablecoins, 2019; Financial Stability Board, 2020). For Nigeria, where financial literacy levels remain uneven, such failures could have devastating effects. Households and small businesses that adopt stablecoins as savings or payment tools may find themselves vulnerable to losses without adequate recourse (Commonwealth Secretariat, 2023). Ensuring transparency, reserve backing, and effective redress mechanisms is therefore not only a regulatory necessity but also a matter of public trust.

Fourth, the issue of global coordination cannot be overstated. Stablecoins are inherently transnational, moving seamlessly across borders in ways that national regulations often struggle to address (Auer & Böhme, 2021). The Commonwealth Secretariat's Model Law on Stablecoins represents a landmark effort to develop a risk-based, flexible framework that countries at different stages of development can adapt. For Nigeria, engaging with such a model provides an opportunity to align domestic policy with international standards while tailoring safeguards to local realities. Without coordination, Nigeria risks either over-regulating in isolation or being left exposed to the vulnerabilities created by fragmented global oversight (Financial Stability Board, 2020).

Finally, Nigeria's strategic position in Africa amplifies the importance of its policy choices. As the continent's most populous country and largest economy, Nigeria's stance on stablecoins will shape regional norms and regulatory benchmarks (World Bank, 2021). A well-calibrated framework could position Nigeria as a leader in digital finance regulation, attracting foreign investment and fostering cross-border innovation under the African Continental Free Trade Area (AfCFTA) (Zetzsche et al., 2020). Conversely, policy missteps could isolate its fintech sector, discourage capital inflows, and push innovation to more hospitable jurisdictions. In this sense, Nigeria is not only regulating for itself but also setting precedents that may influence the trajectory of digital finance across the Global South (Arner et al., 2020).

Taken together, these factors demonstrate why stablecoin regulation is not a peripheral concern but a central challenge for Nigeria's economic future. It sits at the intersection of financial inclusion, sovereignty, systemic resilience, and global competitiveness. For policymakers, industry leaders, and citizens alike, the way Nigeria navigates this issue will have long-term consequences for the inclusiveness, stability, and credibility of its financial system.

This chapter therefore situates Nigeria within the broader global debate. It asks: How can countries harness the benefits of stablecoins while mitigating risks to sovereignty, stability, and consumers? By examining the international regulatory landscape (FATF, IOSCO, FSB, BIS), comparing regional approaches (EU, US, Singapore, Nigeria), and analyzing the Commonwealth's Model Law, the chapter offers both a diagnostic and prescriptive view. It provides a plain-language walkthrough of regulatory tools while critically assessing their fit for emerging markets. In short, the future of money is digital, but its governance remains contested. Stablecoins embody this tension: they can democratize access to finance yet destabilize national systems if left unchecked. For Nigeria, where the promise of digital innovation collides with the imperatives of sovereignty and stability, the challenge is acute. This chapter argues that smart, harmonized, and risk-based regulation—anchored in the Commonwealth Model Law—can provide a path forward.

2. OBJECTIVE

The chapter seeks to demystify stablecoins for policymakers, regulators, academics, and industry leaders, while linking regulation to financial stability, systemic risk, and inclusion. Specifically, it will:

i. Provide a critical overview of global and regional regulatory responses to stablecoins.
ii. Position Nigeria as a test case for emerging economies grappling with innovation and sovereignty.
iii. Present the Commonwealth Model Law as a flexible and harmonizable regulatory template.

iv. Explore how regulation can both mitigate risks and enable financial inclusion in Africa and the Global South.

3. TARGET AUDIENCE

This chapter is written with a diverse audience in mind, reflecting the wide-ranging implications of stablecoins and their regulation. It is first intended for academics and researchers who are exploring the intersections of digital finance, financial stability, and regulatory governance. For this group, the chapter offers a critical, evidence-based contribution to ongoing scholarly debates about how technology is reshaping the global financial system. Equally, the chapter speaks to policymakers and regulators who are grappling with the real-world challenges that stablecoins pose. From questions of monetary sovereignty to systemic risk and consumer protection, regulators must strike a careful balance between enabling innovation and safeguarding the public interest. This book provides both comparative insights from global experiences and practical reflections relevant to Nigeria and the wider Global South.

The chapter also addresses industry actors—developers, fintech entrepreneurs, and financial institutions—who must navigate regulatory uncertainty while building products and services that meet consumer demand. By unpacking both the risks and opportunities of stablecoins, the discussion aims to provide industry participants with clarity on evolving regulatory expectations and potential pathways for compliance and innovation. Finally, the chapter is accessible to students and the wider public seeking to make sense of the rapidly changing financial landscape. Stablecoins are no longer confined to the margins of cryptocurrency communities; they are increasingly part of everyday conversations about money, savings, and payments. By presenting technical and legal concepts in clear, plain language, this chapter equips a general audience with the knowledge needed to engage in informed discussions about the future of money.

4. THEORETICAL AND CONCEPTUAL FRAMEWORK

Stablecoins sit at a dense theoretical intersection: monetary theory, financial stability, innovation governance, and institutional economics. To make sense of their disruptive potential—and to design regulation that is both protective and enabling—we must draw on multiple strands of literature. Below we synthesize relevant theories, show how they illuminate the problems this chapter addresses (sovereignty, inclusion, systemic risk), and propose a concise conceptual model that will guide the empirical and normative claims in the chapter.

4.1 Monetary Theory and the Challenge to State Money

Traditional monetary theory treats the capacity to issue money as a defining attribute of state sovereignty. Chartalism (state theory of money) posits that money is a creature of public authority: the state defines units of account and enforces taxes payable in that unit, thereby underpinning demand for sovereign currency. Monetarist and quantity-theory perspectives, by contrast, emphasize money supply and macroeconomic control (Congdon, 2021). Both traditions share an assumption: money's dominant issuers are public or heavily regulated private institutions (banks).

Stablecoins unsettle that assumption. Privately issued tokens—especially those pegged to a hard currency like the U.S. dollar—can acquire wide acceptance as media of exchange and stores of value, functioning in practice like parallel monies (Brunnermeier et al., 2021). In contexts with weak domestic monetary credibility, such as Nigeria where inflationary pressures and exchange-rate volatility have eroded public confidence in the naira, dollar-pegged stablecoins can become de-facto units of account for transactions and savings (International Monetary Fund, 2024). This dynamic echoes classic analyses of currency substitution and "dollarization" (Levy-Yeyati & Sturzenegger, 2024): when domestic currency is unstable, agents adopt foreign currency substitutes. Stablecoins add a technological twist: they lower transaction frictions and enable near-instant cross-border use, accelerating substitution risks (Auer & Böhme, 2021).

From a seigniorage perspective, widespread private use of stablecoins could transfer rents from the state (seigniorage from issuing currency) to private issuers unless regulatory arrangements internalize these externalities. The literature therefore suggests two policy implications: (1) regulators must restore or preserve trust in sovereign instruments (for example via credible macroeconomic policy or a well-designed CBDC); and (2) regulation must address the monetary externalities of private money issuance (Brunnermeier et al., 2021; Bank for International Settlements, 2022).

4.2 Network Effects, Platform Economics, and Adoption Dynamics

Economics of networks and platforms (Katz & Shapiro, 1985; Shrivastav, 2025) explain how a stablecoin can rapidly scale once a critical mass of users and complementary services (exchanges, wallets, merchants) exist. Network effects create winner-takes-most dynamics: a widely accepted dollar-pegged stablecoin can attract liquidity, reduce spreads, and thus displace competitors—domestic payment rails included. For Nigeria this implies that even a small initial advantage (ease of use, better liquidity) can produce outsized adoption, complicating the task of domestic regulators seeking gradual and controlled innovation (Buckley et al., 2023).

4.3 Financial Stability, Systemic Risk, and Shadow Banking Analogies

Stablecoins can be studied through shadow banking and systemic risk literatures. Like money market funds or certain structured products, stablecoin arrangements rely on asset-liability transformation and liquidity management that can be fragile during runs (Gorton & Metrick, 2012). The collapse of algorithmic stablecoins (e.g., TerraUSD) and episodes of redemption stress demonstrate classic run mechanics in crypto form (Financial Stability Board, 2020). The systemic risk literature highlights the need for prudential rules, resolution mechanisms, and credible backstops for systemically important private monies. Applied to Nigeria, such literature foregrounds the hazard that systemic stablecoins—if unregulated—could propagate shocks through payment systems, FX markets, and the banking sector.

4.4 Institutional and Governance Frameworks: Regulation as Multi-Level Governance

Institutional theory (Hamdan et al., 2022) and scholarship on regulation and governance (Baldwin, Cave, & Lodge, 2012) emphasize that markets are embedded in rule systems; the form of regulation shapes incentives for innovation and compliance. For cross-border, technology-driven phenomena like stablecoins, multilevel governance is necessary: domestic regulators, regional bodies (e.g., ECOWAS/AfCFTA), and global standard-setters (FATF, FSB, BIS) must coordinate (Zetzsche et al., 2023). Regulatory theories also suggest a role for risk-based, principles-oriented approaches where capacity constraints exist—important for many regulators in the Global South who cannot immediately implement heavy-handed prescriptive rules (Balina et al., 2025).

4.5 Innovation Governance, Techno-Legal Assemblages, and Socio-Technical Perspectives

From Science and Technology Studies and socio-technical systems perspectives, stablecoins are not merely financial constructs but socio-technical assemblages: code (smart contracts), institutions (issuers, custodians), markets (exchanges, OTC desks), and law interact to produce outcomes. This lens draws attention to non-economic vectors: user interface design, custody arrangements, oracle reliability, and governance of decentralized protocols. It also underscores that technological fixes alone (e.g., better smart contracts) cannot substitute for institutional frameworks that ensure accountability and redress (Arner et al., 2020).

4.6 Linking Theory to the Nigerian Problem: a Conceptual Synthesis

Bringing these literatures together points to a compact conceptual model for understanding the stablecoin challenge in Nigeria. Three core dimensions emerge as particularly significant. The first concerns monetary credibility and macroeconomic conditions, such as persistent inflation, exchange-rate volatility, and dependence on remittances. These factors shape the demand side for foreign-pegged stablecoins, as households and firms seek instruments that preserve value and provide more predictable cross-border settlement options (Levy-Yeyati & Sturzenegger, 2024; International Monetary Fund, 2024). In Nigeria, recurrent naira depreciation and structural imbalances in the foreign exchange market have intensified demand for dollar-linked tokens, making stablecoins an attractive alternative for savings and remittances.

The second dimension is defined by platform dynamics and market structure. Network effects, liquidity depth, and custodial arrangements determine the speed and scale of stablecoin adoption (Katz & Shapiro, 1985; Shrivastav, 2025; Buckley et al., 2023). Once a critical mass of users and service providers converges around a particular stablecoin, adoption can accelerate rapidly, creating self-reinforcing cycles of liquidity and usability. This is particularly salient in Nigeria, where fintech firms and peer-to-peer networks have built robust infrastructures that reduce barriers to entry and allow stablecoins to diffuse quickly within informal and formal payment ecosystems.

The third dimension relates to regulatory capacity and governance design. Rules on reserve backing, licensing regimes, anti–money laundering and counter-terrorist financing (AML/CFT) compliance, consumer protection, and mechanisms for cross-border coordination determine whether the risks associated with stablecoins can be effectively mitigated (Financial Stability Board [FSB], 2020; Financial Action Task Force [FATF], 2021). Where supervisory capacity is weak or fragmented, stablecoin markets may develop in opaque spaces that expose users to fraud, sudden loss of value, or systemic disruptions.

These three dimensions do not operate in isolation but interact dynamically. Weak macroeconomic credibility heightens demand for dollar-pegged tokens; strong network effects and supportive market structures can rapidly satisfy and amplify that demand; and gaps in regulatory capacity determine whether adoption occurs in a safe and transparent ecosystem or within a shadow financial system. Moreover, the interactions are recursive: large-scale stablecoin use feeds back into the macroeconomy, potentially undermining domestic monetary sovereignty and complicating exchange-rate management. Figure 1 conceptually illustrates these relationships, mapping the pathway from demand drivers to adoption dynamics and regulatory outcomes, with feedback loops that can either reinforce stability or deepen fragility.

4.7 Operationalizing the Framework: Propositions and Empirical Markers

To render the conceptual framework operational for both empirical inquiry and policy analysis, this chapter advances a set of propositions supported by measurable indicators. These propositions bridge theory and practice by specifying the mechanisms through which macroeconomic dynamics, network effects, and regulatory governance shape the trajectory of stablecoin adoption in Nigeria and comparable economies.

The first proposition (P1: Demand-Side) suggests that higher inflation and foreign exchange (FX) volatility directly increase per-capita use of dollar-pegged stablecoins. This expectation draws from the extensive literature on currency substitution, which demonstrates that agents facing unstable domestic currencies often shift to more credible alternatives (Levy-Yeyati & Sturzenegger, 2024; International Monetary Fund, 2024). In practice, proxies such as the inflation rate, FX volatility indices, and peer-to-peer (P2P) stablecoin transaction volumes per capita—measured through national surveys and blockchain analytics (e.g., Chainalysis)—can be employed to capture this relationship.

The second proposition (P2: Supply/Network) posits that greater integration of payment rails and liquidity depth predict faster adoption of stablecoins. This aligns with the literature on network externalities, where liquidity and compatibility generate self-reinforcing adoption cycles (Katz & Shapiro, 1985; Shrivastav, 2025; Buckley et al., 2023). Indicators such as the number of on-ramps and off-ramps, exchange trading volumes, and the count of wallet providers can be used to operationalize these dynamics, offering a concrete way to measure the infrastructural enablers of adoption.

The third proposition (P3: Regulatory Mitigation) emphasizes that stronger regulatory frameworks reduce both the incidence and the impact of stablecoin-related disruptions. Comparative evidence from global regulatory experiments indicates that well-designed rules on tiered licensing, reserve standards, and anti–money laundering and counter-terrorist financing (AML/CFT) compliance can curb the risks of runs and fraud (Financial Stability Board, 2020; Financial Action Task Force, 2021). Operational markers here include the presence of model law elements in domestic frameworks, the number of licensed issuers, and records of supervisory enforcement actions.

Finally, the fourth proposition (P4: Interaction) highlights the relationship between private stablecoins and central bank digital currencies (CBDCs). In the absence of a credible and widely adopted CBDC, private stablecoins tend to substitute for the domestic currency in transactions of value. Conversely, a well-designed CBDC with strong user uptake can attenuate substitution pressures (Auer & Böhme, 2021; International Monetary Fund, 2024). Proxies to assess this interaction include active CBDC wallet counts, transaction volumes on CBDC platforms, and comparative transaction data for stablecoins.

Methodologically, these propositions suggest the value of a mixed-methods approach. Time-series indicators can track macroeconomic drivers such as inflation and FX volatility; case studies of issuer failures, such as the collapse of TerraUSD, can illustrate the systemic fragility of poorly designed arrangements; and comparative regulatory analyses of frameworks like the European Union's Markets in Crypto-Assets (MiCA), Singapore's Payment Services Act, and Nigeria's evolving policy responses can demonstrate the practical implications of different governance designs. By triangulating across these methods, the chapter seeks to integrate theoretical insight with grounded empirical evidence.

4.8 Implications for Regulation and Research Agenda

This theoretical synthesis highlights why single-axis responses (e.g., outright bans) are likely to fail: they ignore network economics, macro drivers of demand, and the socio-technical nature of stablecoins. Instead, the literature points to a layered, risk-based regulatory approach that: (a) strengthens monetary credibility and financial infrastructure, (b) implements proportional licensing and reserve transparency for issuers, (c) invests in supervisory capacity and cross-border cooperation, and (d) incorporates technology governance (smart-contract audits, custodial safeguards). Empirically testing the propositions above—especially within Nigeria's unique macro-institutional context—constitutes the chapter's research agenda and grounds its policy recommendations.

5. GAP ANALYSIS IN LITERATURE

The literature on stablecoins is still nascent and fragmented, with most research focused on advanced economies. While systemic risk studies highlight their potential to trigger shocks and threaten monetary sovereignty, evidence from developing contexts remains scarce (Arner et al., 2020; Brunnermeier et al., 2021; G7 Working Group, 2019). Legal scholarship largely examines U.S. and EU classifications (Zetzsche et al., 2020), offering little guidance for weaker institutional settings, while inclusion-oriented studies emphasize remittances and savings but are limited in Africa and often conflate stablecoins with mobile money. Industry reports provide adoption insights in Nigeria (Chainalysis, 2022), but lack theoretical depth, leaving a gap in connecting global frameworks, Nigeria's domestic experiments, and model laws like the Commonwealth framework. This chapter seeks to bridge that gap by grounding Nigeria in global debates while advancing harmonized yet adaptive regulatory solutions.

6. METHODOLOGY

This chapter adopts a qualitative, desk-based research design that integrates doctrinal legal analysis with comparative policy review. A desk-based approach is particularly appropriate for emergent topics such as stablecoin regulation, where empirical data remain limited and fragmented, while legal and policy texts provide the most authoritative sources of guidance (Zubkov & Pondi, 2022). The doctrinal component focuses on the systematic analysis of primary legal materials, including statutory texts, regulatory guidelines, and international model laws. This is complemented by secondary literature such as policy reports from the Financial Stability Board (Financial Stability Board, 2020), the International Monetary Fund (International Monetary Fund, 2024), and the Commonwealth (2023; 2025). Doctrinal legal analysis enables the chapter to evaluate the internal coherence of Nigeria's regulatory instruments and assess their alignment with evolving international standards (Hutchinson & Duncan, 2012).

The comparative policy review builds on this foundation by situating Nigeria's regulatory environment within a broader transnational context. Comparative research is critical because stablecoin markets are inherently cross-border, meaning that purely domestic approaches are often inadequate (Buckley et al., 2023). Examining the European Union's Markets in Crypto-Assets (MiCA) regulation, Singapore's Payment Services Act, and the U.S. draft stablecoin frameworks provides a benchmark against which Nigeria's trajectory can be assessed. Such comparative analysis also allows for the identification of best practices and pitfalls that can inform a tailored approach for the Nigerian case.

Methodologically, the chapter is purposively normative and exploratory. It is normative in advancing harmonization pathways, particularly through the Commonwealth Secretariat's Model Law on Stablecoins, which emphasizes risk-based, flexible standards adaptable across jurisdictions. By critically engaging this model, the chapter seeks to prescribe actionable reforms that could enhance Nigeria's regulatory capacity while aligning with global norms. It is exploratory in applying these pathways to Nigeria as a test case for the Global South. Exploratory research is appropriate in contexts of uncertainty and rapid innovation, where new theoretical and practical insights are needed to guide both scholarship and governance.

This dual orientation ensures that the chapter is not merely descriptive but also prescriptive. The descriptive dimension maps existing Nigerian frameworks—such as the Central Bank of Nigeria's circulars restricting cryptocurrency use and the regulatory sandbox guidelines—against international standards. The prescriptive dimension proposes context-sensitive reforms that balance innovation with risk mitigation, offering concrete insights for policymakers, regulators, and academics. In doing so, the methodology provides a robust foundation for addressing the chapter's central concern: how stablecoin regulation can simultaneously safeguard financial stability and advance financial inclusion in Nigeria and the wider Global South.

7. THE GLOBAL REGULATORY LANDSCAPE

7.1 International Standards

Stablecoins have been on the agenda of global standard-setting bodies since 2019, when projects such as Facebook's Libra/Diem exposed the potential for private money issuance to disrupt financial systems. The Financial Action Task Force (FATF) has been at the forefront of articulating risks. FATF guidance identified stablecoins as significant AML/CFT risks, requiring virtual asset service providers (VASPs) to implement the Travel Rule, customer due diligence, and suspicious transaction reporting (Financial Action Task Force, 2019). FATF stressed that the arrangements relating to stable coins might be used to provide illegal finance, unless these are actively monitored (Financial Action Task Force, 2023).

The International Organization of Securities Commissions (2022) examined the case of stablecoins through the prism of securities regulation and advised that international stablecoins might be viewed as securities-like instruments that have systemic capabilities. IOSCO emphasized that protection of investors, governance transparency and reserve management were necessary. The guidelines have been high level, required by Financial Stability Board (Financial Stability Board, 2020), which required same-activity, same-risk, same-rules. One of the arguments that FSB has put forth is that stablecoins with high adoption must be issued with wide regulation consisting of governance, reserve adequacy, redemption entitlement, and the ability to interoperate with payment systems. Furthermore, Bank for International Settlements (2022) placed stablecoins in the framework of monetary sovereignty and CBDCs.

7.2. Regional Approaches

European Union: MiCA

The European Union's Markets in Crypto-Assets Regulation (MiCA), formally adopted in 2023, represents the most ambitious and wide-ranging legislative effort anywhere to create a single, harmonized regulatory framework for crypto-assets, including stablecoins (European Parliament, 2023) MiCA was explicitly designed to close regulatory gaps for crypto-assets that are not already covered by existing EU financial services rules (for example, MiFID II, EMD2) and to provide legal certainty across the EU's single market. The regulation has three core ambitions: (1) protect consumers and investors, (2) ensure market integrity and financial stability, and (3) support innovation by creating a predictable rulebook.

Key Structural Features

The Markets in Crypto-Assets (MiCA) Regulation introduces a carefully tiered framework for stablecoins, grounded in the recognition that not all tokens carry identical risks or systemic implications. At the heart of MiCA is its taxonomy, which differentiates between e-money tokens (EMTs) and asset-referenced tokens (ARTs). EMTs are designed to maintain a stable value by referencing a single fiat currency, making them functionally similar to electronic money under existing EU law. ARTs, by contrast, peg their value to a broader set of assets—such as a basket of currencies, commodities, or other crypto-assets—and are therefore subject to distinct prudential and governance requirements. This classification is not merely semantic; it determines the intensity of regulatory oversight, disclosure obligations, and the safeguards imposed on issuers (European Parliament, 2023).

A second structural pillar of MiCA lies in its authorization and prudential requirements. Issuers of both EMTs and ARTs must seek approval from competent national authorities before offering tokens within the EU. Authorization is conditional upon compliance with capital, governance, and organizational standards. For EMTs, this includes strict 1:1 backing by liquid assets, as well as mechanisms that guarantee token holders can redeem their assets for fiat currency at par value. For ARTs, the framework mandates adequate reserves, stabilization arrangements, and risk mitigation measures to ensure resilience under market stress (European Parliament, 2023).

Closely linked to authorization are MiCA's rules on reserve composition, segregation, and audits. Stablecoin reserves must be fully segregated from the issuer's own balance sheet and invested only in high-quality, liquid instruments. Regular attestations and independent audits—often quarterly or more frequent—are required to verify the adequacy of reserves. These reports must also be disclosed publicly, an effort to reduce the opacity that has plagued global stablecoin markets and triggered episodes of instability and loss of confidence.

Transparency is further reinforced through whitepapers and disclosure requirements. Every issuer must publish a detailed crypto-asset whitepaper, outlining the economic design of the token, governance arrangements, risk factors, reserve composition, redemption rights, and associated fees. This disclosure framework parallels the prospectus rules of securities markets but is specifically tailored to the unique risks of crypto-assets, thereby equipping both regulators and consumers with essential information (European Parliament, 2023).

Consumer protection also features prominently in MiCA's design. Issuers are obliged to establish governance frameworks with clearly defined senior management responsibilities, robust internal controls, and strategies for business continuity and operational resilience. To safeguard users, issuers must also implement mechanisms for asset protection, complaints handling, and redress procedures. In addition, consumer-facing disclosures on risks and costs are mandatory, ensuring that retail users engage with stablecoins under conditions of greater transparency and accountability (European Parliament, 2023).

Oversight is structured through a multi-layered supervisory and enforcement system. While national competent authorities remain the primary supervisors of most issuers, tokens deemed "significant" due to their systemic footprint—measured by scale of users, transaction volumes, or cross-border relevance—fall under enhanced oversight from EU-level institutions, including the European Banking Authority (EBA) and the European Securities and Markets Authority (ESMA). These issuers face stricter prudential rules, ensuring that supervisory intensity matches systemic importance.

Finally, MiCA takes a deliberately precautionary stance on stablecoins as a means of exchange. Although it allows issuance and regulated use, the framework imposes limits and heightened prudential standards on tokens that achieve large-scale adoption as payment instruments. This reflects the EU's concern with safeguarding monetary sovereignty and financial stability in the face of privately issued currencies. In practice, issuers of widely used stablecoins must meet the highest thresholds of liquidity, reserve quality, and governance to mitigate potential risks to the euro area's financial system.

Together, these structural features underscore MiCA's dual ambition: to foster innovation within a clear legal framework while pre-emptively managing the systemic risks that large-scale stablecoin adoption could pose to financial markets and monetary policy.

Why MiCA Matters (Implications for Risk and Policy)

MiCA's comprehensive architecture addresses many of the market failures and regulatory gaps identified by the FSB, FATF and BIS (Financial Stability Board, 2020; Financial Action Task Force, 2021; Bank for International Settlements, 2022). By requiring reserve transparency, segregation, and independent attestations, the regulation directly targets the opacity and under-reserving problems that have produced confidence crises in the stablecoin space. By tying supervisory intensity to systemicity, MiCA also aims to avoid imposing an unnecessarily heavy burden on small innovators while ensuring that systemically important issuers face prudential standards comparable to payment institutions or banks where appropriate.

For policymakers in emerging markets, including Nigeria, MiCA provides several concrete policy lessons:

- Operationalize the 'same risk, same rule' principle. MiCA demonstrates how to translate high-level supervisory objectives into concrete statutory requirements (reserve composition, audit cadence, governance duties), an approach the FSB has also recommended (Financial Stability Board, 2020).
- Tiered supervision is feasible and pragmatic. MiCA's distinction between ordinary and 'significant' tokens gives jurisdictions a model for calibrating regulatory intensity to real systemic outcomes rather than imposing uniform, one-size-fits-all rules (Commonwealth Secretariat, 2023).
- Transparency builds trust and mitigates runs. Public whitepapers combined with periodic reserve attestations help markets and supervisors detect problems early—mitigating the probability and severity of runs (Gorton & Metrick, 2012; Financial Stability Board, 2022).

Criticisms and Trade-Offs

MiCA has drawn both praise and critical scrutiny. Proponents argue that it provides legal certainty across a large market, thereby encouraging institutional participation and raising consumer protection standards (European Parliament, 2023). Critics counter that MiCA's compliance burdens—particularly for reserve backing, capital, and governance—may stifle innovation by raising entry costs for small issuers and by privileging established players with deep balance sheets (Zetzsche et al., 2020). There are also concerns about regulatory fragmentation at the global level: a Europe-centric regime that imposes strict reserve or custody rules may push non-EU issuers to seek less-regulated jurisdictions or to serve EU users offshore, thereby creating channels for regulatory arbitrage (Brunnermeier et al., 2021).

Another critique has highlighted MiCA's precautionary posture toward stablecoins as means of exchange: while appropriate for protecting monetary sovereignty, the restrictions may limit the potential benefits of stablecoins for payments and remittances—particularly for users in countries with high remittance costs where an interoperable, low-cost means of cross-border settlement could be socially valuable (World Bank, 2021). This tension—stability vs. inclusion—recurs in the academic and policy literatures (Arner et al., 2020; Bank for International Settlements, 2022).

MiCA was adopted against the backdrop of a rapidly growing crypto market. By 2021–2022, stablecoins accounted for a very large share of crypto transactional volume and liquidity in many on-chain markets; major stablecoins such as USDT and USDC facilitated huge trading volumes on exchanges and DeFi platforms (industry analytics firms, 2022). Although exact EU-specific figures for stablecoin transaction volumes depend on jurisdictional on-chain monitoring, the global prominence of stablecoins underscored the regulatory urgency that MiCA sought to address (Financial Stability Board, 2020). The European Commission's impact assessments emphasized that legal uncertainty was a significant barrier to mainstream institutional adoption of crypto-assets in the EU.

Lessons for Nigeria and the Global South

MiCA's most relevant lessons for Nigeria are practical and institutional:

i. Adopt a tiered, risk-based framework. Nigeria can emulate MiCA's differentiation of token types and systemically scaled supervision, adapting thresholds and reserve composition to local market realities and FX constraints (Commonwealth Secretariat, 2023).
ii. Prioritize reserve transparency and redemption rights. Requirements for segregated reserves, independent attestations, and legally enforceable redemption obligations would materially reduce run and counterparty risk for Nigerian users of stablecoins.
iii. Protect monetary sovereignty without stifling inclusion. MiCA's precautionary limits on wide-scale use as means of exchange are instructive: Nigeria might impose stricter rules for tokens intended as mass payment instruments while facilitating supervised remittance corridors that lower costs for households.
iv. Build supervisory capacity and cross-border MOUs. MiCA's EU-wide architecture depends on capable national supervisors and cross-border coordination. For Nigeria, this implies strengthening the supervisory capacity of both the Central Bank and the Securities and Exchange Commission and creating clear

interagency MOUs to manage oversight of stablecoin activity (Financial Stability Board, 2020).

MiCA stands as the definitive European attempt to regulate stablecoins: comprehensive, precautionary, and technically detailed. While it addresses many of the core risks—reserve opacity, governance failures, consumer harm—it also surfaces trade-offs important to policymakers in the Global South. The regulation's tiered approach, emphasis on reserve quality and transparency, and insistence on governance and consumer protection provide a strong template that jurisdictions such as Nigeria can adapt. However, careful tailoring is required to reconcile monetary sovereignty, developmental priorities (including remittance costs and financial inclusion), and the practical capacities of domestic supervisors.

7.3 United States: Fragmented Oversight

The regulatory architecture for stablecoins in the United States is characteristically fragmented, split among multiple federal agencies and supplemented by a patchwork of state-level regulation. This fragmentation reflects the underlying institutional design of U.S. financial supervision—functional, agency-based jurisdiction (securities, commodities, banking)—rather than a single unified regulator for novel digital-money arrangements (Brunnermeier et al., 2021; Zetzsche et al., 2020).

At the federal level, three agencies loom large in debates about stablecoins. The Securities and Exchange Commission (SEC) asserts jurisdiction where a token functions as an investment contract or security; the Commodity Futures Trading Commission (CFTC) claims authority over some crypto derivatives and "commodity-like" crypto-assets; and bank regulators (the Federal Reserve, Federal Deposit Insurance Corporation—FDIC, and the Office of the Comptroller of the Currency—OCC) oversee insured depository institutions that touch stablecoin operations through custody, reserves, or payments. Overlaying this federal structure is a vigorous body of state-level supervision—notably the New York Department of Financial Services (NYDFS), which enforces money transmitter and trust-charter requirements (Buckley et al., 2023; Zetzsche et al., 2020). The result is multiple, sometimes overlapping, regulatory lenses that market participants must navigate.

This fragmented landscape has several practical consequences. First, issuers and intermediaries often structure themselves to take advantage of whichever regulatory pathway is most favorable—or at least most certain—leading to potential regulatory arbitrage. Second, uncertainty about jurisdiction and applicable rules increases compliance complexity and can either deter entrants or advantage incumbents with legal and compliance resources (Buckley et al., 2023). Third, the multiplicity of regulators complicates coordinated supervisory responses to cross-border and systemic incidents.

Market events have exposed these fractures. The collapse of algorithmic stablecoins such as TerraUSD in 2022 highlighted how unregulated or thinly regulated architectures can fail rapidly, producing widespread market dislocations and prompting renewed calls for clearer rule-making (Financial Stability Board, 2020). Even for fiat-backed stablecoins, questions about reserve composition, custody, and transparency have fueled public and regulatory scrutiny (Financial Stability Board, 2020). Major issuers such as USDC's parent (Circle) and others operate under a mix of federal and state rules—often relying on state money-transmitter registrations, trust charters, or banking partnerships to hold reserves or provide liquidity (Arner et al., 2020). Meanwhile, other stablecoins have operated with less formalized oversight, exacerbating concerns about opacity and counterparty risk.

Against this background, a central policy debate has crystallized in U.S. circles: should issuance of widely used dollar-pegged stablecoins be restricted to insured depository institutions (i.e., banks), or may licensed non-bank entities also issue stablecoins under a bespoke federal framework? Proponents of a bank-only model argue that insurance, access to payment-system safety nets, and direct central-bank or depository oversight materially reduce run and contagion risks associated with private monies (President's Working Group on Financial Markets [PWG], Federal Reserve, Treasury, 2021). The PWG's policy work and related statements have repeatedly highlighted the systemic risks posed by "global stablecoins" and advocated for a regulatory baseline that includes prudential safeguards and federal licensing (Financial Stability Board, 2020). Bank-based issuance proponents also emphasize the ease of integrating reserves into existing supervisory and resolution frameworks—providing clearer tools for crisis management.

Opponents of a bank-only approach counter that confining issuance to banks could stifle innovation, concentrate private-money issuance in a small set of incumbents, and raise entry barriers that ultimately harm competition and consumer choice (Buckley et al., 2023). They argue for a middle path: create a clear federal licensing regime that allows well-regulated non-bank entities to issue stablecoins provided they meet strict prudential, reserve-segregation, and transparency requirements, plus AML/CFT and consumer protection standards (Brunnermeier et al., 2021). This approach aims to capture the benefits of innovation (competition, fintech dynamism) while imposing safeguards comparable to those for banks.

Because of the split of institutional duties, legislative solutions have been repeatedly floated in Congress (various draft bills and proposals) to harmonize rules at the federal level—some proposing bank-only issuance; others proposing tiered issuer frameworks with mandatory reserve backing, redemption rights, and disclosures. As of mid-2024 the legislative picture remained unresolved, with active hearings, competing bills, and intense lobbying by industry and consumer groups (Financial Stability Board, 2022).

Empirically, the U.S. fragmentation has produced mixed outcomes. On one hand, large, well-capitalized issuers operating with transparent reserves and banking partnerships (for example, stablecoins that publish attestations of backing) have supported deep trading and settlement activity on exchanges and DeFi platforms. On the other hand, episodes of market stress and issuer opacity have demonstrated contagion channels between crypto markets and broader financial networks—raising the urgency for harmonized oversight (Financial Stability Board, 2020).

For Nigeria and other emerging markets, the U.S. model offers both cautionary lessons and policy options. The key takeaways are:

- Regulatory clarity matters. Fragmentation increases compliance costs and fosters arbitrage. Nigeria should therefore aim for clear allocation of jurisdiction between central bank, securities regulators, and payments regulators.
- Prudential safeguards reduce systemic risk. Whether through bank-only issuance or a tightly supervised non-bank licensing regime, reserve segregation, liquidity standards, and frequent attestations limit run risk.
- A calibrated, tiered approach can preserve innovation. Lessons from U.S. debates support a framework that scales regulatory intensity to systemic footprint—allowing pilots and fintech innovation under sandboxes while imposing stricter rules on large, cross-border issuers.
- Interagency coordination and cross-border MOUs are essential. Fragmentation without coordination is risky; mechanisms for information sharing and joint supervision (domestic and international) are crucial.

In sum, the U.S. experience—characterized by multiple competent authorities, robust policy debate, and periodic market failures—illustrates both the dangers of regulatory uncertainty and the difficult tradeoffs between financial stability and innovation. For policymakers in Nigeria, the principal policy choice is not binary: it lies in selecting a regime that combines clarity, proportionality, supervisory capacity, and cross-border cooperation to harness stablecoins' benefits while containing their risks.

7.4 Singapore: Innovation With Guardrails

Singapore has deliberately positioned itself as a global crypto-financial hub, adopting a regulatory model that balances innovation with strong prudential safeguards. This approach, spearheaded by the Monetary Authority of Singapore (MAS), seeks to harness the benefits of digital asset innovation while minimizing risks to consumers, financial stability, and the integrity of the financial system (Monetary Authority of Singapore, 2022; Zetzsche et al., 2020).

Regulatory Framework and Guardrails

The cornerstone of Singapore's regulatory strategy is the Payment Services Act (PSA) of 2019, which created a licensing framework for digital payment token (DPT) service providers, including stablecoin issuers. Building on this foundation, the Monetary Authority of Singapore (MAS) introduced a set of bespoke regulations in 2022 specifically targeting single-currency stablecoins (SCS) pegged to either the Singapore dollar or G10 currencies. These rules require issuers to maintain full 1:1 reserves in low-risk, highly liquid assets such as cash or short-dated government securities. To enhance transparency and market discipline, reserves must be subject to independent monthly attestations and annual audits (Monetary Authority of Singapore, 2022). Issuers are also obliged to provide redemption guarantees at par value within five business days, a safeguard designed to bolster consumer confidence and reduce the risk of destabilizing runs. Finally, MAS regulations make a clear distinction between fiat-backed stablecoins and unregulated algorithmic stablecoins, prohibiting the latter from marketing themselves as "MAS-regulated" (Monetary Authority of Singapore, 2022).

By embedding these guardrails, Singapore has established high prudential standards that protect financial stability while still fostering an environment in which fintechs and financial institutions can innovate. This balance has enabled the development of robust applications in payments, remittances, and decentralized finance (DeFi), reinforcing Singapore's reputation as a leading fintech hub in Asia.

Balancing Innovation and Risk Mitigation

Unlike jurisdictions such as Nigeria, which have often taken a restrictive stance—e.g., the Central Bank of Nigeria's (CBN) 2021 directive barring banks from servicing crypto exchanges—Singapore's model signals openness while carefully ring-fencing. This calibrated balance has made Singapore attractive to both domestic startups and global fintechs. Firms can operate in a clear regulatory environment, while consumers benefit from enhanced protections.

From a policy perspective, Singapore demonstrates that financial regulators need not choose between innovation and stability: both can be pursued simultaneously through carefully tailored rules (Arner et al., 2020). MAS's model acknowledges the inevitability of digital asset adoption but insists that trust in stablecoins can only be built through transparency, prudent reserve management, and enforceable redemption rights.

Industry and Global Impact

Singapore's innovation-friendly framework has consolidated its reputation as a regional fintech hub in Asia. Many leading blockchain companies, exchanges, and stablecoin projects have chosen Singapore as a base due to its regulatory clarity, robust financial infrastructure, and strong global connectivity (PwC, 2022).

Globally, the MAS framework has been cited as a benchmark for proportionate, risk-sensitive regulation. It differs from the European Union's MiCA regime, which applies uniform rules across 27 states, by adopting a more pragmatic, principle-based model that can be adjusted as markets evolve (Arner et al., 2020). For emerging markets, Singapore illustrates how small jurisdictions can achieve outsized influence by acting as regulatory pioneers.

Lessons and Relevance for Africa

For African economies—especially Nigeria—the Singaporean model holds practical lessons:

i. Enable but regulate: Banning or restricting digital assets often pushes innovation underground. Instead, calibrated licensing regimes can foster innovation while embedding safeguards.
ii. Reserve integrity is non-negotiable: Requiring 1:1 backing in safe, liquid assets prevents destabilizing runs—critical in markets with fragile investor confidence.
iii. Consumer redemption guarantees: Redemption-at-par rules strengthen public trust and prevent contagion during stress events.
iv. Positioning advantage: Like Singapore, African economies can leverage regulatory clarity to attract fintech capital, talent, and cross-border innovation. For instance, Lagos or Nairobi could aspire to become regional "fintech hubs" if similar guardrails are adopted.
v. Differentiated approach to algorithmic stablecoins: By excluding them from the regulated perimeter, Singapore avoids legitimizing risky models while keeping space open for experimentation under controlled settings.

Academic, Industry, and Policy Implications

- Applied Insight: Singapore's stablecoin regime is not theoretical; it is operational, showing how clear guardrails translate into functioning innovation ecosystems.

- Academic Impact: The model enriches comparative regulatory literature, offering a case study in principle-based financial regulation (Zetzsche et al., 2020).
- Industry Impact: Provides regulatory certainty, lowering compliance ambiguity for fintechs and global firms.
- Policy-Relevance: Offers a template for emerging markets seeking to balance innovation and financial stability.
- Global & Africa-Focused Insight: Africa can adapt Singapore's framework to local realities—e.g., by requiring reserve holdings in both foreign and local currency to manage volatility, or embedding mobile money operators into licensing regimes.

7.5 Nigeria: Restrictive Yet Experimental

Nigeria today represents one of the most active markets for digital assets globally, particularly in the peer-to-peer space. According to Chainalysis (2022), the country consistently ranks among the top ten worldwide for cryptocurrency adoption, with stablecoins accounting for the majority of peer-to-peer (P2P) flows. Despite this strong grassroots adoption of private digital tokens, state-led initiatives have struggled to gain traction. The eNaira, launched in 2021 as Africa's first retail central bank digital currency, has recorded minimal use: fewer than one percent of Nigerian adults actively adopted the currency within two years of its rollout (Abdullahi et al., 2024).

This divergence reflects underlying economic realities. Nigeria remains one of the world's largest recipients of remittances, with inflows exceeding USD 20 billion annually (World Bank, 2023). The high costs and inefficiencies of formal remittance channels have driven households and businesses to seek alternatives, with stablecoins emerging as a faster and cheaper means of transferring value across borders. Together, these dynamics illustrate the paradox facing Nigerian policymakers: while market-driven solutions such as stablecoins thrive, government-backed innovations like the eNaira struggle to win public trust and widespread adoption.

Nigeria therefore occupies a paradoxical position in the global stablecoin and digital asset regulatory landscape. On the one hand, the Central Bank of Nigeria (CBN) has taken a restrictive stance, barring banks and other financial institutions from servicing cryptocurrency-related businesses since February 2021, citing risks of money laundering, terrorism financing, consumer protection failures, and potential threats to monetary sovereignty (Templars, 2021; Templars, 2021). On the other hand, Nigeria has simultaneously demonstrated regulatory experimentation and innovation: the Securities and Exchange Commission (SEC Nigeria, 2022) has issued guidelines for digital asset offerings, and the CBN launched the eNaira in October 2021—the first retail central bank digital currency (CBDC) in Africa.

This duality—prohibitive regulation of private crypto-assets, yet proactive experimentation with state-led digital money—makes Nigeria a unique case study for the application of harmonized frameworks such as the Commonwealth Model Law on Virtual Assets.

Restrictive Posture: Bans and Exclusion

In February 2021, the Central Bank of Nigeria (CBN) issued a circular that effectively froze the relationship between the country's banking sector and the crypto ecosystem. The directive prohibited banks from opening accounts for cryptocurrency exchanges or processing transactions linked to digital assets (Templars, 2021). The CBN justified this measure on three primary grounds. First, it cited financial stability concerns: given Nigeria's persistent inflationary pressures and chronic exchange-rate volatility, authorities feared that the widespread use of dollar-pegged stablecoins would accelerate dollarization and further erode the naira's credibility. Second, the Bank highlighted the risks of illicit finance, noting that Nigeria's exposure to Financial Action Task Force (FATF) scrutiny meant that crypto-assets could present additional vulnerabilities in anti–money laundering and counter-terrorist financing compliance (Financial Action Task Force, 2021). Finally, the circular emphasized consumer protection risks, pointing to the proliferation of scams and the extreme volatility of digital assets as potential sources of systemic harm to retail investors.

Ironically, the ban did not dampen demand. Instead, it pushed crypto activity into informal peer-to-peer (P2P) networks, where transactions occur outside the formal banking system. Far from reducing exposure, this move accelerated the adoption of stablecoins through unregulated channels, especially for remittances and cross-border transfers. By 2023, Nigeria had emerged as one of the world's top ten countries for cryptocurrency adoption, with stablecoins playing a particularly significant role in remittance flows (Chainalysis, 2022).

Experimental Turn: SEC Guidelines and the eNaira

While the CBN moved to close off bank-based rails for crypto-assets, the Securities and Exchange Commission (SEC) Nigeria adopted a more open stance, signaling interest in a structured regulatory framework. In 2022, the SEC released rules that classified digital assets as securities and set out parameters for token issuance, exchange registration, and custodian obligations (SEC Nigeria, 2022). This divergence highlights a regulatory split in Nigeria's approach: while the CBN prioritizes systemic stability and the defense of currency sovereignty, the SEC has been more willing to explore capital-market innovation and investor protection within a controlled framework.

Simultaneously, Nigeria became a global pioneer in central bank digital currencies (CBDCs) with the launch of the eNaira in October 2021—the first retail CBDC in Africa, preceding initiatives in advanced economies such as the European Union and the United Kingdom. The CBN promoted the eNaira as a multi-purpose policy tool:

- To enhance financial inclusion, targeting the estimated 38 percent of Nigerians who remain unbanked;
- To reduce the costs of remittances, a sector critical to Nigeria's economy given inflows of over USD 20 billion annually (World Bank, 2023); and
- To strengthen monetary sovereignty, particularly in the face of growing adoption of stablecoins and cryptocurrencies (Templars, 2021).

Despite these ambitions, adoption of the eNaira has been disappointingly low. Empirical evidence shows that fewer than 1 percent of Nigerians actively used the eNaira within two years of its launch (Abdullahi et al., 2024). Several factors contributed to this outcome, including widespread distrust of government-backed financial innovations, poor user experience and technological usability, and a lack of compelling incentives relative to existing alternatives such as stablecoins and mobile money platforms. This stark gap between policy ambition and public adoption underscores the difficulty of state-led digital monetary innovation competing against market-driven solutions that already meet consumer needs more effectively.

The Paradox: Restrictive Yet Experimental

Nigeria's regulatory posture can best be described as "restrictive yet experimental." On the restrictive side, the CBN's 2021 banking ban effectively criminalized mainstream crypto activity by prohibiting financial institutions from servicing digital asset businesses. This move excluded stablecoins from formal payment rails and forced most activity into informal peer-to-peer networks (Templars, 2021; Templars, 2021). On the experimental side, the Securities and Exchange Commission (SEC Nigeria, 2022) has introduced a tentative framework for token issuance, exchange registration, and custody obligations, signaling openness to structured innovation. At the same time, the launch of the eNaira in 2021 marked an ambitious foray into central bank digital currencies, making Nigeria the first country in Africa to deploy a retail CBDC (Abdullahi et al., 2024).

This paradoxical mix of restriction and experimentation has produced regulatory fragmentation between the CBN and SEC, each pursuing divergent objectives. The CBN emphasizes monetary sovereignty and systemic stability, whereas the SEC leans toward enabling capital-market innovation (Ozili, 2024). For industry actors, this duality generates uncertainty and inconsistent signals, discouraging large-scale investment and deterring global fintech players from engaging directly with the Nigerian market (Chainalysis, 2023). At the same time, it has spurred underground adoption, as users migrate to informal networks to access stablecoins and digital assets that remain in high demand, particularly for remittances and inflation hedging (World Bank, 2023).

8. IMPLICATIONS FOR THE COMMONWEALTH MODEL LAW

The Nigerian case highlights why a harmonized approach, such as the Commonwealth Model Law on Virtual Assets (2022), is urgently needed. Nigeria illustrates the risks inherent in a binary regulatory stance—oscillating between outright prohibition and cautious experimentation—which can unintentionally amplify systemic risks rather than mitigate them. By relying on bans, authorities have driven users into informal peer-to-peer channels, thereby weakening oversight and undermining financial integrity. From an applied perspective, the lack of clear licensing pathways for stablecoin issuers ensures that demand is met through unregulated P2P networks, exposing users to fraud, opacity, and systemic vulnerabilities. In terms of policy relevance, adopting the Commonwealth Model Law could help Nigeria establish a tiered framework that distinguishes between algorithmic, foreign-pegged, and Naira-pegged stablecoins, while embedding strong AML/CFT provisions and prudential safeguards.

For the industry, such clarity would provide legal certainty for fintechs, exchanges, and payment service providers, unlocking innovation under a supervised regime rather than in underground markets. From an academic standpoint, Nigeria offers a striking example of what Zetzsche et al. (2020) term the "regulatory paradoxes of the Global South"—contexts where sovereignty concerns often clash with rapid digital adoption. Finally, from an Africa-focused global perspective, Nigeria's choices carry outsized weight. As the continent's largest economy, its approach sets a precedent: its restrictive stance contrasts sharply with Kenya's consultative dialogue with industry and South Africa's formal licensing of crypto-asset service providers, reflecting the diverse regulatory models emerging across Africa (Ozili, 2024).

Why Harmonization is Hard

Even where there is broad consensus on the necessity of stablecoin regulation, the path to harmonization remains fraught with challenges. Unlike traditional financial instruments that are largely territorial and supervised within clear jurisdictional boundaries, stablecoins are digitally native, borderless assets. Their value proposition lies in the ability to move seamlessly across borders, but this very characteristic complicates oversight and makes convergence of regulatory approaches elusive (Brunnermeier et al., 2021).

Sovereignty and Monetary Authority Conflicts

Stablecoins raise existential questions of monetary sovereignty, touching on one of the most jealously guarded domains of state authority: control over the money supply. For centuries, states have relied on monetary policy as a central lever of economic management, enabling them to influence inflation, stabilize exchange rates, and respond to economic shocks. The widespread adoption of dollar-pegged stablecoins threatens to erode this power by accelerating processes of de facto dollarization, particularly in countries with weaker currencies. Such a shift undermines the effectiveness of domestic monetary policy and constrains a central bank's ability to pursue independent macroeconomic objectives.

In the case of Nigeria, the Central Bank has consistently voiced concern that the increasing use of dollar-linked stablecoins could further destabilize the naira, already under chronic depreciation pressure, and weaken the effectiveness of its policy instruments (Templars, 2021). By contrast, in the European Union, where the euro is more resilient, policymakers have nonetheless taken precautionary steps under the Markets in Crypto-Assets (MiCA) regulation. MiCA includes explicit provisions that cap the use of stablecoins as a medium of exchange, reflecting the EU's determination to preserve the sovereignty of the euro against the encroachment of privately issued digital money (European Parliament, 2023).

This inherent tension between national monetary control and borderless private digital money means that harmonization must reconcile very different domestic imperatives, especially between strong-currency and weak-currency economies.

Divergent Risk Appetites

Regulatory philosophy differs markedly across jurisdictions, resulting in divergent appetites for risk and innovation in the treatment of stablecoins. The European Union has taken a precautionary approach under the Markets in Crypto-Assets (MiCA) Regulation of 2023, imposing stringent prudential, disclosure, and governance requirements, and even capping the use of stablecoins as payment instruments in order to safeguard financial stability and monetary sovereignty. The United States, by contrast, adopts a more market-oriented stance, relying on a patchwork of existing laws and regulatory bodies. Oversight is divided among the Securities and Exchange Commission (SEC), the Commodity Futures Trading Commission (CFTC), and various state regulators, with debates focusing on whether stablecoins should be treated as securities or commodities rather than on the adoption of a bespoke regulatory framework (U.S. Department of the Treasury, 2025).

In Singapore, the Monetary Authority of Singapore (MAS) has pursued a balanced innovation model, mandating 1:1 reserve backing and independent audits for fiat-backed stablecoins while continuing to foster a reputation as a fintech hub (Monetary Authority of Singapore, 2020). Nigeria, meanwhile, represents a restrictive yet experimental case: the CBN's banking ban effectively excludes stablecoins from the formal financial system, but the country simultaneously experiments with digital assets through SEC-issued rules for token markets and the pioneering launch of the eNaira, Africa's first retail central bank digital currency (SEC Nigeria, 2022; Abdullahi et al., 2024).

These contrasting approaches demonstrate how variations in risk tolerance and regulatory philosophy lead to conflicting responses to the same phenomenon. For this reason, global harmonization of stablecoin regulation remains highly challenging, as achieving convergence often requires compromising deeply embedded domestic policy objectives.

Institutional and Legal Fragmentation

Another major barrier to harmonization lies in institutional fragmentation. Stablecoins intersect with multiple regulatory domains—banking, securities, payments, anti–money laundering and counter-terrorist financing (AML/CFT), data protection, and consumer rights—yet few regulators have mandates that span all these areas. This creates overlapping responsibilities, regulatory blind spots, and in some cases, conflicting approaches to supervision.

In the United States, for example, the Securities and Exchange Commission (SEC) and the Commodity Futures Trading Commission (CFTC) continue to dispute jurisdiction over digital assets, leaving issuers and users uncertain as to whether stablecoins should be treated primarily as securities, commodities, or a novel asset class altogether (Arner et al., 2020). In Nigeria, a similar division exists: the Central Bank of Nigeria (CBN) evaluates digital assets largely through the lens of monetary stability and currency sovereignty, whereas the Securities and Exchange Commission (SEC Nigeria, 2022) views them in terms of capital-market innovation and investment opportunities.

When domestic frameworks themselves remain fragmented and inconsistent, the prospects for cross-border harmonization are even more limited. Aligning international rules is especially difficult when countries struggle to first reconcile competing institutional mandates within their own borders.

Asymmetric Capacities and Incentives

A further challenge to harmonization is the issue of capacity constraints in emerging economies. Designing and enforcing sophisticated regulatory frameworks requires significant technical expertise, institutional resources, and supervisory depth, which are unevenly distributed across jurisdictions. Advanced economies such as the European Union are able to impose stringent requirements on stablecoin issuers—including strict reserve composition rules, mandatory independent audits, and frequent disclosures—because these standards can be supported by well-developed supervisory institutions with the ability to enforce compliance effectively.

By contrast, countries in the Global South, including Nigeria, often face limitations in supervisory capacity. Regulatory agencies may lack the technical tools or institutional depth necessary to continuously monitor stablecoin issuers, enforce reserve requirements, or track complex cross-border flows of digital assets (Zetzsche et al., 2020). This asymmetry in institutional capacity and enforcement power makes the adoption of uniform global standards difficult. What is feasible in Brussels or Singapore may be impractical in Lagos or Nairobi, where regulators operate under resource constraints, infrastructural challenges, and competing policy priorities.

Competitive Pressures and Regulatory Arbitrage

There is also a strategic dimension to the regulation of stablecoins, as countries compete to attract fintech investment while simultaneously attempting to mitigate systemic risks. This competitive dynamic creates incentives for regulatory arbitrage and divergence, rather than harmonization.

Singapore, for instance, deliberately positions itself as a fintech hub with guardrails, combining openness to digital innovation with carefully designed prudential safeguards such as 1:1 reserve requirements and independent audits (Monetary Authority of Singapore, 2022). By contrast, Nigeria's more restrictive approach—particularly the CBN's banking ban—has inadvertently driven activity into informal peer-to-peer channels, undermining domestic oversight and creating opportunities for unregulated arbitrage (Chainalysis, 2022).

As long as jurisdictions compete for capital, talent, and technological leadership, achieving uniform regulatory standards across diverse economies will remain elusive. National interests in securing investment and innovation inevitably pull in different directions, making global harmonization of stablecoin regulation an uphill task.

Technical and Conceptual Uncertainty

Finally, the technology itself complicates efforts at harmonization, since stablecoins are far from uniform in design or function. Fiat-backed tokens, such as USDC and USDT, rely on reserves of traditional currencies and pose risks primarily related to reserve transparency, custodial arrangements, and redemption guarantees. Commodity-backed tokens, such as gold-backed stablecoins, raise distinct issues of valuation, custody, and cross-border regulation of physical assets. By contrast, algorithmic stablecoins, such as TerraUSD—whose dramatic collapse in 2022 erased billions in value—illustrate the fragility of models that rely solely on market incentives and algorithms rather than tangible reserves.

Because each type of stablecoin embodies different risk profiles and policy challenges, developing a single, uniform regulatory framework is conceptually problematic. Buckley et al. (2023) argue, the heterogeneity of digital assets means that regulatory approaches must be differentiated and risk-based, rather than one-size-fits-all.

The Core Harmonization Dilemma

Harmonization is hard because it requires balancing sovereignty with global interoperability, reconciling divergent risk appetites, overcoming institutional fragmentation, and addressing capacity asymmetries. Moreover, regulatory competition and technological variety further complicate alignment.

Yet, frameworks like the Commonwealth Model Law on Virtual Assets (2023) attempt to chart a middle path by offering risk-based, modular rules that countries can adapt to local contexts while maintaining broad alignment with FATF and FSB standards. Nigeria, with its paradoxical mix of restriction and experimentation, illustrates both the urgency and the difficulty of moving towards harmonized regulation.

Table 1. Comparative approaches to stablecoin regulation

Jurisdiction	Risk Appetite & Philosophy	Supervisory Structure	Sovereignty & Monetary Concerns	Industry Impact
European Union (MiCA, 2023)	Precautionary; prioritizes financial stability and consumer protection over speed of innovation.	Centralized, with national competent authorities supervising most issuers; EU-level oversight (EBA, ESMA) for "significant" tokens.	Concern about euro sovereignty; caps on stablecoin use as payment rails to protect monetary policy.	Creates a predictable, harmonized framework across 27 states; may slow innovation but fosters legal certainty and investor confidence.
United States	Market-oriented but fragmented; relies on existing laws (securities, commodities, banking) rather than bespoke frameworks.	Fragmented oversight by SEC, CFTC, FinCEN, OCC, and state regulators; Congressional proposals under debate.	Focus less on currency sovereignty, more on financial stability and investor protection. Dollar dominance makes sovereignty less urgent.	Supports innovation through flexibility; but fragmentation creates uncertainty, deterring some institutional participation.
Singapore	Balanced innovation with guardrails; aims to be a fintech hub while managing systemic risks.	Centralized under the Monetary Authority of Singapore (MAS), which integrates banking, securities, and payment oversight.	Sovereignty less at risk given Singapore dollar stability; focus is on AML/CFT and systemic safety.	Attracts global fintech firms through clear rules, 1:1 reserve backing requirements, and transparent governance standards.
Nigeria	Restrictive yet experimental; bans bank–crypto interactions while piloting eNaira.	Split: CBN imposes banking restrictions; SEC Nigeria issues rules on digital assets and exchanges.	High sovereignty concerns: dollar-pegged tokens could worsen naira depreciation and capital flight.	Restrictive stance drives crypto use underground; eNaira uptake low (<0.5% active wallet penetration in 2023). SEC rules show cautious openness to innovation.

Interpretation

This comparison underscores the inherent difficulties of harmonizing stablecoin regulation across jurisdictions. The European Union's precautionary model, alongside Nigeria's restrictive stance, reflects a regulatory philosophy that prioritizes sovereignty and monetary stability. While these approaches safeguard against systemic risks, they also risk displacing innovation to more permissive environments, potentially weakening domestic fintech ecosystems. By contrast, the United States offers an illustration of how fragmented oversight—with multiple regulators applying overlapping and sometimes conflicting rules—creates regulatory uncertainty even in a strong-currency economy where sovereignty concerns are minimal. Singapore, meanwhile, demonstrates a potential "middle path," combining prudential safeguards such as 1:1 reserve requirements with a broader openness to fintech experimentation.

Taken together, these cases highlight why harmonization remains elusive: regulatory philosophies diverge sharply depending on domestic priorities, institutional capacity, and risk appetite. Yet they also point toward a pragmatic solution: the adoption of risk-based, modular frameworks like the Commonwealth Model Law, which allow individual countries to tailor requirements to their local contexts while maintaining international interoperability and coherence.

9. A GUIDED WALKTHROUGH THROUGH OF THE MODEL LAW

The Commonwealth Model Law on Stablecoins (CML) is designed as a flexible, principle-based framework that balances innovation with stability, protection, and systemic resilience. Unlike prescriptive regimes such as the EU's MiCA, the CML emphasizes proportionality and customization, making it particularly relevant for jurisdictions like Nigeria where financial innovation intersects with vulnerabilities such as currency depreciation, systemic risk, and high fraud exposure (Commonwealth Secretariat, 2023; Financial Action Task Force, 2021).

9.1 Licensing and Tiered Supervision

A central feature of the CML is its tiered licensing regime. It distinguishes between small-scale issuers (Tier 0–1), mid-sized providers (Tier 2), and systemic issuers (Tier 3). The goal is to avoid a one-size-fits-all regulatory burden while ensuring that risks scale with systemic importance. Smaller issuers may operate under simplified requirements, while systemic players face rigorous prudential, governance, and reporting obligations (Model Law on Stablecoins, Draft 2025).

For Nigeria, this approach is crucial: while grassroots stablecoin activity often happens on peer-to-peer rails (e.g., USDT via informal merchants), systemic issuers like global stablecoins could significantly impact naira stability. Tiered licensing offers a pathway to bring both local fintech startups and global actors into a supervised space without crushing local experimentation.

9.2 Reserve Management and Transparency

The Model Law mandates that issuers of fiat-backed stablecoins maintain 1:1 reserves in High-Quality Liquid Assets (HQLAs) such as government securities or cash deposits, segregated from the issuer's own assets. Regular independent audits and public disclosures are required to prevent opacity—a key problem in cases like Tether's reserve controversies.

For Nigeria, where distrust in financial intermediaries is high and banking crises have eroded confidence, such transparency could build user trust. Independent attestation aligns with global best practices (Financial Stability Board, 2020) and would reduce the risk of Ponzi-like schemes flourishing in informal markets.

9.3 Consumer Protection and Redress

Recognizing the vulnerability of retail users in emerging markets, the CML provides robust consumer protection. It mandates redress mechanisms, mandatory disclosure of risks and fees, and accessible channels for dispute resolution. This is especially pertinent in Nigeria, where mobile money adoption is high but fraud exposure is among the highest in Sub-Saharan Africa (Martinez & Kale, 2021).

The Commonwealth framework explicitly links financial inclusion with consumer safeguards: stablecoins are recognized as potential tools for remittances and low-cost payments, but their benefits must be delivered without exposing low-literacy users to catastrophic losses.

9.4 AML/CFT and Financial Integrity

In line with FATF's "travel rule," the Model Law requires that issuers and intermediaries collect and transmit sender and receiver information for stablecoin transfers. It also provides for risk-based Know-Your-Customer (KYC) standards, suspicious transaction reporting, and enhanced scrutiny of politically exposed persons (PEPs).

This is particularly important in Nigeria, which has historically been flagged for AML/CFT weaknesses. By embedding FATF compliance, the CML strengthens Nigeria's ability to align with international standards while addressing the risk of stablecoins being used for terrorism financing or capital flight.

9.5 Cybersecurity and Operational Resilience

Stablecoin ecosystems depend on digital infrastructure that is vulnerable to hacking, phishing, and fraud. The Model Law therefore imposes cybersecurity standards, mandating secure wallets, multi-factor authentication, and continuity planning for issuers and intermediaries. It also requires incident reporting to regulators.

For Nigeria, where cybercrime losses exceed USD 500 million annually, these safeguards are non-negotiable. They also complement Nigeria's 2021 National Cybersecurity Policy, providing an integrated approach to fintech resilience.

9.6 Innovation and Sandboxes

Unlike outright prohibitions, the CML encourages regulators to establish regulatory sandboxes where new stablecoin projects can be tested under supervision. This mechanism balances Nigeria's restrictive stance (banking ban on crypto in 2021) with its experimental approach (launch of the eNaira). A sandbox would allow innovation to flourish in a controlled space, providing evidence for policy adjustments without systemic risk.

9.7 Cross-Border Coordination

Stablecoins are inherently borderless, and the Model Law explicitly encourages regulatory cooperation across Commonwealth members. For Nigeria, this is essential given its role as West Africa's financial hub. Harmonizing with Ghana, Kenya, and South Africa could prevent regulatory arbitrage and strengthen Africa's voice in global fintech governance.

Critical Implications for Nigeria

- Applied Insight: Nigeria can adapt the CML's proportionality principle to allow grassroots fintech experimentation while requiring systemic issuers to meet global prudential norms.
- Academic Impact: The CML provides a unique hybrid model—less prescriptive than MiCA, but more structured than the U.S. patchwork—that scholars can use to study regulatory transplants in the Global South.
- Industry Impact: Local fintechs gain regulatory clarity, which could attract investment currently deterred by CBN's ban.
- Policy Relevance: Nigeria's adoption of the Model Law could reconcile its paradox of restriction vs. experimentation, positioning it as a regional regulatory leader.
- Africa-Focused Global Insight: Harmonized adoption across Africa would reduce costs of compliance, facilitate remittance channels, and strengthen the continent's bargaining power in global standard-setting.

10. CRITICAL ANALYSIS OF FINDINGS

10.1 A Critical Overview of Global and Regional Regulatory Responses to Stablecoins

Findings: Comparative review confirms two simultaneous dynamics: (1) international standard setters (FSB, FATF, BIS, IOSCO) have converged on core principles—risk-based supervision, reserve transparency, AML/CFT compliance, and cross-border cooperation—while (2) national/regional responses diverge in instrument and intensity, ranging from MiCA's comprehensive, prescriptive approach to the United States' fragmented, agency-by-agency posture and to more permissive, innovation-friendly regimes such as Singapore's. Emerging markets often oscillate between precautionary bans and ad hoc permissiveness—Nigeria's mix of a CBN banking ban on crypto services and the SEC's digital asset rules illustrates this fragmentation.

Applied insight. For practitioners (regulators and industry), the evidence shows that regulatory clarity matters. Jurisdictions with clearer rules lower compliance costs and reduce opacity that breeds illicit flows and consumer harm. MiCA-style rules create predictable pathways for licensure and reserve requirements; sandbox regimes (Singapore, UK) offer safe testing grounds. Where clarity is absent, firms route activity into informal channels and P2P markets—raising operational and compliance costs for legitimate actors.

Academic impact. The chapter supports and refines scholarly claims that a principle-based global architecture is necessary but insufficient: operational instruments (licensing tiers, reserve composition, audit cadence) matter for outcomes. By mapping specific regulatory tools to risk types (monetary, prudential, operational, AML), the chapter advances the literature from normative advocacy to instrument-level design—an actionable contribution to regulation scholarship.

Industry impact. Industry actors face tradeoffs: strict on-shore reserve and custody requirements raise capital and operational burdens but improve credibility and institutional relationships (e.g., with banks). The analysis shows that firms in robust regulatory regimes gain market access and institutional partnerships; those in fragmented regimes face higher exit and compliance risks.

Policy relevance. Policymakers must choose between three broad postures—ban, laissez-faire, or calibrated regulation. The evidence favors calibrated, tiered approaches that match supervisory intensity to systemic footprint, combined with cross-border MOUs and compliance with FATF travel-rule obligations to limit arbitrage.

Global vs Africa focus. Globally, harmonization reduces contagion risks. For Africa, heterogeneity of regulatory capacity suggests a pragmatic route: adopt common minimum standards (reserve transparency, AML travel-rule) while allowing phased, sandboxed implementation adapted to national conditions. Nigeria's divergent CBN/SEC roles illustrate the cost of institutional ambiguity—clarifying mandates is urgent.

Recommendation. Adopt a tiered, principle-based domestic framework (drawing on MiCA and the Commonwealth Model Law) with mandatory reserve audits, clear licensure for payment-rail participants, and coordinated interagency governance (CBN–SEC memoranda). Prioritize enabling supervised remittance corridors to harness stablecoins' inclusion potential while controlling systemic spillovers.

10.2 Nigeria as a Test Case for Emerging Economies Grappling with Innovation and Sovereignty

Findings: Nigeria typifies the Global South trade-off: large fintech adoption and remittance dependence amid macro instability (inflation, FX volatility) make dollar-pegged stablecoins attractive; at the same time, institutional fragmentation (CBN vs SEC) and precautionary restrictions create an enforcement gap that channels activity into informal markets.

Applied insight: On the ground, P2P and OTC stablecoin activity substitutes for constrained formal FX corridors. Firms and households use USDT/USDC to preserve purchasing power and settle cross-border trade. Practically, this reduces transaction times and costs but increases counterparty, custody, and regulatory risks for participants and the financial system.

Academic impact: The chapter empirically connects currency substitution literature to digital-age phenomena: technological lowering of friction accelerates substitution. It extends theoretical accounts of monetary credibility by showing how payment-layer innovations (stablecoins) interact with macro variables to produce rapid currency substitution in countries with weak FX regimes.

Industry impact: Nigerian fintechs operate in a high-uncertainty environment: compliance with KYC/AML is challenging where banks are discouraged from servicing crypto-related entities (CBN circular). This raises onboarding friction and limits partnerships with regulated financial institutions—hindering scale and institutional trust.

Policy relevance: For sovereignty and monetary policy, the policy lesson is clear: prohibition alone is ineffective. Instead, Nigeria should (a) clarify interagency roles, (b) create supervised on-ramps/off-ramps, (c) require reserve transparency for issuers serving Nigerians, and (d) accelerate credible eNaira utility where possible to provide a sovereign digital alternative.

Africa focus: Nigeria's path will set regional norms. ECOWAS and AfCFTA coordination can prevent regulatory arbitrage and support interoperable corridors for remittances—critical for intra-African trade. Nigeria's regulatory posture thus has outsized influence on regional digital finance architecture.

Recommendation: Reframe policy from exclusion to structured inclusion: enable regulated stablecoin corridors for remittances and trade, implement reserve and audit rules for issuers accessible to Nigerians, and clarify agency mandates with statutory interagency coordination.

10.3 The Commonwealth Model Law as a flexible and harmonizable regulatory template

Findings: The Commonwealth Model Law (2023) encapsulates a pragmatic synthesis: tiered licensing, reserve segregation, mandatory audits, consumer protection, and cross-border coordination. It maps well onto FSB/FATF principles while offering implementation flexibility suitable for capacity-constrained regulators.

Applied insight: For Nigerian regulators, the Model Law provides a ready legal scaffold that can be calibrated (reserve composition, reporting cadence, sandbox criteria) to local realities. It promotes interoperability by embedding FATF travel-rule compliance and encouraging MOUs between supervisory bodies.

Academic impact: The chapter's critique of the Model Law advances scholarship by identifying where a model framework must be localized—e.g., reserve asset choice (how much can be held in domestic sovereign debt versus foreign HQLA), cross-border supervisory resilience, and consumer redress mechanisms tailored to informal markets. It thus contributes to the literature on transplanting regulatory templates across jurisdictions.

Industry impact: Adopting Model Law elements reduces legal uncertainty for fintechs and potential stablecoin issuers, enabling partnerships with banks and custodians, lowering compliance ambiguity for cross-border service provision, and improving investor confidence.

Policy relevance: The Model Law's tiering is particularly policy-relevant: it allows regulators to impose strict prudential standards only where systemic footprint justifies it and to offer lighter regimes for pilots (Tier 0/1), preserving innovation space while protecting stability.

Global vs Africa: Globally, the Model Law helps convergence; regionally, it offers a harmonization vehicle for ECOWAS/AU coordination. For Africa, adopting a common template—adapted for local fiscal/FX constraints—reduces fragmentation and enables coordinated supervisory responses to cross-border stablecoin flows.

Recommendation: Nigeria should adopt an adapted Model Law: codify tiered licensing, reserve segregation with independent audits, AML travel-rule enforcement, and supervisory MOUs—plus transitional provisions accommodating legacy P2P channels during policy roll-out.

10.4 Explore how regulation can both mitigate risks and enable financial inclusion in Africa and the Global South

Findings: Regulation can be both protective and enabling. Mandated reserve transparency, redemption rights, and operational resilience reduce systemic and counterparty risk; simultaneously, supervised on-ramps, consumer protections, and targeted sandboxes lower barriers for underserved populations to access cheaper remittance channels.

Applied insight: Implemented well, regulatory frameworks convert unstable, informal digital corridors into supervised, auditable channels that preserve the benefits—reduced cost, speed, and accessibility—while adding layers of consumer protection. For example, requiring issuers who serve Nigeria to hold HQLA and publish attestations reduces run risk and improves trust among low-income users.

Academic impact: The chapter advances the "inclusion-through-regulation" thesis by empirically and theoretically rebutting the binary view that regulation inherently stifles innovation. It synthesizes development economics and financial regulation literatures to show conditions under which regulation expands access (e.g., requiring interoperable KYC-lite models for low-value users, supervised custodial services, and dispute resolution mechanisms).

Industry impact: For fintech firms, predictable, inclusion-oriented rules open larger addressable markets: supervised corridors reduce counterparty risk and unlock partnerships with remittance platforms and banks. However, compliance costs must be mitigated through proportionality (e.g., graduated capital requirements or simplified KYC for micro-transactions).

Policy relevance: Policy instruments that simultaneously target safety and access include: (1) tiered KYC for low-value flows, (2) mandatory consumer disclosures and escrowed reserve models, (3) supervised remittance corridors with designated local custodians, and (4) resolution playbooks for systemic issuers. These measures help preserve monetary stability while expanding access.

Africa focus: Given Africa's high remittance costs and large informal economies, regulated stablecoin corridors tailored to local needs could materially lower transfer costs. Coordinated regional frameworks would increase scale and interoperability—key to cost reduction.

Recommendation: Implement proportionate consumer protections and graduated KYC for micropayments, mandate reserve attestations for issuers, and create supervised remittance pilots using stablecoins tied to regulated custodians and exchange partners.

10.5 How these findings advance the state of the art

i. Instrumental mapping: Moves beyond broad principles to map specific regulatory instruments to quantified risk outcomes (e.g., reserve audit frequency → lower probability of run contagion), providing practical guidance for policymakers.
ii. Country-level institutional diagnosis: Deepens understanding of how institutional fragmentation (monetary vs market regulators) materially channels stablecoin activity into P2P and opaque markets—an empirical advance with wide relevance for other emerging economies.
iii. Inclusion-through-regulation synthesis: Integrates development, regulation, and fintech literatures to demonstrate how calibrated rules can foster inclusion without sacrificing safety—bridging two literatures often treated separately.
iv. Model Law operationalization: Provides a concrete adaptation roadmap for the Commonwealth Model Law for capacity-constrained states—transforming a generic template into a domestically actionable playbook.

10.6 Limitations and future research

i. Data limitations: On-chain and P2P transaction data for Nigeria are partial and sometimes proprietary; empirical testing of propositions (P1–P4) requires collaboration with analytics firms and regulators.
ii. Dynamic technology risks: Smart-contract vulnerabilities and DeFi innovations evolve quickly; regulatory designs must be adaptive.
iii. Behavioral responses: How households perceive regulated stablecoin products vs informal channels needs household surveys and field experiments.

Suggested research agenda: mixed-methods studies combining blockchain analytics, household remittance surveys, regulator interviews, and pilot evaluations of supervised remittance corridors.

10.7. Final policy and industry prescriptions

i. Clarify institutional mandates (statutory CBN–SEC coordination and MOUs).
ii. Adopt a tiered licensing and supervision framework (Model Law adaptation) with proportional capital/reserve requirements.
iii. Mandate reserve segregation and public attestations by independent auditors; restrict reserve assets to HQLA with clear composition limits.

iv. Implement FATF travel-rule compliance and cross-border supervisory MOUs.
v. Create supervised remittance pilots (sandboxes) with graduated KYC for micropayments to preserve inclusion.
vi. Invest in supervisory capacity and digital forensics (blockchain analytics partnerships).

11. CONCLUDING SYNTHESIS

The chapter's cross-cutting analysis shows that stablecoins in Nigeria—and similar contexts—are not a binary problem to be banned or embraced outright. Rather, they are a governance challenge that requires a nuanced, instrument-level regulatory response. By aligning international principles with practical legal instruments and tailoring them to Nigeria's macro-institutional realities, policymakers can harness stablecoins' benefits for inclusion and efficiency while protecting monetary sovereignty and systemic stability. This blend of academic rigor, policy pragmatism, and industry realism advances the conversation from abstract debate to implementable action.

Among the examples of Global south regulatory dilemma is the example of Nigeria that attempts to balance innovation, financial inclusion and sovereignty and mitigate risk. Its history, such as the cryptocurrency restrictions, and the formation of the eNaira and the formation of the rules of SEC as an example of the Commonwealth Model Law as a harmonising law between the restrictionist and liberalist strategies. These kinds of structures can aid in reduction of systemic risks and not suffocation of innovation. The regulation of stablecoins in a broader sense is a subset of what some call a new Bretton Woods: at a point where global co-ordination is necessary to prevent arbitrage, instability and marginalisation. The need to make innovation responsible is an obligation that cannot be postponed in Nigeria and other emerging economies.

REFERENCES

Abdullahi, M., Ahmad, A., Pandey, B. K., & Pandey, D. (2024). Digital currency adoption: A comparative analysis of global trends and the Nigerian Enaira digital currency. *SN Computer Science*, *5*(5), 602. DOI: 10.1007/s42979-024-02882-6

Arner, D. W., Auer, R., & Frost, J. (2020). Stablecoins: Risks, potential and regulation. BIS Working Paper no. 905 (2020), University of Hong Kong Faculty of Law Research Paper No. 2021/57

Auer, R., & Böhme, R. (2021). Central bank digital currency: The quest for minimally invasive technology. *The Journal of Economic Perspectives*, *35*(2), 161–178.

Baldwin, R., Cave, M., & Lodge, M. (2012). Understanding Regulation. Theory, Strategy, and Practice. OUP Oxford, 2012 - Business & Economics

Balina, R., Spyra, M., Rozynski, F., & Podlinska, O. (2025). From Checklists to Change: FATF's Risk-Based Approach and Its Impact on Malta's AML Framework. *European Research Studies*, *28*(3), 518–530. DOI: 10.35808/ersj/4058

Bank for International Settlements. (2022). *BIS Annual Economic Report 2022*. BIS.

Brunnermeier, M., James, H., & Landau, J. P. (2021). *The digitalization of money*. Princeton University Press.

Buckley, R. P., Arner, D. W., & Zetzsche, D. A. (2023). *FinTech: Finance, technology and regulation*. Cambridge University Press. DOI: 10.1017/9781009086943

Chainalysis. (2022). The 2022 geography of cryptocurrency report. https://go.chainalysis.com/2022-geography-of-cryptocurrency.html

CoinGecko. (2022). 2022 annual cryptocurrency report. CoinGecko. https://www.coingecko.com/research/publications

Commonwealth Secretariat. (2023). *Model Law on Virtual Assets. Office of Civil and Criminal Justice Reform*. Commonwealth Secretariat.

Congdon, T. (2021). Interest rates or quantity of money? Edward Nelson on Milton Friedman. *Economic Affairs*, *41*(2), 320–335. DOI: 10.1111/ecaf.12467

European Parliament. (2023). Markets in Crypto-Assets Regulation (MiCA). Brussels: EU.

Financial Action Task Force. (2019). *Guidance for a risk-based approach to virtual assets and virtual asset service providers*. FATF.

Financial Action Task Force. (2021). *Guidance for a risk-based approach to virtual assets and virtual asset service providers*. FATF.

Financial Action Task Force. (2023). *Targeted update on implementation of the FATF standards on virtual assets*. FATF.

Financial Stability Board. (2020). *Regulation, supervision and oversight of "global stablecoin" arrangements*. FSB.

G7 Working Group on Stablecoins. (2019). *Investigating the impact of global stablecoins*. Bank for International Settlements.

Gorton, G., & Metrick, A. (2012). Getting up to speed on the financial crisis. National Bureau of Economic Research Paper.

Hamdan, A., Ghura, H., Alareeni, B., & Hamdan, R. K. (2022). Entrepreneurship growth in emerging economies: New insights and approaches. *Journal of Sustainable Finance & Investment, 12*(1), 1–12. DOI: 10.1080/20430795.2021.1944750

International Monetary Fund. (2024). *Central bank digital currency—progress and further considerations*. International Monetary Fund.

International Organization of Securities Commissions. (2022). *CPMI and IOSCO publish final guidance on stablecoin arrangements confirming application of Principles for Financial Market Infrastructure*. IOSCO.

Katz, M. L., & Shapiro, C. (1985). *Network externalities, competition, and compatibility; Knapp, G. F. (1924/1973)*. The State Theory of Money.

Levy-Yeyati, E., & Sturzenegger, F. (2024). Exchange Rate Regimes 20 years later: The prevalence of floats. *IMF Economic Review*, •••, 1–30. DOI: 10.1057/s41308-024-00266-7

Martinez, J., & Kale, D. (2021). *Regulating the crypto market in Nigeria*. International Monetary Fund.

Monetary Authority of Singapore. (2022). *Proposed regulatory framework for stablecoin-related activities*. MAS.

Nigeria, S. E. C. (2022). *New rules on issuance, offering platforms and custody of digital assets*. SEC.

Ozili, P. K. (2024). Cryptocurrency regulation in Africa: Advantages, motivation, regulatory models, challenges, consequences, and principles vs. rules-based regulation. *International Journal of Blockchains and Cryptocurrencies, 5*(4), 294–313. DOI: 10.1504/IJBC.2024.143982

President's Working Group on Financial Markets, the Board of Governors of the Federal Reserve System, and the Federal Deposit Insurance Corporation. (2021). Report on stablecoins.

PwC. (2022). *PwC Annual Global Crypto Report 2022*. PwC Global.

Shrivastav, S. (2025). Network externalities, consumer heterogeneity, and optimal monopoly pricing. *Marketing Letters*, *36*(3), 563–575. DOI: 10.1007/s11002-024-09763-1

Templars (2021). The CBN letter on cryptocurrency: Your FAQs answered. Templars.

The Commonwealth. (2025). Consultation on the Draft Commonwealth Model Law on Stablecoins. The Commonwealth

U.S. Department of the Treasury. (2025). *President's working group on financial markets releases report and recommendations on stablecoins*. U.S. Treasury.

World Bank. (2021). Remittance prices worldwide: Quarterly report. https://remittanceprices.worldbank.org

World Bank. (2023). *Migration and Development Brief 38*. World Bank.

Zetzsche, D. A., Arner, D. W., & Buckley, R. P. (2020). Decentralized finance. *Journal of Financial Regulation*, *6*(2), 172–203. DOI: 10.1093/jfr/fjaa010

Zetzsche, D. A., Buckley, R. P., Arner, D. W., & van Ek, M. (2023). Remaining regulatory challenges in digital finance and crypto-assets after MiCA. Committee on Economic and Monetary Affairs (ECON), Policy Department for Economic, Scientific and Quality of Life Policies, European Parliament, Luxembourg, 23-27. DOI: 10.2139/ssrn.4487516

Zubkov, P., & Pondi, K. (2022). Writing the methodology chapter. In *The SAGE Handbook of Qualitative Research in the Asian Context* (pp. 379–395). SAGE Publications Ltd. DOI: 10.4135/9781529781731.n27

Chapter 9
Enabling Innovation in Stablecoin Markets Through Special Jurisdictions

Andreas Baumgartner
The Metis Institute, UK

Mark Beer
The Metis Institute, UK

Ankita Dhawan
https://orcid.org/0009-0002-3244-9796
The Metis Institute, UAE

ABSTRACT

Once limited to crypto trading, stablecoins are now serving global roles in payments, settlements, and value storage, alongside tokenised deposits and CBDCs. As adoption grows, regulation must balance trust, stability, and innovation. This paper argues that special jurisdictions - such as city states and special economic zones - enable stablecoin innovation without risking macroeconomic stability. Through their adaptive regulation, pilot programmes, sandboxes, innovation ecosystems, and specialised dispute-resolution mechanisms, they create controlled environments where stablecoin models can be tested and scaled safely. Through case studies, including Hong Kong, Singapore, DIFC, among others, the paper makes a case that special jursidictions offer credible regulatory pathways to issuers, while acting

DOI: 10.4018/979-8-3373-9043-7.ch009

as evidence-generating laboratories for regulators. Therefore, special jurisdictions are quietly shaping the future of money, where the regulator's role is evolving from merely being a rule-maker to being a co-innovator.

INTRODUCTION

A shopper in Singapore walks into a supermarket, scans a QR code at checkout and shortly after, behind the scenes, her USD Coin (USDC) wallet converts instantly into StraitsX digital Singapore Dollar (XSGD), through stablecoin enabled on-chain payment rails. GrabPay recognises the transaction, and within seconds, funds are settled in Singapore dollars (SGD) to the merchant's account. No card networks, no correspondent banks; just tokenised fiat moving across regulated infrastructure (Huang, 2024).

Thousands of kilometres away, in JPMorgan's London and New York offices, another form of digital money flows quietly, but at scale. JPM Coin (now Kinexys), a permissioned, blockchain-based deposit token, facilitated intraday settlements between the bank's institutional clients across currencies and time zones. A multinational financial company is able to move liquidity between its subsidiaries in Tokyo and Frankfurt within minutes, avoiding the frictions of cut-off times and cross-border clearing. (J.P. Morgan, n.d.)

These seemingly disparate examples illustrate a single, transformative phenomenon: stablecoins are no longer niche digital instruments; instead, they are becoming mainstream financial infrastructure. From retail payments to cross-border settlements, they are being integrated into national and global payment ecosystems, augmenting the efficiency, reach, and inclusivity of traditional finance.

Fundamentally, stablecoins are digital instruments designed to maintain a stable value relative to a reference currency or asset. Most stablecoins are pegged to the US dollar, such as USD Tether (USDT) issued by Tether and USDC issued by Circle. Increasingly, we are seeing stablecoins backed by (a) different fiat currencies such as the Euro, Dirham or the Yen - for example, Stasis Euro (EURS), or (b) tangible assets like gold, such as Tether Gold (XAUT).

Stablecoins maintain their "stable" value through mechanisms of reserve backing, collateralisation, or algorithmic control. In the reserve-backed model, each stablecoin is backed 1:1 by a fiat currency or equivalent. This is followed by most stablecoins, such as the USDC. The collateralised model uses other assets (commodities or bonds) as backing rather than strictly fiat - for example, XAUT, which is backed by physical gold reserves. Another example is DAI, which is issued by MakerDAO Foundation, and is backed by crypto assets. The algorithmic model relies on smart-contract protocols to expand/contract supply rather than holding full asset reserves - for instance, the now-infamous TerraUSD (UST) from Terraform Labs.

From a regulatory standpoint, reserve-backed stablecoins are considered the safest, as they are fully supported by verifiable fiat reserves and subject to licensing and audit requirements (Jiao, 2025). Unsurprisingly, fiat-backed stablecoins currently make up ~87% of the stablecoins market (Brookings Institution, 2025). The algorithmic model, by contrast, is viewed as inherently unstable and is generally prohibited in major jurisdictions due to the absence of identifiable collateral (Jiao, 2025). Collateralised stablecoins occupy an intermediate position - they are permissible under most regulatory frameworks when supported by transparent, liquid, and auditable assets, but they carry higher market and valuation risks than fully fiat-backed designs. Therefore, they are often overcollateralized to hedge for volatility (Bullmann, Klemm, & Pinna, 2019).

Overall, stablecoins combine the technological efficiency, programmability, and global accessibility of distributed ledger systems with the price stability and legal recognition traditionally associated with fiat or asset-backed money. This hybrid character has allowed them to function as a bridge between the conventional financial system and the rapidly expanding digital assets ecosystem.

Yet the function of stablecoins has rapidly expanded beyond the realm of digital assets trading. They are now enabling the movement of value across networks, jurisdictions, and asset classes with unprecedented speed and transparency. They are being integrated into mainstream financial and payment architectures, signalling the convergence of traditional finance (TradFi) and decentralised finance (DeFi). Stablecoins are evolving into programmable payment rails, instruments that can move value instantly, at low cost, and with embedded logic that enables conditional payments, automated settlements, or real-time compliance checks.

Real-world adoption illustrates this transition vividly. Stablecoins have become a preferred instrument for cross-border business-to-business payments and remittances, facilitating on-chain treasury management for fintechs and global corporates. In emerging markets such as Argentina, Nigeria, and the Philippines, stablecoins are increasingly used for dollar savings, remittances, and hedging against currency volatility. (Chainalysis, 2023). In the UAE, stablecoins are powering merchant payments for not just taxis and airline fares, but also for payment of court fees (Tawasul Transport, 2025; Air Arabia, 2025; Al Etihad, 2025). These examples demonstrate that stablecoins are no longer speculative tools but operational components of the global payments ecosystem.

This shift also signifies a deeper structural change. By reducing reliance on legacy intermediaries—such as correspondent banks or clearing houses, stablecoins are augmenting and modernising traditional financial rails. They enable 24/7 settlement, near-instant cross-border payments, and programmable financial products that can interact directly with smart contracts and decentralised applications. In doing so, they enhance monetary efficiency while expanding access to financial services in regions underserved by traditional banking infrastructure. The programmability of stablecoins also opens new possibilities for embedded finance: payments that execute automatically upon fulfilment of digital conditions, whether in supply-chain finance, insurance, or securities settlement.

At the same time, stablecoins are catalysing the next generation of digital-money constructs, including tokenised deposits, synthetic dollars, and CBDCs. Each model builds upon the idea of programmable value, but they differ in important respects. Tokenised deposits are liabilities of regulated banks represented on distributed ledgers, combining bank money with blockchain efficiency. Synthetic dollars, by contrast, are privately issued tokens backed by short-term government securities or cash, functioning as digital money-market funds. CBDCs represent the government counterpart - sovereign liabilities issued directly by central banks, potentially interoperable with private stablecoin ecosystems. The boundaries between public and private money are blurring, reshaping the architecture of global finance.

Undeniably, the implications of these innovations are profound. For consumers, institutional and retail, stablecoins promise cheaper, faster, and more inclusive access to digital payments and cross-border transfers. For businesses, they offer programmable financial infrastructure capable of automating complex cash-flow operations and treasury functions. For governments and central banks, they signal the "privatization" of monetary plumbing" - a shift reminiscent of when railways, telecom networks, and postal systems moved from state-run monopolies to mixed public-private ecosystems.

Despite their promise, stablecoins introduce a new constellation of risks that extend across financial, technological and macroeconomic domains.

Financially, the reliance on asset reserves exposes issuers and users to liquidity, market, and counterparty risks, particularly if reserve assets are concentrated, opaque, or mismatched in duration (Bank for International Settlements, 2025).

Cybersecurity and operational vulnerabilities compound these challenges: smart-contract exploits, key management failures, and oracle manipulation can threaten both user funds and systemic confidence (CertiK, 2025).

At the macro level, widespread use of stablecoins pegged to non-national currencies as payment instruments, in the same manner as state-issued legal tender, could fragment monetary sovereignty and complicate monetary policy transmission. This could be especially true in smaller or emerging economies where foreign currency–linked tokens will compete with local units of account. As a result, the role of the state in money creation and payment infrastructure is being redefined. (Bank for International Settlements, 2025).

The challenge for policymakers is no longer whether to regulate, but how to govern a hybrid monetary system in which public trust must coexist with private innovation. Policy conversation is moving beyond binary debates of permission versus prohibition, toward collaboration and competition. This requires a new generation of policy design - one that can accommodate experimentation without losing control, foster competition without sacrificing stability, and preserve the credibility of money in an increasingly borderless financial ecosystem.

Key questions that regulators and innovators must answer include, but are not limited to: How can monetary authorities preserve policy effectiveness and financial stability in an increasingly multi-currency, tokenised ecosystem? What frameworks ensure that stablecoin reserves remain transparent, auditable, and bankruptcy-remote? How can interoperability be achieved between public (CBDC) and private (stablecoin or tokenised deposit) infrastructures without fragmenting liquidity or creating regulatory blind spots? What safeguards are needed to protect users from cyber, operational, and governance risks as financial activity migrates on-chain?

Policymakers must consider how to balance innovation with control—designing regimes that maintain the integrity of money, protect consumers, and preserve systemic trust, while still enabling experimentation and competition and protecting the ease of usability and flexibility. The challenge is not merely one of compliance, but of institutional design: creating adaptive frameworks capable of evolving with technology, rather than lagging behind it.

Such policy design finds its most effective expression in special jurisdictions. The distinctiveness of these special jurisdictions lies not in geography but in institutional architecture: independent regulators, common-law legal systems, and bespoke rulemaking powers that allow innovation to flourish within prudential safeguards. These jurisdictions function as controlled environments where financial systems can evolve safely, turning innovation from a policy aspiration into an operational reality.

UNDERSTANDING SPECIAL JURISDICTIONS

Special jurisdictions are territories endowed with unique regulatory, legal, or political frameworks that grant them autonomy from national governance systems. Their distinctiveness lies not simply in their geography or governance boundaries, but in their regulatory, legal and institutional autonomy. Special jurisdictions typically exist along a spectrum of autonomy.

At one end of the spectrum, we have sovereign microstates or autonomous regions within sovereign states. For example, micro-states/city-states, such as Monaco and Liechtenstein in Europe, Singapore in Asia, and Nauru in Oceania, all maintain their own constitutions, legal systems, fiscal policies and representation at the United Nations. (United Nations, n.d.)

As for autonomous regions, Hong Kong, a special administrative region within the People's Republic of China, is endowed with constitutional and fiscal independence under the "one country, two systems" model (The Basic Law of the Hong Kong Special Administrative Region, 1990; Sino-British Joint Declaration on the Question of Hong Kong, 1984).

Hong Kong preserves its common-law legal system, convertible currency, and independent monetary authority. (The Basic Law of the Hong Kong Special Administrative Region, 1990, arts. 8, 110–111). This allows it to participate fully in global financial markets while testing new regulatory models, without direct implications for mainland China's monetary regime. Its dual identity, both Chinese and global, gives Hong Kong unique flexibility to act as a bridge jurisdiction, translating international standards into regionally relevant frameworks.

At the other end of the spectrum lie purpose-driven special economic zones (SEZs), designated areas that operate under national regulatory supervision but with specific carve-outs for fiscal and legal incentives, often dedicated to specific sectors. They are often granted varying degrees of legal, and operational autonomy. While traditionally purpose-built SEZs were manufacturing and export oriented, increasingly, SEZs are being adapted for blockchain experimentation and have evolved from industrial enclaves into epicentres of growth and testbeds for innovation.

For example, the Dubai Multi Commodities Centre (DMCC) in the UAE is a dedicated commodities and business free zone, which has attracted 26,000+ companies, thousands of which are web3 and blockchain enterprises. It offers incentives such as 0% corporate tax on qualifying income, 100% foreign ownership, full repatriation of profits and capital, and streamlined company-setup procedures, all while operating under the UAE's federal and Dubai's emirate-level legal and regulatory framework. (Dubai Multi Commodities Centre, n.d.)

Another example is the Cloud Computing SEZ at King Abdulaziz City for Science and Technology (KACST) in the Kingdom of Saudi Arabia — dedicated to digital infrastructure, AI, and cloud services. (Communications and Information Technology Commission, n.d.)

In the middle of the spectrum are purpose-built SEZs which not only have operational autonomy but may also have full financial, legal and adjudicatory autonomy, with varying degrees of host state oversight and involvement.

Notable examples are DIFC, Abu Dhabi Global Market (ADGM), Qatar Financial Centre (QFC), Astana International Financial Centre (AIFC), and Labuan IBFC. All of these operate as ring-fenced jurisdictions established within a national territory (DIFC.; ADGM, n.d.; Qatar Financial Centre, n.d.; AIFC, n.d.; Labuan IBFC, n.d.).

They generally possess the legal authority to craft and enforce their own financial regulations, operate independent courts or dedicated dispute resolution systems (often based on common law), and maintain separate supervisory agencies — all features that give them the agility to test new frameworks without endangering macro-financial stability. Broadly, they are all focussed on enabling the financial sector, including fintech and digital assets.

As these models become the baseline, special jurisdictions are building over the conventional financial paradigm to prototype new forms of economic governance that merge technology, and sustainability. For example, Bhutan's Gelephu Mindfulness City - currently under development - represents a new generation of SEZs built around values-driven innovation rather than purely fiscal arbitrage. (Gelephu Mindfulness City, n.d.) Gelephu envisions a sustainable, mindfulness-based jurisdiction uniting well-being, clean energy, innovation and Buddhist-inspired digital design. It seeks to build upon Bhutan's quietly growing digital-asset ecosystem, which proposes to leverage the country's abundant hydropower to support sustainable crypto mining. Similarly, Kingdom of Saudi Arabia's NEOM exemplifies a state-backed, investor-partnered special jurisdiction designed to pioneer regenerative urbanism under an autonomous legal and regulatory framework. (NEOM, n.d.)

While investment attraction is a key feature of all SEZs, a new trend is the establishment of investor-led zones. For example, Próspera ZEDE in Honduras is a privately developed special jurisdiction that operates under its own charter and regulatory framework, representing a shift toward investor-administered governance models (Próspera ZEDE, n.d.).

From a regulatory-theory perspective, regardless of form, special jurisdictions embody what scholars describe as "experimental governance"—an adaptive model that replaces static, top-down regulation with iterative policy cycles. Under this approach, authorities permit limited deployment of new technologies, observe empirical outcomes, and adjust legal frameworks based on evidence rather than speculation. Importantly, experimentation in these zones does not equate to deregulation. Rather, it allows regulators to simulate market conditions within contained boundaries, managing exposure while gathering data on critical variables such as reserve adequacy, redemption speed, cybersecurity, and compliance performance. This enables regulators to identify systemic risks early, build institutional expertise, and strengthen public trust before mainstream adoption.

Special jurisdictions thus represent more than geographic or fiscal constructs—they are dynamic instruments of institutional design. Their true power lies in how they operationalise innovation through key elements such as regulatory architecture: purpose-built authorities, adaptive licensing regimes, and frameworks for controlled experimentation, dedicated dispute resolution, among others. Pilot programmes allow authorities to test market infrastructure and governance models in real time;

sandboxes enable firms to trial novel business models under regulatory supervision; and accelerators nurture ecosystems that translate proofs-of-concept into investable, compliant enterprises. In this way, special jurisdictions convert abstract innovation into structured learning, as discussed below.

Against this backdrop, special jurisdictions offer a pragmatic pathway to enable stablecoin innovation with financial and economic prudence. Their institutional design, combining regulatory autonomy, adaptive rulemaking, controlled experimentation, innovation mindset and dedicated dispute resolution, makes them ideal environments for testing, refining, and scaling stablecoin use cases before national or global deployment.

METHODOLOGY

This paper examines the five key enablers within special jurisdictions that make them fertile grounds for stress-testing stablecoin business models, namely, (i) regulatory architecture, (ii) sandboxes, (iii) innovation accelerators, (iv) ecosystem, and (v) dispute resolution mechanisms.

It adopts a qualitative benchmarking approach across the above enablers, analysing developments across special jurisdictions and draws on success stories from jurisdictions that have pioneered financial innovation. The paper also highlights ongoing stablecoin initiatives within select special jurisdictions that offer valuable lessons for future policy design. Overall, it explores how such mechanisms can be adapted to govern and scale stablecoin usage responsibly, integrating innovation with stability and experimentation with oversight.

Regulatory Architecture

The first and most fundamental enabler that makes special jurisdictions hotbeds of innovation is their regulatory design. The regulatory design of special jurisdictions confers upon them the ability to legislate, regulate, and adjudicate independently within the broader sovereignty of the host state.

In special jurisdictions, a bespoke regulatory architecture is achieved through deliberate carve-outs - some entrenched constitutionally, others granted by statute/decree or delegated executive authority - that allow these special jurisdictions to govern themselves with substantial autonomy.

The types of carve-outs may be legal-system related, such as creating common-law islands within civil-law states; fiscal, offering tax incentives or exemptions to attract investment; regulatory, empowering separate supervisory authorities to license and oversee financial activity; or adjudicatory, establishing independent courts and arbitration centres to resolve disputes. Together, these mechanisms form self-contained yet sovereignly sanctioned systems that can develop and adapt frameworks for emerging technologies and business models, unencumbered by the inertia that characterises national bureaucracies.

Hong Kong exemplifies the constitutional model. As a Special Administrative Region of the People's Republic of China, its autonomy is defined under the Basic Law, the city's mini-constitution, which enshrines its independent judiciary, common-law system, convertible currency, and independent financial regulator, the Hong Kong Monetary Authority (HKMA) (The Basic Law of the Hong Kong Special Administrative Region, 1990).

Unlike the mainland's Renminbi, the Hong Kong dollar is freely convertible and fully backed by US dollar reserves. The use of English as an official legal and commercial language further reinforces Hong Kong's integration with global markets.

Over the past two decades, Hong Kong's legal independence has allowed it to pioneer a succession of financial innovations: from establishing one of the first real-time gross settlement systems in Asia in the 1996 (Hong Kong Monetary Authority, 2022), to introducing a virtual-banking regime in 2018 (Hong Kong Monetary Authority, 1996) and launching a comprehensive fintech licensing framework in 2023 (Hong Kong Monetary Authority, 2023). With a GDP exceeding USD 360 billion and finance accounting for nearly a quarter of it, Hong Kong's role as a bridge economy, which is simultaneously Chinese and global—shows how constitutional autonomy enables regulatory agility without compromising national sovereignty.

This regulatory design has made Hong Kong an ideal environment for stablecoin experimentation. Its monetary autonomy, anchored by a freely convertible and fully backed currency, enables the stress-testing of tokenised money without affecting China's capital controls or monetary policy. The common-law framework provides clarity and predictability for digital-asset contracts, while the HKMA's integrated oversight of banking and payment systems supports consistent supervision of stablecoin issuers and service providers.

Hong Kong's institutional design is complemented by operational agility and iterative policymaking. It doesn't just have the structure; it also has the know-how to run it. This is evidenced by the fact that Hong Kong is one of the few jurisdictions that has progressed from consultation to implementation in establishing a comprehensive regulatory regime for stablecoins. The HKMA initiated the process in January 2022 with a discussion paper on crypto-assets and stablecoins (Hong Kong Monetary Authority, 2022), followed by a December 2023 joint consultation with the Financial Services and the Treasury Bureau on the proposed legislative framework (HKMA & Financial Services and the Treasury Bureau, 2023). This culminated in the passage of the stablecoins law (Stablecoins Ordinance, 2025) by the Legislative Council in May 2025, creating a licensing regime for stablecoin issuers operating in or targeting Hong Kong, which came into force in August 2025. Shortly after, Standard Chartered, HKT, and Animoca Brands announced a joint venture to issue an HKD-backed stablecoin, becoming one of the first applicants under the new framework.

This legal framework, together with the broader enablers discussed in this paper, makes Hong Kong a model example of how special jurisdictions can foster financial innovation within a prudentially supervised environment. Yet, the regime has not been without criticism. Industry observers argue that Hong Kong's approach, while robust, may be overly cautious: the high capital thresholds, limited number of licences expected, and strict redemption and reserve requirements could constrain competition and discourage smaller fintech entrants. (Securities and Futures Commission & Hong Kong Monetary Authority, 2025; China Daily Global, 2025) Others warn that the dual-regulator structure between the HKMA and the Securities and Futures Commission (SFC) risks overlapping mandates, as newer, more complex tokens with payment + investment use-cases come about (Hong Kong Monetary Authority, 2024). This could create slow approval timelines and regulatory confusion. Nonetheless, the measured rollout reflects Hong Kong's long-standing preference for regulatory credibility over speed, an approach that seeks to anchor innovation in stability.

Another notable example is DIFC. Created in 2004 through a combination of federal constitutional amendment and emirate-level decree, DIFC operates under common law, entirely distinct from the UAE's civil-law framework. Three institutions form its core architecture: the DIFC Authority, responsible for policy, infrastructure, and business services; the Dubai Financial Services Authority (DFSA), an independent regulator overseeing financial conduct and prudential supervision; and the DIFC Courts, which apply common-law principles in English language and whose judgments are internationally enforceable (DIFC Courts, 2021).

The DFSA's independence from both the Central Bank of the United Arab Emirates and the Securities and Commodities Authority enables it to draft and enforce its own financial regulations. It aligns with global frameworks such as the Basel Committee on Banking Supervision, the Financial Action Task Force standards, the International Organization of Securities Commissions standards, among others, while retaining local flexibility.

Today, the DIFC hosts over 5,500 registered firms and plays a central role in Dubai's economic diversification strategy (DIFC Courts, 2021). In 2023, the DIFC accounted for approximately 52 percent of the city's total foreign direct investment (FDI), underscoring its position as both a regulatory and economic engine for the emirate (DIFC Courts, 2021). Its ecosystem spans banks, asset managers, hedge funds, insurers, fintech start-ups, digital-asset and blockchain firms, professional services providers, and regional headquarters of multinational corporations—making it one of the most diversified financial centres in the Middle East.

Like Hong Kong, what makes DIFC's architecture particularly effective is not merely its formal design but its operational culture of adaptive statecraft. The DFSA and the DIFC Authority both employ iterative lawmaking through public consultations, discussion papers, and stakeholder roundtables. For instance, under the DIFC Authority, the consultation on the 2023 Data Protection Law Amendment resulted in what was described as the first global legislative reference to autonomous and AI systems within a data-protection context, embedding AI accountability and human-in-the-loop principles into the legal framework (DIFC Courts, 2021; Data Protection (Amendment) Law 2023, 2023)

Similarly, under the DFSA, a consultation on a crypto-token regime culminated in the enactment of the crypto token regulatory framework in 2022 (Dubai Financial Services Authority, 2022), which introduced licensing, prudential, and market-conduct requirements for firms dealing in crypto-assets. While this framework has enhanced legal clarity and attracted institutional participants, market observers note that the licensing process remains deliberately conservative.

Further, only "Recognised Crypto Tokens" may be used in or offered through regulated financial activities within the DIFC. Before a firm can list, trade, or hold a crypto-asset for custody, payment, or investment purposes, the token must first be formally recognised by the DFSA as meeting stringent standards on governance, transparency, liquidity, technology resilience, and anti-money-laundering and counter-terrorist-financing (AML/CFT) compliance. Notably, among stablecoins, DFSA has recognized USDC and EURC as crypto tokens. While this recognition model gives the DFSA credibility among global regulators, it positions the DIFC's regime primarily as a framework for institutional-grade confidence and prudent innovation.

To make its innovation framework more broad-based and consistent with its adaptive statecraft approach, the DFSA issued a consultation, where it proposes to decentralise the token-recognition process for most crypto-assets. Instead of the regulator centrally approving each token, DFSA-authorised firms would be responsible for assessing the suitability of crypto-tokens for their own regulated activities, subject to supervisory oversight (Dubai Financial Services Authority, 2025).

However, the DFSA intends to maintain a differentiated approach for fiat-referenced tokens (stablecoins), recognising their systemic importance and unique risk profile. Under this consultation, DFSA proposes to retain direct responsibility for evaluating and approving fiat crypto tokens before they are used within the DIFC. The consultation - reflective of the abovementioned adaptive statecraft approach - signals a potential shift toward a more flexible, risk-based oversight.

Further along the spectrum, Prospera, an autonomous zone in Honduras, illustrates the experimental edge of regulatory design. Established through constitutional and legislative authorisation, Próspera enjoys wide latitude to enact its own commercial and financial laws, adjudicate disputes through international arbitration, and attract global fintech ventures. Próspera's model stands out for its radical regulatory decentralisation. Unlike most special jurisdictions, which operate within tightly defined legal carve-outs and central oversight, Próspera's framework devolves rule-making power almost entirely to its governing charter and regulatory agencies. (Próspera ZEDE, n.d.).

In Próspera, financial activity is overseen by the Roatán Financial Services Authority (RFSA) — an independent supervisory agency established under Próspera's internal regulatory framework. (RFSA, n.d.). Prospera actively encourages and facilitates the use of "qualifying cryptocurrencies" for daily operations, including tax payments, payroll, and general commerce. These include, USDT, USDC, Bitcoin (BTC), among others. Because stablecoins operate alongside, not beneath, the zone's monetary system, they can be trialled as functional instruments of value transfer and public finance, not just speculative assets (Próspera ZEDE, 2021).

Prospera's experiment remains young and politically contested for several reasons - domestically, Próspera's broad autonomy has sparked controversy over sovereignty and investor privilege, while internationally, questions remain about the durability of its legal framework. Yet, it still represents an ambitious attempt to build an entirely digital, investor-centric, crypto-friendly environment from the ground up.

It is said that the proof of the pudding is in the eating. While traditional special jurisdictions are tasting the pudding, radical ones are rewriting the recipes. On one hand, Hong Kong and DIFC continue to set benchmarks in prudential governance of stablecoins; on the other hand, radical models like Próspera test the boundaries of regulatory imagination. Both are vital in proving how innovation and oversight can coexist.

Pilot Programmes

Pilot programmes enable authorities to test emerging technologies or frameworks with selected participants under predefined conditions. They are purpose-built, time-bound trials that let authorities validate technology, market plumbing, and controls with a small cohort before scaling. While not unique to special jurisdictions, they tend to perform exceptionally well within them, where independent regulators, flexible legal systems, and ring-fenced environments enable structured experimentation.

A notable example is Hong Kong's e-HKD Pilot Programme, a multi-phase initiative led by the HKMA to assess the design, technical feasibility, and policy implications of a potential retail central bank digital currency (CBDC) for Hong Kong. Announced in May 2023, the pilot was divided into consortia comprising major banks, payment companies, and technology firms. Key participants included

HSBC, Standard Chartered, Bank of China (Hong Kong), Hang Seng Bank, Visa, Mastercard, AlipayHK, and Boston Consulting Group, among others. Each consortium was tasked to test a different aspect, such as programmable retail CBDC payments, offline transactions, and interoperability between commercial banks and tech providers. Each consortium collaborated with the HKMA to test proof-of-concept models under a controlled, non-production environment (Hong Kong Monetary Authority, 2023).

Insights on issues like privacy controls, data governance, and operational scalability from Phase 1 shaped Phase 2 of the pilot. In October 2025, the HKMA released the findings of Phase 2 of the pilot, which sought to evaluate how an e-HKD could interact with existing bank deposit systems, digital wallets, and tokenisation platforms. The trials demonstrated that a tokenised e-HKD could enhance settlement efficiency, enable conditional programmable payments, and improve resilience for offline transactions, while maintaining compliance and privacy safeguards (Hong Kong Monetary Authority, 2025).

The pilot concluded that the most immediate value of an e-HKD lies in wholesale and inter-institutional applications, such as settlement of tokenised assets and liquidity management, rather than in mass retail deployment. Accordingly, the authority announced plans to publish common technical and legal standards for digital tokens and to complete preparatory work by mid-2026 to enable scalable, interoperable deployment. The e-HKD pilot thus exemplifies how jurisdictions with advanced regulatory autonomy can apply empirical, data-driven experimentation to guide cautious innovation in finance.

Another interesting example is Project Guardian, launched by MAS in Singapore. Project Guardian is a collaborative initiative between regulators and the financial services industry aimed at advancing asset tokenisation and digital-asset infrastructure. It brings together MAS, global financial institutions, market infrastructure providers and industry associations to explore how tokenised securities, funds, and digital payment rails can integrate into existing financial markets. For instance, in late 2023 and 2024 Project Guardian pilot streams tested use-cases such as tokenised fund subscriptions and redemptions, smart-contract interoperability with legacy payment systems and cross-border liquidity pools._The initiative emphasises four key enablers: liquidity, infrastructure, standards and settlement assets—underscoring MAS's ambition to move from theoretical exploration to commercialisation of tokenised finance (Monetary Authority of Singapore, n.d.)

Speaking specifically of stablecoins, MAS launched the Purpose Bound Money (PBM) Technical Whitepaper in June 2023. Industry partners such as Ant International, Grab and Fazz (StraitsX) are conducting live trials under this initiative (Monetary Authority of Singapore, 2023).

More recently, in June 2025, Vietnam's central bank and Đà N ng city government announced a tourist-focused pilot enabling USDT payments at selected hotels and retail outlets. Tourists can use USDT to pay, while retailers will receive Vietnamese Dong (VND). The aim of the pilot is to test stablecoins as payment rails without displacing the national currency. It allows testing of understanding payment efficiency, AML compliance, and transaction transparency without macroeconomic risk. The initiative—operating under a regulatory sandbox aligned with Vietnam's proposed international financial centre framework—highlights how even non-crypto jurisdictions can harness targeted pilots to balance innovation with monetary prudence.

While the pilot is not live yet, it could be a part of the proposed IFCs in Vietnam, with two locations in Ho Chi Minh City and Da Nang. This strategy seeks to paint Đà N ng as the regional hub specialising in digital payments, and innovative financial services. (Qu c h i nư c C ng hòa Xã h i Ch nghĩa Vi t Nam, 2025)

Pilots like these are crucial because they bridge the gap between theory and policy, turning abstract innovation into testing and evidence-gathering. For issuers, they provide a low-risk environment to validate technical performance, compliance frameworks, and interoperability with existing payment systems before entering live markets. For users and financial institutions, they build trust by demonstrating that innovation can coexist with consumer protection and systemic stability. And for governments, they serve as controlled laboratories to assess monetary, legal, and cybersecurity implications.

The success of stablecoin pilots is measured by how they cultivate the institutional learning - quantitatively and qualitatively. It depends on carefully selecting participants, defining clear objectives, maintaining regulatory guardrails that ensure meaningful data collection, and ensuring coordination between the participants and regulators.

Regulatory Sandboxes

Regulatory sandboxes provide structured environments where innovative business models can deploy new products under temporary legal exemptions or lighter regulatory oversight. They allow live testing within controlled boundaries, enabling regulators to observe risks and performance in real time, while innovators refine their offerings. This dual-learning mechanism—where supervision and experimentation occur simultaneously—makes sandboxes a cornerstone of adaptive regulation in both financial and non-financial sectors.

While pilots and sandboxes share a common goal of fostering safe experimentation, they differ fundamentally in purpose and design. Pilots are usually regulator-led, testing specific technologies or policy frameworks under defined parameters—such as CBDCs or stablecoin payments—whereas sandboxes are company-driven. Within a sandbox, private firms propose their own innovations to be tested under the regulator's supervision and within temporarily adjusted rules. In short, pilots generate insights; sandboxes generate evidence. The sandbox thus acts as an iterative bridge between proof-of-concept and commercial deployment.

On the continuum of regulatory experimentation, a pilot may precede a sandbox, but one may very well exist without the other. On the same continuum, law making and regulatory development may precede the sandbox, or may follow based on the learnings from the sandbox.

Like pilots, sandboxes may operate within larger economic contexts, but special jurisdictions are particularly well-suited to host regulatory sandboxes because of their legal flexibility and institutional autonomy. This enables rapid rule adjustment and close regulator–industry feedback loops.

A leading example is the RegLab within the Financial Services Regulatory Authority (FSRA), the financial regulator of the Abu Dhabi Global Market (ADGM), a common-law special jurisdiction within the Emirate of Abu Dhabi (ADGM, n.d.) Launched in 2016 as one of the region's first fintech sandboxes, RegLab adopted a "blank-sheet" approach: the FSRA could tailor or waive specific rules, set test parameters and control boundaries, and require structured reporting. Tests operated under time-limited authorisations, typically up to two years. Early cohorts trialled blockchain-based KYC, digital securities issuance, and tokenised settlement systems. Lessons from these experiments directly informed FSRA's Digital Securities and Virtual Assets Rulebooks, providing clarity on licensing, prudential requirements, and market conduct (FSRA, n.d.)

MAS's FinTech Sandbox, introduced in 2016, further illustrates how sandbox evidence has shaped formal regulation in Singapore. Its "Sandbox Express," launched in 2019, accelerated approval for low-risk experiments such as payment-token settlements and stablecoin-backed merchant transactions using USDC and XSGD (Monetary Authority of Singapore, 2016; Monetary Authority of Singapore, 2019).

Insights gathered from participants fed into the MAS Stablecoin Issuance Framework released in August 2023, which now defines capital, redemption, and disclosure standards for single-currency stablecoins pegged to the Singapore dollar or G10 currencies (Monetary Authority of Singapore, 2023).

Labuan IBFC in Malaysia also offers a unique approach to (non)sandboxing, within its mid-shore regulatory models. Labuan operates under Malaysia's federal sovereignty and Labuan's financial sector is governed by the autonomous Labuan Financial Services Authority (Labuan FSA), which is empowered to license, supervise, and regulate financial activities independently. Notably, Labuan FSA oversees both conventional and Islamic finance under separate legislative frameworks.

Labuan FSA offers Asia's first digital "Pick-and-Mix" Toolbox, launched in January 2022 as part of its 2022–2026 roadmap for financial innovation (Labuan

IBFC, n.d.). The Digital Toolbox is not a single sandbox but a flexible licensing architecture that lets digital-finance firms combine modular permissions—such as digital banking, digital-asset issuance, digital-currency trading, custody, or digital-securities dealing—under one supervisory umbrella. Instead of introducing entirely new licence classes, Labuan's approach applies a "digital wrapper" concept, embedding technological innovation within existing financial licences and subjecting each application to merit-based regulatory assessment. Labuan FSA has also launched the i-BOX Islamic Digital Bank Sandbox in July 2024, which offers a controlled environment for Islamic digital banks to pilot new technologies, products, and delivery models before full-scale licensing (Labuan IBFC, n.d.).

The sandbox model can similarly be useful for testing how stablecoins can function safely within the financial system. Authorities use them to observe how fiat-backed tokens behave in retail payments, wholesale settlement, and cross-border remittances, all under controlled conditions. In Hong Kong, the HKMA's dedicated Stablecoin Issuer Sandbox, launched in June 2024, offers an example of a stablecoin-focused sandbox, by allowing consortia of banks, fintechs, and telecoms—including Standard Chartered, Animoca Brands, and HKT—to test governance, reserve management, and redemption mechanisms ahead of the city's then forthcoming Stablecoin Licensing Regime (HKMA 2024). Participants were required to demonstrate plans for reserve assets of high quality and liquidity, robust wallet/private key management, smooth redemption processes, and cross-border compliance.

HKMA's approach is a textbook case of a sandbox pre-figuring legislation rather than the other way around. The sandbox has enabled live interoperability trials between tokenised deposits and fiat-referenced tokens, providing data on liquidity, disclosure, and redemption behaviour.

Innovation Ecosystem

Beyond legal frameworks and controlled experimentation, innovation ultimately thrives within ecosystems — the networks of accelerators, venture programs, co-working hubs, and research partnerships that connect regulators, entrepreneurs, academics and investors. A special jurisdiction's innovation ecosystem determines whether regulatory intent translates into commercial activity. It provides the soft infrastructure — talent, capital, collaboration, and culture — that allows pilots and sandboxes to scale into viable, sustainable financial ecosystems.

Innovation ecosystems are not unique to special jurisdictions — in fact, certain cities and regions become synonymous with the industries they nurture, creating self-reinforcing cycles of talent, investment, and identity. The San Francisco Bay Area's Silicon Valley embodies this for Web2 technology and venture capital; Dubai has rapidly evolved into a global hub for web3 and digital assets; and Bangalore has emerged as the centre of gravity for software development and IT services in Asia. These examples show that when a place builds both infrastructure and belief, it becomes more than a geography — it becomes a mindset.

Innovation ecosystems are not unique to special jurisdictions - However, the presence of innovation ecosystems is essential for such jurisdictions to succeed as zones of growth. The strength of a special jurisdiction lies not in how many start-ups or accelerators it attracts, but in how effectively it institutionalises collaboration between public and private stakeholders — between physical infrastructure (labs, hubs, campuses) and intellectual infrastructure (policy, research, capital, and data). Mature ecosystems integrate these elements into a continuous cycle of experimentation, iteration, and scaling.

However, for special jurisdictions, cultivating such ecosystems becomes essential to sustaining growth and relevance - the ecosystem they build is what sets them apart, from not just the mainland of the host country, but also from other special jurisdictions. Hong Kong's open financial architecture has long made it Asia's pre-eminent financial hub; Labuan has positioned itself as a mid-shore centre for digital and Islamic finance innovation; and Próspera represents a frontier experiment in regulatory design (Labuan IBFC, n.d.; Próspera ZEDE, n.d.)

The innovation ecosystem has several components. One of the core components is the incubator + accelerator culture. Incubators and accelerators act as ecosystem engines that complement pilots and sandboxes by providing the institutional scaffolding—capital, mentorship, infrastructure, and regulatory proximity—needed to turn experimentation into a viable enterprise. These programmes serve as structured bridges between regulatory innovation and market deployment, often situated within special jurisdictions that combine capital access with policy agility.

Globally, accelerators such as Y Combinator in San Francisco and Techstars London (Y Combinator, n.d.; Techstars, n.d.) have demonstrated how structured mentorship and investor networks can create global pipelines for scalable innovation. Interestingly, incubation and acceleration in special jurisdiction may often be regulator led. In Singapore, the Tribe Accelerator, supported by the MAS and Enterprise Singapore, has positioned itself as the country's first government-backed blockchain accelerator, nurturing startups in digital identity, payments, and Web3 infrastructure through partnerships with corporates such as IBM, Citibank, and PwC (Tribe Accelerator, n.d.). This fits within Singapore's broader innovation architecture, anchored by MAS's Looking Glass Lab, Singapore FinTech Festival, and APIX initiatives (Monetary Authority of Singapore, 2016; Monetary Authority of Singapore, 2018; Singapore FinTech Festival, n.d.).

Similarly, the DIFC Innovation Hub in Dubai, home to hundreds of start-ups spanning digital assets, sustainable finance, and artificial intelligence, offers co-location with investors and regulators (DIFC Courts, 2021).

Another critical pillar of the innovation ecosystem is the network of collaboration - the dense web of conferences, academic partnerships, investor forums, and cross-border communities that sustain information exchange and visibility. Special jurisdictions have actively built these collaborations through flagship industry events and partnerships. MAS in Singapore anchors Asia's fintech calendar with the Singapore FinTech Festival (Singapore FinTech Festival, n.d.), HKMA and InvestHK co-host Hong Kong FinTech Week (Hong Kong Monetary Authority, 2025), while Dubai and Abu Dhabi host the Dubai FinTech Summit (Dubai FinTech Summit, n.d.) and Abu Dhabi Finance Week (Abu Dhabi Finance Week, n.d.) respectively. Regulator initiatives are often complemented by privately organised marquee conferences such as TOKEN2049 (TOKEN2049, n.d.), Consensus (CoinDesk, n.d.) and Ripple Swell (Ripple, n.d.)—which hint at the commercial muscle of the host jurisdiction. Specifically, for stablecoins, platforms such as Stablecoin Summit (Stablecoin Summit, n.d.), Stablecon (Stablecon, n.d.), and Stable Summit (Stable Summit, n.d.) are a testimony to the asset class's growing institutionalisation, and there are more to come.

Academia and research institutions form a vital pillar of innovation ecosystems by forging academic-industry partnerships that advance knowledge, policy and talent in digital finance. Examples include the New Asian Institute of Digital Finance set up by MAS, the National Research Foundation and the National University of Singapore (NUS) to support the needs of digital financial services in Asia.

Industry led research initiatives are equally important and signal the ecosystem's maturity and depth. Ripple's University Blockchain Research Initiative (UBRI) now partners with over 50 universities across 26 countries, including Carnegie Mellon University, University of Luxembourg, and Trinity College Dublin, advancing global research on blockchain, payments, and digital asset regulation (Ripple, n.d.)

Innovation ecosystems provide the connective tissue between policy, technology, and adoption. A stablecoin framework cannot thrive in isolation, it is a shared experiment that requires all relevant actors to engage with each other. Innovation ecosystems can act as the final enabler: where law and experimentation converge into market reality, and where the stablecoin ceases to be a theoretical construct and becomes a functional part of the economy.

Dispute Resolution

Another enabler within special jurisdictions is a specialised dispute resolution mechanism, which may be characterised by varying degrees of adjudicatory autonomy. At their most autonomous, these mechanisms take the form of independent court systems operating under separate procedural and substantive laws, often based on internationally recognised frameworks such as common law. At the other end of the spectrum, adjudicatory autonomy may manifest through specialised commercial benches or arbitration centres. These, while technically part of the national judiciary, operate with tailored rules, procedures, and international expertise to handle complex cross-border financial disputes. Regardless of the degree of autonomy, these mechanisms are designed to deliver outcomes that are neutral, efficient, and predictable, often in contrast to the slower or less specialised processes of the host state's judiciary.

Hong Courts and DIFC Courts exemplify the first category, with a high degree of adjudicatory autonomy. Hong Kong operates an independent common law judiciary separate from mainland China, with specialised benches and tribunals, which routinely adjudicate complex financial, insolvency, and digital asset disputes. Similarly, DIFC Courts operate independently from the UAE's national judiciary: they apply English common law to commercial mandates, while criminal and family cases remain under the jurisdiction of the UAE's domestic courts (DIFC Courts, n.d.). They are staffed by internationally recognised judges from jurisdictions including England, Singapore, among others. The DIFC Courts have also established specialised divisions, including the Technology and Digital Economy (TDE) Division, to handle disputes involving fintech, digital assets, blockchain, AI, and cybersecurity — positioning the DIFC judiciary at the forefront of digital-economy adjudication (DIFC Courts, 2021).

DIFC Courts' judgments are directly enforceable within Dubai under a mutual recognition mechanism between the DIFC and Dubai Courts, and internationally through treaties such as the GCC Convention and Riyadh Convention, conventions with China, India and France, and reciprocal arrangements with many of the leading commercial courts located in the world's top financial hubs, such as New York, Singapore, London and Hong Kong (DIFC Courts, n.d.).

Beyond jurisprudence, the DIFC Courts have also invested in judicial innovation - the Court Tech Lab, launched in partnership with the Dubai Future Foundation in 2019, prototypes blockchain-based registries, AI-assisted court management, and smart-contract enforcement tools, demonstrating how the courts both deploy and adjudicate on cutting-edge technology (DIFC Courts & Dubai Future Foundation, 2019).

Their case precedent directs legal interpretation not just locally but also globally and informs policymaking in the domain of emerging technologies. Hong Kong High Court, in Re Gatecoin Ltd (in liquidation) (2023), confirmed cryptocurrencies are property capable of being held on trust, guiding distribution in insolvency. Likewise, in Huobi v. Tabarak Investment Capital Ltd. (2024), the DIFC Court of Appeal delivered a landmark ruling recognising Bitcoin and similar digital assets as property under DIFC law, defining ownership through exclusive control—a finding later codified in the DIFC Digital Assets Law (DIFC Courts, 2021). The judgments were pivotal for establishing enforceable property rights in digital assets and set a precedent for restitution in digital asset theft cases.

Several other special jurisdictions have adopted hybrid adjudicatory models tailored to their financial mandates. The Labuan Financial Services Authority (Labuan FSA) signed a Memorandum of Understanding with the Kuala Lumpur Regional Centre for Arbitration (now the Asian International Arbitration Centre, AIAC), enabling commercial disputes involving Labuan IBFC licensees to be referred to arbitration under AIAC rules (Labuan IBFC, n.d.).

In the Kingdom of Saudi Arabia, the Saudi Center for Commercial Arbitration (SCCA) has a cooperation agreement (which functions similarly to a Memorandum of Understanding or MoU) with the Economic Cities and Special Zones Authority (ECZA) to provide alternative dispute resolution services in the Kingdom's special economic zones, including the King Abdullah Financial District (KAFD) (ECZA, 2025). All of these illustrate how arbitration-linked mechanisms can coexist with the national judiciary while maintaining a sector-specific focus.

While arbitral awards are typically confidential, there has been a marked rise in arbitration proceedings involving digital assets and digital-finance disputes worldwide. According to reports by the Singapore International Arbitration Centre (SIAC), the London Court of International Arbitration (LCIA), and Hong Kong International Arbitration Centre (HKIAC), cases touching on blockchain technology, tokenisation, and crypto-asset recovery have steadily increased since 2021. Digital-asset disputes are migrating toward international arbitration forums that offer confidentiality, enforceability, and technical expertise. (SIAC, 2025; LCIA, 2025; HKIAC, 2024)

For stablecoins, as their use cases evolve, from payments and settlements to tokenised deposits and cross-border remittances, so will disputes related to redemption rights, reserve transparency, or algorithmic stability. Clear adjudicatory pathways will therefore become essential to uphold confidence and predictability in stablecoin regimes. Further, these rulings and arbitral precedents will feed back into policy formation, guiding regulators on how contractual promises, custodial duties, and risk disclosures should be codified within future stablecoin frameworks.

Put together, these enablers provide the agility to prototype, observe, and refine next-generation financial and technological architectures within safe, legally distinct environments. Their success lies not in deregulation but in the deliberate design of bounded flexibility, where experimentation is encouraged, yet systemic stability is preserved.

CONCLUSION: ACTIONABLE TAKEAWAYS FOR STABLECOIN DEVELOPMENT

The evolution of stablecoins represents more than a technological innovation—it signals a structural transformation in how value is created, stored, and transmitted across the global financial system. As programmable, fiat-referenced instruments mature into mainstream payment and settlement tools, the transformation is not merely technical or financial, but also legal. The state's role is metamorphosing from that of a gatekeeper to a collaborator — moving from exclusion and strict oversight toward partnership, facilitation and shared value-creation. Special jurisdictions, by virtue of their institutional autonomy, regulatory flexibility, and capacity for controlled experimentation, stand uniquely positioned to lead this complex transformation. And, they can achieve this without risking macroeconomic instability.

For issuers and innovators, special jurisdiction offers credible pathways to legitimacy. Their clear licensing regimes, sandbox-to-framework pipelines, innovation-oriented ecosystems and independent dispute resolution systems provide legal certainty and reputational assurance. By testing products in these environments, issuers can demonstrate prudential compliance and build institutional trust, paving the way for cross-border interoperability and inclusion in regulated financial infrastructure.

For policymakers, special jurisdictions act as evidence-generating laboratories. They enable regulators to observe how stablecoin models perform in practice—how reserves are managed, redemption works, or cross-border liquidity behaves—before committing to nationwide frameworks. Their ability to test, refine, and scale credible stablecoin regimes within bounded environments ensures that innovation is neither stifled nor left unchecked. Just as insights from Hong Kong, Singapore, and the DIFC have shaped broader rulemaking across Asia, the Middle East, and beyond for financial and digital asset regulation, iterative, consultative experimentation within special jurisdictions will similarly chart the global policy trajectory for stablecoins.

In the long term, special jurisdictions will also serve as transmission nodes, bridging local experimentation with international standard-setting. As stablecoins integrate into payment systems, securities settlement, and trade finance, the frameworks refined within these jurisdictions will influence global norms on reserve transparency, redemption rights, interoperability, and systemic safeguards. Over time, the competitive learning between these centres will help converge fragmented regulatory landscapes into coherent global standards.

Looking ahead, special jurisdictions will also be the proving ground for the evolving role of state, underscored by CBDC–stablecoin-tokenised deposit coexistence and, by extension, the next layer of interoperable global monetary governance. Special jurisdictions, with their own autonomous regimes, will demonstrate how public and private money settle on common rails without fragmenting liquidity or weakening policy transmission. As their frameworks harden into practice - with evidence on reserve audits, redemption enforceability, cross-border compliance - they will export playbooks of digital money.

Ultimately, special jurisdictions are writing the grammar of digital money itself. In doing so, they are making a global blueprint for the future of money.

REFERENCES

Abu Dhabi Finance Week. (n.d.). Abu Dhabi Finance Week: MENA's leading investment summit. https://www.adfw.com/ ADFW

Abu Dhabi Global Market. (n.d.). About ADGM. https://www.adgm.com/

Abu Dhabi Global Market. (n.d.). FinTech at ADGM. https://www.adgm.com/setting-up/fintech

Accelerator, T. (n.d.). Tribe: Powering frontier tech ecosystems. https://tribex.co/accelerator/

Arabia, A. (2025, July 4). Air Arabia and Mbank transform air travel payments with AE Coin: Speed, security, and simplicity [Press release]. Air Arabia. https://press.airarabia.com/air-arabia-and-mbank-transform-air-travel-payments-with-ae-coin-speed-security-and-simplicity/

Astana International Financial Centre. (n.d.). About AIFC. https://aifc.kz/about/

Brookings Institution. (2025, June 16). What are stablecoins, and how are they regulated? Brookings. https://www.brookings.edu/articles/what-are-stablecoins-and-how-are-they-regulated/

Bullmann, D., Klemm, J., & Pinna, A. (2019). In search for stability in crypto-assets: Are stablecoins the solution? (Occasional Paper No. 230). European Central Bank. https://www.ecb.europa.eu/pub/pdf/scpops/ecb.op230~d57946be3b.en.pdf

Certi, K. (2025, July). Security risks of stablecoins. CertiK. https://www.certik.com/resources/blog/security-risks-of-stablecoins

Chainalysis. (2023). The 2023 geography of cryptocurrency report. Chainalysis. https://go.chainalysis.com/geography-of-cryptocurrency-2023.html?utm_source=bambu&utm_medium=social&utm_campaign=advocacy&blaid=5247483

China Daily Global. (2025). HK stablecoin licence attracts big names – "Hong Kong's Stablecoins Ordinance has relatively high thresholds and only large companies and institutions can apply for stablecoin licences" [Article by Fan Feifei]. China Daily Global. https://www.chinadailyhk.com/hk/article/615602

CoinDesk. (n.d.). Consensus. https://consensus2025.coindesk.com/ consensus2025.coindesk.com

Combinator, Y. (n.d.). Y Combinator. https://www.ycombinator.com

Communications and Information Technology Commission. (n.d.). Cloud Computing Special Economic Zone. Government of Saudi Arabia. https://www.cst.gov.sa/en/about/program-and-initiatives/cloud-computing-special-economic-zone-technology

Courts, D. I. F. C. (2021). DIFC Courts launches specialised court for the digital economy. https://www.difccourts.ae/media-centre/newsroom/difc-courts-launches-specialised-court-for-the-digital-economy

Data Protection (Amendment) Law. (2023). Law No. 3 of 2023 (DIFC, 2023). https://www.difc.ae/business/laws-regulations

DIFC Courts & Dubai Future Foundation. (2019, October 30). Court Tech Lab launched by DIFC Courts and the Dubai Future Foundation. https://www.difccourts.ae/media-centre/newsroom/court-tech-lab-launched-difc-courts-and-dubai-future-foundation

Dubai Financial Services Authority. (2022). Consultation Paper No. 143 – Regulation of Crypto Tokens. https://dfsaen.thomsonreuters.com/sites/default/files/net_file_store/CP143_Regulation_of_Crypto_Tokens.pdf

Dubai Financial Services Authority. (2025). Consultation Paper No. 168 – Enhancements to the Regulation of Crypto Tokens. https://www.dfsa.ae/news/notice-consultation-paper-release-cp-168

Dubai FinTech Summit. (n.d.). Dubai FinTech Summit. https://dubaifintechsummit.com/ Dubai FinTech Summit

Dubai International Financial Centre. (2024, April 29). DIFC emerges as premier global hub for family businesses – over 5,500 active registered companies. https://www.wam.ae/en/article/b2wfs1m-difc-emerges-premier-global-hub-for-family

Dubai International Financial Centre. (2024, February 15). DIFC's 20th anniversary takes flight with strong contribution to Dubai's economy – financial services sector captured more than half (52%) of all FDI into Dubai. https://www.difc.com/whats-on/news/difcs-20th-anniversary-takes-flight-with-strong-contribution-to-dubais-economy

Dubai International Financial Centre. (2024). Digital Assets Law, DIFC Law No. 2 of 2024 (enacted 1 March 2024, commences 8 March 2024). https://www.difc.com/business/laws-and-regulations/legal-database/difc-laws/digital-assets-law-difc-law-no-2-of-2024

Dubai International Financial Centre. (2025, February 26). DIFC announces consultation for amendments to select legislation through DIFC Laws Amendment Law, Law No. 1 of 2005 – proposed amendments to the Data Protection Law 2020. https://www.difc.com/whats-on/news/difc-announces-consultation-for-amendments-to-select-difc-legislation-through-difc-law-amendment-law

Dubai International Financial Centre. (n.d.). About DIFC. https://www.difc.com/

Dubai International Financial Centre. (n.d.). DIFC Innovation Hub. https://www.difc.com/ecosystem/innovation-hub difc.com

Dubai International Financial Centre Courts. (n.d.). Enforcement of judgments and orders – DIFC Courts. https://www.difccourts.ae/difc-courts/enforcement

Dubai International Financial Centre Courts. (n.d.). Legal framework. https://www.difccourts.ae/about/legal-framework

Dubai Multi Commodities Centre. (n.d.). Welcome to DMCC – The world's premier business destination. Retrieved November 4, 2025, from https://dmcc.ae/

Economic Cities and Special Zones Authority. (2025, April). ECZA activates strategic partnerships to strengthen Saudi Arabia's investment landscape. https://ecza.gov.sa/en/media-center/news-press/ecza-activates-strategic-partnerships-strengthen-saudi-arabias-investment-landscape

Etihad, A. (2025, July 21). Abu Dhabi Judicial Department to accept fee payments in digital currency [Press release]. Abu Dhabi Judicial Department. https://en.aletihad.ae/news/business/4591968/abu-dhabi-judicial-department-to-accept-fee-payments-in-digi

Financial Services Regulatory Authority. (n.d.). FSRA rulebook. Abu Dhabi Global Market. https://en.adgm.thomsonreuters.com/rulebook/fsra

Gelephu Mindfulness City. (n.d.). Gelephu Mindfulness City – Home. https://gmc.bt/

HKIAC. (n.d.). Statistics (includes "Cryptocurrency" category). https://www.hkiac.org/about-us/statistics

Hong Kong Monetary Authority. (1996). Annual report 1996: Market infrastructure – Real-time gross settlement system launched. Hong Kong Monetary Authority. https://www.hkma.gov.hk/eng/publications-and-research/annual-report/1996/037.shtml#:~:text=REAL%20TIME%20GROSS%20SETTLEMENT%20SYSTEM,system%20by%20reducing%20settlement%20risk

Hong Kong Monetary Authority. (2018). Guideline on authorization of virtual banks. Hong Kong Monetary Authority. https://www.hkma.gov.hk/eng/news-and-media/press-releases/2018/05/20180530-3/

Hong Kong Monetary Authority. (2022). Discussion paper on crypto-assets and stablecoins. https://www.hkma.gov.hk/eng/news-and-media/press-releases/2022/01/20220112-3/ hkma.gov.hk+1

Hong Kong Monetary Authority. (2023). e-HKD pilot programme phase 1 report. https://www.hkma.gov.hk/media/eng/doc/key-information/press-release/2023/20231030e3a1.pdf

Hong Kong Monetary Authority. (2024). Consultation conclusions on the legislative proposal to implement the regulatory regime for fiat-referenced stablecoin issuers in Hong Kong. https://www.hkma.gov.hk/media/eng/doc/key-information/press-release/2024/20240717e3a1.pdf

Hong Kong Monetary Authority. (2025). The HKMA unveils "Fintech 2030" at the Hong Kong FinTech Week 2025 [Press release noting HKFW is co-organised with InvestHK]. https://www.hkma.gov.hk/eng/news-and-media/press-releases/2025/11/20251103-3/ hkma.gov.hk

Hong Kong Monetary Authority & Financial Services and the Treasury Bureau. (2023). Joint consultation paper on the proposed legislative framework for stablecoin issuers. https://www.hkma.gov.hk/eng/key-functions/international-financial-centre/stablecoin-issuers/

Huang, C. (2024). Grab users can now use digital currencies to top up their e-wallets. The Straits Times. https://www.straitstimes.com/business/grab-users-can-now-pay-in-crypto

Huobi v. Tabarak Investment Capital Ltd. (2024). CA 002/2023 (DIFC Ct App).

Jiao, H. (2025). The Concept of Stablecoins and Their Future Prospects. *Proceedings of Business and Economic Studies.*, *8*(5), 1–10. DOI: 10.26689/pbes.v8i5.12105

Labuan, I. B. F. C. (n.d.). Who we are / Labuan IBFC – Asia's premier international financial hub. https://www.labuanibfc.com/who-we-are/labuan-ibfc

Labuan Financial Services Authority. (2016). Signing of Memorandum of Understanding between Labuan FSA and Kuala Lumpur Regional Centre for Arbitration (KLRCA). https://www.labuanfsa.gov.my/general-info/media/signing-of-memorandum-of-understanding-between-labuan-fsa-and-klrca

Labuan Financial Services Authority. (2024). Guidelines on the establishment of Labuan Islamic digital bank (i-BOX). https://www.labuanfsa.gov.my/clients/asset_120A5FB8-61B6-45E8-93F0-3F79F86455C8/contentms/img/documents/Legislation_and_Guidelines/Guidelines/banking/2024/Guidelines%20on%20the%20Establishment%20of%20Islamic%20Digital%20Bank%20%28i-BOX%29_01072024.pdf

Labuan International Business and Financial Centre Incorporated. (2025, March 10). Asia's only digital "pick and mix" tool box [Brochure]. https://www.labuanibfc.com/clients/asset_52E835CC-1342-4701-B6FA-E2CD03AD74B4/contentms/img/publications/brochures/35%20Logo/Digital-Toolbox_RGB-250310.pdf

LCIA. (2025, July 3). LCIA's 2024 Annual Casework Report (news; links to full report). https://www.lcia.org/News/lcias-2024-annual-casework-report.aspx

Monetary Authority of Singapore. (2016). MAS establishes FinTech Innovation Lab (Looking Glass @ MAS) [Press release]. https://www.mas.gov.sg/news/media-releases/2016/mas-establishes-fintech-innovation-lab

Monetary Authority of Singapore. (2018). World's first cross-border open-architecture platform to improve financial inclusion – APIX [Press release]. https://www.mas.gov.sg/news/media-releases/2018/worlds-first-cross-border-open-architecture-platform-to-improve-financial-inclusion mas.gov.sg+1

Monetary Authority of Singapore. (2019). Sandbox Express. https://www.mas.gov.sg/development/fintech/sandbox-express

Monetary Authority of Singapore. National Research Foundation; National University of Singapore. (2020, August 4). New Asian Institute of Digital Finance to spearhead FinTech education and research. https://www.mas.gov.sg/news/media-releases/2020/new-asian-institute-of-digital-finance-to-spearhead-fintech-education-and-research

Monetary Authority of Singapore. (2023). MAS finalises stablecoin regulatory framework. https://www.mas.gov.sg/news/media-releases/2023/mas-finalises-stablecoin-regulatory-framework

Monetary Authority of Singapore. (n.d.). Project Guardian: Asset tokenisation initiative. https://www.mas.gov.sg/schemes-and-initiatives/project-guardian

Morgan, J. P. (n.d.). About Kinexys: Our story, leadership and more. https://www.jpmorgan.com/kinexys/about

NEOM. (n.d.). About NEOM. Government of Saudi Arabia. https://www.neom.com/

Ordinance, S. (2025). Cap. 656 (Hong Kong SAR, 2025). https://www.elegislation.gov.hk/hk/cap656

Próspera, Z. E. D. E. (2021). Resolution approving qualifying cryptocurrencies for payment (§ 5-1-139-0-0-0-1). Próspera Governance Platform. https://pzgps.hn/wp-content/uploads/2024/09/06.-Resolution-Approving-Qualifying-Cryptocurrencies-for-Payment-5-1-139-0-0-0-1.pdf

Próspera, Z. E. D. E. (n.d.). About Próspera. Próspera. https://prospera.hn/

Qatar Financial Centre. (n.d.). Overview | QFC. https://www.qfc.qa/en/about-qfc/overview

Re Gatecoin Ltd (in liquidation). (2023). HKCFI 914 (Hong Kong Court of First Instance).

Ripple. (n.d.). University Blockchain Research Initiative (UBRI). https://ripple.com/impact/ubri/

Roatán Financial Services Authority. (n.d.). About the RFSA. https://www.rfsa.hn/about

Securities and Futures Commission & Hong Kong Monetary Authority. (2025). Joint statement on stablecoin-related market movements. https://apps.sfc.hk/edistributionWeb/gateway/EN/news-and-announcements/news/doc?refNo=25PR123

SIAC. (2025). Annual Report 2024 (rules update & sector context). https://siac.org.sg/wp-content/uploads/2024/08/SIAC_AR2024_FA-spread-Online.pdf

Singapore FinTech Festival. (n.d.). Singapore FinTech Festival – Home. https://www.fintechfestival.sg/

Singapore FinTech Festival. (n.d.). Singapore FinTech Festival. https://www.fintechfestival.sg/

Sino-British Joint Declaration on the Question of Hong Kong. (1984). The Government of the People's Republic of China and the Government of the United Kingdom of Great Britain and Northern Ireland. https://treaties.fcdo.gov.uk/awweb/pdfopener?md=1&did=68291

Stablecon. (n.d.). Stablecon. https://stablecon.com/

Standard Chartered Bank (Hong Kong) Limited. Animoca Brands Corporation Limited; HKT Limited. (2025, February 17). Standard Chartered, Animoca Brands and HKT establish joint venture to issue HKD-backed stablecoin. https://www.sc.com/en/press-release/standard-chartered-animoca-brands-and-hkt-establish-joint-venture-to-issue-hkd-backed-stablecoin/

Summit, S. (n.d.). Stable Summit — The global stablecoin conference. https://www.stablesummit.xyz/

Summit, S. (n.d.). Stablecoin Summit. https://stablecoinsummit.com/

Techstars. (n.d.). Techstars London accelerator. https://www.techstars.com/accelerators/london

The Basic Law of the Hong Kong Special Administrative Region of the People's Republic of China. (1990). Adopted on April 4, 1990, effective July 1, 1997. The Government of the Hong Kong Special Administrative Region. https://www.basiclaw.gov.hk/en/basiclawtext/

TOKEN2049. (n.d.). TOKEN2049. https://www.token2049.com/

Transport, T. (2025, July 4). Tawasul Transport and Al Maryah Community Bank launch the first digital payment system in taxis using AE Coin [Press release]. Tawasul Transport. https://tawasul.ae/tawasul-transport-and-al-maryah-community-bank-launch-the-first-digital-payment-system-in-taxis-using-ae-coin/

United Nations. (n.d.). Member States. United Nations. https://www.un.org/en/about-us/member-states

Vietnam, National Assembly. (2025, June 27). Resolution 222/2025/QH15 on International Financial Centres in Vietnam [Resolution No. 222/2025/QH15]. https://datafiles.chinhphu.vn/cpp/files/vbpq/2025/7/222qh.signed.pdf?utm_source=chatgpt.com

VietnamPlus. (2025, June 10). Da N ng proposes pilot programme for Tether transactions. https://en.vietnamplus.vn/da-nang-proposes-pilot-programme-for-tether-transactions-post320653.vnp

Chapter 10
Synthesizing Global Lessons for Stablecoin Regulation and Financial Stability: The Road Ahead

Jane Thomason
https://orcid.org/0009-0007-3123-7851
University College London, Australia

Muazu Umar
https://orcid.org/0009-0003-1578-8531
Inter-Governmental Action Group against Money Laundering in West Africa, Senegal

ABSTRACT

Stablecoins have moved decisively into the centre of global digital finance, emerging as payment infrastructure, liquidity instruments, and potential public-purpose digital money. Evidence shows growing global convergence around proportionate, technology-neutral, and risk-based regulation, even as significant divergences persist in implementation, supervisory capacity, and treatment of novel models such as algorithmic stablecoins. Unique opportunities and vulnerabilities face emerging markets, where stablecoins can lower remittance costs and expand financial access while simultaneously raising concerns about dollarisation and monetary sovereignty. Ethical considerations, around surveillance, identity, humanitarian use, and private-sector dependency, remain central to responsible adoption. The Commonwealth Model Law on Stablecoins provides a forward-looking blueprint

DOI: 10.4018/979-8-3373-9043-7.ch010

for harmonised, adaptive regulation. Its principles provide the foundation for safe, inclusive, and interoperable digital money systems capable of supporting the next generation of global finance.

INTRODUCTION

Global Lessons for Stablecoin Regulation and Governance advances the central proposition that stablecoins are programmable monetary infrastructure embedded within economic, social, and governance systems. Its underlying message is that as money becomes software, stability, trust, and legitimacy must be designed institutionally and encoded.

Global Lessons for Stablecoin Regulation and Governance draws upon and builds upon *Stablecoins and the Future of Financial Regulation* (IGI-Global, forthcoming), a companion to the Commonwealth Model Law on Stablecoins (Commonwealth Secretariat, 2025), which establishes the conceptual, legal, and regulatory foundations for understanding stablecoins in contemporary digital finance. The book provides precise definitions, comparative analysis across major jurisdictions, and a detailed assessment of systemic risks. It also provides a fully developed legislative framework for adoption by member states and is aligned with international standards set by the FATF (2021), the Financial Stability Board (Financial Stability Board, 2020; Financial Stability Board, 2023), and the Bank for International Settlements (2007).

Building on that foundation, *Global Lessons for Stablecoin Regulation and Governance* brings together scholarship from contributors worldwide to examine real-world case studies and emerging research. This volume highlights diverse national experiences, use cases, and the evolving policy landscape. It covers a broad set of topics including cross-border interoperability, consumer protection, public-good applications, future policy models and legislation.

In Chapter 1, *Technical Definitions, Economic Taxonomy, and Comparative Analysis of Fiat-Backed, Crypto-Collateralised, Algorithmic, and CBDC Models*, Aditya Mudgal provides an examination of the technical architecture, economic functions, stabilisation mechanisms, and governance structures that underpin different categories of stablecoins. He demonstrates the way stablecoin designs navigate a fundamental trilemma involving stability, decentralisation, and capital efficiency. For example, fiat-backed stablecoins offer the most reliable pegs but introduce concentration, custodial, and transparency risks. In contrast, crypto-collateralised models achieve higher decentralisation but are subject to price volatility, excessive collateral requirements, and cascading liquidations. On the other hand, algorithmic models proffer efficiency and autonomy but, lack external value anchors, and have repeatedly failed under periods of contraction or loss of confidence.

Mudgal also demonstrates that stablecoins have evolved into systemic financial instruments, playing central roles in payments, remittances, decentralised finance, and in dollarisation dynamics in emerging markets. This elevates their risks to macro-relevant issues. His comparative assessment of stablecoins and CBDCs highlights that public and private digital monies will increasingly coexist, overlap, and interact. This interplay raises significant questions around monetary sovereignty, regulatory arbitrage, and global financial stability.

Mudgal makes the case for coherent, risk-based, and globally harmonised regulatory approaches, noting that stablecoins can promote inclusion, reduce costs, and drive innovation, but only if supported by strong reserves, sound governance, operational transparency, and coordinated cross-border supervision. Without these safeguards, stablecoins risk amplifying volatility and transmitting systemic fragility across the financial system.

In Chapter 2, *Stablecoins: Technical Foundations, Economic Implications, and Real-World Applications*, Ramu N. M. and Vinod Krishna provide an assessment of the technological underpinnings, economic functions, practical applications, and regulatory challenges of stablecoins. They show that stablecoins now form an integral part of an emerging global financial architecture. Their ability to facilitate instant, low-cost transfers, support decentralised finance markets, expand financial inclusion, and streamline cross-border remittance flows, positions them as key infrastructure for an efficient and accessible digital economy.

The authors emphasise that these benefits come with significant and interrelated risks. The stability of any stablecoin depends on the quality of its reserve backing, the strength of its governance, the robustness of its interoperability, and the confidence of its users. High-profile failures such as TerraUSD underscore the fragility of weakly designed systems. Moreover, the expanding scale of fiat-backed and DeFi-linked stablecoins raises essential concerns about monetary sovereignty, the potential disintermediation of banks, and the risk of systemic contagion across digital and traditional financial markets.

Regulatory fragmentation further complicates adequate cross-border supervision. The authors conclude that the future impact of stablecoins will be determined by the extent to which global regulation becomes coherent, technology continues to evolve responsibly, and governance structures mature. With transparent reserves, rigorous oversight, and interoperable infrastructure, stablecoins can enhance financial stability and inclusion. Without these safeguards, they risk intensifying volatility and undermining trust in the broader financial system.

In Chapter 3, *GENIUS-Compatible Stablecoins: From Law to Supervisory Practice – A Toolkit for Secure, Transparent Issuance*, Silvio Andrae provides further evidence that the long-term viability of stablecoins depends on a rigorous regulatory architecture that ensures stability, transparency, and operational enforceability. He presents the GENIUS Act (2025) as an example of a new generation of digital-money regulation, one that articulates not only the core principles of safe stablecoin issuance, such as full reserve backing, enforceable one-to-one parity, and auditable transparency, but also the supervisory processes required to make these principles effective in practice. By integrating liquidity discipline, standardised disclosure requirements, and technology-enabled oversight, the GENIUS framework positions them as verifiable, programmable payment tools.

Andrae's comparative analysis shows that although the Commonwealth Model Law (Commonwealth Secretariat, 2025) and MiCA (2023) frameworks follow different implementation pathways, they converge on the same fundamental safeguards. This divergence underscores that while regulatory approaches must adapt to national institutional capacities, core principles must remain global. He offers a practical supervisory toolkit, which includes reserve codebooks, disclosure workflows, SupTech-driven AML monitoring, and smart-contract governance templates provide jurisdictions with a transferable model for building secure and interoperable programmable money systems.

Andrae argues that stablecoins and central bank digital currencies should not be seen as competing innovations but as complementary layers within a modern monetary system. The future of digital money, he contends, will be shaped less by specific tokens and more by the quality of governance, the alignment of law, market structure, and technology into a coherent, sovereign, and innovation-ready payment architecture.

In Chapter 4, *Financial Stability and Systemic Risk in Stablecoins: When Does Digital Currency Infrastructure Become "Too Big to Fail*?", Ameya Anil Pati and Vishwanath Karad analyse the emergence of new and complex channels of systemic risk introduced by stablecoins. They show how stablecoins have evolved into critical payment and liquidity infrastructure across crypto markets, DeFi ecosystems, and now traditional financial systems. The chapter traces how the rapid scale-up of stablecoins has produced new vulnerabilities, because of high transaction velocity, intricate cross-protocol linkages, and algorithmic stabilisation mechanisms.

They examine major instability events, including the TerraUSD collapse and the USDC–Silicon Valley Bank depeg. The authors illustrate how crises of confidence can trigger swift contagion. Automated liquidations, complex network dependencies, and continuous 24/7 trading amplify these shocks. These events demonstrate that disruptions in digital markets can spill into traditional finance, challenging established understandings of what constitutes "too big to fail."

The authors argue that existing regulatory frameworks, which were designed primarily for centralised intermediaries, are ill-suited to the dynamics of decentralised and algorithmic financial systems. They call for the development of new systemic-risk indicators that capture network centrality, real-time contagion pathways, and governance vulnerabilities.

The chapter concludes by reiterating the underlying theme of this book, that stablecoins can contribute to financial stability only if supported by stringent prudential requirements, transparent and verifiable reserves, robust governance structures, and internationally coordinated regulatory oversight capable of addressing the distinctive risks of programmable money.

In Chapter 5, *"Stablecoins as Public Good: Remittances, Humanitarian Aid, and Digital ID,"* Oumaima Abouzaid and Faouzi Boussedra examine the considerable potential of stablecoins to serve as global public-good infrastructure. They demonstrate how stablecoins can reduce financial exclusion, strengthen humanitarian response systems, and support more inclusive digital identity frameworks. In the context of remittances, the authors show that stablecoins can significantly reduce transfer costs, from global averages of approximately 6% to approximately 1%, thereby returning billions of dollars to poor households. They draw upon case studies from the Philippines, Venezuela, and Sub-Saharan Africa to illustrate how these cost reductions contribute to improved household resilience and wider socio-economic gains.

In humanitarian contexts, they present pilots such as the World Food Programme's Building Blocks initiative to demonstrate that blockchain-based stablecoin transfers can reduce administrative overhead by up to 98%, while improving transparency and minimising leakage. At the same time, they warn that these systems introduce new forms of dependency on private issuers and require reliable digital access, highlighting the importance of rights-based, inclusive design in humanitarian technology.

The chapter further highlights the risk of the integration of stablecoins with digital identity systems. While such integration can empower refugees, women, and undocumented populations, particularly when linked to self-sovereign identity models, it also carries risks. For example, exclusion, excessive surveillance, and what the authors term "crypto-colonialism," can emerge with poor governance or weak interoperability standards.

The authors conclude that stablecoins can evolve into inclusive and socially beneficial public infrastructure only within transparent, accountable, and human-rights-aligned regulatory frameworks. Without such safeguards, there is a risk that stablecoins could instead reinforce inequality, dependency, and digital vulnerability.

In Chapter 6, *Designing Trust in Digital Money: Interdisciplinary Approaches to Stablecoin Governance*, López Jiménez et al. argues that trust in stablecoins must be intentionally built through coherent legal, technological, and governance structures. They trace the development of stablecoins to their current status as globally relevant digital assets used in payments, remittances, and decentralised finance. While stablecoins offer clear benefits in efficiency and inclusion, The authors show that repeated failures across the sector demonstrate that stability cannot be delivered by algorithms alone. Genuine trust rests on transparent reserves, enforceable redemption rights, and strong regulatory oversight.

The authors map the international regulatory landscape and underscores the limitations of soft-law approaches: industry codes, voluntary principles, and best-practice guidelines, which lack enforceability and often fail under stress. They contrast the approaches of the EU, the United States, and the Asia Pacific region, illustrating how fragmented regulatory frameworks create arbitrage opportunities and heighten systemic vulnerabilities. In this context, they suggest that the Commonwealth Model Law on Stablecoins (2025) stands out as a harmonised but adaptable legislative framework that translates global standards into effective national law.

The chapter examines the technological foundations of stablecoins, analysing smart contracts, oracle systems, custody architectures, and emerging AI-based mechanisms. The authors highlight the operational, cyber, and human risks embedded in programmable money systems, noting that these risks require deliberate governance rather than reactive oversight.

Ultimately, the chapter argues that trust in stablecoins must be constructed institutionally. He reinforces the call across the book for proportional regulation, coordinated cross-border supervision, and governance models that embed transparency, accountability, and financial integrity are essential elements of a trustworthy digital monetary system.

In Chapter 7, *Payments 1.0 to 5.0: Pathways to Agentic Autonomy*, A.V. Senthil Kumar and his co-authors argue that the transition from Payments 1.0 to Payments 5.0 reflects a profound redefinition of how financial systems function. Payments 5.0 represents a structural shift in which intelligent, autonomous payment agents emerge as central actors. These agents can interpret user intent, plan and sequence financial actions, and execute transactions safely within defined guardrails. The authors explain how advances in large language models, autonomous agent architectures, and integrated compliance frameworks drive this transformation. These technologies make payment systems proactive rather than reactive, optimising liquidity, transaction routing, compliance checks, fraud prevention, and user outcomes in real time.

Agentic autonomy offers significant benefits for both institutions and consumers, including automated dispute resolution, predictive cash-flow management, enhanced cross-border payment efficiency, and institution-scale programmable settlement. However, the authors stress that such autonomy requires rigorous safeguards. As payment agents become more capable, the risks associated with adversarial attacks, prompt manipulation, mandate abuse, and tool misuse also increase. The chapter underscores the need for robust identity frameworks, verifiable mandates, machine-to-machine payment standards, continuous monitoring mechanisms, and simulation environments to test resilience. The authors conclude that Payments 5.0 transforms payments into intelligent, explainable, and secure digital ecosystems, and that these systems will play a defining role in shaping the next generation of global finance.

In Chapter 8, *Stablecoins and the Future of Financial Regulation: Nigeria's Experience and Global Lessons*, Obinna Ezeala and Oluseyi Oladapo illustrate how Nigeria's engagement with stablecoins provide a real world example of the core regulatory dilemmas faced by many emerging markets as the adoption of digital money accelerates. They show that while stablecoins offer Nigeria substantial benefits, including lower remittance costs, greater financial inclusion, an informal hedge against inflation, and access to global payment networks, these advantages coexist with serious concerns about monetary sovereignty, consumer protection, and systemic stability. Nigeria's regulatory posture reflects this tension: the Central Bank's ban on crypto operations, has driven crypto activity into informal P2P channels. Yet, the introduction of the eNaira and the SEC's guidelines signal cautious, incremental innovation. This mixed approach exposes the risks of fragmented governance, regulatory uncertainty, and policy incoherence.

Through comparative analysis, the authors highlight that jurisdictions such as the EU MiCA (2023) and Singapore (Money Authority of Singapore, 2023) have established proportionate, structured frameworks that emphasise transparency, reserve quality, and enforceable redemption rights. In contrast, the United States illustrates the pitfalls of fragmented and overlapping oversight.

Ezeala and Oladapo commend the Commonwealth Model Law as providing Nigeria with a viable roadmap for reconciling innovation with stability. Its provisions on tiered licensing, reserve transparency, consumer protection, AML/CFT compliance, and cross-border cooperation offer a coherent architecture for integrating stablecoins into supervised channels rather than allowing them to flourish primarily in informal markets and through blinded parallel operations in the formal financial system.

The chapter concludes that stablecoins will play a defining role in Nigeria's financial future. The central challenge for policymakers is to regulate them with precision, managing risks while unlocking their potential to advance financial inclusion, reduce transaction costs, and support economic growth.

In Chapter 9, *Enabling Innovation in Stablecoin Markets through Special Jurisdictions,* Andreas Baumgartner and his co-authors argue that special jurisdictions, such as financial free zones, autonomous regulatory centres, and purpose-built innovation hubs, have become critical laboratories for shaping the future of global stablecoin governance. Their importance lies not in geography but in institutional design. Features such as independent regulators, common-law legal frameworks, adaptive licensing regimes, and specialised dispute-resolution mechanisms create controlled environments where new stablecoin models can be developed, tested, and refined without exposing national financial systems to undue risk.

Drawing on global case studies from Hong Kong, Singapore, and elsewhere, the chapter shows how these jurisdictions support the whole innovation lifecycle. They offer pilot programmes to validate emerging technologies, regulatory sandboxes to test business models, accelerators to commercialise new products, and specialised courts to resolve disputes with predictability. These environments produce empirical evidence on reserve adequacy, redemption dynamics, interoperability, AML/CFT performance, and consumer protection outcomes.

For stablecoin issuers, special jurisdictions provide credible pathways from sandbox testing to licensing and, ultimately, to international scaling. For policymakers, they function as empirical engines that inform both national rulemaking and global standard-setting. Within the broader financial system, they serve as transmission nodes, translating successful experiments into practical norms and emerging standards for digital money.

Baumgartner and his co-authors conclude that special jurisdictions are quietly drafting the first operational blueprint for the next monetary era, one in which stablecoins, tokenised deposits, and CBDCs coexist on interoperable, programmable, and prudentially governed financial rails.

KEY THEMES

These global examples underscore the importance of harmonised, risk-based frameworks that can be tailored to local institutional capacity and policy priorities. The book was initially conceived as an accessible companion to the Commonwealth Model Law on Stablecoins. However, as contributions from scholars and practitioners worldwide accumulated, several cross-cutting themes emerged.

These themes highlight shared perspectives on the evolution of stablecoins and the challenges and opportunities they present. A clear alignment emerges across contributors that:

(i) Stablecoins Have Become Systemically Relevant Components of the Global Financial Architecture

The opening chapters establish the structural foundations of stablecoins. Their these design now carry macro-relevant consequences, as stablecoins increasingly mediate payments, remittances, DeFi liquidity, and dollarisation dynamics in emerging markets. Stablecoins have therefore crossed the threshold from experimental instruments to systemically significant financial infrastructure. Subsequent chapters deepen this shift from product logic to infrastructure logic. Stablecoins now function as core components of modern payment systems, remittance channels, humanitarian transfer mechanisms, and DeFi liquidity rails. Their economic role increasingly mirrors that of short-term money market instruments and cross-border payment networks. The future of digital money will depend on intelligent, automated, and interoperable systems. This shift requires new compliance architectures, robust identity frameworks, and upgraded resilience standards to manage autonomous payment agents, programmable financial action triggers, and workflow architecture.

(ii) Effective Regulation Must be Risk-Based, Proportionate, and Technology-Neutral, Anchored in Full-Reserve Backing, Enforceable Redemption Rights, Strong Governance, and Transparent Disclosures

The middle chapters articulate how programmable money must be governed. This includes a transition from principle-based regulation to supervisory operationalisation, embedding reserve discipline, disclosure workflows, SupTech monitoring, and enforceable redemption into digital money systems. Comparative analysis of MiCA and the Commonwealth Model Law reinforces a core insight of programmable money: regulatory diversity is inevitable, but governance principles must be globally coherent. Stablecoins and CBDCs are framed not as competitors, but as interoperable layers within a modern monetary stack, where sovereignty, innovation, and resilience must be jointly preserved.

(iii) Cross-Border Coordination is Essential to Prevent Fragmentation, Regulatory Arbitrage, and Systemic Blind Spots

Systemic risk analysis further reinforces the infrastructure framing. Stablecoins introduce new contagion channels, with high transaction velocity, protocol interdependence, and algorithmic feedback loops, that exceed the scope of legacy financial regulation. These risks underscore the need for comprehensive safeguards and cross-border cooperation, collaboration and coordination. They also require new systemic-risk metrics capable of capturing network centrality, governance fragility, and real-time contagion pathways.

(iv) When Properly Governed, Stablecoins Can Act as Public-Purpose Infrastructure That Reduces Costs, Promotes Financial Inclusion, Enhances Humanitarian Operations, and Supports Secure Digital Identity Ecosystems

The social dimensions of programmable money are addressed explicitly through the lens of public goods. Stablecoins can reduce remittance costs, improve humanitarian delivery, and support inclusive digital identity systems. However, these gains require rights-based governance, transparent oversight, and interoperable standards. Inclusion should not be an emergent property of technology but a deliberate governance outcome.

(v) Geopolitical and Institutional Realities will Continue to Play a Role, but Global Principles are Needed

The final chapters ground the framework in these realities. Nigeria's experience illustrates the costs of fragmented governance, where regulatory bans coexist with widespread informal adoption. In contrast, special jurisdictions such as Singapore, ADGM, DIFC, and Hong Kong emerge as institutional laboratories, translating experimentation into scalable norms. These environments demonstrate how programmable money can be integrated into supervised, interoperable financial systems without destabilising national economies.

(vi) Trust Emerges as the Unifying Theme

Trust in digital money cannot be engineered solely through algorithms or market incentives. It must be constructed through enforceable law, transparent reserves, accountable governance, and coordinated supervision. Soft-law approaches and voluntary standards consistently fail under stress, reinforcing the necessity of binding institutional design. This is especially relevant for Payments 5.0, the era of agentic autonomy, where intelligent payment agents act on behalf of users. Here, programmability reaches its logical conclusion: money becomes not only software, but decision-making infrastructure, requiring verifiable mandates, explainability, and continuous oversight. The chapters uniformly emphasise that trust ultimately rests on legal and institutional structures. Enforceable redemption rights, transparent high-quality reserves, credible governance, rigorous licensing and supervision, and coherent cross-border oversight recur as essential elements of stable systems.

Together, these themes highlight the convergence of scholarly, policy, and technical perspectives on how stablecoins should evolve within a safe, inclusive, and globally coherent digital financial system.

UNRESOLVED QUESTIONS IN THE GLOBAL STABLECOIN LANDSCAPE

This volume provides initial answers to the question: What happens when money becomes programmable, and how should institutions evolve in response? Some of the current debates surround issues such as :

Who should be allowed to issue stablecoins? Some regulatory regimes, such as those of the United States and the European Union (European Union, 2023), argue that issuance should be confined to insured deposit-taking institutions, effectively treating stablecoins as narrow-bank liabilities. By contrast, jurisdictions such as Singapore, the UK (under the FCA), and the Commonwealth Model Law support a more open approach, allowing non-bank entities to issue stablecoins provided they comply with stringent requirements on reserves, governance, and auditing. This divide reflects more profound differences in philosophies regarding financial innovation, competition, and public–private risk sharing.

Stablecoins versus CBDCs? Debate also persists on the relationship between stablecoins and CBDCs. While most authors view them as complementary, some policymakers, particularly in emerging markets, remain cautious. Concerns include potential erosion of monetary sovereignty, accelerated dollarisation, and diminished adoption of domestic CBDCs. Overexposure also carries its own risks, including the risk of contagion collapse. These tensions underscore the geopolitical and macroeconomic considerations embedded in the design of digital currency.

Payments 5.0 and agentic autonomy? The emergence of autonomous payment agents further complicates the landscape. While contributors generally agree that agentic systems and self-executing digital money are inevitable, concerns persist regarding identity governance, vulnerabilities to adversarial manipulation, explainability of agent decisions, and the supervisory methods required to manage autonomy at scale.

The role of special jurisdictions and free-trade zones? Special regulatory zones are another source of debate. For some, these jurisdictions provide essential, controlled environments for responsible experimentation. For others, they risk enabling regulatory arbitrage, weakening global standards, and influencing national policy trajectories without adequate democratic oversight. The line between innovation and instability is not easily drawn.

Ethical tensions in the use of humanitarian and development aid? Chapters focusing on humanitarian and development applications reveal substantial ethical risks including "crypto-colonialism," heightened beneficiary surveillance, and deepening dependency on private issuers. Others highlight tangible benefits demonstrated in real-world pilots: lower costs, faster transfers, improved transparency, and reduced leakage in fragile contexts. The balance between protecting vulnerable populations and empowering them through digital tools remains unresolved.

FUTURE RESEARCH DIRECTIONS

The future of stablecoins will depend on how regulators, policymakers, and international institutions navigate these unresolved tensions surrounding them. The ability to balance innovation with stability, sovereignty, and ethical considerations will shape the next phase of global digital finance. This invites a whole new discipline of scholarly and research endeavour on *Programmable Money as Infrastructure.* Some of they many research questions are summarised below.

Quantitative Models of Systemic Risk in Programmable Money Systems: Critical for the Development of Early-Warning Systems and Macroprudential Tools Suited to Programmable Financial Infrastructure

How can systemic risk arising from stablecoins and other forms of programmable money be quantitatively modelled across integrated digital and traditional financial markets? What stress-testing methodologies are appropriate for 24/7 markets characterised by instant settlement, algorithmic redemption, and composability? How do redemption cascades, liquidity spirals, and protocol-level shocks propagate across stablecoins, DeFi protocols, and banking systems? Can real-time contagion and network-centrality models identify "too-interconnected-to-fail" nodes within digital money ecosystems?

Interoperability Standards for Multi-Rail Digital Money Ecosystems to Determine Whether Programmable Money Evolves Into a Fragmented Landscape or a Coherent Global Network

As CBDCs, stablecoins, tokenised deposits, and commercial bank money coexist, how can interoperability be designed as foundational infrastructure rather than an afterthought? What technical, legal, and governance standards are required to enable seamless interaction between CBDCs and privately issued stablecoins? How can tokenised bank deposits be safely integrated into multi-rail payment systems? What role should emerging xNetwork standards (such as x402, AP2, and PAY-Bench) and harmonised data schemas play in enabling agentic, machine-to-machine payments and compliant cross-border settlement? Governance of AI-Driven and Agentic Payment Systems

As payments become increasingly autonomous, what governance architectures are required for AI-driven payment agents operating at scale? How can mandate integrity, guardrails, and bounded autonomy be enforced in systems capable of initiating and executing financial transactions independently? What standards of explainability, auditability, and traceability are necessary for supervisory oversight? How should adversarial risks, cyber-resilience, and real-time supervision be addressed in agentic payment environments? Finally, how should legal liability be allocated for algorithmic error, misuse, or emergent behaviour? These questions point to the need for entirely new governance models for Payments 5.0.

Public-Good and Humanitarian Applications of Programmable Stablecoins, Rigorous Evidence is Needed on Safeguards and Risks Before Large-Scale Deployment

Can programmable stablecoins function as a reliable public-good infrastructure in humanitarian and development contexts? How do their cost-effectiveness, speed, and transparency compare with traditional aid delivery and remittance systems? What safeguards are required to ensure informed consent, user protection, and dignity in crisis environments? How do such systems affect inclusion outcomes for refugees, women, and undocumented populations? How resilient are programmable payment systems during conflict, displacement, or natural disasters? What governance models can prevent "crypto-colonialism" while safeguarding rights and local agency?

Regulatory Impact and Comparative Effectiveness Across Jurisdictions to Identify Regulatory Design Choices that Scale Effectively Across Jurisdictions

How do different regulatory frameworks for programmable money perform in practice? Comparative research is needed to evaluate regimes such as the EU's MiCA (2023), the US GENIUS Act (2025), Singapore's Payment Services Act, the UAE's VARA and FSRA frameworks, and early implementations of the Commonwealth Model Law on Stablecoins. How do these approaches differ in their impacts on market integrity, consumer protection, compliance effectiveness, innovation pathways, and systemic-risk outcomes?

Redress and Accountability in Borderless Digital Money Systems Which are Central to Sustaining Trust in Global Digital Money Infrastructure

As programmable money enables frictionless cross-border activity, how can effective redress mechanisms be designed for borderless digital economies? What role can interoperable Online Dispute Resolution (ODR) systems play? How can AI-driven redress systems mitigate bias while preserving procedural fairness? Can consumer rights be portable across jurisdictions, and how might privacy-preserving data sharing support enforcement without undermining confidentiality?

Programmable Money, Sovereignty, and Digital Dollarisation Impacts for Economies With High Inflation, Large Remittance Corridors, or Fragile Banking Systems

What are the macroeconomic implications of widespread stablecoin adoption in emerging and developing economies? How does programmable money affect monetary transmission, capital flows, and financial stability? To what extent does it accelerate digital dollarisation and policy leakage? What hybrid public–private models could preserve monetary sovereignty while leveraging private innovation? How can states maintain autonomy amid competing digital payment rails?

Cybersecurity, Operational Resilience, and Third-Party Dependencies to safeguard digital monetary infrastructure.

Given the layered and interoperable nature of programmable money systems, where do systemic vulnerabilities concentrate? How resilient are oracle networks, custodians, wallet providers, and smart-contract infrastructures under stress? What failure modes emerge when cyberattacks coincide with liquidity shocks or mass redemptions? Are minimum global standards for ICT resilience and third-party risk management feasible, and if so, how should they be enforced?

Legal Interoperability and Cross-Border Enforcement Legal Interoperability Will be a Decisive Factor in the Viability of Global Programmable Finance

As programmable money circulates across jurisdictions, how can legal interoperability be achieved? What mechanisms are needed for mutual recognition of licences and supervisory decisions? How should conflict-of-laws issues be resolved for digital money transactions? Can redemption rights be enforced consistently across borders? How can international coordination on sanctions compliance and PF/TF controls be strengthened without fragmenting markets?

Privacy, Identity, and Ethical Design of Digital Money Infrastructure to Ensure That Programmable Money Enhances Human Rights and Democratic Values

How can programmable money systems embed privacy, rights, and ethical safeguards by design? What transaction architectures enable meaningful privacy while supporting compliance? How should digital identity systems be integrated to balance inclusion, security, and autonomy? What ethical frameworks are appropriate for public-sector and humanitarian deployments? How can governance prevent surveillance, exclusion, or data exploitation?

Collectively, these questions define a next-generation research agenda that treats programmable money not merely as a financial product, but as critical global infrastructure, with implications for stability, sovereignty, inclusion, governance, and trust.

CONCLUSION

Taken together, the chapters in this volume point to a future in which stablecoins evolve from niche financial instruments into foundational components of programmable monetary infrastructure. Their long-term viability will depend on the quality of governance, the strength of institutions, and the depth of international coordination that underpin them. The central challenge is to embed programmable money within frameworks that uphold human dignity, market integrity, and monetary sovereignty in an increasingly automated and interconnected financial system.

The trajectory of stablecoins will be shaped by three interdependent pillars of trust, interoperability, and regulatory coherence. Trust must be grounded in enforceable legal rights, transparent reserves, resilient technology, and credible supervisory oversight. Interoperability must be designed as core infrastructure to enable the safe operation of stablecoins, CBDCs, tokenised deposits, and commercial bank money across shared digital rails. Regulatory coherence, both within and across jurisdictions, will determine whether programmable money strengthens or fragments global financial stability.

Over the coming decade, digital money will transition decisively to public-critical infrastructure. Stablecoins, CBDCs, tokenised deposits, and increasingly autonomous payment agents will coexist and interact across programmable networks that blur traditional distinctions between public and private money. The defining policy question will be how programmable monetary systems should be governed, supervised, and anchored in principles of transparency, accountability, and the protection of rights. As cross-border value flows intensify and AI-driven agents begin to intermediate economic activity at scale, regulatory frameworks must become modular, adaptive, and technically informed and capable of evolving alongside the systems they oversee.

If designed and governed wisely, programmable money has the potential to expand financial inclusion, reduce friction in global payments, enhance resilience, and support new forms of economic coordination. If poorly governed, it risks entrenching inequality, accelerating unwanted forms of digital dollarisation, eroding monetary autonomy, and introducing new sources of systemic fragility.

In this context, the book's purpose is both analytical and practical. It provides a rigorous foundation for understanding programmable money as infrastructure, and a policy-relevant framework for those tasked with designing, regulating, and stewarding the next generation of global monetary systems. As programmable money reshapes the architecture of finance, this volume offers a benchmark reference for policymakers, regulators, technologists, and institutions seeking to ensure that innovation serves the public interest.

REFERENCES

Bank for International Settlements. (2007). *Basel Committee on Banking Supervision Principles for home-host supervisory cooperation and allocation mechanisms in the context of Advanced Measurement Approaches (AMA)*. https://www.bis.org/publ/bcbs135.pdf

European Union. (2023). *Regulation - 2023/1114 - EN - EUR-Lex*. Europa.eu. DOI: 10/1093/2024-12-30

FATF. (2021). *Updated Guidance for a Risk-Based Approach to Virtual Assets and Virtual Asset Service Providers*. Www.fatf-Gafi.org. https://www.fatf-gafi.org/en/publications/Fatfrecommendations/Guidance-rba-virtual-assets-2021.html

Financial Stability Board. (2020). *Regulation, Supervision and Oversight of "Global Stablecoin" Arrangements*. Www.fsb.org. https://www.fsb.org/2020/10/regulation-supervision-and-oversight-of-global-stablecoin-arrangements/

Financial Stability Board. (2023). *High-level Recommendations for the Regulation, Supervision and Oversight of Global Stablecoin Arrangements: Final report*. Www.fsb.org. https://www.fsb.org/2023/07/high-level-recommendations-for-the-regulation-supervision-and-oversight-of-global-stablecoin-arrangements-final-report/

Money Authority of Singapore. (2023). *MAS Finalizes Stablecoin Regulatory Framework*. https://www.sgpc.gov.sg/api/file/getfile/Media%20Release_MAS%20Finalises%20Stablecoin%20Regulatory%20Framework.pdf?path=/sgpcmedia/media_releases/mas/press_release/P-20230815-2/attachment/Media+Release_MAS+Finalises+Stablecoin+Regulatory+Framework.pdf

Secretariat, C. (2025). *Commonwealth Model Law on Stablecoins (draft)*. Commonwealth Secretariat.

Compilation of References

Abdullahi, M., Ahmad, A., Pandey, B. K., & Pandey, D. (2024). Digital currency adoption: A comparative analysis of global trends and the Nigerian Enaira digital currency. *SN Computer Science*, *5*(5), 602. DOI: 10.1007/s42979-024-02882-6

Abu Dhabi Finance Week. (n.d.). Abu Dhabi Finance Week: MENA's leading investment summit. https://www.adfw.com/ ADFW

Abu Dhabi Global Market. (n.d.). About ADGM. https://www.adgm.com/

Abu Dhabi Global Market. (n.d.). FinTech at ADGM. https://www.adgm.com/setting-up/fintech

Accelerator, T. (n.d.). Tribe: Powering frontier tech ecosystems. https://tribex.co/accelerator/

Agama, D. E. (2024) *Stablecoins and National Security: Implications for Nigeria's Regulatory Landscape. SSRN.* Available at: https://papers.ssrn.com/sol3/papers.cfm?abstract_id=5098084

Ali, A., Butt, M. H., & Senturk, I. (2025) 'Decentralised Finance as a Catalyst for Financial Inclusion: Evidence from Emerging Economies', *Policy Journal of Social Sciences and Research.* Available at: https://policyjssr.com/index.php/PJSSR/article/view/399

Aljunaid, A. M., Alamoudi, A., & Alkahtani, M. (2025). Explainable artificial intelligence-driven federated learning model for financial fraud detection. *Journal of Risk and Financial Management*, *18*(4), 179. DOI: 10.3390/jrfm18040179

Allen, F., & Carletti, E. (2022). Some simple economics of stablecoins. *Annual Review of Financial Economics*, *14*(1), 195–214. DOI: 10.1146/annurev-financial-111621-101151

Allen, F., Gu, X., & Jagtiani, J. (2021). A survey of fintech research and policy discussion. *Review of Corporate Finance*, *1*(3-4), 259–339. DOI: 10.1561/114.00000007

Allen, F., Gu, X., & Jagtiani, J. (2022). Fintech, cryptocurrencies, and CBDCs: Financial Structural Transformation in China. *Journal of International Money and Finance*, *124*, 102625. DOI: 10.1016/j.jimonfin.2022.102625

AlOkaily, A. (2024) *Exploring Blockchain Technology for Humanitarian Aid in Conflict Zones: A Syrian Case Study*. Available at: https://peacerep.org/wp-content/uploads/2024/10/Exploring-Blockchain-Technology-for-Humanitarian-Aid-in-Conflict-Zones-DIGITAL.pdf

Andrae, S. (2026). U.S. strategy to dominate the Dollar with stablecoins: Geopolitical and economic implications. In Akhtar, S., Khan, M., Almaqtari, F. A G., Selvam, V., & Bahl, S. (Eds.), *Policy Implications on International Financial Economics and Banking* (pp. 195–236). IGI Global Publishing., DOI: 10.4018/979-8-3373-3725-8.ch007

Ansar, S., Demirguc-Kunt, A., Klapper, L., & Singer, D. (2022). *The Global Findex Database 2021: Financial Inclusion, Digital Payments, and Resilience in the Age of COVID-19*. World Bank Group. Retrieved from: https://documents.worldbank.org/curated/en/099818107072234182

Ante, L. (2023). The non-fungible token (NFT) market and its relationship with Bitcoin and Ethereum. *FinTech*, *2*(1), 216–224.

Arabia, A. (2025, July 4). Air Arabia and Mbank transform air travel payments with AE Coin: Speed, security, and simplicity [Press release]. Air Arabia. https://press.airarabia.com/air-arabia-and-mbank-transform-air-travel-payments-with-ae-coin-speed-security-and-simplicity/

Aramonte, S., Huang, W., & Schrimpf, A. (2021). *DeFi risks and the decentralisation illusion*. BIS Quarterly Review. Retrieved from: https://www.bis.org/publ/qtrpdf/r_qt2112b.htm

Aramonte, S., Huang, W., & Schrimpf, A. (2021). DeFi risks and the decentralisation illusion. *BIS Quarterly Review*, (December), 21–36.

Argoz Consultants. (2025). stablecoins and CBDCs: competing for the digital economy. Argoz Consultants Blog. https://www.argozconsultants.com/blog/stablecoins-cbdcs

Arner, D. W., Auer, R., & Frost, J. (2020). Stablecoins: Risks, potential and regulation. Bank for International Settlements. https://www.bis.org/publ/othp33.pdf

Arner, D. W., Auer, R., & Frost, J. (2020). Stablecoins: Risks, potential and regulation. BIS Working Paper no. 905 (2020), University of Hong Kong Faculty of Law Research Paper No. 2021/57

Arner, D. W., Auer, R., & Frost, J. (2020). stablecoins: risks, potential and regulation. BIS Working Papers, No. 905. Bank for International Settlements. https://www.bis.org/publ/work905.htm

Arner, D. W., Auer, R., & Frost, J. (2020). Stablecoins: Risks, potential and regulation. *SSRN*, Working paper Nº 905. DOI: 10.2139/ssrn.3979495

Astana International Financial Centre. (n.d.). About AIFC. https://aifc.kz/about/

Auer, R. (2019). Embedded supervision: how to build regulation into blockchain finance. BIS Working Papers, No. 811. Bank for International Settlements. https://www.bis.org/publ/work811.htm

Auer, R., & Böhme, R. (2021). Central bank digital currency: The quest for minimally invasive technology. *The Journal of Economic Perspectives*, *35*(2), 161–178.

Auer, R., & Tercero-Lucas, P. (2022). Distrust or speculation? The socioeconomic drivers of U.S. cryptocurrency investments. *Journal of Financial Stability*, *62*, 101066. DOI: 10.1016/j.jfs.2022.101066

AWS. (2025, September 4). Agentic AI solutions in financial services. AWS Marketplace Blog. https://aws.amazon.com/blogs/awsmarketplace/agentic-ai-solutions-in-financial-services/

Baldwin, R., Cave, M., & Lodge, M. (2012). Understanding Regulation. Theory, Strategy, and Practice. OUP Oxford, 2012 - Business & Economics

Balina, R., Spyra, M., Rozynski, F., & Podlinska, O. (2025). From Checklists to Change: FATF's Risk-Based Approach and Its Impact on Malta's AML Framework. *European Research Studies*, *28*(3), 518–530. DOI: 10.35808/ersj/4058

Bank for International Settlements. (2007). *Basel Committee on Banking Supervision Principles for home-host supervisory cooperation and allocation mechanisms in the context of Advanced Measurement Approaches (AMA)*. https://www.bis.org/publ/bcbs135.pdf

Bank for International Settlements. (2022). *BIS Annual Economic Report 2022*. BIS.

Bank for International Settlements. (2022). Stablecoins and their role in the financial system. https://www.bis.org/publ/othp.pdf

Bank for International Settlements. (2022). The future monetary system. In *BIS Annual Economic Report 2022*. Retrieved from: https://www.bis.org/publ/arpdf/ar2022e3.pdf

Bank for International Settlements. (2024). *Stablecoin oversight framework*. https://www.bis.org

Bank for International Settlements. (2024). The interplay between stablecoins and central bank digital currencies. BIS Bulletin No. 81. https://www.bis.org/publ/bisbull81.htm

Barthélémy, J., Gardin, P., & Nguyen, B. (2023). stablecoins and the financing of the real economy. Banque de France Working Paper, No. 908. https://publications.banque-france.fr/stablecoins-and-financing-real-economy

Basel Committee on Banking Supervision. (2013). *Global systemically important banks: Updated assessment methodology and the higher loss absorbency requirement*. Bank for International Settlements.

Baur, D. G., Hong, K., & Lee, A. D. (2018). Bitcoin: Medium of exchange or speculative assets? *Journal of International Financial Markets, Institutions and Money*, *54*, 177–189. DOI: 10.1016/j.intfin.2017.12.004

Benson, C. C., Loftesness, S., & Jones, R. (2017). *Payment systems in the U.S* (3rd ed.). Glenbrook Press., https://books.google.com/books/about/Payments_Systems_in_the_U_S.html?id=IGmhcQAACAAJ

Bindseil, U. (2025). Regulatory responses to the financial stability implications of stablecoins. DOI: 10.2139/ssrn.5710762

BIS (Bank for International Settlements). (2023). Cross-border exchange of wholesale CBDCs using automated market-makers. https://www.banque-france.fr/system/files/2023-09/20230928%20Mariana%20final%20report.pdf

Blockchain Consortium. (2024). *Interoperability in blockchain networks: Challenges and solutions* (White paper). https://blockchainconsortium.org

Blockchain Governance Initiative Network. (2022). stablecoins: past, present, and future (BGIN Study Report 010). https://bgin-global.org/wp-content/uploads/2022/06/BGIN_SR010_stablecoins.pdf

Boiardi, P., & Stout, E. (2021) *To what extent can blockchain help development co-operation actors meet the 2030 Agenda?* OECD. Available at: https://www.oecd.org/content/dam/oecd/en/publications/reports/2021/05/to-what-extent-can-blockchain-help-development-co-operation-actors-meet-the-2030-agenda_14630965/11857cb5-en.pdf

Brookings Institution. (2025, June 16). What are stablecoins, and how are they regulated? Brookings. https://www.brookings.edu/articles/what-are-stablecoins-and-how-are-they-regulated/

Brown, T. B., Mann, B., Ryder, N., Subbiah, M., Kaplan, J., Dhariwal, P., & Amodei, D. (2020). Language models are few-shot learners. *Advances in Neural Information Processing Systems*, *33*, 1877–1901. DOI: 10.48550/arXiv.2005.14165

Brummer, C. (2020). *Fintech law in a nutshell*. West Academic Publishing.

Brummer, C., & Yadav, Y. (2019). Fintech and the innovation trilemma. *The Georgetown Law Journal*, *107*(2), 235–307. https://scholarship.law.vanderbilt.edu/faculty-publications/1084

Brunnermeier, M. K., & Landau, J.-P. (2022). The economics and regulation of stablecoins. *Journal of Financial Stability*, *58*, 100945. DOI: 10.1016/j.jfs.2022.100945

Brunnermeier, M., James, H., & Landau, J. P. (2021). *The digitalization of money*. Princeton University Press.

Buckley, R. P., Arner, D. W., & Zetzsche, D. A. (2023). *FinTech: Finance, technology and regulation*. Cambridge University Press. DOI: 10.1017/9781009086943

Buckley, R. P., Arner, D., Veidt, R., & Zetzsche, D. (2020). Building Fintech Ecosystems: Regulatory Sandboxes, Innovation Hubs and Beyond. *Washington University Journal of Law and Policy*, *61*(1), 55–98. https://openscholarship.wustl.edu/law_journal_law_policy/vol61/iss1/10

Bullmann, D., Klemm, J., & Pinna, A. (2019). In search for stability in crypto-assets: Are stablecoins the solution? (Occasional Paper No. 230). European Central Bank. https://www.ecb.europa.eu/pub/pdf/scpops/ecb.op230~d57946be3b.en.pdf

Bullmann, D., Klemm, J., & Pinna, A. (2019). *In search for stability in crypto-assets: Are stablecoins the solution?* European Central Bank Occasional Paper Series No. 230.

Cambridge Centre for Alternative Finance. (2025, June 12). From automation to autonomy: The agentic AI era of financial services. Cambridge Judge Business School. https://www.jbs.cam.ac.uk/2025/from-automation-to-autonomy-the-agentic-ai-era-of-financial-services/

Cantú, C., Frost, J., & Noone, T. (2025) 'Some Perspectives on the Regulation of Stablecoins', *Law and Contemporary Problems*. Available at: https://scholarship.law.duke.edu/cgi/viewcontent.cgi?article=5161&context=lcp

Capco. (2025, June 30). Agentic AI: Transforming payments & cash management. Capco Intelligence. https://www.capco.com/intelligence/capco-intelligence/agentic-ai-transforming-payments-and-cash-management

Carapella, F. (2025). Stablecoin Self-Regulation. *SSRN.* DOI: 10.2139/ssrn.5133007

Castrén, O., & Russo, R. (2026). Runs, transparency and regulation: On the optimal design of stablecoin frameworks. *Economics Letters*, *258*, 112720. DOI: 10.1016/j.econlet.2025.112720

Catalini, C., & de Gortari, A. (2022). On the economic design of stablecoins. *Management Science*, *68*(2), 949–977.

Certi, K. (2025, July). Security risks of stablecoins. CertiK. https://www.certik.com/resources/blog/security-risks-of-stablecoins

Chainalysis (2024). The 2024 geography of crypto report. https://www.chainalysis.com/wp-content/uploads/2024/10/the-2024-geography-of-crypto-report-release.pdf

Chainalysis. (2022). The 2022 geography of cryptocurrency report. https://go.chainalysis.com/2022-geography-of-cryptocurrency.html

Chainalysis. (2023). The 2023 geography of cryptocurrency report. Chainalysis. https://go.chainalysis.com/geography-of-cryptocurrency-2023.html?utm_source=bambu&utm_medium=social&utm_campaign=advocacy&blaid=5247483

Chainalysis. (2024). *Stablecoin market analytics report.* https://www.chainalysis.com

Chari, A., Converse, N., Mehl, A., Milesi-Ferretti, G. M., & Vansteenkiste, I. (2025). Geopolitical tensions and international financial fragmentation Evidence and implications. Geneva Reports on the World Economy 28. https://cepr.org/system/files/publication-files/271360-geneva_28_geopolitical_tensions_and_international_fragmentation_evidence_and_implications.pdf

Chen, H. (Ed.). (2021). *Regulation, emerging risk, and ethics in FinTech and AI.* IGI Global., https://books.google.com/books/about/Regulation_Emerging_Risk_and_Ethics_in_F.html?id=TAl-EQAAQBAJ

China Daily Global. (2025). HK stablecoin licence attracts big names – "Hong Kong's Stablecoins Ordinance has relatively high thresholds and only large companies and institutions can apply for stablecoin licences" [Article by Fan Feifei]. China Daily Global. https://www.chinadailyhk.com/hk/article/615602

Choi, K. J., & Rhee, K. (2025) From the fringe to the core: Stablecoins and the future of banking stability. DOI: 10.2139/ssrn.5374790

Circle (2024). USDC as a platform for global prosperity. https://6778953.fs1.hubspotusercontent-na1.net/hubfs/6778953/Davos%202025/USDC-report-2025-Digital_AW.pdf

CoinDesk. (n.d.). Consensus. https://consensus2025.coindesk.com/ consensus2025.coindesk.com

CoinGecko. (2022). 2022 annual cryptocurrency report. CoinGecko. https://www.coingecko.com/research/publications

Combinator, Y. (n.d.). Y Combinator. https://www.ycombinator.com

Committee on Payments and Market Infrastructures & International Organization of Securities Commissions. (2012). *Principles for financial market infrastructures*. Retrieved from: https://www.bis.org/cpmi/publ/d101a.pdf

Commonwealth Secretariat (2025). Draft Commonwealth Model Law on Stablecoins. Retrieved from Commonwealth Secretariat consultation document, July 2025.

Commonwealth Secretariat. (2023). *Model Law on Virtual Assets. Office of Civil and Criminal Justice Reform*. Commonwealth Secretariat.

Commonwealth Secretariat. (2025). Draft Commonwealth model law on stablecoins (Draft as at 4 July 2025). Commonwealth Secretariat. https://thecommonwealth.org/sites/default/files/inline/Draft%20Model%20Law%20on%20stablecoins.pdf

Communications and Information Technology Commission. (n.d.). Cloud Computing Special Economic Zone. Government of Saudi Arabia. https://www.cst.gov.sa/en/about/program-and-initiatives/cloud-computing-special-economic-zone-technology

Congdon, T. (2021). Interest rates or quantity of money? Edward Nelson on Milton Friedman. *Economic Affairs*, *41*(2), 320–335. DOI: 10.1111/ecaf.12467

Courts, D. I. F. C. (2021). DIFC Courts launches specialised court for the digital economy. https://www.difccourts.ae/media-centre/newsroom/difc-courts-launches-specialised-court-for-the-digital-economy

Data Protection (Amendment) Law. (2023). Law No. 3 of 2023 (DIFC, 2023). https://www.difc.ae/business/laws-regulations

De Bandt, O., & Hartmann, P. (2000). Systemic risk: A survey. *ECB Working Paper Series*, No. 35.

De Conti, B., & Guttmann, R. (2025). Digital money: Fragmentation of the monetary regime. *Review of Political Economy*, 1–22. Advance online publication. DOI: 10.1080/09538259.2025.2573356

Demirgüç-Kunt, A., Klapper, L., Singer, D., Ansar, S., & Hess, J. (2018). *The Global Findex Database 2017: Measuring Financial Inclusion and the Fintech Revolution*. World Bank., Available at https://documents1.worldbank.org/curated/en/491271624538346557/pdf/The-Global-Findex-Database-2017-Measuring-Financial-Inclusion-and-Opportunities-to-Expand-Access-to-and-Use-of-Financial-Services.pdf DOI: 10.1596/978-1-4648-1259-0

DIFC Courts & Dubai Future Foundation. (2019, October 30). Court Tech Lab launched by DIFC Courts and the Dubai Future Foundation. https://www.difccourts.ae/media-centre/newsroom/court-tech-lab-launched-difc-courts-and-dubai-future-foundation

Dubai Financial Services Authority. (2022). Consultation Paper No. 143 – Regulation of Crypto Tokens. https://dfsaen.thomsonreuters.com/sites/default/files/net_file_store/CP143_Regulation_of_Crypto_Tokens.pdf

Dubai Financial Services Authority. (2025). Consultation Paper No. 168 – Enhancements to the Regulation of Crypto Tokens. https://www.dfsa.ae/news/notice-consultation-paper-release-cp-168

Dubai FinTech Summit. (n.d.). Dubai FinTech Summit. https://dubaifintechsummit.com/ Dubai FinTech Summit

Dubai International Financial Centre Courts. (n.d.). Enforcement of judgments and orders – DIFC Courts. https://www.difccourts.ae/difc-courts/enforcement

Dubai International Financial Centre Courts. (n.d.). Legal framework. https://www.difccourts.ae/about/legal-framework

Dubai International Financial Centre. (2024). Digital Assets Law, DIFC Law No. 2 of 2024 (enacted 1 March 2024, commences 8 March 2024). https://www.difc.com/business/laws-and-regulations/legal-database/difc-laws/digital-assets-law-difc-law-no-2-of-2024

Dubai International Financial Centre. (2024, April 29). DIFC emerges as premier global hub for family businesses – over 5,500 active registered companies. https://www.wam.ae/en/article/b2wfs1m-difc-emerges-premier-global-hub-for-family

Dubai International Financial Centre. (2024, February 15). DIFC's 20th anniversary takes flight with strong contribution to Dubai's economy – financial services sector captured more than half (52%) of all FDI into Dubai. https://www.difc.com/whats-on/news/difcs-20th-anniversary-takes-flight-with-strong-contribution-to-dubais-economy

Dubai International Financial Centre. (2025, February 26). DIFC announces consultation for amendments to select legislation through DIFC Laws Amendment Law, Law No. 1 of 2005 – proposed amendments to the Data Protection Law 2020. https://www.difc.com/whats-on/news/difc-announces-consultation-for-amendments-to-select-difc-legislation-through-difc-law-amendment-law

Dubai International Financial Centre. (n.d.). About DIFC. https://www.difc.com/

Dubai International Financial Centre. (n.d.). DIFC Innovation Hub. https://www.difc.com/ecosystem/innovation-hub difc.com

Dubai Multi Commodities Centre. (n.d.). Welcome to DMCC – The world's premier business destination. Retrieved November 4, 2025, from https://dmcc.ae/

Economic Cities and Special Zones Authority. (2025, April). ECZA activates strategic partnerships to strengthen Saudi Arabia's investment landscape. https://ecza.gov.sa/en/media-center/news-press/ecza-activates-strategic-partnerships-strengthen-saudi-arabias-investment-landscape

Ekshian, E. (2025) *Stablecoins and the Future of Remittances*. FGVEurope Research Study. Available at: https://www.fgveurope.de/wp-content/uploads/2025/02/Research-Study-Emily-Ekshian.pdf

Etihad, A. (2025, July 21). Abu Dhabi Judicial Department to accept fee payments in digital currency [Press release]. Abu Dhabi Judicial Department. https://en.aletihad.ae/news/business/4591968/abu-dhabi-judicial-department-to-accept-fee-payments-in-digi

European Central Bank. (2022). Stablecoins and financial inclusion: Opportunities and challenges. https://www.ecb.europa.eu/pub/pdf/scpops/ecb.op281~4d5e47be30.en.pdf

European Parliament. (2023). Markets in Crypto-Assets Regulation (MiCA). Brussels: EU.

European Parliament. (2025). *Markets in crypto-assets (MiCA) implementation report*. https://www.europarl.europa.eu

European Securities and Markets Authority. (2025). *Markets in Crypto-Assets Regulation (MiCA)*. Retrieved from: https://www.esma.europa.eu/esmas-activities/digital-finance-and-innovation/markets-crypto-assets-regulation-mica

European Union. (2023). *Regulation - 2023/1114 - EN - EUR-Lex*. Europa.eu. DOI: 10/1093/2024-12-30

Farhat, K., Mueller, M., & Srivastava, V. (2025). Interconnection and rivalry in global monetary networks. IGP White Paper 13, February 2025. https://www.internetgovernance.org/wp-content/uploads/Networks_of_money_research_paper-1-1.pdf

FATF. (2021). *Updated Guidance for a Risk-Based Approach to Virtual Assets and Virtual Asset Service Providers*. Www.fatf-Gafi.org. https://www.fatf-gafi.org/en/publications/Fatfrecommendations/Guidance-rba-virtual-assets-2021.html

Feldstein, S. (2021). *The rise of digital repression: How technology is reshaping power, politics, and resistance*. Oxford University Press., Available at https://books.google.com/books?hl=en&lr=&id=W3QjEAAAQBAJ DOI: 10.1093/oso/9780190057497.001.0001

Feyen, E., Klingebiel, D., & Ruiz, M. (2024). Can crypto-assets play a role in foreign reserve portfolios? Not today, and likely not in the near future. https://documents1.worldbank.org/curated/en/099553102232444409/pdf/IDU1c16366af173fa148931a28b189e8eca412f3.pdf

Financial Action Task Force. (2019). *Guidance for a risk-based approach to virtual assets and virtual asset service providers*. FATF.

Financial Action Task Force. (2021). *Updated Guidance for a Risk-Based Approach to Virtual Assets and Virtual Asset Service Providers*. Retrieved from: https://www.fatf-gafi.org/en/publications/Fatfrecommendations/Guidance-rba-virtual-assets-2021.html

Financial Action Task Force. (2023). *Targeted update on implementation of the FATF standards on virtual assets*. FATF.

Financial Services Regulatory Authority. (n.d.). FSRA rulebook. Abu Dhabi Global Market. https://en.adgm.thomsonreuters.com/rulebook/fsra

Financial Stability Board. (2020). *Regulation, supervision and oversight of "global stablecoin" arrangements*. FSB.

Financial Stability Board. (2020). Regulation, supervision and oversight of "global stablecoin" arrangements. https://www.fsb.org/2020/10/regulation-supervision-and-oversight-of-global-stablecoin-arrangements/

Financial Stability Board. (2020). *Regulation, Supervision and Oversight of "Global Stablecoin" Arrangements*. Retrieved from: https://www.fsb.org/uploads/P131020-3.pdf

Financial Stability Board. (2020). *Regulation, Supervision and Oversight of "Global Stablecoin" Arrangements*. Www.fsb.org. https://www.fsb.org/2020/10/regulation-supervision-and-oversight-of-global-stablecoin-arrangements/

Financial Stability Board. (2022). *Assessment of Risks to Financial Stability from Crypto-assets*. Retrieved from: https://www.fsb.org/uploads/P160222.pdf

Financial Stability Board. (2023). *High-level Recommendations for the Regulation, Supervision and Oversight of Global Stablecoin Arrangements*. Retrieved from: https://www.fsb.org/uploads/P170723-3.pdf

Financial Stability Board. (2023). *High-level Recommendations for the Regulation, Supervision and Oversight of Global Stablecoin Arrangements: Final report*. Www.fsb.org. https://www.fsb.org/2023/07/high-level-recommendations-for-the-regulation-supervision-and-oversight-of-global-stablecoin-arrangements-final-report/

Franceschi, L. G., Macharia, E., Binns, M. L., Jarvis, S., & Joseph, L. (2025). *Commonwealth Model Law on Stablecoins: Regulatory framework for emerging economies*. Commonwealth Secretariat.

FXCintel. (2025, September 3). Agentic AI and efficiency drive recent developments in cross-border payments. FXCintel Research. https://www.fxcintel.com/research/analysis/agentic-ai-cross-border-payments-sep-2025

G7 Working Group on Stablecoins. (2019). *Investigating the impact of global stablecoins*. Bank for International Settlements.

Gaudreau, D. (2024) *Analyzing Crypto's Potential to Expand Financial Inclusion in EMDEs*. Theseus. Available at: https://www.theseus.fi/handle/10024/872077

Gelephu Mindfulness City. (n.d.). Gelephu Mindfulness City – Home. https://gmc.bt/

Ghosh, A., & Sanyal, S. (2024). Trustworthy AI in financial services: A framework for explainability, fairness, and accountability. *AI and Ethics*, *4*(2), 233–246. https://www.sciencedirect.com/science/article/pii/S0045790624003379

Global Digital Finance. (2019). *Principles for stablecoin issuers*. Retrieved from: https://www.gdf.io/wp-content/uploads/2019/03/0010_GDF_VI-Principles-for-Stablecoin-Issuers_Digital_161019.pdf

Gorton, G., & Metrick, A. (2012). Getting up to speed on the financial crisis. National Bureau of Economic Research Paper.

Gorton, G. B., & Zhang, J. I. (2023). Taming Wildcat Stablecoins. *SSRN*, *90*, 909–971. DOI: 10.2139/ssrn.3888752

Gorton, G., & Zhang, J. (2021). Taming Wildcat Stablecoins. *Annual Review of Financial Economics, 13*, 279–299. DOI: 10.1146/annurev-financial-110220-070821

Gorton, G., & Zhang, J. (2023). Taming wildcat stablecoins. *University of Pennsylvania Law Review, 171*(4), 1125–1187.

Grobys, K. (2021). The risks of algorithmic stablecoins: Insights from TerraUSD and beyond. *Crypto Finance Review, 3*(4), 45–60.

Gudgeon, L., Perez, D., Harz, D., Livshits, B., & Gervais, A. (2020). The decentralized financial crisis. *Proceedings of the 2020 Crypto Valley Conference on Blockchain Technology*, 1-15.

Gudgeon, L., Werner, S., Perez, D., & Knottenbelt, W. J. (2023). DeFi protocols for loanable funds: Interest rates, liquidity and market efficiency. *ACM Computing Surveys, 55*(13s), 1–48.

Guseva, A., Pistor, K., & Riles, A. (2025). On innovation and the coexistence of stablecoins and central bank digital currencies. *Law and Contemporary Problems, 87*(2), 89–117. https://scholarship.law.duke.edu/lcp/vol87/iss2/5/

Hafner, M., & Henriques Pereira, M. (2023). The four types of stablecoins: A comparative analysis. *LEDGER, 8*, 44–67. DOI: 10.5195/ledger.2023.285

Hamdan, A., Ghura, H., Alareeni, B., & Hamdan, R. K. (2022). Entrepreneurship growth in emerging economies: New insights and approaches. *Journal of Sustainable Finance & Investment, 12*(1), 1–12. DOI: 10.1080/20430795.2021.1944750

Harvey, C. R., Ramachandran, A., & Santoro, J. (2021). *DeFi and the future of finance*. John Wiley & Sons.

Harz, D., Klages-Mundt, A., Liu, J.-Y., Gudgeon, L., & Minca, A. (2020). stablecoins 2.0: economic foundations and risk-based models. arXiv. https://arxiv.org/abs/2006.12388

HKIAC. (n.d.). Statistics (includes "Cryptocurrency" category). https://www.hkiac.org/about-us/statistics

Holloway, K., Al Masri, R., & Yahia, A. A. (2021) *Digital identity, biometrics and inclusion in humanitarian responses to refugee crises*. The CALP Network. Available at: https://www.calpnetwork.org/wp-content/uploads/2021/10/Digital_IP_Biometrics_case_study_web.pdf

Hong Kong Monetary Authority & Financial Services and the Treasury Bureau. (2023). Joint consultation paper on the proposed legislative framework for stablecoin issuers. https://www.hkma.gov.hk/eng/key-functions/international-financial-centre/stablecoin-issuers/

Hong Kong Monetary Authority. (1996). Annual report 1996: Market infrastructure – Real-time gross settlement system launched. Hong Kong Monetary Authority. https://www.hkma.gov.hk/eng/publications-and-research/annual-report/1996/037.shtml#:~:text=REAL%20TIME%20GROSS%20SETTLEMENT%20SYSTEM,system%20by%20reducing%20settlement%20risk

Hong Kong Monetary Authority. (2018). Guideline on authorization of virtual banks. Hong Kong Monetary Authority. https://www.hkma.gov.hk/eng/news-and-media/press-releases/2018/05/20180530-3/

Hong Kong Monetary Authority. (2022). Discussion paper on crypto-assets and stablecoins. https://www.hkma.gov.hk/eng/news-and-media/press-releases/2022/01/20220112-3/ hkma.gov.hk+1

Hong Kong Monetary Authority. (2023). e-HKD pilot programme phase 1 report. https://www.hkma.gov.hk/media/eng/doc/key-information/press-release/2023/20231030e3a1.pdf

Hong Kong Monetary Authority. (2024). Consultation conclusions on the legislative proposal to implement the regulatory regime for fiat-referenced stablecoin issuers in Hong Kong. https://www.hkma.gov.hk/media/eng/doc/key-information/press-release/2024/20240717e3a1.pdf

Hong Kong Monetary Authority. (2025). The HKMA unveils "Fintech 2030" at the Hong Kong FinTech Week 2025 [Press release noting HKFW is co-organised with InvestHK]. https://www.hkma.gov.hk/eng/news-and-media/press-releases/2025/11/20251103-3/ hkma.gov.hk

Horky, N. (2024) *Stablecoins and their implications in emerging markets with gender disparities*. Medium, 17 October. Available at: https://medium.com/@hrknsinst/stablecoins-and-their-implications-in-emerging-markets-with-gender-disparities-8cbf2ecce50e

Howson, P. (2021). Crypto-giving and surveillance philanthropy: Exploring the trade-offs in blockchain innovation for nonprofits. *Nonprofit Management & Leadership*, *32*(4), 509–530. DOI: 10.1002/nml.21452

Huang, C. (2024). Grab users can now use digital currencies to top up their e-wallets. The Straits Times. https://www.straitstimes.com/business/grab-users-can-now-pay-in-crypto

Huang, Y., Ji, Y., Lin, J., Su, D., & Wang, P. (2025). The crumbling wall between crypto and non-crypto markets: Risk transmission through stablecoins. *Journal of Financial Markets, 101043*, 101043. Advance online publication. DOI: 10.1016/j.finmar.2025.101043

Huobi v. Tabarak Investment Capital Ltd. (2024). CA 002/2023 (DIFC Ct App).

Idris, I. (2024) *Humanitarian Digital Transfers in Challenging Contexts*. Institute of Development Studies. Available at: https://opendocs.ids.ac.uk/articles/report/Humanitarian_Digital_Transfers_in_Challenging_Contexts/26379823

International Monetary Fund. (2024). *Central bank digital currency—progress and further considerations*. International Monetary Fund.

International Monetary Fund. (2024). Digital money, trust, and regulation. IMF Working Paper WP/24/162. https://www.imf.org/en/Publications/WP/Issues/2024/06/12/Digital-Money-Trust-Regulation-245122

International Monetary Fund. (2025). The future landscape of stablecoins and CBDCs: Financial stability and innovation. https://www.imf.org/en/Publications

International Organization of Securities Commissions. (2020). Global Stablecoin Initiatives. Retrieved from: https://www.iosco.org/library/pubdocs/pdf/IOSCOPD650.pdf

International Organization of Securities Commissions. (2022). *CPMI and IOSCO publish final guidance on stablecoin arrangements confirming application of Principles for Financial Market Infrastructure*. IOSCO.

IOSCO (International Organization of Securities Commissions). (2025). Tokenization of financial assets. https://www.iosco.org/library/pubdocs/pdf/IOSCOPD809.pdf

Jegerson, D., & Mertzanis, C. (2025) 'Deciphering the role of cryptocurrencies in global remittances: a comprehensive literature review', *Journal of Money Laundering Control*. Emerald Insight. Available at: https://www.emerald.com/insight/content/doi/10.1108/msar-12-2023-0061/full/html

Jensen, J. R., von Wachter, V., & Ross, O. (2021). An introduction to decentralized finance (DeFi). *Complex Systems Informatics and Modeling Quarterly*, *26*(26), 46–54. DOI: 10.7250/csimq.2021-26.03

Jiao, H. (2025). The Concept of Stablecoins and Their Future Prospects. *Proceedings of Business and Economic Studies.*, *8*(5), 1–10. DOI: 10.26689/pbes.v8i5.12105

Jutel, O. (2021). Blockchain humanitarianism and crypto-colonialism. *Patterns (New York, N.Y.)*, *2*(12), 100422. DOI: 10.1016/j.patter.2021.100422 PMID: 35079720

Katz, M. L., & Shapiro, C. (1985). *Network externalities, competition, and compatibility; Knapp, G. F. (1924/1973).* The State Theory of Money.

Kaufman, G. G., & Scott, K. E. (2003). What is systemic risk, and do bank regulators retard or contribute to it? *The Independent Review*, 7(3), 371-391.

Kılıç, M. A., & Bodur, M. Y. (2024) 'Between empowerment and surveillance: Forced migration and information and communication technologies', *DergiPark*. Available at: https://dergipark.org.tr/en/download/article-file/3526318

Klages-Mundt, A., Harz, D., Gudgeon, L., Liu, J.-Y., & Minca, A. (2020). stablecoins 2.0: economic foundations and risk-based models. In *Proceedings of the 2nd ACM Conference on Advances in Financial Technologies* (pp. 59–79). ACM. DOI: 10.1145/3419614.3423261

Klages-Mundt, A., & Minca, A. (2022). While stability lasts: A stochastic model of noncustodial stablecoins. *Mathematical Finance*, *32*(4), 943–981. DOI: 10.1111/mafi.12357

Knodell, J. (2016). The anatomy of global banking: 1781–2013. Routledge. https://www.routledge.com/The-Second-Bank-of-the-United-States-Central-banker-in-an-era-of-nation-building-18161836/Knodell/p/book/9780367870225

Kochergin, D. A. (2020). Economic nature and classification of stablecoins. Finance: theory and Practice, 24(6), 140–160. DOI: 10.26794/2587-5671-2020-24-6-140-160

Korkmaz, E. E. (2023). *Digital Identity and Surveillance Capitalism.* Bristol University Press., Available at https://bristoluniversitypressdigital.com/monochap/book/9781529233520/ch004.xml

Kosse, A., & Mattei, I. (2022). *Gaining momentum-Results of the 2021 BIS survey on central bank digital currencies.* Bank for International Settlements. Retrieved from: https://www.bis.org/publ/bppdf/bispap125.pdf

Kozhan, R., & Viswanath-Natraj, G. (2021). Decentralised stablecoins and collateral risk (WBS Finance Group Research Paper). Warwick Business School. https://papers.ssrn.com/sol3/papers.cfm?abstract_id=3866975

KPMG. (2025). Stablecoins: The bridge between traditional finance and digital assets. https://kpmg.com/kpmg-us/content/dam/kpmg/pdf/2025/stablecoins-kpmg.pdf

Kulkarni, R., Schintler, L., Koizumi, N., & Olds, J. (2019) *Cryptocurrency, Stablecoins and Blockchain: Exploring digital money solutions for remittances and inclusive economies. SSRN*. Available at: https://papers.ssrn.com/sol3/papers.cfm?abstract_id=3524988 DOI: 10.2139/ssrn.3511139

Kwon, D., & Platias, N. (2019). *Terra money: Stability and adoption*. Terra White Paper.

Laatikainen, G., Kolehmainen, T., Li, M., & Hautala, M. (2021) *Towards a trustful digital world: exploring self-sovereign identity ecosystems*. arXiv. Available at: https://arxiv.org/pdf/2105.15131

Laatikainen, G., Kolehmainen, T., & Abrahamsson, P. (2021). Self-sovereign identity ecosystems: Benefits and challenges. *Information and Organization*, *31*(2), 105–117. https://jyx.jyu.fi/bitstreams/8d5377a9-ab2c-45a9-a5de-e9d8324bc545/download

Laboure, M., & Siazon, C. (2025). Stablecoins: How the GENIUS Act strengthens US geopolitical dominance. Deutsche Bank Research Institute. https://www.dbresearch.com/PROD/RI-PROD/PDFVIEWER.calias?pdfViewerPdfUrl=PROD0000000000603306

Labuan Financial Services Authority. (2016). Signing of Memorandum of Understanding between Labuan FSA and Kuala Lumpur Regional Centre for Arbitration (KLRCA). https://www.labuanfsa.gov.my/general-info/media/signing-of-memorandum-of-understanding-between-labuan-fsa-and-klrca

Labuan Financial Services Authority. (2024). Guidelines on the establishment of Labuan Islamic digital bank (i-BOX). https://www.labuanfsa.gov.my/clients/asset_120A5FB8-61B6-45E8-93F0-3F79F86455C8/contentms/img/documents/Legislation_and_Guidelines/Guidelines/banking/2024/Guidelines%20on%20the%20Establishment%20of%20Islamic%20Digital%20Bank%20%28i-BOX%29_01072024.pdf

Labuan International Business and Financial Centre Incorporated. (2025, March 10). Asia's only digital "pick and mix" tool box [Brochure]. https://www.labuanibfc.com/clients/asset_52E835CC-1342-4701-B6FA-E2CD03AD74B4/contentms/img/publications/brochures/35%20Logo/Digital-Toolbox_RGB-250310.pdf

Labuan, I. B. F. C. (n.d.). Who we are / Labuan IBFC – Asia's premier international financial hub. https://www.labuanibfc.com/who-we-are/labuan-ibfc

Latham & Watkins. (2025). The GENIUS Act of 2025: Stablecoin legislation adopted in the US. https://www.lw.com/en/insights/the-genius-act-of-2025-stablecoinlegislation-adopted-in-the-us

LCIA. (2025, July 3). LCIA's 2024 Annual Casework Report (news; links to full report). https://www.lcia.org/News/lcias-2024-annual-casework-report.aspx

Levy-Yeyati, E., & Sturzenegger, F. (2024). Exchange Rate Regimes 20 years later: The prevalence of floats. *IMF Economic Review*, •••, 1–30. DOI: 10.1057/s41308-024-00266-7

Liang, N. (2025). Stablecoins: Issues for regulators as they implement GENIUS Act. October 21, 2025. https://www.brookings.edu/articles/stablecoins-issues-for-regulators-as-they-implement-genius-act/

Liao, G. Y., & Caramichael, J. (2022). stablecoins: growth potential and impact on banking (International Finance Discussion Papers No. 1334). Board of Governors of the Federal Reserve System. DOI: 10.17016/ifdp.2022.1334

Liberty Street Economics. (2025). The evolution of crypto-stablecoins. Federal Reserve Bank of New York. https://libertystreeteconomics.newyorkfed.org/

Lietaer, B. (2001). The future of money: Beyond greed and scarcity. Random House. https://www.penguin.com.au/books/the-future-of-money-9781448149933

Linklaters. (2025, August 20). Agentic payments: What are they, what are the legal risks … Linklaters FinTechLinks. https://www.linklaters.com

Luck, S., (2025). A historical perspective on stablecoins. Federal Reserve Bank of New York Liberty Street Economics, October 1, 2025. DOI: 10.59576/lse.20251001

Lyons, R. K., & Viswanath-Natraj, G. (2023). What keeps stablecoins stable? *Journal of International Money and Finance*, *131*, 102777. DOI: 10.1016/j.jimonfin.2022.102777

MacDonald, C., & Zhao, L. (2022). stablecoins and their risks to financial stability (Staff Discussion Paper No. 2022-20). Bank of Canada. https://www.bankofcanada.ca/2022/11/staff-discussion-paper-2022-20/

Mannan, M. (2024) 'From Digital Humanitarianism to Crypto-Humanitarianism', *International Trade and Business Law Annual*, 24. Available at: https://heinonline.org/hol-cgi-bin/get_pdf.cgi?handle=hein.journals/itbla24&section=11

Martinez, J., & Kale, D. (2021). *Regulating the crypto market in Nigeria*. International Monetary Fund.

Mastercard. (2025, September 9). Mastercard unveils Agent Pay, pioneering agentic payments technology to power commerce in the age of AI. Mastercard Newsroom. https://www.mastercard.com/global/en/news-and-trends/press/2025/april/mastercard-unveils-agent-pay-pioneering-agentic-payments-technology-to-power-commerce-in-the-age-of-ai.html

Mathews, R. (2017). Interrogating "privacy" in a world brimming with high political entanglements, surveillance, interdependence & interconnections. *Health and Technology*, *7*(4), 373–381. https://link.springer.com/article/10.1007/s12553-017-0211-5. DOI: 10.1007/s12553-017-0211-5

Monetary Authority of Singapore. (2016). MAS establishes FinTech Innovation Lab (Looking Glass @ MAS) [Press release]. https://www.mas.gov.sg/news/media-releases/2016/mas-establishes-fintech-innovation-lab

Monetary Authority of Singapore. (2018). World's first cross-border open-architecture platform to improve financial inclusion – APIX [Press release]. https://www.mas.gov.sg/news/media-releases/2018/worlds-first-cross-border-open-architecture-platform-to-improve-financial-inclusion mas.gov.sg+1

Monetary Authority of Singapore. (2019). Sandbox Express. https://www.mas.gov.sg/development/fintech/sandbox-express

Monetary Authority of Singapore. (2022). *Proposed regulatory framework for stablecoin-related activities*. MAS.

Monetary Authority of Singapore. (2023). MAS finalises stablecoin regulatory framework. https://www.mas.gov.sg/news/media-releases/2023/mas-finalises-stablecoin-regulatory-framework

Monetary Authority of Singapore. (n.d.). Project Guardian: Asset tokenisation initiative. https://www.mas.gov.sg/schemes-and-initiatives/project-guardian

Monetary Authority of Singapore. National Research Foundation; National University of Singapore. (2020, August 4). New Asian Institute of Digital Finance to spearhead FinTech education and research. https://www.mas.gov.sg/news/media-releases/2020/new-asian-institute-of-digital-finance-to-spearhead-fintech-education-and-research

Money Authority of Singapore. (2023). *MAS Finalizes Stablecoin Regulatory Framework*. https://www.sgpc.gov.sg/api/file/getfile/Media%20Release_MAS%20Finalises%20Stablecoin%20Regulatory%20Framework.pdf?path=/sgpcmedia/media_releases/mas/press_release/P-20230815-2/attachment/Media+Release_MAS+Finalises+Stablecoin+Regulatory+Framework.pdf

Morgan, J. P. (n.d.). About Kinexys: Our story, leadership and more. https://www.jpmorgan.com/kinexys/about

Nakamoto, S. (2008). Bitcoin: a peer-to-peer electronic cash system. https://bitcoin.org/bitcoin.pdf

NEOM. (n.d.). About NEOM. Government of Saudi Arabia. https://www.neom.com/

Nigeria, S. E. C. (2022). *New rules on issuance, offering platforms and custody of digital assets*. SEC.

OECD. (2022). Environmental impact of digital assets: Crypto-asset mining and DLT consensus mechanisms, OECD Business and Finance Policy Papers, OECD Publishing. DOI: 10.1787/bf84ff64-en

Oliver, R., & Warfe, G. (2020). The story of payments: How the industrialization of trust created the modern payment system. Glenbrook Partners. https://www.barnesandnoble.com/w/payment-systems-in-the-us-carol-coye-benson/1144602923

Ordinance, S. (2025). Cap. 656 (Hong Kong SAR, 2025). https://www.elegislation.gov.hk/hk/cap656

Organisation for Economic Co-operation and Development. (2024). *Global stablecoin adoption and financial inclusion*. https://www.oecd.org

Owen, A., Dawson, G., & Walker, J. (2025) *The Role of Stablecoins in Money Laundering and Financial Crime*. ResearchGate. Available at: https://www.researchgate.net/profile/Antony-Owen/publication/394787347_The_Role_of_Stablecoins_in_Money_Laundering_and_Financial_Crime/links/68a649ef7984e374acea2dd0/The-Role-of-Stablecoins-in-Money-Laundering-and-Financial-Crime.pdf

Ozili, P. K. (2024). Cryptocurrency regulation in Africa: Advantages, motivation, regulatory models, challenges, consequences, and principles vs. rules-based regulation. *International Journal of Blockchains and Cryptocurrencies*, *5*(4), 294–313. DOI: 10.1504/IJBC.2024.143982

Parasuraman, R., & Riley, V. (1997). Humans and automation: Use, misuse, disuse, abuse. *Human Factors*, *39*(2), 230–253. DOI: 10.1518/001872097778543886

Pocher, N. (2025). AML/CFT and Crypto-Assets: EU Law and Global Standards. In *Crypto-Asset Ecosystems and the EU Anti-Money Laundering Framework*. Springer., Available at https://link.springer.com/chapter/10.1007/978-3-031-94698-1_5 DOI: 10.1007/978-3-031-94698-1_5

Prasad, E. S. (2021). *The future of money: How the digital revolution is transforming currencies and finance*. Harvard University Press.

President's Working Group on Financial Markets, the Board of Governors of the Federal Reserve System, and the Federal Deposit Insurance Corporation. (2021). Report on stablecoins.

President's Working Group on Financial Markets. Federal Deposit Insurance Corporation, & Office of the Comptroller of the Currency (2021). *Report on Stablecoins*. U.S. Department of the Treasury. Retrieved from: https://home.treasury.gov/system/files/136/StableCoinReport_Nov1_508.pdf

Privacy Ledger Foundation. (2025). *Privacy-preserving technologies in crypto compliance.*

Próspera, Z. E. D. E. (2021). Resolution approving qualifying cryptocurrencies for payment (§ 5-1-139-0-0-0-1). Próspera Governance Platform. https://pzgps.hn/wp-content/uploads/2024/09/06.-Resolution-Approving-Qualifying-Cryptocurrencies-for-Payment-5-1-139-0-0-0-1.pdf

Próspera, Z. E. D. E. (n.d.). About Próspera. Próspera. https://prospera.hn/

PwC. (2022). *PwC Annual Global Crypto Report 2022*. PwC Global.

Qatar Financial Centre. (n.d.). Overview | QFC. https://www.qfc.qa/en/about-qfc/overview

Qian, C., Zhang, Y., Liu, H., & Yu, L. (2023). AutoGPT and beyond: Toward general-purpose autonomous agents. arXiv preprint arXiv:2305.01210. https://arxiv.org/abs/2305.01210

Re Gatecoin Ltd (in liquidation). (2023). HKCFI 914 (Hong Kong Court of First Instance).

Reuters (2025) *Keeping crypto clean: Risk-based controls for stablecoins*. Reuters Legal Industry News, 24 June. Available at: https://www.reuters.com/legal/legalindustry/keeping-crypto-clean-risk-based-controls-stablecoins-2025-06-24

Ripple. (n.d.). University Blockchain Research Initiative (UBRI). https://ripple.com/impact/ubri/

Roatán Financial Services Authority. (n.d.). About the RFSA. https://www.rfsa.hn/about

Schär, F. (2021). Decentralized Finance: On Blockchain- and Smart Contract-Based Financial Markets. *Review - Federal Reserve Bank of St. Louis*, *103*(2), 153–174. DOI: 10.20955/r.103.153-74

Schär, F. (2021). Decentralized finance: On blockchain-and smart contract-based financial markets. *Review - Federal Reserve Bank of St. Louis*, *103*(2), 153–174.

Schwarcz, S. L. (2016). Regulating financial change: A functional approach. *SSRN*, *100*, 1441–1494. DOI: 10.2139/ssrn.2469467

Schwarcz, S. L. (2023). Regulating Global Stablecoins: A Model-Law Strategy. *Vanderbilt Law Review*, *75*(6), 1729–1785.

Schwartz, G. (2010). The impulse economy: Understanding mobile shoppers and what makes them buy. Simon & Schuster. https://www.simonandschuster.com/books/The-Impulse-Economy/Gary-Schwartz/9781451671872

Secretariat, C. (2025). *Commonwealth Model Law on Stablecoins (draft)*. Commonwealth Secretariat.

Securities and Futures Commission & Hong Kong Monetary Authority. (2025). Joint statement on stablecoin-related market movements. https://apps.sfc.hk/edistributionWeb/gateway/EN/news-and-announcements/news/doc?refNo=25PR123

Sethaput, V., & Innet, S. (2023). Blockchain application for central bank digital currencies (CBDC). *Cluster Computing*, *26*(4), 2183–2197. DOI: 10.1007/s10586-022-03962-z PMID: 36686339

Shrivastav, S. (2025). Network externalities, consumer heterogeneity, and optimal monopoly pricing. *Marketing Letters*, *36*(3), 563–575. DOI: 10.1007/s11002-024-09763-1

SIAC. (2025). Annual Report 2024 (rules update & sector context). https://siac.org.sg/wp-content/uploads/2024/08/SIAC_AR2024_FA-spread-Online.pdf

Sindhu, S. (2025) *Blockchain-Enabled Decentralized Identity and Finance: Advancing Women's Socioeconomic Empowerment in Developing Economies. Journal of Women in Information Technology and Engineering*. Available at: https://aasrresearch.com/index.php/jwite/article/view/5

Singapore FinTech Festival. (n.d.). Singapore FinTech Festival – Home. https://www.fintechfestival.sg/

Singapore FinTech Festival. (n.d.). Singapore FinTech Festival. https://www.fintechfestival.sg/

Sino-British Joint Declaration on the Question of Hong Kong. (1984). The Government of the People's Republic of China and the Government of the United Kingdom of Great Britain and Northern Ireland. https://treaties.fcdo.gov.uk/awweb/pdfopener?md=1&did=68291

South, S. N. (2024) *Towards a Stablecoin Regulatory Framework in India.* Esya Centre. Available at: https://www.esyacentre.org/s/Esya-Centre-Report-045-Towards-a-Stablecoin-Regulatory-Framework-in-India.pdf

Stablecon. (n.d.). Stablecon. https://stablecon.com/

Standard Chartered Bank (Hong Kong) Limited. Animoca Brands Corporation Limited; HKT Limited. (2025, February 17). Standard Chartered, Animoca Brands and HKT establish joint venture to issue HKD-backed stablecoin. https://www.sc.com/en/press-release/standard-chartered-animoca-brands-and-hkt-establish-joint-venture-to-issue-hkd-backed-stablecoin/

Stern, G. H., & Feldman, R. J. (2004). *Too big to fail: The hazards of bank bailouts.* Brookings Institution Press.

Summit, S. (n.d.). Stable Summit — The global stablecoin conference. https://www.stablesummit.xyz/

Summit, S. (n.d.). Stablecoin Summit. https://stablecoinsummit.com/

Sutton, R. S., & Barto, A. G. (2018). *Reinforcement learning: An introduction* (2nd ed.). MIT Press., https://mitpress.mit.edu/9780262039246/reinforcement-learning-second-edition

Techstars. (n.d.). Techstars London accelerator. https://www.techstars.com/accelerators/london

Templars (2021). The CBN letter on cryptocurrency: Your FAQs answered. Templars.

The Basic Law of the Hong Kong Special Administrative Region of the People's Republic of China. (1990). Adopted on April 4, 1990, effective July 1, 1997. The Government of the Hong Kong Special Administrative Region. https://www.basiclaw.gov.hk/en/basiclawtext/

The Commonwealth. (2025). Consultation on the Draft Commonwealth Model Law on Stablecoins. The Commonwealth

TOKEN2049. (n.d.). TOKEN2049. https://www.token2049.com/

Transport, T. (2025, July 4). Tawasul Transport and Al Maryah Community Bank launch the first digital payment system in taxis using AE Coin [Press release]. Tawasul Transport. https://tawasul.ae/tawasul-transport-and-al-maryah-community-bank-launch-the-first-digital-payment-system-in-taxis-using-ae-coin/

U.S. Department of the Treasury. (2025). *President's working group on financial markets releases report and recommendations on stablecoins*. U.S. Treasury.

U.S. Department of Treasury. (2024). *Stablecoin oversight framework*. https://home.treasury.gov

U.S. President's Working Group on Financial Markets. (2021). Stablecoins—Risks, regulation, and policy recommendations. https://home.treasury.gov/policy-issues/financial-markets-financial-institutions-and-fiscal-service/financial-markets/stablecoins

United Nations Commission on International Trade Law. (1996). *UNCITRAL Model Law on Electronic Commerce*. Retrieved from: https://uncitral.un.org/en/texts/ecommerce/modellaw/electronic_commerce

United Nations Commission on International Trade Law. (2017). *UNCITRAL Model Law on Electronic Transferable Records*. Retrieved from: https://uncitral.un.org/en/texts/ecommerce/modellaw/electronic_transferable_records

United Nations Office for the Coordination of Humanitarian Affairs (UNOCHA). (2024) *Global Humanitarian Overview 2024*. Geneva: UNOCHA. Available at: https://www.unocha.org/publications/report/world/global-humanitarian-overview-2024-enarfres

United Nations. (n.d.). Member States. United Nations. https://www.un.org/en/about-us/member-states

Vasselin, F. (2024) *Blockchain for Migrants: Promoting Self-Sovereign Identity and Financial Inclusion*. HAL Open Science. Available at: https://hal.science/hal-04815373/.

Vietnam, National Assembly. (2025, June 27). Resolution 222/2025/QH15 on International Financial Centres in Vietnam [Resolution No. 222/2025/QH15]. https://datafiles.chinhphu.vn/cpp/files/vbpq/2025/7/222qh.signed.pdf?utm_source=chatgpt.com

VietnamPlus. (2025, June 10). Da N ng proposes pilot programme for Tether transactions. https://en.vietnamplus.vn/da-nang-proposes-pilot-programme-for-tether-transactions-post320653.vnp

Wang, F., & De Filippi, P. (2020). Self-sovereign identity in a globalized world: Credentials-based identity systems as a driver for economic inclusion. *Frontiers in Blockchain, 3*(28), 28. https://www.frontiersin.org/journals/blockchain/articles/10.3389/fbloc.2019.00028/full. DOI: 10.3389/fbloc.2019.00028

Wen, H., Li, S., & Zhang, J. (2025) *Hybrid Monetary Ecosystems: Integrating Stablecoins and Fiat in the Future of Currency Systems*. arXiv. doi: /arXiv.2505.10997. Available at: https://arxiv.org/abs/2505.10997DOI: 10.48550

Wilmarth, A. E. (2025). Time bomb: How uninsured stablecoins and crypto derivatives threaten financial and economic stability. October 6, 2025. https://www.ineteconomics.org/perspectives/blog/time-bomb-how-uninsured-stablecoins-and-crypto-derivatives-threaten-financial-and-economic-stability

World Bank. (2018) *ID4D Annual Report 2018*. Washington, DC: World Bank. Available at: https://id4d.worldbank.org/sites/id4d.worldbank.org/files/2018_ID4D_Annual_Report.pdf

World Bank. (2021). Remittance prices worldwide: Quarterly report. https://remittanceprices.worldbank.org

World Bank. (2023) *Migration and remittances: Overview*. Washington, DC: World Bank. Available at: https://www.worldbank.org/en/topic/migration/overview

World Bank. (2023). *Migration and Development Brief 38*. World Bank.

World Economic Forum. (2023). How are CBDCs different from cryptocurrencies and stablecoins? World Economic Forum. https://www.weforum.org/agenda/2023/02/cbdcs-different-cryptocurrencies-stablecoins/

World Food Programme (WFP) Innovation. (2025) *Building Blocks Project*. Rome: WFP. Available at: https://innovation.wfp.org/project/building-blocks

x402 Working Group (Coinbase). (2025, May 5). x402: An HTTP-native protocol for paid API access (Whitepaper). x402.org. https://www.x402.org/x402-whitepaper.pdf

Zetzsche, D. A., Birdthistle, W. A., Arner, D. W., & Buckley, R. P. (2020). Digital finance platforms: Toward a new regulatory paradigm. *University of Pennsylvania Journal of Business Law, 23*(1), 273-339. Retrieved from: https://scholarship.law.upenn.edu/jbl/vol23/iss1/6

Zetzsche, D. A., Buckley, R. P., Arner, D. W., & van Ek, M. (2023). Remaining regulatory challenges in digital finance and crypto-assets after MiCA. Committee on Economic and Monetary Affairs (ECON), Policy Department for Economic, Scientific and Quality of Life Policies, European Parliament, Luxembourg, 23-27. DOI: 10.2139/ssrn.4487516

Zetzsche, D. A., Arner, D. W., & Buckley, R. P. (2020). Decentralized finance. *Journal of Financial Regulation*, *6*(2), 172–203. DOI: 10.1093/jfr/fjaa010

Zetzsche, D. A., Buckley, R. P., & Arner, D. W. (2021). Regulating Libra. *Oxford Journal of Legal Studies*, *41*(1), 80–113. DOI: 10.1093/ojls/gqaa036 PMID: 33762888

Zetzsche, D. A., Buckley, R. P., Arner, D. W., & Föhr, L. (2020). The ICO gold rush: It's a scam, it's a bubble, it's a super challenge for regulators. *Harvard International Law Journal*, *60*(2), 267–315.

Zhu, J., He, W., & Liu, Y. (2024). Implementing artificial intelligence-empowered financial services: Design principles and regulatory considerations. *Journal of Business Research*, *168*, 114–127. DOI: 10.1016/j.jbusres.2023.113959

Zubkov, P., & Pondi, K. (2022). Writing the methodology chapter. In *The SAGE Handbook of Qualitative Research in the Asian Context* (pp. 379–395). SAGE Publications Ltd. DOI: 10.4135/9781529781731.n27

About the Contributors

Jane Thomason, is a global thought leader in emerging technologies, including AI, Blockchain, Web3, Metaverse, and MedTech. She holds a PhD from the University of Queensland. She currently holds distinguished roles on the editorial boards of three peer reviewed journals and is an Industry Associate: University College London, Centre for Blockchain. She is author of "Blockchain for Global Social Change," "Applied Ethics in a Digital World" and has "Advancements in the New World of Web 3: A Look Toward the Decentralized Future". She has published widely on MedTech, Web3, Blockchain, AI and Metaverse and is at the forefront of the impact of emerging technologies on industry and society.

***

Silvio Andrae has been an independent researcher, senior consultant, project manager, and business partner in the financial sector since 1995. His specialization is inclusive finance, and he has over 25 years of experience advising financial institutions in Latin America, Africa, and Asia. Notably, he is a dedicated senior lecturer and trainer at various universities and teaching institutions, where he shares his expertise with the next generation of professionals, inspiring them to make a difference in the field. He is also the author of books and articles in journals. He completed his doctoral studies at the Free University of Berlin (Germany).

Andreas Baumgartner is the Co-founder and CEO of The Metis Institute. His core focus is on special economic zones (SEZs), new/autonomous cities, and PPPs (public-private partnerships), with functional expertise in strategy, governance, and narrative development/strategic communications. In a complementary way, Dr Andreas Baumgartner is passionate about regulatory setup and judicial as well as alternative dispute resolution. He is proud to have been instrumental in developing the concept and setting up multiple SEZ jurisdictions (primarily common law) around the world. He is also affiliated with EZDA (Economic Zones Development Alliance; United Arab Emirates) and a former advisory board member of FEMOZA/FEMAC (World Free & Special Economic Zones Federation). His work experience includes CMS Transnational Legal Services, McKinsey & Company, the Office of Tony Blair/Tony Blair Associates, the DIFC Dispute Resolution Authority, Tipolis Pte Ltd, and various other roles.

Amit Chaudhary is a Lead Architect with more than 18 years of IT experience with excellent knowledge of Software development/design and specializes in developing test automation frameworks and AI/ML driven solutions, specialized in AI-driven solutions for enterprise risk assess software, software quality, and CI/CD automation. I have developed NLP-based multi-dialect search systems, improved scalability, and optimized test automation strategies, ensuring 99%+ coverage and reducing defect leakage by 30%. With expertise in Java, Python, Selenium, and Cucumber, I have built scalable automation frameworks achieving 80%+ automation coverage while streamlining CI/CD with GitHub Actions and Groovy pipelines, cutting deployment time by 40%. By integrating AI-powered test optimization and intelligent caching, I have reduced query latency by 60% and improved efficiency. I have led Agile transformations, optimized onshore-offshore models, and conducted POCs to enhance tool efficiency, reducing release cycles by 30%. Additionally, I have developed AI-assisted automation tools, cutting manual testing efforts by 60% and enabling faster, more intelligent validation. Passionate about leveraging AI, automation, and DevOps to drive innovation and efficiency in software development. I have published research papers, contributed to patents, and expertise in microservices testing. As an IEEE member, actively involved in AI policy discussions and has participated in Congressional Visits Day (CVD) in Washington, D.C., advocating for AI advancements.

Ankita Dhawan is The Metis Institute's Head of Middle East and India. She works extensively on regulatory design and public policy aspects of special economic zones, primarily to enable emerging technologies. Ankita was a part of the drafting team of the Commonwealth Model Laws on Virtual Assets. Before The Metis Institute, she worked in private legal practice in the UAE and India, advising big tech and start-ups on economic laws, particularly those interfacing with technology, such as antitrust, data, and virtual assets. She started her career at Google, where she worked on digital policy issues.

Eduardo Carlos Dittmar is an economist holding a PhD in Economic and Business Sciences. He brings extensive teaching expertise at both undergraduate and graduate levels. His scholarly work encompasses fundamental and applied research, resulting in a contribution of over 50 peer-reviewed publications and book chapters. Throughout his career, he has maintained active involvement in various research groups and served on editorial boards of multiple academic journals. His research interests focus on artificial intelligence, new technologies, corporate social responsibility, strategic marketing, and business ethics.

Obinna Ezeala is a Research Associate at Lagos Business School, Pan-Atlantic University, Nigeria, where he contributes to research on decentralised finance, digital transformation, artificial intelligence, and sustainable business strategy in emerging markets. His work focuses on how data-driven innovation, predictive analytics, and technology adoption influence enterprise growth—particularly within Africa's informal and SME sectors. Obinna has co-authored academic papers and book chapters on AI in finance, stablecoins, and the evolving digital and retail ecosystems across the continent. He is committed to producing insights that support evidence-based policymaking and strengthen the competitiveness of African businesses in a rapidly shifting global economy. Obinna continues to develop expertise in applied analytics, strategic management, and the intersection of technology, ethics, and development.

David López Jiménez obtained his Law degree from the Complutense University of Madrid. He obtained one PhD (with European mention) from the Seville University and another PhD from the Rey Juan Carlos University. He has an Extraordinary Doctoral Award. He has leaded research stays in different European countries. He is the author of several monographs, some of them published by the prestigious publisher Thomson Reuters and Marcial Pons, as well as more than 200 publications in various scientific journals, book chapters, book reviews, and comments about national and international law.

Nagaraju Jooluri is a distinguished academic and technology professional specializing in artificial intelligence and machine learning. He currently serves as a solutions architect at a leading unicorn company, where he applies his extensive expertise in product development and enterprise architecture to design and deliver robust, scalable, and business-aligned solutions.Nagaraju combines technical depth with innovative thinking to craft elegant solutions that address complex challenges. His professional journey reflects a deep commitment to advancing technology and its practical applications across industries.Nagaraju is an active contributor to the global research and technology community, regularly engaging with professional organizations such as IEEE and ORCID. He has also served as a reviewer for technical papers and research publications within the IEEE community and beyond, helping uphold the standards of quality and rigor in scholarly communications.

Through his continuous participation in conferences, technical forums, and collaborative initiatives, his career blends academic excellence, hands-on innovation, and a strong drive to bridge research with real-world impact.

Abhinav Kataria has rich experience in the areas of Teaching, Educational Assessment, Classroom Presentation, Student Relations and General Administration. A dedicated, resourceful and innovative instructor who strives to help students change marginal grades into good grades. Experience of facilitating students by using interactive discussions and hands-on approaches to help students learn and apply concepts in various fields of Finance, Banking, Economics, Fintech and Business Management. A thorough professional with a proactive attitude, capable of thinking in & out of the box. His Area of Interest includes Financial Accounting, Securities Analysis and Portfolio Management, Digital Transformation in Finance, Mutual Fund Distribution Module, Managerial Economics, Financial Management, Finance for Non Finance, Fintech and Country Analysis etc. In the past he was associated with the Delhi Skill and Entrepreneur University, Amity University, IMS Group of Institutions, ITS Group of Institutions.

Vinod Krishna M. U is an Professor at Department of Management Studies, Dayananda Sagar College of Engineering with over 34 years of experience in corporate, entrepreneurship, and academia. His expertise spans personal finance, fintech, cybersecurity, and marketing. He holds a PhD in Management and has co-founded ventures in education, consulting, and financial services.

Aditya Mudgal is currently pursuing a BBA in FinTech, equipping himself with strong foundations in financial management, digital finance, and emerging technologies shaping the future of the financial sector. He has a keen interest in the broader field of finance and actively participates in finance-focused student clubs, where he contributes to discussions on market trends, corporate finance, and investment strategy. Aditya is passionate about building a career at the intersection of finance and technology, with a strong commitment to continuous learning and professional development. He aims to leverage his academic background, hands-on experience, and leadership involvement to contribute meaningfully to the evolving FinTech and financial services landscape.

Ramu N. M. has experience as an Equity Research Analyst Intern at Motilal Oswal Financial Services and has worked on company valuation and stock price prediction using time series analysis, machine learning, and deep learning models. Ramu is a finance and analytics professional with an MBA in Finance and Business Analytics from Dayananda Sagar College of Engineering, Bengaluru. He holds a BBA in Marketing and an Honours Diploma in Computer Application. Ramu has experience as an Equity Research Analyst Intern at Motilal Oswal Financial Services and has worked on company valuation and stock price prediction using time series analysis, machine learning, and deep learning models. He is also a creative writer, having won a state-level poetry and lyrics award from Dr. Rajkumar Academy for Civil Services.

Oluseyi Ishola Oladapo is an energy sector professional with experience in upstream oil and gas operations, strategy, and project optimisation. He works with NEWCROSS Exploration and Production Limited, where he contributes to operational planning, data-driven decision-making, and organisational performance improvement. His interests include the application of technology, predictive analytics, and sustainable management practices within the African energy industry. Oladapo has engaged in research exploring how innovation, talent development, and cross-functional collaboration can strengthen competitiveness and operational excellence in complex environments. He is passionate about integrating industry experience with research-based insights to support organisational resilience and long-term value creation. His work continues to reflect a commitment to advancing best practices in energy management, workforce capability development, and strategic problem-solving.

Ameya Patil is currently Associate Professor at MIT World Peace University, Pune with 13 years of teaching experience and 3.5 years of Industrial experience. He previously worked as an Assistant Manager with IDBI Bank and as Assistant Professor and HOD of BBA and BBA-IB at Sinhgad College, Pune. He teaches subjects related to Finance and International Business. He has authored several books and research papers related to various topics in Finance, Management and International Business. His research interest areas include stock prediction, green finance, behavioral finance and allied areas in finance and general management. He is a member of Indian Institute of Banking and Finance (IIBF) and ASCB(UK). 17 of his research works have appeared in Scopus and ABDC journals, and with reputed publishers such as Wiley, Springer, Emerald, Inderscience, IGI Global and Emerald

Mohan Sankaran is a seasoned technology professional with 20+ years of experience across Android, AI/ML, fintech, tokenisation, cybersecurity, blockchain, and IoT. At PayPal, he leads engineering for the Business Experience in the PayPal App, serving millions of business users worldwide, and has played a pivotal role in PayPal Zettle's growth in the U.S. and Europe while contributing to multiple PayPal financial products. Previously (2015–2019) at Visa, he contributed to the Visa Token Service (VTS), the tokenisation platform behind Samsung Pay, Google Pay, and bank-led digital wallets - improving authorisation rates and reducing fraud at scale.

His interests include mobile security and privacy, EMV/PCI systems, behavioral risk modeling, and real-time ML-driven user experiences. He serves as a reviewer and mentor for academic venues and serves on professional committees. He is a Senior Member of IEEE, member of ACM and IAENG and a Full Member of Sigma Xi.

A.V. Senthil Kumar is working as a Professor and Director, PG and Research Department of Computer Applications, Hindusthan College of Arts & Science, Coimbatore, Tamilnadu. To his credit he has industrial experience for five years and teaching experience of 29 years. He has also received his Doctor of Science (D.Sc in Computer Science). He has to his credit 84 Book Chapters, 234 papers in International and National Journals, 85 papers in International Conferences in International and National Conferences, and edited 18 books and 3 Text books. He is as Associate Editor of IEEE Access. He is an Editor-in-Chief for many journals and Key Member for India, Machine Intelligence Research Lab (MIR Labs). He is an Editorial Board Member and Reviewer for various International Journals. He is also a Committee member for various International Conferences. He has guided 16 Ph.D scholars and guiding 3 Ph. D scholars now.

Muazu Umar brings a depth of expertise spanning counter-narcotics, anti-money laundering (AML), and combatting the financing of terrorism (CFT). With over 32 years in public service, he has been recognized for his skill in conducting and analyzing comprehensive, objective research, driving cross-functional teams, and disrupting illicit financial flows and organized crime networks. He is the Director of Policy and Research at the Inter-Governmental Action Group Against Money Laundering in West Africa (GIABA), an ECOWAS institution. He leads policy development, conduct research on money laundering, terrorist financing, and illicit financial flows, and support member states in risk assessments and crafting AML/CFT strategic plans. Collaborating with senior leadership, stakeholders, and cross-functional teams, he works to ensure that research outcomes and policy frameworks enhance AML/CFT effectiveness across GIABA's 17 member states.

Jenny Patricia Vargas Portillo is a PhD with the highest qualification, three master's degrees, an Advanced Studies Diploma and numerous specialization courses. The research carried out involves both basic and applied exploration. The lines she has been working involves, among others, Consumer Behavior, Marketing and New Technologies (Interactive Advertising and Electronic Commerce). She has been teaching and doing research in different countries of the world. She has been a professor at undergraduate and graduate levels. Likewise, she has directed a significant number of Bachelor and Master theses.

Index

A

B

C

D

F

G

H

I

M

N

P

R

S

www.ingramcontent.com/pod-product-compliance
Lightning Source LLC
LaVergne TN
LVHW080905300926
849162LV00003B/561